# THE NEW CAMBRIDGE SHAKESPEARE

FOUNDING GENERAL EDITOR
Philip Brockbank

GENERAL EDITOR
Brian Gibbons, *Professor of English Literature, University of Zürich*

ASSOCIATE GENERAL EDITORS
A. R. Braunmuller, *Professor of English, University of California at Los Angeles*
Robin Hood, *Senior Lecturer in English, University of York*


## THE SECOND PART OF KING HENRY VI

Shakespeare's plays about the reign of Henry VI, written at the beginning of his career, were for a long time undervalued. This was because of doubts about their authorship and because of the difficulties of determining their theatrical provenance. Recently, however, a series of outstanding productions by the RSC and other companies has demonstrated their theatrical vitality, their conventions have been better understood in the light of new critical methods, and their innovative and sceptical questioning of Elizabethan orthodoxies has been understood in the light of revisionist readings of the history of Shakespeare's own times. The Wars of the Roses haunted the Elizabethans, as is shown by the number of authors who wrote about them. Shakespeare's account was the most ambitious, the most dramatically innovative, and politically the most radical.

This is the first major edition for over thirty years of *The Second Part of King Henry VI*. It takes account of recent discoveries concerning Shakespeare's early career, and pays particular attention to recent theatrical history, relating readings generated by modern performances to new ideologically positioned accounts of the history and politics of Shakespeare's age. *Part 2* offers a searing account of aristocratic sedition and a portrait of a relationship between the king and his Protector, Good Duke Humphrey, which is as complex as that between Prince Hal and his father Bullingbrook. It concerns itself with the nature of history, the role of conscience, and the relation between law and equity. It also contains a complex reading of the kind of event the the Tudor régime had cause to fear, a popular uprising, led in this instance by Jack Cade.

# THE NEW CAMBRIDGE SHAKESPEARE

# THE SECOND PART OF
# KING HENRY VI

*Edited by*
## MICHAEL HATTAWAY

*Professor of English Literature,*
*University of Sheffield*

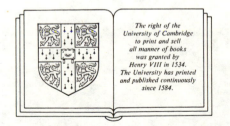

The right of the
University of Cambridge
to print and sell
all manner of books
was granted by
Henry VIII in 1534.
The University has printed
and published continuously
since 1584.

## CAMBRIDGE UNIVERSITY PRESS

*Cambridge*
*New York   Port Chester*
*Melbourne   Sydney*

Published by the Press Syndicate of the University of Cambridge
The Pitt Building, Trumpington Street, Cambridge CB2 1RP
40 West 20th Street, New York, NY 10011, USA
10 Stamford Road, Oakleigh, Melbourne 3166, Australia

First published 1991

Printed in Great Britain at the University Press, Cambridge

*British Library cataloguing in publication data*

Shakespeare, William, *1564–1616*
[Henry VI, part 2] The second part of King Henry VI.
1. Drama in English. Shakespeare, William, 1564–1616 –
Texts
I. [Henry VI, part 2]  II. Title  III. Hattaway, Michael
822.33

*Library of Congress cataloguing in publication data*

Shakespeare, William, 1564–1616.
[King Henry VI. Part 2]
The second part of King Henry VI / edited by Michael Hattaway.
      p.      cm. – (The New Cambridge Shakespeare)
Includes bibliographical references.
ISBN 0-521-37330-1. – ISBN 0-521-37704-8 (pbk.)
1. Henry VI. King of England, 1421–1471 – Drama.  I. Hattaway,
Michael. II. Title.  III. Series: Shakespeare, William, 1564–1616.
Works.  1984.  Cambridge University Press.
PR2815.A2H38  1990
822.3'3 – dc20  90-1324 CIP

ISBN 0 521 37330 1 hardback
ISBN 0 521 37704 8 paperback

# THE NEW CAMBRIDGE SHAKESPEARE

The *New Cambridge Shakespeare* succeeds *The New Shakespeare* which began publication in 1921 under the general editorship of Sir Arthur Quiller-Couch and John Dover Wilson, and was completed in the 1960s, with the assistance of G. I. Duthie, Alice Walker, Peter Ure and J. C. Maxwell. *The New Shakespeare* itself followed upon *The Cambridge Shakespeare*, 1863–6, edited by W. G. Clark, J. Glover and W. A. Wright.

*The New Shakespeare* won high esteem both for its scholarship and for its design, but shifts of critical taste and insight, recent Shakespearean research, and a changing sense of what is important in our understanding of the plays, have made it necessary to re-edit and redesign, not merely to revise, the series.

The *New Cambridge Shakespeare* aims to be of value to a new generation of playgoers and readers who wish to enjoy fuller access to Shakespeare's poetic and dramatic art. While offering ample academic guidance, it reflects current critical interests and is more attentive than some earlier editions have been to the realisation of the plays on the stage, and to their social and cultural settings. The text of each play has been freshly edited, with textual data made available to those users who wish to know why and how one published text differs from another. Although modernised, the edition conserves forms that appear to be expressive and characteristically Shakespearean, and it does not attempt to disguise the fact that the plays were written in a language other than that of our own time.

Illustrations are usually integrated into the critical and historical discussion of the play and include some reconstructions of early performances by C. Walter Hodges. Some editors have also made use of the advice and experience of Maurice Daniels, for many years a member of the Royal Shakespeare Company.

Each volume is addressed to the needs and problems of a particular text, and each therefore differs in style and emphasis from others in the series.

PHILIP BROCKBANK
*Founding General Editor*

# CONTENTS

# ILLUSTRATIONS

Illustrations 1 and 7 are reproduced by permission of the British Library; 6, 10, 12, 15 (photograph Gordon Goode), 16 (Tom Holte Theatre Photographic Collection) by permission of the Shakespeare Centre Library, Stratford-upon-Avon; 13 from the RSC Collection, with the permission of the Governors of the Royal Shakespeare Theatre; 14 from the Walker Art Gallery, Liverpool; 2, 3, 5, 8, 17, 18 by permission of Joe Cocks Photography, Stratford-upon-Avon; 19 by permission of The Museum of London and Andrew Fulgoni (photographer).

# PREFACE

*Henry VI Part 2* is, without doubt, a major play. It addresses some of the major concerns of *Julius Caesar*, having at its centre the murder of a national leader. It probes a relationship between the young king and his Protector Gloucester that is as complex as that between Prince Hal and Henry IV. It contains a portrayal of a major rebellion which I have tried to re-examine in the light of new social history and cultural theory.

It is in the theatre, however, that the value and dramatic potential of this and the other *Henry VI* texts have been truly demonstrated. In the decades since the last major editions, those of John Dover Wilson (The New Shakespeare, 1952) and Andrew S. Cairncross (New Arden, 1957), Stratford and London have seen major productions of versions of this history cycle (1964 and 1977), a shortened version went on a national tour (1987–8), and a shortened version appeared at Stratford in late 1988. Reviews of those productions have turned into some of the most perceptive critical appraisals of these plays.

The editions of Wilson and Cairncross, along with that of Norman Sanders (New Penguin, 1981), created major advances in our knowledge of these texts. To these editors I owe a debt for their major work on the lexical problems of the text, although I have been surprised how much there was still to do. Cairncross's edition offered challenging but unendorsable views on the history of the text. The Oxford edition of *The Complete Works* (1986), wherein *2 Henry VI* (known there as *The First Part of the Contention*) was prepared by William Montgomery and Gary Taylor, along with the apparatus in *William Shakespeare: A Textual Companion* (1987), appeared after my own work was well advanced. The work of these editors has been perpetually stimulating and often provocative. My own edition, however, will be found to be far less interventionist than theirs. I had prepared a draft of this edition and of that of *3 Henry VI* before turning to my final work on *1 Henry VI*. Working on the plays in this order persuaded me that *critical* arguments exist in plenty for the case that Shakespeare wrote his plays in the order of history, arguments that have not been taken sufficient note of by those scholars who have approached the problems of authorship and composition from textual propositions alone.

To the late Philip Brockbank I am grateful for much encouragement and the loan of his PhD thesis, which not only records pioneering work on the sources of the sequence but which generated a series of articles that were really the first to treat the plays as a major achievement. These stood virtually alone and certainly unchallenged for a critical generation. My own work confirms Brockbank's pioneering but not yet accepted contention that Shakespeare drew far more from Holinshed than from Hall. Marilynne Robinson also loaned me her PhD thesis, which, in its handling of the sources of the play and careful intelligent probing of the subtext of the relationship between Henry and Gloucester, is the fruit of labours important as those of Brockbank; I am ashamed to admit how long I had it. Michael Freeman, Leonard Goldstein, Ronald Knowles, William Montgomery, and Eric Rasmussen all generously offered me the fruits of research before publication.

Librarians at the Universities of Kent, Sheffield, Texas, and at the British and London Libraries have been consistently helpful; so have the staff of the Oxford Text Archive who provided me with electronic copies of the Folio and Quarto texts which were an invaluable aid in checking the text I had established. Mary White and Sylvia Morris at the Shakespeare Centre Library in Stratford could not have been more helpful in guiding me through their archives and, in particular, helping me with the choice of illustrations. To colleagues at Kent and Sheffield I am grateful for sabbatical leaves which hastened the advancement of this work. Dr Pamela Mason disagreed constructively with me over the productions we had seen, and Professor Dominique Goy-Blanquet argued the toss over the meaning of the play and directed me to useful French material. Professor Brian Gibbons, my general editor, was perceptive, courteous – both when critical and encouraging – and unfailingly prompt to respond to what I sent him. Professor Patrick Collinson introduced me to the new wave of political, religious, and social historians of the period. My colleague, Professor Norman Blake, demonstrated by his painstaking scrutiny of my manuscript that divisions between Departments of Literature and Language are more imagined than real. Thanks to Sarah Stanton of Cambridge University Press for her patience and sage suggestions. C. Walter Hodges' drawings served, as always, to stimulate and not just to illustrate.

*University of Sheffield*                                                                                                    M. H.

# ABBREVIATIONS AND CONVENTIONS

Shakespeare's plays, when cited in this edition, are abbreviated in a style modified slightly from that used in the *Harvard Concordance to Shakespeare*. Other editions of Shakespeare are abbreviated under the editor's surname (Cairncross, Dyce) unless they are the work of more than one editor. In such cases, an abbreviated series name is used (Cam., Johnson Var.) When more than one edition by the same editor is cited, later editions are discriminated with a raised figure (Collier²). All quotations from Shakespeare, except those from *1–3 Henry VI*, use the lineation of *The Riverside Shakespeare*, under the textual editorship of G. Blakemore Evans.

## 1. Shakespeare's plays

| | |
|---|---|
| *Ado* | *Much Ado About Nothing* |
| *Ant.* | *Antony and Cleopatra* |
| *AWW* | *All's Well That Ends Well* |
| *AYLI* | *As You Like It* |
| *Cor.* | *Coriolanus* |
| *Cym.* | *Cymbeline* |
| *Err.* | *The Comedy of Errors* |
| *Ham.* | *Hamlet* |
| *1H4* | *The First Part of King Henry the Fourth* |
| *2H4* | *The Second Part of King Henry the Fourth* |
| *H5* | *King Henry the Fifth* |
| *1H6* | *The First Part of King Henry the Sixth* |
| *2H6* | *The Second Part of King Henry the Sixth* |
| *3H6* | *The Third Part of King Henry the Sixth* |
| *H8* | *King Henry the Eighth* |
| *JC* | *Julius Caesar* |
| *John* | *King John* |
| *LLL* | *Love's Labour's Lost* |
| *Lear* | *King Lear* |
| *Mac.* | *Macbeth* |
| *MM* | *Measure for Measure* |
| *MND* | *A Midsummer Night's Dream* |
| *MV* | *The Merchant of Venice* |
| *Oth.* | *Othello* |
| *Per.* | *Pericles* |
| *R2* | *King Richard the Second* |
| *R3* | *King Richard the Third* |
| *Rom.* | *Romeo and Juliet* |
| *Shr.* | *The Taming of the Shrew* |
| *STM* | *Sir Thomas More* |
| *Temp.* | *The Tempest* |

| TGV | *The Two Gentlemen of Verona* |
| Tim. | *Timon of Athens* |
| Tit. | *Titus Andronicus* |
| TN | *Twelfth Night* |
| TNK | *The Two Noble Kinsmen* |
| Tro. | *Troilus and Cressida* |
| Wiv. | *The Merry Wives of Windsor* |
| WT | *The Winter's Tale* |

## 2. Other works cited and general references

| | |
| --- | --- |
| Abbott | E. A. Abbott, *A Shakespearian Grammar*, 1878 edn (references are to numbered paragraphs) |
| Alexander | *William Shakespeare, The Complete Works*, ed. Peter Alexander, 1951 |
| Arber | E. Arber, *A Transcript of the Registers of the Company of Stationers of London 1554–1650*, 5 vols., 1875–94 |
| Baldwin | T. W. Baldwin, *Shakspere's 'Small Latine & Lesse Greeke'*, 2 vols., 1944 |
| Bell | J. Bell ed., *Shakespeare's Plays*, 9 vols., 1774 |
| Bentley | G. E. Bentley, *The Jacobean and Caroline Stage*, 7 vols., 1941–68 |
| Boswell-Stone | W. G. Boswell-Stone, *Shakespeare's Holinshed: The Chronicle and the Historical Plays Compared*, 1896 |
| Brewer | E. C. Brewer, *The Dictionary of Phrase and Fable*, n.d. |
| Brockbank | J. P. Brockbank, 'Shakespeare's historical myth: a study of Shakespeare's adaptations of his sources in making the plays of *Henry VI* and *Richard III*', unpublished PhD dissertation, University of Cambridge, 1953 |
| Bullough | Geoffrey Bullough, *Narrative and Dramatic Sources of Shakespeare*, 8 vols., 1957–75 |
| Cairncross | *2 Henry VI*, ed. Andrew S. Cairncross, 1957 (New Arden) |
| Cam. | *Works*, ed. William Aldis Wright, 9 vols., 1891–3 (Cambridge Shakespeare) |
| Capell | *Mr William Shakespeare his Comedies, Histories, and Tragedies*, ed. Edward Capell, 10 vols., 1767–8 |
| Cartwright | Robert Cartwright, *New Readings in Shakespeare*, 1866 |
| Cercignani | F. Cercignani, *Shakespeare's Works and Elizabethan Pronunciation*, 1981 |
| Chambers | E. K. Chambers, *The Elizabethan Stage*, 4 vols., 1923 |
| Collier | *Works*, ed. John P. Collier, 8 vols., 1842–4 |
| Collier[2] | *Works*, ed. John P. Collier, 1853 |
| Collier MS | Perkins' Second Folio, 1632 (Huntington Library) |
| Colman | E. A. M. Colman, *The Dramatic Use of Bawdy in Shakespeare*, 1974 |
| conj. | conjecture |
| Dekker, *ND* | Thomas Dekker, *Non Dramatic Works*, 5 vols., 1884–6 |
| Delius[2] | *Werke*, ed. Nicolaus Delius, 7 vols, 1854–[61] |
| Dent | R. W. Dent, *Shakespeare's Proverbial Language: An Index*, 1981 (references are to numbered proverbs) |
| *DNB* | *Dictionary of National Biography* |
| Drayton | Michael Drayton, *Works*, ed. J. W. Hebel, 5 vols, 1951 |

| | |
|---|---|
| Dyce | *The Works of William Shakespeare*, ed. Alexander Dyce, 6 vols., 1857 |
| Dyce$^2$ | *The Works of William Shakespeare*, ed. Alexander Dyce, 9 vols., 1864–7 |
| Eds | Various editors |
| *ELR* | *English Literary Renaissance* |
| *ES* | *English Studies* |
| F | *Mr William Shakespeares Comedies, Histories, and Tragedies*, 1623 (First Folio) |
| F2 | *Mr William Shakespeares Comedies, Histories, and Tragedies*, 1632 (Second Folio) |
| F3 | *Mr William Shakespeares Comedies, Histories, and Tragedies*, 1664 (Third Folio) |
| F4 | *Mr William Shakespeares Comedies, Histories, and Tragedies*, 1685 (Fourth Folio) |
| Fabyan | Robert Fabyan, *The New Chronicles of England and France*, 1516, reprinted 1811 |
| Farmer | Richard Farmer, in Johnson Var. (see below) |
| *FQ* | Edmund Spenser, *The Faerie Queene*, ed. A. C. Hamilton, 1977 |
| Freeman | *Henry VI, Part Two*, ed. Arthur Freeman, 1967, (Signet) |
| Grafton | Richard Grafton, *A Chronicle at Large of the History of The Affayres of England*, 1569, reprinted in 2 vols., 1809 |
| Griffiths | Ralph A. Griffiths, *The Reign of King Henry VI*, 1981 |
| Hall | Edward Hall, *The Union of the...Families of Lancastre and Yorke*, 1548, reprinted 1809 (page references are to the 1809 edn) |
| Halliwell | *The Complete Works of Shakespeare*, ed. James O. Halliwell, 16 vols., 1853–65 |
| Hanmer | *The Works of Shakspear*, ed. Thomas Hanmer, 6 vols., 1743–4 |
| Hart | *2 Henry VI*, ed. H. C. Hart, 1909 (Arden) |
| Hattaway | Michael Hattaway, *Elizabethan Popular Theatre*, 1982 |
| Henslowe | *Henslowe's Diary*, ed. R. A. Foakes and R. T. Rickert, 1961 |
| Holinshed | Raphael Holinshed, *Chronicles of England, Scotland, and Ireland*, second edition, 1587, reprinted in 6 vols., 1808 (unless otherwise specified, page references are to vol. III of the 1808 edn) |
| Hudson | *The Complete Works of William Shakespeare*, ed. Henry N. Hudson, 11 vols., 1851–6 |
| Hulme | Hilda M. Hulme, *Explorations in Shakespeare's Language*, 1962 |
| Irving | *The Works of William Shakespeare*, ed. Henry Irving and Frank A. Marshall, 8 vols., 1888–90 |
| Johnson | *The Plays of William Shakespeare*, ed. Samuel Johnson, 8 vols., 1765 |
| Johnson Var. | *The Plays of William Shakespeare*, ed. Samuel Johnson and George Steevens, 10 vols., 1773 |
| Jonson | C. H. Herford and P. and E. Simpson eds, *The Works of Ben Jonson*, 11 vols., 1925–52 |
| Keightley | *The Plays of Shakespeare*, ed. Thomas Keightley, 6 vols., 1864 |
| Kittredge | *The Complete Works of Shakespeare*, ed. George Lyman Kittredge, 1936 |
| Kökeritz | Helge Kökeritz, *Shakespeare's Pronunciation*, 1953 |
| Long | John H. Long, *Shakespeare's Use of Music: The Histories and Tragedies*, 1971 |

| | |
|---|---|
| Mahood | M. M. Mahood, *Shakespeare's Wordplay*, 1957 |
| Malone | *The Plays and Poems of William Shakespeare*, ed. Edmond Malone, 10 vols., 1790 |
| Mason | John Monck Mason, *Comments on...Shakespeare's Plays*, 1785 |
| McKerrow | Unpublished edition of *2 Henry VI*, cited in Wells and Taylor (see below) |
| *Metamorphoses* | Ovid, *Metamorphoses*, trans. Arthur Golding (1567), ed. J. F. Nims, 1965 |
| *Mirror* | *The Mirror for Magistrates*, ed. Lily B. Campbell, 1938 |
| Montgomery | 'The Contention of York and Lancaster: a critical edition', ed. William Montgomery, unpublished D Phil dissertation, University of Oxford, 1985 |
| Munro | *The London Shakespeare*, ed. John Munro, 6 vols., 1958 |
| Nashe | Thomas Nashe, *Works*, ed. R. B. McKerrow, 5 vols., 1904–10, revised by F. P. Wilson, 1958 |
| Neilson | *The Complete Dramatic and Poetic Works of William Shakespeare*, ed. William Alan Neilson, 1906 |
| Noble | Richmond Noble, *Shakespeare's Biblical Knowledge*, 1935 |
| *NQ* | *Notes and Queries* |
| obs. | obsolete |
| *OED* | *Oxford English Dictionary* |
| Onions | C. T. Onions, *A Shakespeare Glossary*, revised by Robert D. Eagleson, 1986 |
| Oxford | *William Shakespeare: The Complete Works*, ed. Stanley Wells and Gary Taylor, 1986 |
| Partridge | Eric Partridge, *Shakespeare's Bawdy*, 1968 edn |
| *PBSA* | *Papers of the Bibliographical Society of America* |
| Pelican | *The Second and Third Parts of King Henry the Sixth*, ed. Robert K. Turner Jr and George Walton Williams, 1967 |
| Plutarch | *The Lives of the Noble Grecians and Romanes*, trans. Thomas North, 8 vols., 1928 ed. |
| *PMLA* | *Publications of the Modern Language Association of America* |
| Pope | *The Works of Shakespear*, ed. Alexander Pope, 6 vols., 1723–5 |
| *PQ* | *Philological Quarterly* |
| Q1 | *The First part of the Contention betwixt the two famous Houses of Yorke and Lancaster*, 1594; prepared in facsimile by William Montgomery, 1985 |
| Q2 | *The First Part of the Contention betwixt the two Famous Houses of York and Lancaster*, 1600 |
| Q3 | *The Whole Contention between the two Famous Houses, Lancaster and York*, 1619; prepared in facsimile by Charles Praetorius, 1886 |
| Reed | *The Plays of William Shakespeare*, [ed. Isaac Reed], 10 vols., 1785 |
| *Ren. Drama* | *Renaissance Drama* |
| *RES* | *Review of English Studies* |
| Riverside | *The Riverside Shakespeare*, ed. G. Blakemore Evans, 1974 |
| Robinson | Marilynne S. Robinson, 'A new look at Shakespeare's *Henry VI*, *Part II*: sources, structure, and meaning', unpublished PhD dissertation, University of Washington, 1977 |
| *RORD* | *Research Opportunities in Renaissance Drama* |

| | |
|---|---|
| Rowe | *The Works of Mr William Shakespear*, ed. Nicholas Rowe, 6 vols., 1709 |
| Rowe$^2$ | *The Works of Mr William Shakespear*, ed. Nicholas Rowe, 2nd edn, 6 vols., 1709 |
| Rowe$^3$ | *The Works of Mr William Shakespear*, ed. Nicholas Rowe, 3rd edn, 8 vols., 1714 |
| Sanders | *2 Henry VI*, ed. Norman Sanders, 1981 (New Penguin) |
| SB | *Studies in Bibliography* |
| Schmidt | Alexander Schmidt, *Shakespeare-Lexicon*, 1866 edn |
| Scott-Giles | C. W. Scott-Giles, *Shakespeare's Heraldry*, 1950 |
| SD | stage direction |
| SEL | *Studies in English Literature* |
| Seymour | E. H. Seymour, *Remarks... upon the Plays of Shakespeare*, 2 vols., 1805 |
| SH | speech heading |
| Shakespeare's England | *Shakespeare's England: An Account of the Life and Manners of his Age*, ed. Sidney Lee and C. T. Onions, 2 vols., 1916 |
| Singer | *The Dramatic Works of William Shakespeare*, ed. Samuel Weller Singer, 10 vols., 1826 |
| Singer$^2$ | *The Dramatic Works of William Shakespeare*, ed. Samuel Weller Singer, 10 vols., 1856 |
| Sisson | Charles Sisson ed., *Works*, 1954 |
| Sisson, *New Readings* | C. J. Sisson, *New Readings in Shakespeare*, 2 vols., 1956 |
| SQ | *Shakespeare Quarterly* |
| S.St. | *Shakespeare Studies* |
| S.Sur. | *Shakespeare Survey* |
| Staunton | *The Plays of William Shakespeare*, ed. Howard Staunton, 3 vols., 1858–60 |
| Steevens | *The Plays of William Shakespeare*, ed. George Steevens and Isaac Reed, 4th edn, 15 vols., 1793 |
| Stow | John Stow, *The Survey of London*, 1603 edn, reprinted in Everyman Library, n.d. |
| subst. | substantively |
| Sugden | E. H. Sugden, *A Topographical Dictionary to the Works of Shakespeare and his Fellow Dramatists*, 1925 |
| Theobald | *The Works of Shakespeare*, ed. Lewis Theobald, 7 vols., 1733 |
| Theobald$^2$ | *The Works of Shakespeare*, ed. Lewis Theobald, 8 vols., 1740 |
| Thomas | K. V. Thomas, *Religion and the Decline of Magic*, 1971 |
| Thomson | W. H. Thomson, *Shakespeare's Characters: A Historical Dictionary*, 1951 |
| Tilley | M. P. Tilley, *A Dictionary of the Proverbs in England in the Sixteenth and Seventeenth Centuries*, 1950 (references are to numbered proverbs) |
| TLN | Through line numbering |
| Vaughan | Henry H. Vaughan, *New Readings and Renderings of Shakespeare's Tragedies*, 3 vols., 1886 |
| Walker | William S. Walker, *Critical Examination of the Text of Shakespeare*, 3 vols., 1860 |
| Warburton | *The Works of Shakespeare*, ed. William Warburton, 8 vols., 1747 |

| Wells and Taylor, *Textual Companion* | Stanley Wells and Gary Taylor, *William Shakespeare: A Textual Companion*, 1987 |
| White | *Works*, ed. Richard Grand White, 12 vols., 1857–66 |
| Williams | Penry Williams, *The Tudor Regime*, 1979 |
| Wilson | *2 Henry VI*, ed. J. Dover Wilson, 1952 (New Shakespeare) |

Unless otherwise specified, biblical quotations are given in the Geneva version (1560).

# INTRODUCTION

## Henry VI: the reign and the plays

If men did know what shining fetters, gilded miseries, and painted happiness thrones and sceptres were, there would not be so frequent strife about the getting or holding of them.

Ben Jonson, 'Character principis' in Discoveries[1]

*Henry VI Part 2* is a fine, important, and undervalued play. Its scope is ambitious in that it attends to the large and public concerns of dynastic wars, and yet it is able to uncover, by exposing the very theatricality of those at the centre of the political stage, the most complex web of petty jealousies and private agonies. This human interest, however, depends upon a clarity of historical analysis that can be understood only if a reader or spectator attends closely to the play's particular analytic techniques and does not interpret it in terms of any grand design. This introduction will therefore begin by arguing that Shakespeare, unlike Edmund Spenser, for example,[2] did not slavishly endorse 'the Tudor Myth': this play and the group of plays to which it belongs do *not* propose simply that God had led England through the troubled times of dissension between Lancastrian and Yorkist dynasties to fulfil her destiny with the enthronement of Henry Tudor as Henry VII. If there is a grand design it is only dimly glimpsed, for the emphasis of Shakespeare, if not always of his characters, rests firmly upon efficient and not final causes. He had, at the opening of the sequence, laid down a challenge to all those who linked historical change to the mysteries of divine retribution by having a Messenger respond unequivocally to the suggestion that it was the sin of treachery that caused the loss of France. 'No treachery', he retorts tersely, 'but want of men and money' (*1 Henry VI* 1.1.69).[3] The political thrust of *Part 2* is likewise a demonstration that it is internal dissension, in particular seditious squabbling among the nobility, that damaged England's power and authority abroad. We are reminded of Kyd's report of Marlowe's table talk: 'That things esteemed to be done by divine power might have as well been done by observation of [i.e. what is observed in] men'.[4] Moreover, it can be argued, the variety of styles found throughout the sequence contributes to the analysis and need not be taken as evidence of multiple authorship or revision, but rather of perspectivism, a dramatic cross-examination from differing points of view, embodied in different dramatic styles, of the issues raised and events enacted on the stage. From the

---

[1] Jonson, VIII, 62.
[2] *FQ*, III, iii, 48–9.
[3] See Michael Hattaway (ed.), *1H6*, 1990, pp. 13–16.
[4] Harleian MS 6849, fol. 218.

I

theatrical shorthand techniques Shakespeare used to depict the battles between England and France in *Part 1*, through the developing complexities of character in the events of *Part 2* – which is centred around the death of good Duke Humphrey of Gloucester and the rebellion of York – to the opposition of tormented Henry VI and murderous Richard of Gloucester[1] under Edward IV in *Part 3*, Shakespeare demonstrated a quite extraordinary capacity to 'set a form upon that indigest'.[2] The heroical idioms and scenical strutting of *1 Henry VI* disappear from the stage to be replaced by more workaday theatrical registers as Shakespeare traces the wane of England's glory and the mounting ferment of political intrigue.[3]

Rather than beginning, therefore, with a description of the 'transgressions against history'[4] that Shakespeare was guilty of in his *Henry VI* plays – his account, that is, of the period from the funeral of Henry V in 1422 to the battle of Tewkesbury in 1471 – or a rehearsal of arguments over what parts of the plays Shakespeare may or may not have written,[5] let us consider what might have drawn him to this complicated chapter in the history of fifteenth-century England. Complicated it is, and so it was inevitable that its very wealth of incident led the dramatist to begin his career as a writer of history plays by concentrating as much on actions and their outcomes as on personalities and their motives: he could not avoid investigating politics and the secular as well as morality and the theological.

Unlike the reigns of Henry V and Richard III, that of Henry VI was not dominated by the personality of its monarch – Edward IV's rule during the last years of Henry's 'reign' is stark evidence of this. Rather it was a period of war between nations (the Hundred Years War) and within the kingdom (the Wars of the Roses). It was also a time of dynastic strife which manifested itself in both aristocratic factionalism and popular insurrection, a sequence of contests between allegiance to the monarchy and alliance between peers. Shakespeare offered to the playhouse audiences of sixteenth-century London a deliberate rearrangement of historical events into dramatic themes. For this reason, therefore, the plays are best regarded not simply as 'adapted history' or as vehicles for dramatic biography, but as a set of complex essays on the *politics* of the mid fifteenth century – essays which, of course, also offer reflections on Shakespeare's own times. For it was only after he had in this way learned to convert chronicle into political analysis that he turned to the kind of history that thrusts personality out into the foreground of the action: *Richard II*, *Henry IV*, and *Henry V* were written after the *Henry VI* plays and *Richard III*. The great sequence of studies of the history and politics of England was not composed in the order of the chronology of her Plantagenet rulers.

[1] Youngest son of York, and later Richard III.
[2] *John* 5.7.26; see Larry Champion, 'The search for dramatic form: *1, 2, 3 Henry VI*', in *Perspective in Shakespeare's English Histories*, 1980, pp. 12–53.
[3] For a general analysis of the style of the play see David Riggs, *Shakespeare's Heroical Histories: 'Henry VI' and its Literary Tradition*, 1971; L. C. Knights, 'Rhetoric and insincerity' and Wolfgang Clemen, 'Some aspects of style in the *Henry VI* plays', in P. Edwards, I.-S. Ewbank, G. K. Hunter (eds.), *Shakespeare's Styles: Essays in Honour of Kenneth Muir*, 1980, pp. 1–8 and 9–24; James C. Bulman, *The Heroic Idiom of Shakespearean Tragedy*, 1985, pp. 26–44.
[4] Theobald, IV, p. 390 n.
[5] See below, p. 59 n. 5, and M. Hattaway (ed.), *1H6*, 1990, pp. 41–3.

1   An army camp. A cut from Holinshed, *Chronicles of England, Scotland, and Ireland*, 1577

### THE LOSS OF FRANCE AND THE WARS OF THE ROSES

Henry VI came to the throne as a nine-month-old infant in 1422,[1] and while he was a minor England was ruled through a council, his uncle 'good' Duke Humphrey of Gloucester being Protector. During Henry's reign, despite the heroism on the field of battle of John Talbot, first Earl of Shrewsbury, and the overthrow and capture of the champion of the French, Joan, la Pucelle (see *1 Henry VI* 5.3–4), the French territory won back for England by virtue of his heroic father Henry V's victory at Agincourt in 1415 (*Henry V* 4.1–8) had been, by 1453, recovered by his maternal uncle, Charles VII of France.

In *1 Henry VI*, Shakespeare moved from the funeral of Henry V through to the marriage of his son. He took us through a sequence of battles at Orléans (*1 Henry VI* 1.2ff.), Rouen, and Bordeaux (3.2ff. and 4.2ff.),[2] leading to a truce which was called at Tours in 1444 (5.4) and which centred on a politic marriage for Henry (arranged with an eye to his own benefit by the Earl of Suffolk) with Margaret of Anjou, a cousin to King Charles. Although *1 Henry VI* thus ended, unhistorically, with an English triumph, Shakespeare demonstrated *en route* that the empire had been irremediably weakened and that this was principally caused by internal sedition.

---

[1]   Ralph Griffiths, *The Reign of King Henry VI*, 1981, offers a modern history of the reign; see also K. B. McFarlane, *England in the Fifteenth Century*, 1982. W. G. Boswell-Stone, *Shakespeare's Holinshed, the Chronicle and the Historical Plays Compared*, 1896, reprints passages from the sources in the order Shakespeare deployed them; Peter Saccio, *Shakespeare's English Kings*, 1977, offers a modern account of the dramatic chronicle provided by Shakespeare.

[2]   Rouen in fact was not taken by the French until 1449–50, and the fighting at Bordeaux took place nine years *after* the truce of Tours in 1444.

*Part 1*, therefore, constituted a historical prologue, a demonstration of the way in which the Hundred Years War affected the Wars of the Roses, which are dramatised in *Parts 2* and *3*. The title of the 'bad Quarto' of *Part 2*, *The First Part of the Contention betwixt the two Famous Houses of York and Lancaster*, therefore, need not suggest that Shakespeare might have begun writing his sequence with the second play,[1] but simply that he was following Holinshed, who clearly announced his intention of attending to happenings in England after he had completed his account of the Treaty of Tours:

Whilst the wars between the two nations of England and France ceased...the minds of men were not so quiet, but that such as were bent to malicious revenge sought to compass their prepensed purpose, not against foreign foes and enemies of their country, but against their own countrymen and those that had deserved very well of the commonwealth.[2]

Margaret's coronation in 1445 marks the beginning of *2 Henry VI*. This play concentrates largely on the conspiracy of Buckingham, Somerset, and Cardinal Beaufort, Bishop of Winchester, to take power from Humphrey of Gloucester, Protector of the kingdom and father figure to the king, and on civil tumult, the Wars of the Roses. These had begun when Henry's cousin Richard, third Duke of York, laid claim to the throne. The claim was based on the grounds that York was the maternal great-great-grandson of Lionel Duke of Clarence, third son of Edward III (1327–77), whereas Henry was great-grandson of John of Gaunt, Duke of Lancaster, the fourth son (see Appendix 1, pp. 225–6). York chose as his badge a white rose, while the Lancastrians, led by York's enemy Somerset, wore red roses (*1 Henry VI* 2.4). (Henry VI's claim was further weakened by the fact that his grandfather Henry IV – 'Bullingbrook' – was commonly held to have usurped the throne and murdered the childless Richard II in 1400.) Moreover, rebellion broke out in Ireland, and York, who was assigned to put it down, took the opportunity to make his army serve his own ambition (*2 Henry VI* 3.1), winning the first battle of St Albans on 22 May 1455. This is depicted in the final sequence of *2 Henry VI*.

Henry was compelled to acknowledge York as heir apparent to the crown in 1460 (*3 Henry VI* 1.1), but York was defeated and savagely killed at the battle of Wakefield at the end of that year (*3 Henry VI* 1.3–4), a battle in which the barbarous Cliffords played a prominent part on the Lancastrian side. The Yorkists were defeated again at the second battle of St Albans in February 1461 (*3 Henry VI* 2.1), but the Lancastrians then withdrew north while York's eldest son Edward was proclaimed as King Edward IV in London. The next month Edward marched northwards and won the battle of Towton, which established him on the throne (*3 Henry* 2.3–6),[3] and Henry took refuge in Scotland (his wife and son going into exile in France) until he was captured (*3 Henry VI* 3.1). He was imprisoned in the

---

[1] See pp. 56–68.
[2] Holinshed, p. 210.
[3] The famous scene (*3H6* 2.5) in which the king sees a father who has killed his son and a son who has killed his father is fictitious.

Tower (*3 Henry VI* 3.1) from 1465 until 1470, when he was restored to the throne by the 'Kingmaker', Earl of Warwick (*3 Henry VI* 4.2 and 4.6). Warwick had been enraged by the news that Edward, 'taking counsel of his own desire',[1] had made an impolitic marriage with the widow Elizabeth, Lady Grey (*3 Henry VI* 3.2) while Warwick was abroad negotiating for the hand of a French princess for the new king. In April 1471, after losing the battle of Barnet, in which Warwick was killed (*3 Henry VI* 5.2–3), Henry fell into the hands of Edward again, and Queen Margaret was defeated by Edward's younger brother Richard of Gloucester at the battle of Tewkesbury the next month (*3 Henry VI* 5.4–5). Henry was recommitted to the Tower, where, on the night of Edward's return, he was murdered (*3 Henry VI* 5.6) – it is supposed by Gloucester. The sequence ends with a brief appearance by Edward's twelve-year-old son, later Edward V, who also was to be murdered in the Tower by Gloucester, along with his brother Richard.[2]

The reign, then, was a pattern of disorder, a mirror for Shakespeare's contemporaries of the disasters of the type of dynastic strife, centred on personal ambition rather than any desire for reform, which could so easily have broken out upon the death of Elizabeth. Francis Bacon was to rejoice at the succession of King James, fearing that without it:

after Queen Elizabeth's decease, there must follow in England nothing but confusions, interreigns, and perturbations of estate, likely far to exceed the ancient calamities of Lancaster and York.[3]

Not only were there 'vertical' divisions between the noble factions: the reign witnessed division between the populace and the élite in the Jack Cade rebellion.[4] In his handling of this event, Shakespeare defined a distinct group or even class consciousness[5] for his rebels, although the text also demonstrates the way in which political conflagration occurred when the horizontal divisions manifest in popular discontent were exacerbated by aristocratic dissension.[6]

To dramatise all this was massively ambitious, innovative – there were no popular plays on English history before the Armada in 1588 – and potentially radical (see pp. 6–8). A dramatic sequence as long as this must also have created distinctive theatrical conventions – as modern revivals have demonstrated. It would have been expensive to perform in sequence without recourse to a standardised repertory style with some uniformity in costumes and with doubling – which may

---

[1] Hall, p. 366.
[2] See *Richard III* 4.3; Richard III, of course, was to be defeated and killed by Queen Elizabeth's Tudor grandfather, Henry VII, at the battle of Bosworth in 1485, so uniting the white rose with the red.
[3] *The Beginning of the History of Great Britain*, in *Works*, Spedding, Ellis and Heath (eds.), 15 vols., 1857–74, VI, pp. 276–7.
[4] See *2 H6* 4.2–3, 5–9.
[5] On this notion in the period, see J. A. Sharpe, *Early Modern England: A Social History, 1550–1760*, 1987, p. 121; see also Michael Hattaway, 'Rebellion, class consciousness, and Shakespeare's *2 Henry VI*', *Cahiers élisabéthains* 33 (1988), 13–22.
[6] For an account of the military power of aristocratic magnates in the 1590s see Sharpe, p. 160.

itself have made telling political comments on the action. These plays are not vehicles for star performers, although modern actors have amassed great reputations from playing in them.

Political plays fell out of favour in the Jacobean period, and in the eighteenth century the plays disappeared almost completely from the canon of performed works. Perhaps they were too radical and anti-establishment; the female characters, moreover, were not objects of sentiment but seekers after power.[1] For the nineteenth century, they were unsuited for performance on naturalistic stages – and perhaps their anatomy of empire was too critical. In our own times literary critics have found them disappointingly based on narrative rather than significant structure, lacking both psychologically complex characters and the kinds of verbal density that Shakespeare was to attain in his later plays. But this is to ignore the particular theatrical qualities that modern directors have found in them and their tough-minded anatomy of the political nation of England.

## The play: a political documentary

### FROM *1 HENRY VI* TO *2 HENRY VI*

*1 Henry VI* may well have been written written to show how the history of a nation is never to be understood in isolation. The Wars of the Roses, which form the subject of the second two parts of the sequence, can be fully understood only in the context of the Hundred Years War, dramatised incidents from which formed the substance of the first play. *1 Henry VI* portrayed the decline of England's empire over France and the accompanying decay of the ideals of feudalism that had sustained the order of the realm. That play also established themes – the deaths of the old Titans from the reign of Henry V, the attacks on Duke Humphrey the Protector, the origins of the York–Lancaster quarrel, and Suffolk's bid for power through his intimate relationship with Queen Margaret – but all the events of the play were presented as much for their potential as for their actual significance, so that the end was no conclusion. Just as *1 Henry VI* began with a funeral, the traditional end of tragedy, so *2 Henry VI* begins with a marriage, the traditional end of comedy. These inverted dramatic patterns help create a new and 'open' form, the political play – perhaps in fact all Shakespeare's history plays ought to be redesignated 'political plays'.

In *Part 2* the political focus is on the way the loss of empire breeds further insurrection: by the colonised, by the nobles, and by the people. In this play France is, to all intents and purposes, finally lost (3.1.83–5), Ireland erupts in revolt

---

[1] So we read in the introduction to Bell's *Edition of Shakespeare's Plays*, 1774: 'National transactions, however important they may be in their nature and consequences, are not likely to have a very popular effect, as they tend chiefly to indulge political reflection, but have very little to gratify taste. Such pieces as this are also very barren of female characters and affecting circumstances, without which the drama is too defective. Shakespeare has herein adhered to facts, and maintained just preservation of character, without producing one striking scene: it is not therefore to be recommended for representation' (VII, 89).

(3.1.282–4), and York is laying claim to the throne and not just jostling for authority. To further their cause, the Yorkist party have fomented a popular revolt led by York's creature, Jack Cade. No republican freedom, however, will emerge from the decay of empire, but merely the loosing upon the kingdom of the wars of the barons. These events conspire to undermine the power of the king and even the monarchy: Shakespeare, after writing the long prelude of *Part 1* in which he sketched out the swelling acts of his imperial themes, now turns to a closer examination of how, as the Lieutenant interrogating Suffolk puts it, 'reproach and beggary / Is crept into the palace of our king' (4.1.101–2).

RADICAL HISTORIOGRAPHY

Shakespeare, in fact, while seeming in this text to be both anti-aristocratic and, on occasion, anti-plebeian, can still be radical. His radicalism comes not just from allegiance to one estate in the realm, but is to be understood in its literal sense: it derives from an ability to root out the causes of political dilemmas, to demonstrate the partiality of contesting explanations of particular events – while showing that there is no easy way of discriminating between one set of values and another – and from a tendency to demolish myth through demystification. Shakespeare's history serves as an art of demonstration, rather than, as it had been in the hands of medieval chroniclers, an art of interpretation. Interpretation, wrote Walter Benjamin, 'is not concerned with an accurate concatenation of definite events, but with the way these are embedded in the great inscrutable course of the world'.[1]

Such enquiry could appear 'oppositional': on 12 November 1589 the Privy Council had written to the Archbishop of Canterbury, the Lord Mayor of London, and the Master of the Revels asking them each to appoint someone to scrutinise all plays performed in and about the City of London because the players had taken 'upon themselves to handle in their plays certain matters of divinity and state unfit to be suffered'.[2] There is no sign in the Folio version of the play of certain passages found in the Quarto, and this may well be the result of censorship consequent upon this instruction.[3] The sequence which shows Cade at the height of his power (4.5.0 SD – 4.6.5) may equally have been censored.[4] This suggests that not only were *playhouses* seen as centres of disorder and riot but that the *plays* performed in them could appear subversive.

The writing of history, as we have seen, entails the making of political statements. At the end of *Henry V*, Shakespeare, looking back to his earlier work, has the Chorus say of the hero of that play:

---

[1] Walter Benjamin, 'The storyteller', in his *Illuminations*, trans. H. Zohn, 1970, p. 96.
[2] Chambers, IV, 306; several cancelled pages in the 1587 edition of Holinshed dealing with the Babington plot and recent events in Scotland and Ireland indicate that his *Chronicles* were in fact censored; see Janet Clare, '"Greater themes for insurrection's arguing": political censorship of the Elizabethan and Jacobean stage', *RES* 38 (1987), 169–183.
[3] See Appendix 2, pp. 230–3; Cairncross, pp. xxv–xxix; Clare, 'Greater themes'.
[4] See Textual Analysis, pp. 219–20.

> Fortune made his sword,
> By which the world's best garden he achieved,
> And of it left his son imperial lord.
> Henry the Sixth, in infant bands crowned King
> Of France and England, did this king succeed,
> Whose state *so many had the managing*
> *That they lost France and made his England bleed.*

(Epilogue, 6–12, emphasis added)

With its stress on the way man 'manages his own state', makes his own history, *2* and *3 Henry VI* share with Marlowe's *Edward II* the quality of documentary.[1] Moreover, Shakespeare refuses to glamorise any of the events which precipitated change. After dramatising emblematically in *Part 1* the origin in the Temple Garden of the Wars of the Roses, he now shows us, with a gesture towards the Genesis myth perhaps, a world 'after the garden' in which political deals are struck as individuals compete for power. Shakespeare's reading of the troublesome reign of Henry VI, accordingly, takes its nature *not* from the visitation of divine vengeance for an original sin (the deposition and murder of Richard II) committed two generations before but from the aspirations of particular estates.[2] Even Edward Hall, one of Shakespeare's principal sources for the sequence, sardonically offers in the course of his chronicle a secular alternative to the model of providentially ordered history he had earlier set out in the 'Introduction into the History of King Henry the Fourth', with which his chronicle began:[3]

For many of the nobility, and more of the mean estate, wisely pondering the estate and condition of the realm, perceiving more loss than increase, more ruin than advancement, daily to ensue; remembering also that France was conquered, and Normandy was gained by the French people in short space, thought with themselves and imagined that the fault of all these miserable chances happened either because the king was not the true inheritor to the crown, or that he or his council were not able of wit, policy, and circumspection to rule and govern so noble a realm, or so famous a region.[4]

King Henry might invoke the idea of divine judgement, as for example when he hears of Gloucester's death (3.2.136–40), but Shakespeare's laying out of motive, event, and consequence offers spectators no real demonstration that the troubles of the kingdom are the *consequence* of divine displeasure or retribution. God's purposes are in no way to be deduced from the play.

In this fallen world no political value is left untested – and in performance the

---

[1] See Hattaway, chap. 6.

[2] Holinshed (p. 208) does ascribe to God displeasure at the marriage of Henry with Margaret of Anjou and relates the events of reign to this (see Appendix 1, p. 221); Hall (p. 205) calls the marriage 'infortunate and unprofitable'.

[3] Hall, pp. 1–2; E. M. W. Tillyard took this part of Hall's text as the key to the whole 'cycle' of history plays and let it inform his reading of *2H6* – see *Shakespeare's History Plays*, 1944, pp. 147ff.; compare J. P. Brockbank, who argues that Shakespeare reproduces a scheme of retributive justice he finds in the chronicles, but recoils from it by investing scenes of retribution with an atmosphere of horror. See 'The frame of disorder – *Henry VI*', in J. R. Brown and B. Harris (eds.), *Early Shakespeare*, 1961, p. 90.

[4] Hall, p. 219.

text may have been coloured even more with populism. Early in the play Gloucester invokes the old military values that informed *Part 1*. When he realises that Suffolk has given away many of the remaining French provinces his outburst reads thus in the Folio text:

> What, did my brother Henry spend his youth,
> His valour, coin, and people in the wars?
> Did he so often lodge in open field,
> In winter's cold and summer's parching heat,
> To conquer France, his true inheritance?
> And did my brother Bedford toil his wits
> To keep by policy what Henry got? (1.1.75–81)

Q1's version of the text, which may contain material the gist of which was censored, or which may record what a player, himself sceptical of the court's version of honour, thought of Suffolk's betrayal, reads like this:

> What, did my brother Henry toil himself
> And waste his subjects for to conquer France?
> And did my brother Bedford spend his time
> To keep in awe that stout unruly realm? (TLN 101–4)

The emphasis changes from a focus on the heroism and honour of the English champions to the *cost* of their wasteful struggle to conquer and control. Later Lord Say will pay with his life because Cade's rebels hold him responsible not only for the actual loss of Normandy but for high subsidies they had to pay to prosecute these wars (see 4.7.17–18).

Without the monarch's imperial control, all of these conflicting political and economic forces serve to lay bare the nature of the rest of the institutional fabric of the kingdom. One of the central events of the play, the murder of good Duke Humphrey of Gloucester, symbolises the extinction of equity, the final term of Saturnian rule incarnate in Henry V, just as the death of Talbot in *1 Henry VI* stood for the end of feudal valour. Hall describes Gloucester thus: 'the duke, being very well learned in the law civil, detesting malefactors and punishing their offences, got great malice and hatred of such as feared to have condign reward for their ungracious acts and mischievous doings'.[1] The murder of such a figure marks a change in the nature of the state: the play seems to embody Machiavelli's model of political degradation, as illustrated in the *Discorsi*:

I must...observe that some of the writers on politics distinguished three kinds of government, viz. the monarchical, the aristocratic, and the democratic; and maintain that the legislators of a people must choose from these three the one that seems to them most suitable. Other authors, wiser according to the opinion of many, count six kinds of governments, three of which are very bad, and three good in themselves, but so liable to be corrupted that they become absolutely bad. The three good ones are those which we have

---

[1] Hall, p. 209; Humphrey became proverbial as an exemplary statesman: in a work by Thomas Dekker, a character is described as being so depraved that 'he would revolt from Duke Humphrey' (*The Meeting of Gallants at an Ordinarie*, 1604, sig. B2ʳ).

just named; the three bad ones result from the degradation of the other three, and each of them resembles its corresponding original, so that the transition from the one to the other is very easy. Thus monarchy becomes tyranny; aristocracy degenerates into oligarchy; and the popular government lapses readily into licentiousness.[1]

In *2 Henry VI*, in the absence of a strong monarchy, we see what is, in effect, an oligarchy. Popular rule under Cade collapses into anarchy. The decline into tyranny will be complete when Richard III mounts the throne. In such a world men revert to their atavistic states:[2] Clifford's evocation of Medea's archaic savagery at the end of the play is a measure of how family bonds – the *pietas* of the ancients emblematized in his second figure of Aeneas – are swept aside by the will to power and revenge:

> Meet I an infant of the house of York,
> Into as many gobbets will I cut it
> As wild Medea young Absyrtis did;
> In cruelty will I seek out my fame.
> > [*He takes his father's body up on his back.*]
> Come, thou new ruin of old Clifford's house:
> As did Aeneas old Anchises bear,
> So bear I thee upon my manly shoulders;
> But then Aeneas bare a living load,
> Nothing so heavy as these woes of mine. (5.2.57–65)

Henry VI too was haunted by his father, and in *Part 3*, at the battle of Towton, he will see a son who has killed his father and a father who has killed his son. Thus are brought home to him the evils he has created by failing to control the peers of England.

The radical nature of Shakespeare's historical analysis can be seen from another perspective by comparing the trilogy with 'history' plays on similar themes written about a decade later, in 1599: *Sir John Oldcastle*, for example, a collaboration by Drayton, Hathway, Munday, and Wilson, or Thomas Heywood's *Edward IV*. These were produced when Queen Elizabeth was confronting the crisis posed by the insubordinate but popular Earl of Essex.[3] The former deals in part with the rebellion of the Earl of Cambridge, York's father, and treats it as a simple case of treachery,[4] and the latter takes the absolute power of the monarchy for granted: the institution is revered by the populace and the sensual failings of the hero happily condoned. Neither play attempts the great confrontations of authority with power which are the true subjects of Shakespeare's histories.

---

[1] Niccolo Machiavelli, *The Discourses*, i.ii., trans. L. Ricci, 1950 edn, pp. 111–12.
[2] See Robinson, pp. 16–19.
[3] See J. E. Neale, *Queen Elizabeth I*, 1952 edn., chap. 21.
[4] Drayton, *Works*, i, 420–6; compare his 'Duke Humphrey to Eleanor Cobham', 90–110, in *England's Heroical Epistles*, 1619 (*Works*, ii, 226).

GREATNESS AND GOODNESS

Monarchical rule does not depend merely upon the power of office but upon the personal authority of the ruler.[1] After the titanic rule of Henry V, England under his pious young son contained a partial power vacuum into which all the malcontent factions seen forming in *1 Henry VI* were drawn. Throughout *Part 1* the king and the kingdom had been protected by the valour of Talbot and the testy magistracy of Duke Humphrey of Gloucester, who had foiled the plans of his uncle the Cardinal of Winchester to take over the government of England. Talbot is now dead, and in this play Henry attains his majority and dismisses Gloucester, throwing 'away his crutch / Before his legs be firm to bear his body' (3.1.189–90). Henry has an overweening confidence that his virtue can stand alone, and an inability to understand that, as Machiavelli had demonstrated, monarchical authority derives as much from the way he is perceived as from anything else. To his courtiers he seems merely a holy fool, a man who, according to his wife, is more interested in observing antiquated papal rituals than in wielding his imperial sceptre. This may, however, be too simple a view of his character. Rather, within the welter of the political action he stands – in the main – for goodness, and in this play the hard question is put: is greatness in a monarchy to be built upon goodness, or is it only to be won through 'policy', the skills Machiavelli deemed necessary for the acquisition and maintenance of princely power? Like Machiavelli, Shakespeare emerges as a realist and does not align himself with those Christian humanists who tended to assert that only a good man could be a great man.[2]

Henry, however, obviously considered himself as one who should play the two roles of emperor and shepherd, the great man and the good man, roles that were supposed to be combined in the person of the Holy Roman Emperor.[3] His marriage had done something to restore empire by joining the houses of England and France,[4] although the league was not to last long. Sometimes Shakespeare gives us an imperious Henry who realises that moral virtue is not enough and who can be politic and ruthless:

> Tell him I'll send Duke Edmund to the Tower –
> And, Somerset, we will commit thee thither,
> Until his army be dismissed from him.                              (4.9.38–40)

However, all too often, especially after the death of Duke Humphrey, Henry's religious inclinations blind him to political realities: his tendency to perceive men

---

[1] These notions can be explored in Richard Tuck, '*Power* and *authority* in seventeenth-century England', *The Historical Journal* 17 (1974), 43–61.

[2] The relationship between these concepts was explored, for example, in Virgilian epigrams translated by Chapman and included in his *Petrarch's Seven Penitential Psalms*, 1612 (*Poems*, ed. P. B. Bartlett, 1941, pp. 227–30).

[3] Compare *3H6* 2.5, and see Frances Yates, *Astraea*, 1975, pp. 25–6.

[4] In this connection compare the praise of Charles V, sprung from the union of Austria and Aragon and celebrated by Ariosto, *Orlando Furioso*, trans. Sir John Harington, 1591, XV, xxi, ff.

2  Ralph Fiennes as Henry and Penny Downie as Margaret in Adrian Noble's 1988 Stratford production

as instruments of God's will[1] makes him peculiarly ineffectual, destined for goodness but not for greatness. He looks constantly to heaven for miracles: those around him (and the audience) are far more pragmatic concerning these matters. 'They say miracles are past, and we have our philosophical persons to make modern and familiar, things supernatural and causeless:'[2] these lines from *All's Well that Ends Well* point to a long-running debate over whether, by Shakespeare's time, the age of miracles was in fact well past.[3] Before the demonstration early in the play that the restoration of Saunder Simpcox's sight was a fraud, Henry had been all too ready to take it as a miracle; he likewise treats the news of the putting down of the Cade rebellion in 4.9 as a miracle, although the previous scene has demonstrated to the audience that it was put down by the lion-and-fox tactics of Clifford. Henry's goodness is thereby rendered impotent by the sheer strength of the forces ranged against him and the machinations of 'the great' – including his wife Margaret.

But personality is not to be isolated from event. *2 Henry VI*, like all of Shakespeare's political plays, not only offers us chronicles and portraits of great men but analyses the meshing of personality and situation and anatomizes institutions and not just events. Central to its concerns is an analysis of the function of the monarchy itself and an examination of the relationship between the personality of Henry VI and the role he has to play. The king had to serve two functions: the symbolic, mystical, quasi-divine role as incarnation of the body politic of the kingdom, 'a corporation in himself that liveth ever',[4] and the role of a 'natural' man subject to the vicissitudes of change, the whips and scorns of office. The conflict between these two 'bodies', the politic and the natural, the discrepancy between ideals and realities, was all too noticeable in Shakespeare's time – it is manifest in the interrupted ceremonies which are such a notable feature of the history plays,[5] and in the way, within the estate of nobility, allegiance falls prey to alliance. The nature of the institution itself, in other words, was perceived to be subject to strain.

In *Part 1* we saw that Henry was not introduced merely as a martyr king,[6] and in

---

[1] Compare *3H6* 4.6.18.

[2] *AWW* 2.3.1–2.

[3] Thomas, pp. 92–3 etc.

[4] Dr John Cowell, *The Interpreter or Book Containing the Signification of Words*, 1607, s.v. 'King', quoted in E. H. Kantorowicz, *The King's Two Bodies*, 1957.

[5] See Michael Hattaway (ed.), *1H6*, pp. 14–21.

[6] 'In 1494, Pope Alexander VI ordered the appointment of a commission to investigate the reports of the numerous miracles of Henry VI said to have occurred in many parts of England, and a magnificent chapel in Westminster Abbey – now known as the Chapel of Henry VII – was prepared to receive the mortal remains of Henry VI' (H. Mutschmann and K. Wentersdorf, *Shakespeare and Catholicism*, 1952, p. 354). The unsuccessful attempt by Henry VII to have Henry VI canonised by Pope Julius is described by Bacon: 'The general opinion was, that Pope Julius was too dear, and that the king would not come to his rates. But it is more probable that the pope...knowing that King Henry the Sixth was reputed in the world abroad but for a simple man, was afraid it would but diminish the estimation of that kind of honour, if there were not a distance kept between innocents and saints' (*Bacon's History of the Reign of King Henry VII*, ed. J. R. Lumby, 1881, p. 207; compare Holinshed, p. 325, Hall, p. 304).

*Part 2* his predicament does not come just from his personality but rather from the conditions of the body politic. Like Hamlet and like characters in *King John*, he has to confront an intractable political problem: the conflicting and irreconcilable claims of those who held the crown by possession and those who wanted it held by right. Shakespeare compounds the ethical dilemma by making York obviously cravenly ambitious – most of the time – and making Henry party to the cause and not just judge of it. Henry, in other words, faced a political as well as an ethical dilemma, compounded by the fact that his own rule was part of the problem.

LAW, JUSTICE, AND THE 'MIRROR SCENES'

The play is particularly concerned with the nature and workings of law in such a society. It used to be argued that Shakespeare measured men against an ideal moral order, indicating that actions could be measured against laws that had their origins in the natural and ultimately the divine. Critics were inclined to look to theologians such as Richard Hooker, who was committed to looking for correspondence between the heavenly order and terrestrial practice,[1] rather than to historians such as William Harrison, who interrupted his survey of the laws of England with a sceptical observation that might have astounded a previous generation:

For what hath the meditation of the law of God to do with any precise knowledge of the law of man, sith they are several trades and incident to divers persons.[2]

In England under Henry, law bears little relation to divinity and stands divorced from equity. The regnal and judiciary roles of the king's court are hopelessly confused, so that the status of the institution itself is compromised. The Duchess of Gloucester, having been enticed into treason by *agents provocateurs* planted by her political adversaries, is banished, and the prosecution of her case makes it easier for the court – in a scene where it has been actually constituted as a parliament – to find a pretext to have her husband murdered before his case can come to trial. The age's conversion of self-interest into policy, of law into expediency, is proclaimed by the Bishop of Winchester, Cardinal Beaufort, himself:

> That he should die is worthy policy;
> But yet we want a colour for his death:
> 'Tis meet he be condemned by course of law. (3.1.235–7)

The feudal ritual of trial by combat (archaic by Shakespeare's day although, significantly, the form preferred by King Henry[3]) is reduced to the grotesque fight between the drunken armourer and his apprentice – Shakespeare developed this scene from a couple of sentences in the chroniclers, who do not specify what

[1] See Richard Hooker, *Of the Laws of Ecclesiastical Polity*, 1593, Book 1.
[2] F. J. Furnivall (ed.), *Elizabethan England* (London, n.d.), p. 51.
[3] See 3.2.232–5; for trial by battle see Thomas, pp. 260–1 and G. Holderness, L. Potter, and J. Turner, *Shakespeare: The Play of History*, 1988, pp. 26–32.

the treasonable remarks were.[1] It serves to mirror the realities of the play: instead of seeing justice determined by God with regard to the rights of the adversaries, here we see simply a trial of might. The tone of the encounter is caught by the terse marginal gloss on the event that we find in Holinshed: 'Drunkenness the overthrow of right and manhood'.[2] The fight, moreover, was occasioned by the accident of one of the petitions reaching Suffolk. This lord prevents the right of the other petitioners to have their complaints heard by the Protector[3] and takes only one forward: it is in Suffolk's interest to broadcast the supposed treachery of York. Justice, already subservient to power, becomes propaganda, and the process of the trial is reduced to sickening show as a sober man beats a drunken man to death.[4] Looked at from a converse point of view, the scene suggests that the Duke of York's claim to the throne might be right in law, but that his prosecution of his case will destroy the commonwealth.

In this trial scene the outcome is dictated by main force – and the apprentice is, significantly, rewarded by the king. Moreover, after Horner has been struck down and has confessed his treason, York attributes the victory of the apprentice to divine intervention – but equally to more secular cause: 'Fellow, thank God, and the good wine in thy master's way' (2.3.89–90). Henry, on the other hand, characteristically exposes his inability to perceive any of the realities of the moment:

> Go, take hence that traitor from our sight,
> For by his death we do perceive his guilt;
> And God in justice hath revealed to us
> The truth and innocence of this poor fellow,
> Which he had thought to have murdered wrongfully.                      (2.3.93–7)

The Horner duel is one mirror sequence that reflects on the themes of justice and equity in the political world. Another, for which Shakespeare went to a complementary source, Foxe's *Acts and Monuments of Martyrs*, is the false miracle in which Saunder Simpcox claims to have recovered his sight and demonstrates that he can immediately distinguish colours (2.1). Simpcox's fraud is peremptorily exposed by Duke Humphrey in a manner that seems essentially populist. His demonstration is theatrical and convincing, his motives are just, and yet his methods – which include the torture of whipping – may be of dubious propriety.[5] For Humphrey, like Angelo when he is examining Pompey in *Measure for Measure* (2.1), converts an examination into a summary trial, a procedure introduced shortly before the time of the play as a way of getting malefactors to confess and of

---

[1] Hall, pp. 207–8; Holinshed, p. 210, has the servant hanged – Shakespeare has him rewarded (see Appendix 1, p. 222).
[2] Holinshed, p. 210; see p. 30 n. 2.
[3] Williams, p. 22.
[4] For the willingness of Tudor monarchs to prosecute people as obscure as Horner for treason, see Kevin Sharpe, *Early Modern England: A Social History 1550–1750*, 1987, p. 108.
[5] For a warning to Tudor princes to confine their punishments to what was decreed by law, see John Aylmer, *An Harborowe for Faithfull and Trewe Subjectes*, 1559, sigs. Hiiᵛ – Hiv.

3    The Saunder Simpcox sequence in Terry Hands's 1977 Stratford production

avoiding the corruption of jurors.[1] Humphrey's disregard for the forms of justice serves to make him more vulnerable to York's charge at the Parliament of Bury that he devised 'strange tortures for offenders' (3.1.122).

It may be possible to read this scene allegorically:[2] it is only by custom and not by virtue that men's true colours are to be perceived, and 'colour' is a significant pun – it means pretext. Simpcox, in other words, perceives men's pretensions to rank. What is also notable about the sequence is the way his wife's plea to Humphrey, 'Alas, sir, we did it for pure need' (2.1.154), falls completely on deaf ears. Monarch, episcopacy, and aristocracy are oblivious to the economic plight of their inferiors. Even before the death of Humphrey, Astræa seems to have been totally banished from this declining world.

After the death of Humphrey the people want to take the law into their own hands and wreak their revenge on Suffolk and the court (3.2.235ff.). Later we hear: 'The first thing we do, let's kill all the lawyers' (4.2.63). But although there is something invigorating in the carnivalesque radicalism of the Cade scenes, the rebels are easily converted from their cause, and their mob cruelty makes it

---

[1]  See William Lambarde's handbook for justices of the peace, *Eirenarcha*, 1581, p. 431, and Williams, p. 228. Later Gloucester will be accused of devising punishments contrary to 'form of law' (3.1.38).
[2]  I am indebted for some aspects of my reading of this scene to a private communication from Ronald Knowles.

apparent that their kind of summary justice is no better than that exercised by the political élite. Justice is compromised by revenge – as it is when York slays Old Clifford. Although York claims that his deed expresses 'justice and true right' (5.2.25), we feel that he, against the judgement of his better self perhaps, is simply avenging his family's honour. Later, Young Clifford will exact a bloody payment from York's son Rutland and then from York himself.[1]

Equity and justice are explored in another mode in 2.2, where York expounds his claim to the throne. Technically, according to the law of primogeniture, his claim is correct, but the catalogue of his ancestry is impossible for a playhouse audience to follow. (Significantly it was mangled in the reported texts from which Q derives.)[2] It is the liturgy of a man obsessed, and Warwick, in a comic moment, speaks with terse irony when he asks, 'What plain proceedings is more plain than this?' (2.2.53). Later, in 4.2, Cade will parody the claim. Shakespeare is a realist: the restoration of the *de jure* line will cause more harm than the occupation of the throne by a man who *de facto* wears the crown.

As Harrison claimed (see p. 13), therefore, there is no easy relationship between equity and justice, between Law and the laws of a kingdom. Or, as Marilynne Robinson put it: 'The point Shakespeare is making is very subtle and finely honed. The implication of all these scenes is that poetic justice – and retribution precise enough to seem divine – cannot substitute for the regular and scrupulous functioning of the law.'[3]

## DRAMATIC STRUCTURE

In *1 Henry VI*, Shakespeare explored archetypes as he wrote his prologue to his account of the Wars of the Roses. In *Part 2*, he traces the alliances and factions of the reign, evokes in imagery those predatory animals that roam the garden of the state.[4] The stage fights of *Part 1* took on the qualities of ritual combats between the great powers of England and France, male and female, right versus right, as Joan la Pucelle led her country to victory and herself to degradation and death: the play depicted the deaths of the titanic survivors of an *ancien régime*. The particular conspiracies and allegiances we see forged and forging in *Part 2* demonstrate the end of political consensus. Now it is a question of right versus might: motives are concealed behind pretexts; concern for the commonweal conceals desire for private wealth. Power remains in the hands of the patriciate but, as in *Part 1*, although the people have only a small role to play, the actions of the nobles are scrutinized from what may well be a populist point of view.

The play might at first sight seem to be a mirror for magistrates, a demonstration, in the mould of medieval tragedy, of the remorseless turning of Fortune's wheel and the consecutive falls of great men. (In fact, 'fortune' appears

---

[1] See *3H6* 1.3–4.
[2] See Appendix 2, pp. 234–5.
[3] Robinson, p. 146.
[4] James L. Calderwood, 'Shakespeare's evolving imagery: *2 Henry VI*', *ES* 48 (1967), 482–93; Virginia M. Carr, 'Animal imagery in *2 Henry VI*', *ES* 53 (1972), 408–12.

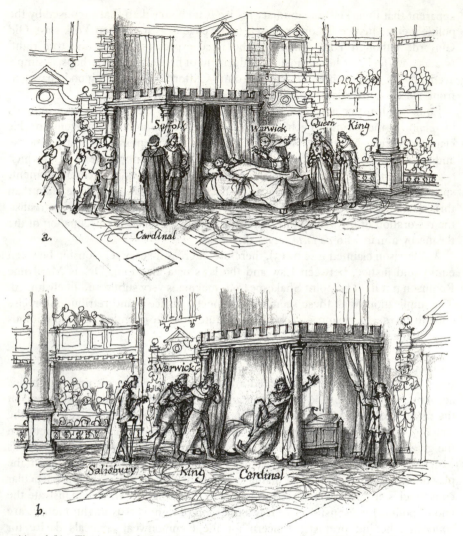

4 (a) and (b)   The 'putting forth' and 'discovery' of beds in Act 3, by C. Walter Hodges

only four times in the play as opposed to sixteen occurrences in *3 Henry VI*.) After
good Duke Humphrey of Gloucester has gone, Winchester, Suffolk, Stafford,
Say, Cade, Somerset, and Clifford die according to a strong dramatic rhythm. The
pattern of this, one of Shakespeare's earliest plays, would thereby seem to
anticipate some accounts of his latest, *Henry VIII*, which is structured about the
falls of Buckingham, Cromwell, and Wolsey. But in *2 Henry VI* Shakespeare is less
interested in this simple dramatic pattern, an 'anthology of falls':[1] rather he is

[1] Frank Kermode, 'What is Shakespeare's *Henry VIII* about?', in W. A. Armstrong (ed.), *Shakespeare's
Histories*, 1972, pp. 256–69.

concerned with the particular *political* allegiances that may make the details of the *plot* difficult to follow but which bring out the significance of the *action* in high relief.[1] In *The Prince* Machiavelli had shown how different men might prepare and act out different parts: in his *Discorsi* he showed the multiplicity of causes that might obtain in the interaction of Nature and Fortune. Shakespeare's analysis is as complex.

The political centre of the play is the bond between Henry and Gloucester. The king's supporters include Somerset, the Cliffords, as well as Buckingham and the Staffords. This Lancastrian alliance is threatened from three quarters: by the dynastic claim of York, by the long-standing rivalry between Gloucester and his uncle Cardinal Beaufort, Bishop of Winchester, and by the adulterous relationship between Queen Margaret and Suffolk. The loyalty of the Nevilles, the Earl of Salisbury and his son the Earl of Warwick, is shattered by Henry's inability to maintain dominion over France (1.1.106ff.), and they are the first to commit themselves whole-heartedly to the Yorkist cause (2.2.53ff.). The court is threatened further by the enmity between Gloucester's wife Eleanor and Queen Margaret (1.3.133ff.) as well as that between Warwick and Suffolk (3.2.158ff.). Around them all York lays his conspiratorial mines so that these political engineers will be hoist with their own petards:

> I am not your king
> Till I be crowned and that my sword be stained
> With heart-blood of the house of Lancaster;
> And that's not suddenly to be performed
> But with advice and silent secrecy.
> Do you as I do in these dangerous days:
> Wink at the Duke of Suffolk's insolence,
> At Beaufort's pride, at Somerset's ambition,
> At Buckingham, and all the crew of them,
> Till they have snared the shepherd of the flock,
> That virtuous prince, the good Duke Humphrey:
> 'Tis that they seek; and they, in seeking that,
> Shall find their deaths, if York can prophesy.          (2.2.64–76)

The narrative action, then, concentrates on the eclipse of Lancastrian power. This is marked by the death of Gloucester, which comes as the climax to Act 3, and the subsequent end of his old adversary Winchester. Act 4 begins with a fustian speech from the Lieutenant who will execute Suffolk, which may seem to turn all that follows to a vision of hell – its function is not unlike the Porter's scene in *Macbeth*.

> The gaudy, blabbing, and remorseful day
> Is crept into the bosom of the sea;
> And now loud-howling wolves arouse the jades
> That drag the tragic melancholy night,

---

[1] Emrys Jones notes that a 'characteristic of the early Shakespeare is the unflagging invention, the profusion of thematically pointed episode and incident' (*The Origins of Shakespeare*, 1977, p. 166).

> Who, with their drowsy, slow, and flagging wings
> Clip dead men's graves, and from their misty jaws
> Breathe foul contagious darkness in the air. (4.1.1–7)

But although a lot of what follows is mindless and barbaric, it is difficult to argue that Act 4 with its chronicle of various populist uprisings is a simply a grim vision of rule under the iron age of the people. For in this play, unlike *Part 1*, the commons do come to stand for values that are worth taking seriously, even if the action of the play suggests a frightening and inevitable disparity between the embodiment of a political idea and a political idea as idea. (There is, equally, a demonstration of the way that the idea of hierarchy which the aristocrats express is distorted by their embodiment of it.)

The sequence begins with the summary execution of Suffolk, who pays with his life for what is seen to be his part in all the ills of the kingdom. The Pirate Lieutenant's indictment (4.1.70ff.) reveals a complete understanding of the political situation, and a determination, typical of nearly all popular revolt in the early modern period, to protect the monarchy from 'reproach and beggary' (4.1.101). There follows the dramatisation of the Cade rebellion, which, like the Falstaff scenes in the *Henry IV* plays, stands not as 'comic relief' but as a vision both of the limits of government and of the consequences of aristocratic factionalism. Immediately the Cade rebellion is over, York's claim to the throne moves to the centre of the action.[1]

Like *1 Henry VI*, the play had begun with a public ceremony, the first meeting, after their proxy marriage, between Henry and Margaret; it ends raggedly, again like the earlier play, with the couple in flight, vanquished at St Albans by 'dogged York, that reaches at the moon' (3.1.158). Like *1* and *2 Henry IV*, moreover, the play is only partly about the personality of the king whose name furnishes it with a title.[2] It is about a segment of the reign – the full title of Q1 summarises the political activity we have analysed: *The First part of the Contention betwixt the two famous Houses of Yorke and Lancaster, with the death of the good Duke Humphrey: And the banishment and death of the Duke of Suffolke, and the Tragicall end of the proud Cardinall of Winchester, with the notable Rebellion of Iacke Cade: And the Duke of Yorkes first claime vnto the Crowne.* All of these events create a theme: the relationship between the power and the authority of the monarchy. The political climax of the play comes in 5.1, where York has triumphed over the king. There Shakespeare exposes the limits of monarchical authority when the obedience upon which the king's own power rests is in dispute. The 'body politic' is empowered by the 'body natural', and not vice versa. The clinching moment comes when Salisbury opposes his conscience to the Lancastrian claims for automatic loyalty:

KING HENRY For shame! In duty bend thy knee to me,
That bows unto the grave with mickle age.

---

[1] Interesting structural comparisons can be drawn with *Julius Caesar* concerning the relationships between the deaths of Caesar and Duke Humphrey and the rise of Brutus and York.

[2] See Larry S. Champion, *Perspective in Shakespeare's English Histories*, 1980, p. 5.

SALISBURY My lord, I have considered with myself
        The title of this most renownèd duke;
        And in my conscience do repute his grace
        The rightful heir to England's royal seat.
KING HENRY Hast thou not sworn allegiance unto me?
SALISBURY I have.
KING HENRY Canst thou dispense with heaven for such an oath?
SALISBURY It is great sin to swear unto a sin,
        But greater sin to keep a sinful oath.                    (5.1.173–83)

It is a key moment, a demonstration of Shakespeare's radicalism in that he is
asking the kind of question that princes did not want to be asked: as a Bishop of
Winchester, Stephen Gardiner (1483–1555) wrote in 1553, 'Obedience is due,
but how far the limits requiring obedience extend, that is the whole question to be
demanded.'[1] The gloss in the Geneva Bible (1560) to Romans 13.5 – 'Wherefore
ye must be subject, not because of wrath only, but also for conscience' –
appropriates the biblical text into anti-papist polemic, but implicitly admits that
rebellion might be a matter of conscience: 'For no private man can contemn that
government which God hath appointed without the breach of his conscience; and
here [St Paul] speaketh of civil magistrates: so that Antichrist and his cannot wrest
this place to establish their tyranny over the conscience.' Marlowe made a jest in
earnest that was recorded in his table talk on the matter: 'all the apostles were
fishermen and base fellows neither of wit nor worth...Paul only had wit, but he
was a timorous fellow in bidding men to be subject to magistrates against his
conscience.'[2]

    Not that Salisbury can be taken as a simple moral positive. We may be aware
here of a distinction between legalism and lawfulness, or we might conjecture that
although Salisbury's cause is just, his motives may be more pragmatic: is York
likely to be a better (because stronger) king than Henry?

    The rest of the act demonstrates York's consolidation of his authority by main
strength with the killing of Old Clifford and Somerset. Shakespeare demonstrates
that it is the 'rebel' York who is a man of conscience while, with brilliant irony,
Clifford, the king's champion at this point, is a monster, a Tamburlaine-like killing
machine.[3]

## CADE

Affairs at court and on the battlefield occupy most of the play, but Act 4 contains
an important inset, Jack Cade's rebellion, which adds a dimension at once comic

---

[1] *Concerning True Obedience*, cited in J. W. Allen, *A History of Political Thought*, 1928, p. 128; see R. E.
   Burckhardt, 'Obedience and rebellion in Shakespeare's early histories', *ES* 55 (1974), 108–17;
   Frances A. Shirley, *Swearing and Perjury in Shakespeare's Plays*, 1979, pp. 80–1.
[2] Recorded by the informer Richard Baines, MS Harleian 6848, fol. 185–6; see Peter Milward,
   *Shakespeare's Religious Background*, 1973, p. 219.
[3] See 5.1–2.

5   Oliver Cotton as Cade in Adrian Noble's 1988 Stratford production of '*The Rise of Edward IV*'

and horrific to the portrayal of insurrection and mutiny.[1] Since the appearance
in 1959 of C. L. Barber's *Shakespeare's Festive Comedy*, scholars have been
accustomed to relate drama to occasion, in particular to patterns of holiday and
recreation, and the Cade episodes have been explained according to this model.

[1]  Some of what follows appears in my article 'Rebellion, class consciousness, and Shakespeare's *2
Henry VI*', *Cahiers élisabéthains* 33 (1988), 13–22.

Barber himself describes the sequence as 'an astonishingly consistent expression of anarchy by clowning'.[1] Barber's book now seems to be apolitical, in fact to be written according to a Freudian paradigm, in that his key formulation is that the comic experience may be defined as a process of release leading to clarification and social harmony. This play does not end harmoniously, and issues, if they are clarified, are not resolved.

More recently critics have been offered a similar but political model, that constructed by Mikhail Bakhtin, who would argue that in comedy we encounter the elements of carnival – demotic, satirical, deflationary, extra-institutional, devoted to the celebration of community and local solidarity at the expense of national interest or hierarchical order[2] or 'the specialized appreciation of durable literary values'.[3] What, though, is the function of carnival? Is it a riot that turns to insurrection as took place in Shakespeare's day at Romans,[4] or is it merely a safety valve?[5] Is it a moment when, in this case through a theatrical re-presentation, society ritually purges itself of what are commonly taken to be its undesirable elements, in a mode similar to the way in which, on Shrove Tuesday, the apprentices in ritual disorder sacked brothels and theatres?[6] This was a period of turmoil, as the success of the rebellion demonstrates. Does carnival reveal how the ranks of governors were able to draw upon internalized ideological constraints in the people, given that they had limited powers of coercion at their disposal? Did the conjuring of disorder demonstrate the seeming necessity of order? As Machiavelli[7] and Weber[8] demonstrated, authority is predicated upon disorder.

In the theatre, are endings necessarily conclusions? We shall be looking at a populist uprising that is defeated – should we resist the temptation that besets all adherents of historicism to empathise with the victors?[9] Are the questions posed in the course of the play more important than the historical and dramatic answers it offers?

In his long soliloquy at the end of the Parliament scene (3.1), York reveals that he has stirred up the rebellion of Jack Cade, whose wild martial strength and politic skills he had observed in Ireland.[10] The imagery of the lines taps into the vein of witchcraft and conjuring that runs through the play, but again we are aware of the realities of power at York's disposal. York in fact hopes to convert a typical medieval revolt against aristocratic tyranny[11] into a full-scale popular rebellion which would enable him to seize the throne.

---

[1] *Shakespeare's Festive Comedy*, 1959, p. 13.

[2] See Mikhail Bakhtin, *Rabelais and his World*, trans. Helene Iswolksky, 1984.

[3] Michael D. Bristol, *Carnival and Theater*, 1985, p. 4.

[4] See Emmanuel Le Roy Ladurie, *Le Carnaval de Romans*, 1979.

[5] For a critique of this model, see Bristol, p. 27.

[6] Hattaway, p. 49.

[7] G. H. Sabine, *A History of Political Theory*, 1959, p. 294.

[8] David Little, *Religion, Order, and Law*, 1970, pp. 20–1.

[9] Walter Benjamin, quoted by Bristol, p. 7.

[10] 'York calls Cade his "substitute", but he is also his alter ego, his carefully-hidden demon. These two are never on stage at the same time, and could well and profitably be played by the same actor' (Robinson, p. 120).

[11] Williams, p. 322.

The wind that York blew through the kingdom, as Hall aptly puts it,[1] provides one cause for popular insurrection, and this was the cause that was most widely propounded when the rebellion was discussed in Shakespeare's time. Cade's rebellion had been described by Stephen Gardiner as simply an extension of the Yorkist revolt, a general manifestation of the way 'the license of the people comes from the factions of the nobles',[2] and Holinshed begins his account of the rebellion by stating that 'those that favoured the Duke of York...procured a commotion in Kent'.[3] We must, however, like Shakespeare, consider a second cause, the efficient cause, which is the 'furious rage of the outrageous [i.e. outraged] people' against those responsible for the loss of Anjou – notably the 'flagitious' Suffolk, 'the abhorred toad and common nuisance of the realm of England'.[4] Shakespeare points to the importance of this by showing the execution of Suffolk in the scene that comes just before the beginning of the rebellion. By indicating these two instances of popular outrage against England's loss of self-esteem, he indicates that in part Cade's rebellion was a spontaneous uprising: aristocratic rebellion is the *catalyst* rather than the *cause* of popular revolt over specific social issues[5] – a distinction that is blurred by Hall, who refers to Cade and his followers simply as 'proud rebels'.[6] It may also be notable that the rebels do not mention the death of Duke Humphrey – they are reacting against conditions rather than events. Their own poverty and England's loss of empire are linked in their minds because the taxes for the French wars had weighed heavily upon them. This is why they are so proud to have captured Lord Say, who was held to be responsible for these. In order to amplify these grievances Shakespeare went beyond the chroniclers' treatment of the uprising in the context of the Yorkist rebellion[7] and incorporated into the sequence details taken from the account of another rebellion, that of Wat Tyler in the reign of Richard II.[8] This was, moreover, no local riot as were most of the Plantagenet and Tudor uprisings: Cade and his followers captured London.

Shakespeare indeed may be underlining divisions in society that are deep enough to be called class divisions. I acknowledge that from drama and theatre history alone we cannot recreate a model that would enable us to measure the radical thrust offered by the political drama of Shakespeare and his contemporaries. But it is possible to offer a coherent reading of some of the drama that would question the conclusion the editors of a recent and most distinguished collection of

---

[1] Hall, p. 219.

[2] Stephen Gardiner, *A Machiavellian Treatise*, ed. and trans. Peter Samuel Donaldson, 1975, p. 121.

[3] Holinshed, p. 220.

[4] Hall, p. 219.

[5] Williams, p. 313.

[6] Hall, p. 220.

[7] Holinshed has flattering things to say about Cade – see Appendix 1, pp. 227–8. For an account of the Cade scenes which argues that Cade represented the antithesis of everything Shakespeare stood for, see Richard Wilson, '"A mingled yarn": Shakespeare and the cloth workers', *Literature and History* 12 (1986), 164–81.

[8] See Appendix 1, pp. 228–9.

essays in social history would offer to us. Working from an analysis of cultural models, patterns of behaviour, and local community, Anthony Fletcher and John Stevenson conclude that 'a class society had not in our period yet arrived'.[1]

I cannot dispute their conclusion if I work from the same material and the same premises. But it seems that yet again literary critics have something to offer the cultural historians. Jonson may have been working from a background in medieval social theory, but *Volpone* and *The Alchemist* offer a thorough indictment of contemporary entrepreneurial rapacity. In this play it is not simply a cultural difference marked by manners of speech or behaviour: the *economic* chasm between those with silk coats and those with leather aprons gapes wide in this sequence and might be seen as a reactive protest to the sumptuary laws of the Elizabethan period,[2] themselves surely a manifestation of a hierarchical society's obsession with rank at a time of political crisis.[3] Seen from this perspective, the *Henry VI* plays offer a searing indictment of aristocratic factionalism and the haughtiness of prelates.[4] The nobility in this set of plays does constitute a class – or, if we prefer, an élite – defined by the conflict between individual aspirations of its members and everything that constitutes the interest of the plebeians.[5]

The social composition of the rebels needs some preliminary analysis. The rebellion is certainly not just an occasion for 'mechanicals' to be forced into their customary stage role of clowns,[6] for the disorder includes not only the marginal and dispossessed. As in many of the uprisings of the early modern period (including Kett's rebellion of 1549), we find here no 'peasants' revolt', but a group dominated by the middling sort of rural artisans or 'handicraftsmen' (4.2.8),[7] including a tanner, a butcher, and a weaver. The two kinds of division – horizontal between social groups and vertical between political factions – described by Emmanuel Le Roy Ladurie in his account of an analogous insurrection which occurred in France in 1580,[8] intersect, therefore, at this historical moment.

Not that the Cade rebellion is just a social documentary: it has its part to play in the construction of the drama. Duke Humphrey foresaw the mischief that York was brewing and deployed theatrical metaphors that might seem to turn political action into theatrical game.

---

[1] Anthony Fletcher and John Stevenson, *Order and Disorder in Early Modern England*, 1985, p. 4; some evidence of class antagonism is cited by Keith Wrightson, *English Society 1580–1680*, 1982, p. 150.
[2] See N. B. Harte, 'State control of dress and social change in pre-industrial England', in D. C. Coleman and A. H. John (eds.), *Trade, Government and Economy in Pre-Industrial England*, 1976, pp. 132–65.
[3] See Lawrence Stone, *The Crisis of the Aristocracy 1558–1641*, 1965.
[4] See John Foxe, quoted by Bullough, p. 127.
[5] See E. P. Thompson, 'Patrician society, plebeian culture', *Journal of Social History* 7 (1974), pp. 382–405.
[6] See Anat Feinberg, 'The representation of the poor in Elizabethan and Stuart drama', *Literature and History* 12 (1986), 152–63.
[7] See Diarmaid MacCulloch, 'Kett's rebellion in context', in Paul Slack (ed.), *Rebellion, Popular Protest and the Social Order in Early Modern England*, 1984, pp. 39–62.
[8] Ladurie, *Le Carnaval de Romans*.

> But [my death] is made the prologue to their play:
> For thousands more, that yet suspect no peril,
> Will not conclude their plotted tragedy. (3.1.151–3)

Indeed, the uprising of the commons becomes a shadow play of the substantial quarrel between the aristocrats: the first lines of the first plebeians we meet suggest that they are wielding weapons that are obviously theatrical properties, the traditional mock weapons borne by fools and soldier clowns in Tudor interludes.[1] York's description of Cade as a 'Morisco' (3.1.365), a morris dancer, also places him in this tradition of revelry or ritual misrule. This does not mean, however, that the episode is thereby depoliticized:[2] on the contrary, carnival served to legitimise protest by imposing ritual forms upon it.[3] Subversion is equated with celebration. Moreover, Cade's genealogy is a parody (4.2.31ff.) of the genealogy of York: like his master, he uses *de jure* arguments to mask his tyrannical ambitions. (Compare the parody in the Horner episode of the aristocratic form of justice, the trial by combat.) As Ronald Knowles writes, 'ultimately Cade is an inverted image of authority, both its distorted representative and its grotesque critic'.[4]

It is impossible, therefore, to argue, as Tillyard did, that the Cade scenes simply offer the 'impious spectacle of the proper order reversed',[5] producing a homiletic demonstration of the evils of rebellion – the play would scarcely have been a success in the popular playhouses if they had. If, in order to explain a political play, we invoke a metaphysical 'order', we have to be careful, as we translate it to the social sphere, to ask ourselves, 'Whose order?' Riot and 'disorder' are not synonymous.[6] Although Dick the Butcher in 4.2 witheringly exposes in his asides the contradictions of Cade's claims (27ff.), and Holland in 4.7 mocks Cade's justice, the audience is simultaneously made aware that matters of real moment for the people are being raised. Shakespeare seems to have wanted to set his spectators laughing and then demonstrate that this combination of noble provocation and popular combustion is no laughing matter.

---

[1] See 4.2.1ff.; compare *TN* 4.2.126 and *1H4* 2.4.137; and see David Wiles, *Shakespeare's Clown*, 1987, pp. 121–2.

[2] François Laroque, "Shakespeare et la fête populaire: le carnaval sanglant de Jack Cade", *Réforme, Humanisme, et Renaissance* 11 (1979), 126–30. Laroque argues that Cade's 'jacquerie' turns to carnival, an inversion of the normal order. For carnival see also Peter Burke, *Popular Culture in Early Modern Europe*, 1978, pp. 182ff.; for a critique of Burke and an attempt to use the anthropological categories of Victor Turner to explain Elizabethan carnival, see Wiles, *Shakespeare's Clown*, pp. 172ff.

[3] See Thomas Pettitt ('"Here comes I, Jack Straw": English folk drama and social revolt', *Folklore* 95 (1984), 3–20) who points out that the historical Jack Cade may have used the Whitsun festivities of 1450 to forward or cover his enterprise, and that the Great Revolt of 1381 led by Wat Tyler (who may have used the carnival name of 'Jack Straw' – see Holinshed, II, 736) reached its climax, as Holinshed pointed out (*ibid.*), on Corpus Christi day (13 June); for the ritual roles of butchers (consider Dick the Butcher) in carnivals see Michael D. Bristol, 'Lenten Butchery: legitimation crisis in *Coriolanus*' in Jean E. Howard and Marion F. O'Connor (eds), *Shakespeare Reproduced*, 1987, pp. 207–24.

[4] In a private communication.

[5] *Shakespeare's History Plays*, p. 183.

[6] Slack, *Rebellion*, pp. 1–2.

6  H. Bunbury, *Dick the Butcher and the Clerk of Chartham*, 1795. Six years after the French Revolution the rebels have become heroes, their adversary a grotesque

   The disorder of the revolt in fact generates glimpses of an alternative order, of political radicalism: 'we are in order when we are most out of order' (4.2.164).[1] Bullough ignores the paradox and, following the chroniclers, unwarrantably uses this line to claim that Shakespeare thus brands the rebels as a 'rabble'.[2] No, Cade's rebellion in Shakespeare's text is a political act and not a moral aberration or manifestation of base passion, as riots are portrayed in Ariosto, Spenser, and Drayton,[3] or of duncical folly, as John of Leiden's anabaptist rebellion at Münster in 1534[4] was portrayed in Nashe's *The Unfortunate Traveller* (1594).[5] There is in *2 Henry VI* no speech proclaiming that obedience to authority was

[1]  See M. E. James, 'The concept of order and the northern uprising of 1569', *Past and Present* 60 (1973), 59–83; K. Wrightson, 'Two concepts of order', in J. Brewer and J. Styles (eds.), *An Ungovernable People*, 1980, pp. 21–46.
[2]  Bullough, p. 96. See also C. A. Patrides, '"The beast with many heads": Renaissance views on the multitude', *SQ* 16 (1965), 241–6; Christopher Hill, 'The many-headed monster' in *Change and Continuity in Seventeenth-Century England*, 1974, pp. 181–204.
[3]  *Orlando Furioso*, VI.60–70; *FQ*, II, ix, 13–17, V.ii.30–54; Drayton refers to 'that rake-hell Cade', *Poly-Olbion*, XXII, 531 (*Works*, IV, 438).
[4]  For this and anabaptism generally see Norman Cohn, *The Pursuit of the Millennium*, 1970 edn, pp. 261ff.
[5]  Nashe, *Works*, II, 232–41.

enjoined upon men by St Paul, as there is in *Sir Thomas More* (*c.*1595).[1] Sir Thomas More says to the rebels in that play:

> What do you, then,
> Rising against him that God himself installs,
> But rise 'gainst God? (2.4.128–30)

Cade's rebels seek reformation (4.2.53) and liberty (4.2.158), not anarchy, and a production could bring out, without denying or suppressing Cade's extremism and, at least in the opening of the sequence, a 'profound sense of legitimacy'[2] that we might weigh against the consuming appetites of the rulers. The demands of the rebels are a mixture of those categorised by E. P. Thompson as belonging to 'the moral economy of the crowd'[3] and more millenarian demands: they are not simply reacting to violations of a time-hallowed order of landed society such as the loss of common land by enclosure (4.2.56–7)[4] and the loss of their 'ancient freedom' (4.8.24), but are proposing a new egalitarian and libertarian order (see 4.2.1ff.).

Their utopia is a utopia of reconstruction as much as one of escape.[5] A tract of 1589 by Bishop Cooper, a contribution to the Marprelate debate, indicates how the rebels' ideas were part of the currency of debate at the time of the play's composition: 'At the beginning (say they), when God had first made the world, all men were alike, there was no principality; then was no bondage or villeinage: that grew afterwards by violence and cruelty. Therefore why should we live in this miserable slavery under those proud lords and crafty lawyers, etc.'[6]

In most critical accounts of the play, however, the rebels have been branded as a rabble – indeed, it is still a commonplace to claim that Shakespeare, like Horace, hated the profane mob.[7] The followers of Cade *are* described as a '*rabblement*' in the opening stage direction to 4.8, but it is important to note that, in the period, the word could be used without contempt (*OED* Rabble 2). If critics do generate some sympathy in themselves for the plebeian cause, they tend to water it down by pointing out that Cade's economic reforms seem to derive from the land of Cockaigne.[8] Cade may well, on the contrary, through the insistent and

---

[1] See the text in C. F. Tucker Brooke (ed.), *The Shakespeare Apocrypha*, 1908, 2.4.112ff.; on the history of the play, see Carol A. Chillington, 'Playwrights at work: Henslowe's, not Shakespeare's, *Book of Sir Thomas More*', *ELR* 10 (1980), 439–79; for St Paul, see pp. 18–20 above.

[2] Slack, *Rebellion*, p. 1.

[3] E. P. Thompson, 'The moral economy of the crowd', *Past and Present* 51 (1971), 76–136; Sharpe, p. 110.

[4] Suffolk is accused of enclosing by one of the Petitioners early in the play (1.3.19–20).

[5] See Lewis Mumford, *The Story of Utopia*, 1922, p. 15.

[6] T. Cooper, *An Admonition to the People of England*, 1589, ed. E. Arber, 1895, p. 118 (cf. pp. 144–5, 148, 159, 168–9); quoted by Christopher Hill, *The World Turned Upside Down*, 1975 edn, p. 115. The Bishop used the sentiments as an argument for suppressing Presbyterians.

[7] See D. Goy-Blanquet, 'Pauvres Jacques: chroniques et spectacles en Angleterre au xvi^e siècle', in Elie Konigson (ed.), *Figures théâtrales du peuple*, 1985, pp. 49–74.

[8] See Gormon Beauchamp, 'The dream of Cockaigne: some motives for the utopias of escape', *The Centennial Review* 25 (1981), 345–62.

demagogic rhythms of his prose, be offering an oblique comment on the massive price rises of Shakespeare's period:[1]

There shall be in England seven half-penny loaves sold for a penny, the three-hooped pot shall have ten hoops, and I will make it felony to drink small beer; all the realm shall be in common and in Cheapside shall my palfrey go to grass.                                          (4.2.54–7)

This deprivation caused by inflation, moreover, coupled with the violence of the gentry, was a likely cause of the breakdown of the traditional corporate orders of the common people.[2]

We can demonstrate the emergent ideological claims of the rebels by examining Shakespeare's deployment of source materials. Hall wrote little about the emerging 'manifesto' of the rebels, noting only that the 'Kentishmen be impatient in wrongs, disdaining of too much oppression, and ever desirous of new change and new-fangleness'.[3] Accordingly, as we have seen, Shakespeare turned from Hall to 'Holinshed's or Grafton's account of the Peasants' Revolt of 1381, regarded as representative of popular revolts, and led by a[nother] Kentishman', John Ball.[4]

Act 4, Scene 2 opens with a conversation (1–25) between two artisans of unspecified vocations, Bevis and Holland, which reveals a thoroughgoing radicalism, a desire to put down gentlemen and magistrates and install a new order of workers. Their rich prose, informed by both chop-logic and messianic discourse, is both comic and serious, and their aspirations derive from the kind of egalitarianism that inspired John Ball, whose catch-phrase question 'When Adam delved and Eve span, / Who was then a gentleman?'[5] was well known:[6]

BEVIS      Come and get thee a sword, though made of a lath: they have been up these two
           days.
HOLLAND    They have the more need to sleep now then.
BEVIS      I tell thee, Jack Cade the clothier means to dress the commonwealth, and turn
           it, and set a new nap upon it.
HOLLAND    So he had need, for 'tis threadbare. Well, I say, it was never merry world in
           England since gentlemen came up.
BEVIS      O miserable age! Virtue is not regarded in handicraftsmen.
HOLLAND    The nobility think scorn to go in leather aprons.

---

[1] See D. M. Palliser, *The Age of Elizabeth*, 1983, chap. 5; John Walter and Keith Wrightson argue that dearth could, in fact, often 'serve as an active element in the maintenance of social stability', 'Dearth and the social order in early modern England', in Slack, *Rebellion*, p. 108; inflation is attributed to high consumption by aliens and strangers (foreigners) in *Sir Thomas More* 2.4.
[2] Emile Durkheim, *The Division of Labour in Society*, 1935.
[3] Hall, p. 219.
[4] Bullough, pp. 96, 128–33.
[5] Holinshed, cited Bullough, p. 133. Ball speaks the lines in the anonymous *Life and Death of Jack Straw* (1593–4; Bullough, p. 139, lines 82–3); see Norman Cohn, *The Pursuit*, pp. 198–204; for a contemporary argument against equality, see Sir John Cheke, *The Hurt of Sedition*, written in 1549 and included in the 1587 edition of Holinshed's *Chronicles* (III, 1042–55).
[6] See Hill, *The World Turned Upside Down*, pp. 114–5; Charles Hobday, 'Clouted shoon and leather aprons: Shakespeare and the egalitarian tradition', *Renaissance and Modern Studies* 23 (1979), 69–78.

BEVIS        Nay more, the king's council are no good workmen.
HOLLAND  True: and yet it is said, 'Labour in thy vocation': which is as much to say, as let
             the magistrates be labouring men; and therefore should we be magistrates.
BEVIS        Thou hast hit it: for there's no better sign of a brave mind than a hard hand.

(4.2.1–15)

Even though, as we have seen, the first line of the sequence signals that the rebels
are playing well-known parts, both as rebels and as clowns, the scene draws the
audience towards an alternative and populist vantage-point from which they might
continue to view the main action. The scene gains an added resonance with the
entrance of Dick the Butcher, a member of a trade prominent in the Kett rebellion
of 1549,[1] who shares their apocalyptic vision. Unlike the cabals of the nobles, the
gathering represents a group and not a faction.[2]

Unfortunately for these radical artisans, however, as we have seen, York's
creature Cade hijacks the leadership of the revolt. (We might compare the way in
which the Münster rebellion turned into a dictatorship ruled by Jan Bockelson as
John of Leiden.)[3] Now Cade's brand of radicalism, as opposed to that of his
fellows, is, like most of the aspirations that emerged during the course of the
rebellions of the Tudor period,[4] informed by conservatism and megalomania –
there will be no egalitarianism in Cade's commonwealth or true communism. For
although 'all the realm shall be in common' (4.2.56–7), Cade will be king, and
riches will be distributed as an act of largesse to enhance Cade's rule. (Hall does
note that the Kentish men were partly roused by 'fair promises of liberty'.)[5]

In Ball's revolt, the grievances of the insurgents resulted in a ritual act of
supplication to the king against the nobles. Here, Cade's ambition prevents this
traditional solution, and the rebels are disbanded by Clifford's invocation of the
fear of French invasion (4.8.31ff.). Given that the rebellion was in part an
extension of the revolt of York, the treatment of the rebels by his arch-enemy
Clifford is notable. Clifford does not point out that they have been misled by the
treachery of York but appeals to their national sense of honour. This manifests an
extraordinary *esprit de corps*, perhaps reflecting part of a change in the ideology of
honour that occurred between the time of the action and the time of play's
composition. Before Kett's rebellion of 1549, it has been argued, espousal of
honour by the nobility had a subversive potential – as we see in the action of the
play. After this watershed, new concepts of order and obedience 'branded

---

[1] Slack, *Rebellion*, p. 52. The Kett rebellion was the last (until 1607) large-scale protest movement,
   although various plots and conspiracies punctuated the reign of Elizabeth; about the time that the
   play was written there were localized protests by the oppressed against enclosures and the cost and
   effects of the wars in the Netherlands (see Williams, pp. 326, 342–3 and B. Sharp, *In Contempt of
   All Authority*, 1980).
[2] See Robert Ornstein, *A Kingdom for a Stage*, p. 26.
[3] See Cohn, *The Pursuit*, pp. 271ff.; a contemporary account of the anabaptist revolt was provided by
   Joannes Philippson (Sleidanus), *A Famous Chronicle of Our Time Called Sleideane's Commentaries*,
   trans. J. Daus, 1560, Book 10, folios 129ff., although there is no evidence that Shakespeare knew
   this work.
[4] See Slack, *Rebellion*, p. 6.
[5] Hall, p. 220.

dissidence as the activity only of the brutal and ignorant "commons".[1] The commons are branded for actions for which the peers were responsible.

In the theatre, on the other hand, the rebels might well take on the characteristics of a mob.[2] Dick the Butcher, so sceptical of Cade's claims to rule, is caught up in the excitement of the massacres, and if Shakespeare arouses our sympathy, he is careful to prevent our being carried away on a tide of hysterical empathy by showing the slaughter of the Clerk of Chartham, executed because he could read and write.[3] Although this may appear as a horrendous example of mindless violence, it may equally reflect on the abuse of benefit of clergy, the privilege claimed by the literate that enabled them to escape execution by virtue of being able to read and write. We might remember how later in the sequence Cade furthers his cause by a species of populist justice in his campaign against the lawyers (part of the case of the rebels in *The Life and Death of Jack Straw*)[4] and the lettered. His indictment of the Lord Say (4.7.19ff.), although muddled, does demonstrate how learning and literacy could function as tools of oppression.

But it is the mode of the representation that is of interest. I want to point out how this surge of dispensation of justice by the people may well have been seen from a double perspective, with a degree of horror but also with a degree of glee as the privileged get their comeuppance. My evidence comes from the source. Shakespeare again turned from his principal source, Hall, but this time to Holinshed. The unruly commons, he wrote, put precept into practice:

beheading all such men of law, justices, and jurors as they might catch and lay hands upon, without respect of pity, or remorse of conscience, alleging that the land could never enjoy her native and true liberty till all those sorts of people were dispatched out of the way.

This talk liked well the ears of the common uplandish people, and by the less conveying the more, they purposed to burn and destroy all records, evidences, court-rolls, and other muniments, that the remembrance of ancient matters being removed out of mind, their landlords might not have whereby to challenge any right at their hands.[5]

This is written from the point of view of orthodox morality, but it would seem that Shakespeare may have caught the tone of these sequences not from the text but from the marginal glosses. For against the first of those two paragraphs we read 'Lawyers, justices, and jurors brought to "blockam feast" by the rebels'.[6] This

[1] Slack, *Rebellion*, p. 13, drawing upon Mervyn James, *English Politics and the Concept of Honour 1485–1642, Past and Present*, Supplement No. 3, 1978; for the gentry's withdrawal from armed political demonstrations in the sixteenth century, see Fletcher and Stevenson, *Order and Disorder*, p. 10.

[2] On crowd scenes in this and other plays see Margot Heinemann, 'How Brecht read Shakespeare', in Jonathan Dollimore and Alan Sinfield (eds.), *Political Shakespeare*, 1985, p. 226.

[3] On the tenuousness of a firm division between literate and non-literate social classes, see Fletcher and Stevenson, *Order and Disorder*, pp. 11–12. It may be that the Clerk is executed as a scapegoat for those who escaped hanging by claiming 'benefit of clergy', i.e. having the rudiments of literacy, displayed by knowing their 'neck-verse' (the beginning of Psalm 51); see 4.7.35–6 n.

[4] Bullough, pp. 144, 519; for later Leveller hostility to lawyers see Hill, *The World Turned Upside Down*, pp. 103, 133–6, 194.

[5] Holinshed, II, 737.

[6] The phrase 'blockam feast', which is not recorded in *OED*, is found in *Mirror*, 'John, Earl of Worcester', 118. This sardonic populist tone is to be heard elsewhere in the margins, as, for

7  An execution. The illustration accompanies an account of lawyers being brought to 'blockam feast'
in Holinshed, 1577

reconstitutes the slaughter into a carnival of violence, enacted in the grisly display
whereby the heads of the executed Lord Say and Sir James Cromer are made to
kiss at the end of their pikes (4.7.112–3). Against the second we read, 'The next
way to extinguish right'. This deftly inverts argument of the text, for whereas
Holinshed intended his reader to understand the way in which the nobles were
deprived of their rights, this second gloss offers the example as a means for so
doing.[1] Moreover the fate of Say and Cromer stands as an awful revenge of the
people upon the justices: like Duke Humphrey, Lord Say thought of himself as an
upright judge and, like Duke Humphrey, he meets his end after a perfunctory 'trial
upon examination' (see p. 14).

The same dialogic technique is used in the account of Cade in *A Mirror for
Magistrates*, 1559. The verse 'tragedy' is headed 'How Jack Cade Traitorously
Rebelling against his King was for his Treasons and Cruel Doings Worthily
Punished', but the prose gloss which follows the poem notes that God always uses
rebels to his glory: 'For when kings and chief rulers suffer their under-officers to
misuse their subjects and will not hear nor remedy their peoples' wrongs when
they complain, then suffereth God the rebel to rage and to execute that part of his
justice which the partial prince would not.'[2]

After the rebels have been deflected from their aims, Cade is killed in a garden
by a man called Iden: does this scene mark some kind of moral positive, and is this

example, when the death of the Duke of York is explained as 'a purchase of God's curse with the
pope's blessing' (Holinshed, p. 269 and see p. 14 above).
[1]  Compare the attack on book learning by the Münster anabaptists (see Cohn, p. 267).
[2]  *Mirror*, pp. 171, 178.

8  Act 4, Scene 7 in Adrian Noble's 1988 Stratford production – the number of heads has been multiplied

poetic justice? Cade *is* a rebel and even may stand indicted in the eyes of some of the audience for diverting the energies of the commons' insurrection. But the spectacle of his death is no more enlightening than that of Horner. Although Shakespeare, with true magnanimity, demonstrates how Cade provokes Iden into attacking him, we see a strong man slaughtering a starving one as a sober man had earlier in the play beaten to death a drunken one (2.3). When Iden learns who Cade is, he shows as he kills him no stoic calm, certainly no Christian forgiveness, just hatred – wishing he 'might thrust his soul to hell'.[1] (Is this class hatred?)

---

[1]  4.10.72.

Perhaps Cade's emaciated state is an emblematic comment on his spent force as a political figure and his moral bankruptcy as an individual. Iden, moreover, having entered to proclaim his abhorrence of the court and courtly ambitions at the opening of the scene, at its close goes off in triumph to court to claim the honour that he knows will be his reward. The Kentish garden turns out to be another failed paradise in which ideals are vitiated by ambition.

These sequences stand, therefore, not only as echoes but as retorts to the crescendos of violence sounded by the nobles, in particular the murder of Duke Humphrey.[1] The ills of the nation, moreover, derive not just from the rampant will to power displayed by the aristocrats, but from their conspicuous consumption. Margaret's lines about Dame Eleanor serve not only to mark her disdain for an upstart but also to offer a clue to a modern director:

> She sweeps it through the court with troops of ladies
> More like an empress than Duke Humphrey's wife.
> Strangers in court do take her for the queen:
> She bears a duke's revenues on her back
> And in her heart she scorns our poverty.          (1.3.72–6)

Winchester's death scene (3.3) – he does not 'die well' – is a demonstration that the wealth massed by the cardinal is not sufficient to save him from death. Cupidity is the root of all suffering. The sequence is significantly placed just before the scene in which summary justice is meted out to Suffolk, who had swallowed 'the treasure of the realm' (4.1.74).

AFFAIRS AT COURT

The play opened in the realm of international diplomacy. In the first scene Shakespeare employed the familiar device of the interrupted ceremony: the grand tableau of the greeting of king and queen was jolted into confusion. Contention had been brought home to England, as was registered by the way Gloucester faltered as he realised what the new league had cost the country. He dropped the paper containing the bad tidings. (1.1.50), and his ancient enemy Winchester picked it up and continued to read, doubtless in such a way that the recital of Suffolk's doings became an implicit indictment of the rule of Henry and Gloucester. The little sequence ended with the king's defensive and precipitate investiture of Suffolk – Henry had, after all, instructed Suffolk to 'agree to any covenants'[2] in his negotiations to secure the hand of Margaret. Strains in the body politic were already apparent, and, ironically, the two political adversaries Gloucester and York were in complete agreement over the blow to England's authority caused by the loss of France.[3] After the exit of the king and queen,

---

[1] The exhibition of Gloucester's corpse could well have quoted the stage image of the exhibition of Henry V's corpse in *Part 1*. Stage directions indicate that it was 'discovered', but it may well have been then thrust out on the stage, the contorted features a travesty of the order supposed to be figured forth in his trial.

[2] *1H6* 5.5.88.

[3] See 1.1.120–32.

9  The stage and principal characters for the opening of the play, denoting their Yorkist and
Lancastrian allegiances, by C. Walter Hodges

10   *The Witch of Eye* from the Boydell Collection

Gloucester stepped forward as a kind of chorus – again a point of stasis – to lament the loss of France, but, as he ended, the ancient bickerings between him and his cardinal uncle Winchester were renewed. In fact this was the last we saw of the foreign quarrel: the focus thenceforth was on the twists and turns of the contentions of York and Lancaster. The lords clustered in antic movement until they went out to leave York in soliloquy with the audience, just as Winchester had been left at the end of 1.1 of *1 Henry VI*.

This long speech of York, in which he takes the audience into his confidence, reveals that his interest in the 'public good' (1.1.196) might in fact be a useful weapon in his personal vendetta against the Lancastrians. Whereas Gloucester had spoken for England's honour, York reveals that he sees kingdoms as commodities, and that his real interest is in private gain. The 'canker of ambitious thoughts' (1.2.18) has spread from the theatre of nations to the stage of England's kingdom: in the next scene we see it grow inwards to make desolation in the family.

Eleanor, Humphrey's low-born wife, is consumed by ambition for the crown and is desirous of displacing Margaret. Her treacherous ambitions, displayed early in the play, may seem incidental to York's conspiracy, but Shakespeare's treatment of her motives and the effects of her actions is characteristically complex and repays some analysis. First, she is not, any more than is Queen Margaret, a mere stage villain. Since, as we have seen, her agents are in fact double agents, an audience may well conclude that she was condemned for crimes she intended but did not in fact commit. Like Joan of Arc in the first play, she resorts to witchcraft in an attempt to divine the future, but whereas Joan's conjuration scene[1] had offered insight into her despair, here the conjuring serves as a further demonstration of aristocratic ambition. (Both scenes show strong women seized by men in a demonstration of male triumphalism.) Prophesying could be a prelude to malefice (the doing of harm by means of magic), and any magic was regarded as a threat to the authority of the monarchy:[2] in 1563 a statute was published, encouraged by 'concern of the Government at the amount of treasonable activity which took the form of false prophecies, astrological predictions, and other amateur conjuring'.[3] Sir John Harington wrote of prophecies: 'The wise sort for the most part do utterly scorn them, yet I find they give a presage and leave an impression in their minds that seem most to scorn them';[4] in *Richard II* the Bishop of Carlisle is immediately arrested for the prophecy he delivers as Bullingbrook ascends the throne of Richard.[5] Here, in *2 Henry VI*, Eleanor is already the dupe of the priest and the witch, but, like the comic scenes in *Doctor Faustus*, the sequence serves a double function: it exploits hocus-pocus to create a theatrical spectacle[6] and turns Eleanor into a figure at once deservedly repaid for her ambition and yet pathetic. Accordingly, the trickery of the priest and Bolingbroke should be transparent to the audience – who then find their allegiances to the tricksters confounded when York and Buckingham break in to seize them and the lady.

As so often, Shakespeare is employing in this scene two levels of consciousness: although the sequence serves as an elaborate snare for an over-reaching woman, the 'Spirit' prophesies the deaths of the three great personages of the play, a simple device for dramatic irony. Its obvious fictiveness, in other words, serves two purposes: to deceive Dame Eleanor and to tell the audience of the outcome of the action.

The downfall of Dame Eleanor is part of a prolonged attack on Duke Humphrey made from several quarters. Margaret is her immediate enemy,[7] but the queen is equally concerned to obliterate Humphrey's role as Protector of her husband. Although the origins of his fall are political, the sequence in which he is accused (1.3.117–32) has a ritual feeling[8] which simultaneously exposes the suspect nature of the charges cooked up by Gloucester's antagonists – Suffolk,

---

[1] *1H6* 5.3.
[2] See Kurt Tetzeli von Rosador, 'The Power of Magic: from *Endimion* to *The Tempest*', *S. Sur.* (forthcoming).
[3] A. Macfarlane, *Witchcraft in Tudor and Stuart England*, 1970, p. 14. See also Hill, *Upside Down*, chap. 6. Thomas, pp. 470–86, gives a full account of the political uses to which prophecies were put throughout the sixteenth century.
[4] *A Tract on the Succession to the Crown*, cited Thomas, p. 470.
[5] *R2* 4.1.136–53; see also George Puttenham, *The Arte of English Poesie*, 1589, p. 218, whose account of the dangers of prophecies includes references to Jack Straw, Jack Cade, and Kett.
[6] Sprague, p. 116, describes how effective it can be in the theatre.
[7] See 1.3.70–77 and 133.
[8] Emrys Jones, *Origins*, p. 42.

11   Act 1, Scene 4: the conjuration scene, by C. Walter Hodges

Winchester, Buckingham, and the queen – and establishes his fall as a turning-point in the action. Immediately after Dame Eleanor has been sentenced, Henry, unprompted by his wife, asks Duke Humphrey to resign his staff (2.3.22ff.). The action is uncharacteristically bold and scarcely compassionate. In the scene where Humphrey is arraigned in Parliament it is notable that the king does not publicly support the erstwhile Protector (3.1.139–41). He makes a notable profession of grief (3.1.198ff.), but it is not clear from the text whether this is to be regarded as a semi-soliloquy or a public statement. If the former, we should be inclined to take the king at his word; if the latter, it may be that the king is proclaiming an inability to help the Protector precisely because he is not certain that he wants the Protector to be helped. The relationship between King Henry and Gloucester, in fact, is emerging as being as complex as that between Prince Hal and his two father figures, Henry IV and Falstaff.

Certain modern historians suspect that the king himself might have colluded in the destruction of Gloucester,[1] although none of the chroniclers goes so far. They do, however, underline the rift that opened up between Gloucester and the rest of the court after Suffolk had prevailed and been rewarded by the king for bringing Margaret to him.[2] Shakespeare shows that Margaret was among those who plotted Humphrey's death (3.1.223ff.), a role which is made more obvious in *The First Part of the Contention...*:[3] with regard to Henry himself, Shakespeare offers occasions from which we might deduce motives, but leaves the causes of the king's actions unclear. If he was not simply driven to it by his wife, perhaps the motive is Oedipal and derives from conflict between generations: Humphrey had acted as father as well as Protector to the infant monarch.[4] Fathers and sons figure largely in Shakespeare's plays, and the moment is a rite of passage into adulthood. By surrendering his staff, however, Gloucester hands over the administration of the realm to a monarch who may know what is right but who is unable to control what is wrong. Gloucester could do that: when giving up the Protector's staff of office, he proclaims

> Ah, thus King Henry throws away his crutch
> Before his legs be firm to bear his body.
> Thus is the shepherd beaten from thy side
> And wolves are gnarling who shall gnaw thee first.                    (3.1.189–92)

Events will prove Gloucester right.

When Gloucester is eventually arrested in 3.1 and the king listens passively to the charges against him, the measure of Lancastrian degradation is complete – the scene ends with York's soliloquy in which he reveals how he is ready to turn his policies into power and has harnessed the energies of Jack Cade to his own cause. Henry's motives are again in doubt in the next scene, when he learns from Suffolk that Gloucester is dead. After recovering from his faint, he does not deliver a praise of the dead man but turns and pours vitriol on Suffolk's head (3.2.39ff.). He does not actually accuse him of the murder, although he terms Suffolk a basilisk whose looks can kill. It may be, therefore, that his emotion is caused by his cuckoldry, a conjecture that is further confirmed when, a speech or so later, the queen protests her love far too much. Just as the fall of Eleanor was opportunistically seized upon by her enemies, the death of Gloucester may serve a king who feels that he is now ready to command. (It also serves the Nevilles, who, completely aware of the conspiracy to kill Humphrey (2.2.69–75), raise the commons against the court – a subtle way of advancing their Yorkist cause.) The king is yet again silent in 3.2 when he sees Gloucester's corpse and fails to respond to those who note that Gloucester was murdered – his silence this time perhaps

---

[1] See B. Wilkinson, *A History of England in the Fifteenth Century*, 1964, p. 17; Ralph A. Griffiths, *The Reign of King Henry VI*, 1981, pp. 497–8.
[2] Holinshed, p. 207; Hall, p. 204.
[3] See Appendix 2, pp. 231–2.
[4] The complexities of the relationship are masterfully explored by Robinson.

being generated by unexpressed guilt which leads him to order Suffolk's banishment rather than his death (3.2.295–7).[1] Henry will pay dearly for having failed to put justice before scruple and expediency.

Action has so far been dictated by the *natures* of the protagonists. But, just as Machiavelli demonstrated, although history is made by men's natures, character issuing in action, event and situation are equally important. In *2 Henry VI*, Shakespeare has, as it were, pushed the clash of nations off-stage. The momentum acquired by nationalist movements, however, gives them a power beyond the control of individuals, and Shakespeare dramatises their effect. *1 Henry VI* gave us full understanding of the origins of these political surges: in *2 Henry VI* this knowledge creates an ironic perspective on King Henry's providentialism, rendering it comic and inadequate. On the loss of France: 'Cold news, Lord Somerset; but God's will be done (3.1.86);[2] and in the final fight after we have witnessed Richard's savage slaughter of Somerset: 'Can we outrun the heavens? Good Margaret, stay' (5.2.73).

The first of these 'surges' occurs in 3.1 when Somerset enters to announce starkly that all the French territories and all the king's interest in them have been lost. With an eye to the main chance, Suffolk seizes on the news as a pretext for arresting Gloucester.[3] In the same scene news comes of rebellion in Ireland, whither York is dispatched with an army which he then can use to move towards the crown. His soliloquy at the end of the scene shows how he too has the capacity to seize the opportunity:

> Faster than spring-time showers comes thought on thought,
> And not a thought but thinks on dignity.
> My brain, more busy than the labouring spider,
> Weaves tedious snares to trap mine enemies.
> Well, nobles, well: 'tis politicly done
> To send me packing with an host of men;
> I fear me you but warm the starvèd snake
> Who, cherished in your breasts, will sting your hearts.
> 'Twas men I lacked, and you will give them me:
> I take it kindly, yet be well assured
> You put sharp weapons in a madman's hands.
>
> (3.1.337–47)

The verse has an assured maturity in which metaphors, although proverbial, enliven the lines to give the impression of an exploring consciousness. The confidences York entrusts to the audience suggest the Vice from the old morality plays or the stage 'Machiavel', but his *Realpolitik*, his awareness that power will come only if he can command the necessary resources, again implies a radical historiography. France was lost through 'want of men and money' (*1 Henry VI*, 1.1.69): England may, with the help of these necessities, be won. What makes the

---

[1] This would seem to be confirmed by his refusal to judge Winchester after hearing the latter's deathbed confession of his part in Gloucester's murder (3.3.9–11).
[2] The line ironically echoes York's 'Cold news for me, for I had hope of France' (1.1.234).
[3] See 3.1 headnote.

speech even more notable is that York gives a remarkable impression of self-disdain. Like Macbeth, he is not at all enamoured of the new 'politique' self, practising 'tedious snares', that he feels forced upon him by this change of fortune. He clearly feels the force of what he calls "*sancta majestas*" (5.1.5). For all his bloody talk, he watches and waits for some better chance to make his move. His secrecy seems to be largely compounded of reluctance.[1]

## PUBLIC LIVES AND PRIVATE SORROWS

Political machinations breed domestic distress. In this play, more than in the first part of the sequence, Shakespeare is able to move inward towards the consciousness of his characters. We can see this in two scenes of separation: that in which Duke Humphrey bids farewell to his wife, bound for penitential exile in the Isle of Man, and that of the parting of Margaret and Suffolk, who had been thrown together by the chance of war, and whose love had grown as they played their true roles in the proxy marriage and their feigned roles when marriage with the king turned their liaison to adultery. In the former scene, Humphrey shows both an emblematic awareness of the transitoriness of earthly glory and a noble pity for the person of his wife, paraded barefoot over the flinty streets. Neither he nor she, however, is willing to display in public the affection they feel for one another. Instead, Eleanor warns her husband of the politic snares that lie ahead for him; he, in his self-righteousness, ignores not only her pleas for more than stoic comfort, but her warnings. Her warnings are justified, it seems, for a herald appears to summon him to a parliament for which he had not given his assent. But he steadfastly refuses the gesture of affection his wife craves and leaves the stage without a final embrace:

> ELEANOR What, gone, my lord, and bid me not farewell?
> GLOUCESTER Witness my tears, I cannot stay to speak.                (2.4.84−5)

Less successful, it may seem, is 3.2, where Margaret and Suffolk are left on stage after Suffolk's banishment to bid farewell for, as it turns out, the last time. Both fling curses at the departed king, and the curses are built formally, studded with personification and emblem, the lines end-stopped and generally divided firmly into two hemistiches. Suffolk's lines turn to rant, but he is appeased by Margaret, whose new-found figures give her an unwonted sincerity:

> And these dread curses, like the sun 'gainst glass
> Or like an over-chargèd gun, recoil
> And turn the force of them upon thyself.                          (3.2.330−2)

In Suffolk's language, too, images of common life begin to appear:

> Well could I curse away a winter's night
> Though standing naked on a mountain top

---

[1] Robinson, p. 248.

> Where biting cold would never let grass grow,
> And think it but a minute spent in sport. (3.2.335–8)

But the scene reverts to stale Petrarchisms:

> O, let me entreat thee cease. Give me thy hand
> That I may dew it with my mournful tears;
> Nor let the rain of heaven wet this place
> To wash away my woeful monuments. (3.2.339–42)

It is obvious that the effect is generated more by the situation than by the personalities of the protagonists[1] – we might compare the leave-taking of Hotspur and his wife in *1 Henry IV*, 2.3, which offers a far more subtle mixture of affection and anger. More successful is Margaret's speech in 3.2, in which bad conscience causes her to blame her husband for the death of their love just after she has connived at plans for the murder of Gloucester. Her tactic is to remind him of the emotion she felt as the ship brought her to England for her marriage. Her self-dramatisation and inflation of emotion serves not only to expose her wiles to the audience but to explore the sea change which her entry into the political arena has brought about in her own sense of self:

> I stood upon the hatches in the storm;
> And when the dusky sky began to rob
> My earnest-gaping sight of thy land's view,
> I took a costly jewel from my neck –
> A heart it was, bound in with diamonds –
> And threw it towards thy land. The sea received it,
> And so I wished thy body might my heart:
> And, even with this, I lost fair England's view,
> And bid mine eyes be packing with my heart,
> And called them blind and dusky spectacles
> For losing ken of Albion's wishèd coast.
> How often have I tempted Suffolk's tongue –
> The agent of thy foul inconstancy –
> To sit and witch me as Ascanius did
> When he to madding Dido would unfold
> His father's acts commenced in burning Troy. (3.2.103–18)

The play ends with apocalypse: Old Clifford, the last of a gallery of fathers, is succeeded by the new generation:

> Y. CLIFFORD Shame and confusion! All is on the rout;
> Fear frames disorder, and disorder wounds
> Where it should guard. O war, thou son of hell,
> Whom angry heavens do make their minister,

---

[1] John Arthos, *Shakespeare: The Early Writings*, 1972, writes: 'So the lords and ladies of Montemayor and Sidney and Shakespeare are, as it were, always removing themselves from the currents of their adventures to come forth singly upon the scene to utter in a self-dramatizing way the correspondence of their feelings to the world in which they are enmeshed' (p. 178). Emrys Jones (*Origins*) demonstrates that the scene derives from Ovid's *Heroides*.

Throw in the frozen bosoms of our part
Hot coals of vengeance! Let no soldier fly.
He that is truly dedicate to war
Hath no self-love, nor he that loves himself
Hath not essentially but by circumstance
The name of valour. [*Seeing his dead father*] O let the vile world end,
And the premised flames of the last day
Knit earth and heaven together!...
                    Even at this sight
My heart is turned to stone: and while 'tis mine,
It shall be stony.
                                      (5.2.31–51)

The rant of these first lines suggests that the civil war has an eschatological dimension, but, as the speech continues, the audience becomes aware that the violence and suffering derive rather from the political strategies of the aristocratic factions. 'As Clifford speaks...he degenerates from a chivalric warrior to a Senecan revenger.'[1]

Salisbury, the 'winter lion' (5.3.2), is the last character to enter. A grotesque figure of martial will in an 'old feeble body' (5.3.13), he serves like Cade as an emblem of rebellion, York's will in the body politic. In *1 Henry VI* Shakespeare ended the play with an unhistorical victory for the English. In the case of *2 Henry VI* the chroniclers record a reconciliation between Henry and York after the first Battle of Saint Albans:[2] Shakespeare ends the second play with a celebration of York's victory, but there is no reconciliation. Instead, the trumpets blare out to herald the invasion of the king's parliament by the victor.

## Stage history

No performances of the play are known to have taken place between those which were mounted during Shakespeare's lifetime from March 1592 (see pp. 59–61 below) and the closing of the theatres. In 1681, after the Restoration, John Crowne's expanded adaptation of Acts 1–3 of the play was produced by the Duke's Company at Dorset Garden Theatre with the title of '*Henry the Sixth, the First Part, With the Murder of Humphrey Duke of Glocester* [*sic*]'.[3] The production delivered a political charge, cutting the Cade rebellion and making Cardinal Winchester a villain for a time of Popish troubles. An anti-papist slant was also imposed on the play by Ambrose Philips, who, at Drury Lane on 15 February 1723, produced *Humfrey Duke of Gloucester*, a five-act tragedy founded on the first three acts of the play but containing only about thirty lines from Shakespeare. Eleanor is innocent, framed by Margaret, Suffolk, and Winchester, and York and Salisbury and

---

[1] James C. Bulman, *The Heroic Idiom of Shakespearean Tragedy*, 1985, p. 39.
[2] See 5.3 headnote.
[3] John Genest, *Some Account of the English Stage from the Restoration in 1660 to 1830*, 10 vols., 1832, I, 302–4; George C. D. Odell, *Shakespeare from Betterton to Irving*, 2 vols., 1920, I, 63–7; see also Hazelton Spencer, *Shakespeare Improved*, 1927, pp. 310–13; A. C. Sprague, *Shakespeare's Histories: Plays for the Stage*, 1964, pp. 110–23.

12   H. François Gravelot's engraving of *The Death of Winchester*, in Hanmer, 1743

13   Sir Joshua Reynolds, *The Death of Winchester*

14   H. Fuseli, *The Death of Cardinal Beaufort*

Warwick become political allies and friends of Gloucester. Colley Cibber took the part of Winchester, the role that seized the imagination of those who produced illustrations of the play.[1] Five months later Theophilus Cibber produced a further compilation at Drury Lane, compiled this time almost entirely from lines by Shakespeare taken from Act 5 of *2 Henry VI* and Acts 1–2 of *3 Henry VI*.[2]

   At the beginning of the nineteenth century the play was produced by Edmund Kean as part of J. H. Merivale's five-act adaptation, *Richard Duke of York* (1817), a compilation of the three parts of the play performed at Dury Lane (with passages from Chapman, Marston, and Webster thrown in) from 15 December 1817.[3] This omitted the Duchess of Gloucester but, unusually for versions of this period, there are brief glimpses of the Cade rebellion.[4] Kean took the star part of York.

[1]   See Plates 12, 13 and 14; also C. B. Hogan, *Shakespeare in the Theatre, 1701–1800*, 2 vols., 1952–7, II, 202–3; Odell, *Shakespeare from Betterton to Irving*, I, 248–50.
[2]   Odell, *Shakespeare from Betterton to Irving*, I, 250–2.
[3]   Charles H. Shattuck, *The Shakespeare Promptbooks*, 1965, p. 154; accounts are given in Genest, *Some Account*, VIII, 636–41 and Odell, *Shakespeare from Betterton to Irving*, II, 128–30. It was not well received: see the review in *The Times* 23 December 1817, and L. L. and C. W. Houtchens (eds.), *Leigh Hunt's Dramatic Criticism*, 1949, pp. 180–2. A contemporary review from *The European Magazine* is reprinted by Gamini Salgado, *Eyewitnesses of Shakespeare*, 1975, pp. 86–7.
[4]   See Plate 6 for a glimpse of the way these scenes might be interpreted after 1789.

Another abridgement of the three parts into three acts was made by Charles Kemble (1775–1854, younger brother to John Philip Kemble), but there is no evidence that it was published or performed in his lifetime.[1]

A later adaptation was that of Robert Atkins, who produced *1 Henry VI* along with the first half of *2 Henry VI* at the Old Vic on 29 January 1923.[2]

*2 Henry VI* was revived at the rough-and-tumble Surrey Theatre in Blackfriars by James Anderson in April 1864 as part of the celebrations connected with the tercentenary of Shakespeare's birth. Anderson derived his text from *The Contention* and *The True Tragedy*, and made use of doubling, playing York and Cade himself.

Bold and dashing...is his performance of ambitious York, whose part he had strengthened...by incorporating...a portion of Warwick's...It falls to Mr Anderson's lot to describe the appearance of Duke Humphrey's body after death; and he took advantage of the situation to ensure himself a remarkable effect, which brought down the plaudits of the house...The fight in [Iden's] garden...was exciting, and Mr Anderson threw considerable humour into it by indicating the weakness he suffered from a five days' fast, and buckling his belt tighter in order to strengthen himself for the task. He died boldly, like a courageous rebel of the true English type, and won our respect even in his fall...Miss Pauncefort's Margaret was exceedingly feeble, and Mrs St.-Henry, as the Duchess of Gloucester, was altogether unequal to the assumption. The getting-up of the drama was admirable; the scenery and costumes being in excellent keeping.[3]

There were productions in Germany and Austria in the nineteenth century, including a notable version at the Burgtheater in Vienna in 1873, in which Mitterwurzer played Winchester.[4]

F. R. Benson produced *2 Henry VI* at Stratford in 1899[5] and the three parts of the play at Stratford on 2, 3, and 4 May 1906[6] – *3 Henry VI* being revived for the first time. The director used a set that, although permanent, could be deployed in the service of illusion. An anonymous reviewer wrote: 'There was no changing of scenery, except of portable furniture, the action was continuous, and the auditors were expected to exercise not only their attention but their imagination. "The Players' House" served for all castles and battlements and balconies: the arras and painted cloths for all backgrounds; curtains gave opportunities for concealment, and ordinary exits and entrances allowed a continuous stream of performers to pass over the proscenium.'[7] Another reviewer wrote: 'A conspicuous feature of the present revival is the care which has been bestowed upon what may be termed the historical and archaeological side of the production. With an Irving-like

[1] It is printed in *The Henry Irving Shakespeare*, 8 vols., 1888, III, 201–46.
[2] See *The [London] Shakespeare [League] Journal* 8 (February, 1923), 57. Rupert Harvey played York; Guy Martineau, the King; and Esther Whitehouse, Margaret. The playbill is reprinted in John Parker, *Who's Who in the Theatre*, 1925.
[3] *The Athenaeum*, 30 April 1864, p. 620.
[4] See E. L. Stahl, *Shakespeare und das Deutsche Theater*, 1947.
[5] The prompt book is in the Shakespeare Centre Library, along with two unpublished volumes of heraldic designs by Alfred Rodway, Benson's expert in this field.
[6] Benson's interpretative note is given by Sprague, p. 112, who also notes that the production is reviewed at length in *The Athenaeum*, 12 May 1906.
[7] *Stratford-upon-Avon Herald*, 11 May 1906.

minuteness of study of detail, Mr F. R. Benson has gone into this deeply and he has wisely secured the best of aid in transporting the atmosphere and colour of a brilliant period of history on to the stage.'[1]

In *2 Henry VI* Benson played Winchester and his wife the queen: 'Mr Benson descends from his kingly pedestal, and takes the character of Beaufort...He is the chief murderer of the unhappy duke, and the scene on his pallet bed [3.3] was a painful piece of acting. The dying wretch perishes in the fearful recollection of his unrepented sins, and in his delirium beholds the spirit of the murdered duke, whose sightless orbs are bent upon him. He looked the very picture of the cruel, keen, politic, turbulent, haughty prelate.'[2] There was little sympathy for Cade and his rebels: 'Mr C. H. Dorcus' Jack Cade was played with the requisite bluster and callousness, but failed to reach the standard attained by Mr Oscar Asche, whose realistic representation will remain in the memory for many long years.'[3]

In the United States the play was performed for the first time at the Pasadena Community Playhouse in California under the direction of Gilmor Brown, from 25–7 July 1935 as part of a season which saw productions of all ten histories,[4] and James Sandoe and Jerry Turner respectively produced the play at the Oregon Shakespeare Festival in 1954 and 1976.[5]

A sequence of notable modern British revivals began when, under Sir Barry Jackson, the whole sequence was directed by Douglas Seale at the Birmingham Repertory Theatre from 1951.[6] The sequence was played in London on successive nights at the Old Vic in 1953.[7] 'Douglas Seale was a director who knew what a clean thrusting style could do for a crowded chronicle. Hence the ultimate triumph at the Vic in Finlay James's setting of triple Gothic arches.'[8] Jack May played the king and Rosalind Boxall Queen Margaret. Seale brought the production again to the Old Vic, where it was played with *Parts 1* and *2* condensed into one performance from 16 October 1957.[9]

The reviewer of *2 Henry VI* in *The Times* wrote, 'Cumulative disorder is the only order of the play and it demands of the actors an explosive vitality...The Birmingham Repertory actors take the challenge, attacking with ringing voice and

[1] *Birmingham Express*, 2 May 1906.
[2] *Stratford-upon-Avon Herald*, 4 May 1906.
[3] *Ibid.*
[4] Louis Marder describes a production of the three parts of the sequence condensed by Arthur Lithgow into a single one-act play and performed in August 1952 at Antioch Area Theatre, Yellow Springs, Ohio: 'History cycle at Antioch College', *SQ* 4 (1953), 57–8; for a similar adaptation performed in Canada, see Ralph Berry, 'Stratford Festival Canada', *SQ* 3 (1981), 176–80.
[5] See James Sandoe, 'King Henry VI, Part 2: Notes during Production', *Theatre Annual* 13 (1955), 32–48, and Alan C. Dessen, 'Oregon Shakespearean Festival, 1976', *SQ* 28 (1977), 244–52; see also Joseph H. Stodder and Lillian Wilds, 'Shakespeare in Southern California and Visalia', *SQ* 31 (1980), 254–74 for an account of productions of *2H6* and *3H6* by Keith Lawrence in Los Angeles.
[6] Seale produced *2H6* in 1951, *3H6* in 1952 (22 July) and *1H6* in 1953 (14 July). See Sir Barry Jackson, 'On producing *Henry VI*,' *S. Sur.* 6 (1953); J. C. Trewin, *Going to Shakespeare*, 1978, p. 20.
[7] The whole sequence was reviewed in *The Times* 15–17 July 1953.
[8] J. C. Trewin, *Shakespeare on the English Stage, 1900–1964*, 1964, p. 225.
[9] *The Times* reviewer felt that the London performances did not match the original ones (17 October 1957).

sterling sincerity...It is clamant emotion more than sumptuous scenery that Old Vic audiences want...[The reviewer praised] Mr Jack King's king, plunging down into the depths of impassioned pity over Humphrey's death, Miss Rosalind Boxall's hooded silent malice as the treacherous queen, the gargoyle menace of Mr Alfred Burke's cardinal, and the sword-sharp ambition of Mr John Arnatt's York'.[1]

Sprague[2] describes an uncut amateur production by the Hovenden Theatre Club in August 1959 that used only ten men and three women. *2 Henry VI* was performed for only a single night.

In 1963 Peter Hall directed John Barton's two-part sequence, *The Wars of the Roses*, a condensation of the three parts of *Henry VI* into two plays, '*Henry VI*' and '*Edward IV*'.[3] This was designed to be part of a revival of all the history plays mounted to celebrate the Shakespeare centenary the following year. Barton not only cut passages, but added material of his own, usually derived from the chronicles.[4] In the programme, John Barton and Peter Hall wrote: 'We are sure that these early plays produced in an unadapted form would show to a modern audience the force of their political and human meaning.' The intention, moreover, seems not to have been to create star vehicles, but to establish a unified company style played on a set that eschewed any kind of historical accuracy or theatrical glamour. The influence of Brecht's notions of history and the theatrical style of his Berliner Ensemble was manifest: 'Hall's policy? To fashion a company that can play together, to and with each other, with only the occasional use of stars with ready-made reputations...Whatever distant historical ends these kings and nobles may be carrying out, it is their individual actions that are determining the sway of the struggle.'[5] David Pryce-Jones missed a sense of doom in this production: 'Now [the barons] are presented merely as the greedy symbols of ambition and power, thwarted by the even greedier symbols of absolutism.'[6] 'There were even titters of protest at some of the decapitations, but the triumph of the production is the even conversational tone with which the discussions are carried forward and the care to avoid ranting, even in dealing with martial bombast.'[7]

Although the conception of the productions was widely praised, many reviewers found the violence of the later parts of the sequence distasteful or disturbing. The sequence was revived at Stratford in 1964, the year in which the Royal

[1] *The Times*, 16 July 1953.
[2] Sprague, p. 114–16. 'In the 1960s the Marlowe Society at Cambridge produced a heavily condensed version of *Parts Two* and *Three* to make a play called *Alarums and Excursions*' (RSC Programme to the 1988 production).
[3] See John Russell Brown, *Shakespeare's Plays in Performance*, 1966, pp. 195–202. A television version of this production was broadcast by the BBC. Barton's text '*Henry VI*' was performed at the Stratford Festival Theatre in Ontario in 1966.
[4] The text is given in J. Barton and P. Hall, *The Wars of the Roses: Adapted for the Royal Shakespeare Company from William Shakespeare's 'Henry VI, Part I, II, III and Richard III'*, 1970.
[5] Bernard Levin, *Daily Mail*, 18 July 1963.
[6] David Pryce-Jones, *Spectator*, 26 July 1963.
[7] Philip Hope-Wallace, *Guardian*, 18 July 1963.

Shakespeare Company first directed Weiss's *Marat/Sade*; the kind of work the company was doing led to the season's being associated not only with Brecht but with a 'theatre of cruelty'. 'In the second of the plays, *Edward IV*, the violence grows to a kind of white heat of blood lust as Yorkists and Lancastrians, abandoning the council table, join the fight in earnest on the battle field where every battle ends in an orgy of savagery'.[1] And J. C. Trewin wrote: 'It is a pity, I think, although Shakespeare demands it, that [Margaret] has to mourn at the last over Suffolk's head [4.4]. These gory properties are always dangerous in performance.'[2] However, this scene was praised when the production was revived in 1964: '[Suffolk's] head is placed where the queen cannot fail to find it. Down a staircase lit only by flickering torches she comes, bearing the head covered with blood in her arms and mourning his death. The king sadly watches her. He picks up a prayer book and all his disillusionment and frustration are put into two of the play's key lines. "Come, wife, let's in and learn to govern better; For yet may England curse my wretched reign"' [4.9.48–9].[3]

David Warner as the king, 'like a holy idiot out of Dostoyevsky',[4] marked his character development by donning 'a grey cloak and [becoming] more bowed, now the complete monk'.[5] Harold Hobson found him 'particularly fine in the supposed miracle scene, where his part is so unemphatic that a lessor actor, with a lesser director, would go unperceived. But, as the fraud is exposed, the king's face is stricken. We see a man's faith, which is all in all to him, momentarily destroyed. Mr Warner is only on the edge of the crowd, but in effect he is the centre of the stage.'[6]

Peggy Ashcroft, playing Margaret, with a French accent as she did throughout, drew unqualified critical acclaim for moving from young girl to the embittered old woman of *Richard III*:[7] 'At the reading of the marriage contract, she eliminates pages of the text simply by a silent debby smirk and shrug at the revelation that she has no dowry.'[8]

Cade's rebels drew more sympathy than they had in previous productions. 'The great ones, almost to a man, are arrogant, savage, and fickle: and so, aping them, are the common people, whose behaviour in Jack Cade's rebellion prompts the reflection that every Government gets the country it deserves.'[9] 'Jack Cade's unruly rabble, on the other hand, have a life and energy lacked by the soldiers, hampered as they are (and doubtless were) by hefty swords, clanking armour – and the rules of chivalrous combat.'[10]

[1] T. C. Worsley, *Financial Times*, 18 July 1963.
[2] J. C. Trewin, *Birmingham Post*, 18 July 1963.
[3] Geoffrey Tarran, *Morning Advertiser*, 3 August 1964.
[4] Alan Brien, *Sunday Telegraph*, 21 July 1963.
[5] Felix Barker, *Evening News*, 18 July 1963.
[6] Harold Hobson, *Sunday Times*, 21 July 1963.
[7] Added to the *Henry VI* sequence in 1964 as part of the centennial performance of the complete cycle of history plays.
[8] Alan Brien, *Sunday Telegraph*, 21 July 1963.
[9] Kenneth Tynan, *Observer*, 21 July 1963.
[10] E. M. A., *Leamington Spa Courier*, 19 July 1963.

15 David Warner and Peggy Ashcroft in Sir Peter Hall's 1963 Stratford production

16   The Council Table in Sir Peter Hall's 1964 Stratford production

Part of the acclaim won for the production derived from the set: 'It is a hard world – shaped in steel, John Bury, the present designer says. He has told us how he has tried to mark the English court by "thick enclosing walls", the English countryside by trees, and France by the use of copper. All is stern, metallic, and ringing. The stage is wide and bare, a sounding-board for fierce words and fierce deeds.'[1] The stage was backed by steel trellis work, and the 'walls' were great triangular structures faced with a pattern of rivetted plates which could be moved like massive city gates. 'We seem to be claustrophobically caught between two swinging metal wings that crush us first from one side then from the other.'[2] Prominent was a large council table which could be thrust out over matching stylised flagstones to the front of the stage, suggesting the domination of lords over monarch. 'The play is admirably produced to show us how behind the scenes decisions are cooked up to be ratified later at this table.'[3] 'The endless succession of sorties and sieges with clanking figures wrestling in half-light actually became restful interludes between the far more dramatic and exciting clashes of ambition and policy.'[4] Also thrust out was a 'push-on-push-off throne and dais...itself a miniature architectural masterpiece, oddly contemporary yet

[1] J. C. Trewin, *Birmingham Post*, 18 July 1963.    [3] T. C. Worsley, *Financial Times*, 18 July 1963.
[2] T. C. Worsley, *Financial Times*, 18 July 1963.    [4] Alan Brien, *Sunday Telegraph*, 21 July 1963.

not without the dignity of history. It would have graced Coventry Cathedral or the Shell Building.'[1]

Instead of historical costumes, actors wore uniform greys, blacks, and browns flecked with gold: '[the barons] are nicely differentiated but not in a fancy Guthrie fashion'.[2] Instead, therefore, of appearing as heroes in a divinely appointed saga, they were operators within a specific political milieu.

A French adaptation of the three *Henry VI* plays and *Richard III* was prepared and directed by Denis Llorca in 1978. It was entitled *Kings, ou les adieux à Shakespeare*, comprised three parts – 'L'été', 'L'automne', and 'L'hiver', with a preliminary adaptation of the deposition of Richard II by Bullingbrook ('Le printemps') – and took the form of a twelve-hour performance that was remarkable for its spectacle and symbolic structure. It was performed at the Maison des arts André Malraux, at Créteil near Paris in May 1979, after being the centrepiece of the festival at Carcassonne the previous summer.[3]

The complete sequence of three plays was directed by Terry Hands at Stratford-upon-Avon for the Royal Shakespeare Company from 12 July 1977.[4] They were staged in conjunction with a revival of Hands's very successful 1975 Stratford production of *Henry V*: Alan Howard played both kings, father and son, to great acclaim. The productions were revived at the Aldwych Theatre in London in April 1978.

The style of production, which was designed by Farrah, was again, like that of *Henry V*, epic in the Brechtian manner. The bare stage with stark simple properties but bold costumes was much praised.[5] 'As the stage was festooned with cannon for Part 1, so it is sown with grass for Part 2; for Part 2 takes us out of France into the English countryside...The fighting this time is of a more intimate brand, no cannon, only swords, clubs, or extemporary weapons.'[6] The stage was 'divided by a rope barrier. On one side king, queen and courtiers perambulate; on the other the lower classes gawp.'[7] 'What we see is the people bursting on to the

---

[1] Ken Griffith, *South Wales Evening Argus*, 19 July 1963.

[2] T. C. Worsley, *Financial Times*, 18 July 1963.

[3] See Marie-Claude Rousseau's account of the discussion of the play at the Société Française Shakespeare (*Actes du congrès*, 1979), and reviews in *Midi Libre*, 18 and 19 July 1978; *La Dépêche du Midi*, 17 July 1978; *Les Nouvelles littéraires*, 20 July 1978; *Le Monde*, 5 August 1978 and 16 May 1979.

[4] The first night of *2 Henry VI* was 30 June. The story of the productions is told by Sally Beauman, *The Royal Shakespeare Company*, 1982, pp. 338–42; see also M. Billington, 'Shakespeare's dance to the broken music of time', *Guardian*, 17 April 1978, p. 8; B. Nightingale, '*Henry VI*', *New Statesman* 94 (22 July 1977), p. 124; J-M. Maguin, 'Review of Terry Hands' RSC Stratford production of *Henry VI*', *Cahiers élisabéthains* 12 (1977), 77–80; G. K. Hunter, 'The Royal Shakespeare Company plays *Henry VI*', *Ren. Drama* 9 (1978), 91–108; G. M. Pearce, 'Review of Terry Hands' RSC London production of *Henry VI*', *Cahiers élisabéthains* 14 (1978), 107–9; D. Daniell, 'Opening up the text: Shakespeare's Henry VI plays in performance', in J. Redmond (ed.), *Themes in Drama I: Drama and Society*, 1979, pp. 247–77; H. D. Swander, 'The rediscovery of Henry VI', *SQ* 29 (1978), 146–63; R. Warren, 'Comedies and histories at two Stratfords, 1977', *S. Sur.* 31 (1978), 141–53.

[5] See the Stage History section of my *1 Henry VI*, pp. 49–51.

[6] B. A. Young, *Financial Times*, 14 July 1977.

[7] R. Cushman, *Observer*, 17 July 1977.

green in the Jack Cade rebellion, like spectators invading the pitch at Lords, and
the nobles reduced to savage animalistic clusters: it's a perfect metaphor for a
play which is, literally, about breaking ranks.'[1] Irving Wardle noted, however,
that the grass which set all scenes outdoors obliged Winchester 'to stagger about
and writhe in the king's arms instead of taking to his bed'.[2]

'[Hands] hasn't found an overpowering single image for the three plays, like the
diamond shaped council-table that dominated [Barton's] *The Wars of the Roses* [see
above]. But he has...evoked a style that admirably suits chronicle plays. It's based
on a minimal setting, roving spotlights, and a bold frontal style of playing that gives
the actors a chance to establish direct lines of contact with the audience.'[3]
Benedict Nightingale claimed that the productions succeeded 'without that
editorializing, moralizing touch which has sometimes spoiled promising productions at Stratford'.[4] After the London revival, the critic of *The Financial Times*
wrote: 'To my mind this is the best Shakespeare production I have ever seen.
There is no scenery, no more than a token growth of grass [in *2 Henry VI*]; but
there is a spare yet powerful use of props – cannon mostly in Part 1 where the war
is on an international scale, the Throne and the benches of Parliament in the
other parts – and there are fine costumes devised so that the wearer is always
recognizable.'[5]

In this play the king comes into his own. 'Mr Howard's Henry is actually neither
saint nor imbecile; he is not even a particularly good man, though he is certainly
a very nice one. He is an innocent (Mr Howard has discovered a staggeringly
virginal walk) who loses his illusions very quickly but gains all the time in
intelligence. He can out-observe any man in the realm but he cannot act on his
insights.'[6] In particular, '[Howard] achieves one thrilling climax by treating the
exile of Suffolk as a demoniac exorcism.'[7]

'Helen Mirren's Margaret of Anjou is not a battle-axe, but a woman who moves
from her passionate love for Suffolk, to a greedy but kindly loving appreciation of
the king, while defending her son's rights against the odds.'[8] She 'has grown
sour and ill-tempered, but is still comparatively young and beautiful'.[9] The *Daily
Mail* critic wrote: 'Helen Mirren's sensual, impetuous, and slightly common
Queen Margaret with McEnery's increasingly disdainful Suffolk have between
them opened a mischievous Pandora's box around the throne.'[10]

'The principals [mostly] come over as interchangeable gangsters...Emrys
James's York goes from strength to strength, now a full-blown reptilian narcissus,

[1] Michael Billington, *Guardian*, 17 April 1978.
[2] Irving Wardle, *The Times*, 14 July 1977.
[3] Michael Billington, *Guardian*, 17 April 1978.
[4] Benedict Nightingale, *New Statesman*, 22 July 1977.
[5] B. A. Young, *Financial Times*, 17 April 1978.
[6] R. Cushman, *Observer*, 17 July 1977.
[7] Irving Wardle, *The Times*, 14 July 1977.
[8] Gavin Millar, *Listener*, 21 July 1977.
[9] B. A. Young, *Financial Times*, 14 July 1977.
[10] Jack Tinker, *Daily Mail*, 14 July 1977.

17   Alan Howard as Henry VI in Terry Hands's 1977 Stratford production (the falcon scene, 2.1)

coaxing irony from out of the recital of his ramshackle pedigree, and passing a white rose to his nostrils as if it had the power of a magic charm.'[1] John Barber noted: 'It is a neat touch in Hands' vigorous production that a minor character, well taken by Barrie Rutter, squats obediently at York's feet later, to underline the poet's moral for his contemporaries: all rebels are one, and a land with two kings has none.'[2] 'Avuncular Gloucester, whom Graham Crowden plays with great sympathy, has now become irascible with age...Peter McEnery's Suffolk flashes across the scene like a shooting star, every sidelong glance proclaiming his arrogance, his handsome figure a fitting target for Margaret's ambition.'[3] 'Julian Glover is a brusque Warwick, so much the kingmaker that he treats the crown like a frisbee, and actually whisks it from claimant to claimant.'[4]

'Jack Cade's rebellion is built up beautifully from small beginnings to general uproar. Cade is played with such understanding by James Laurenson that it is hard not to fall in on his side.'[5] Roger Warren saw him as a John the Baptist figure.[6] At the climax of the rebellion, however, 'a small group of [rebels turned] away in

[1]  Irving Wardle, *The Times*, 14 July 1977.
[2]  John Barber, *Daily Telegraph*, 14 July 1977.
[3]  B. A. Young, *Financial Times*, 14 July 1977.
[4]  Benedict Nightingale, *New Statesman*, 22 July 1977.
[5]  B. A. Young, *Financial Times*, 14 July 1977.
[6]  Warren, 'Comedies and histories at two Stratfords'.

18   The Iden scene in Terry Hands's 1977 Stratford production

disgust from the carnage. There is no single theme running through [the production] and...Terry Hands was wise not to impose one. He is exclusively concerned with fluency.'[1] *The Oxford Times* agreed, describing 'Shakespeare's disillusioned realization that the lower social strata can be as vicious and self-seeking, when power falls into their hands, as the hereditary tyrants among the regality and the nobility. Cade himself seems to be more desperately concerned that his Plantagenet origins shall be acknowledged than he is for the welfare of his rabble of underdog supporters.'[2]

The BBC's television version of the play was broadcast on 9 January 1983. It was produced by Jonathan Miller and directed by Jane Howell. For this, the other two parts of the plays, and *Richard III* a constructivist, anti-illusionist set was used, a seemingly circular playing space – or playground – surrounded by walls and galleries made of old doors and timber. All this and a throne knocked together out of roughly cut timbers suggested perhaps the rickety and improvised structures of institutions as Shakespeare portrayed them. (The Petitioners of 1.3 prised off boards to make an entrance for themselves into the political arena.) The director 'worked with her designers [Oliver Bayldon and John Peacock] to produce a set suggestive of a brightly coloured playground, with Playcraft props, "dressing up" costumes, and armour inspired by the shoulder pads of American football'.[3] It worked well, far better than those productions in the series which were shot on location or which used an illusionistic set. While the text was taken at a rattling pace in *Part 1*, displaying a Brechtian sense of *Spass* (fun), the players spoke in a much more measured pace in *Part 2*, seeking to clarify the story as far as possible.

The king (Peter Benson) was played very much as other characters described him, as a holy fool. Margaret (Julia Foster) was a short but commanding figure who was appalled by the lack of energy of her future spouse the first time she saw him. The theatricality of the duchess's conjuring scene was displayed by showing Margery Jourdain painting up her face before the action began: she also took the part of the spirit who delivered the prophecies. In this production, Dick the Butcher, who demolishes the pretensions to authority of Jack Cade, was, perhaps unfortunately, placed immediately before the camera, his opinions thereby foregrounded and endorsed. Jack Cade became thereby a comic figure, and the rebels were completely demonised by the inclusion of a scene of book-burning redolent of events in Nazi Germany. The lines of Iden which reveal that he sees his capture of Cade as a means of obtaining position at court (4.10.60–4) were cut.

[1] Frank Marcus, *Sunday Telegraph*, 17 July 1977.
[2] Anon, *Oxford Times*, 22 July 1977.
[3] Robert Hapgood, 'Shakespeare on film and television', in Stanley Wells (ed.), *The Cambridge Companion to Shakespeare Studies*, 1986, p. 278; see also Henry Fenwick, 'The production', *The BBC TV Shakespeare: Henry VI Part One*, 1983, pp. 22–3; Michèle Willems, *Shakespeare à la télévision*, 1987, pp. 79–92, 157–78; Graham Holderness, 'Radical potentiality and institutional closure: Shakespeare in film and television', in J. Dollimore and A. Sinfield (eds.), *Political Shakespeare*, 1985, pp. 192ff. Other reviews are to be found in J. C. Bulman and H. R. Coursen (eds.), *Shakespeare on Television*, 1988, pp. 292–96.

In 1986 the English Shakespeare Company under the artistic direction of Michael Pennington and Michael Bogdanov began to mount, for a national tour, seven of Shakespeare's histories under the title of *The Wars of the Roses*.[1] The *Henry VI* texts were condensed into two plays: *Henry VI: House of Lancaster*, and *Henry VI: House of York*. *2 Henry VI* was shortened: the court scenes were arranged into the second half of the former play, which ended with Queen Margaret receiving the head of Suffolk, and the Cade sequences were arranged into the first half of the latter. The plays received their first performances on 14 and 15 December 1987 at the Theatre Royal in Bath. Bogdanov directed, and Pennington played Jack Cade. The plays were performed in a box formed by black screens, and much use was made of recorded classical music. In the first play, costumes and a certain amount of weaponry were taken from styles of the First World War, although swords were also occasionally used. Contemporary punk styles with allusions to the National Front were used for the Cade sequences, but the main part of the production evoked the styles of the Second World War. Paul Brennen, a tall, thin, and almost totally bald actor, played the king, June Watson was Margaret, and Colin Farrell was Gloucester.

The Royal Shakespeare Company produced another adaptation, *The Plantagenets*, at Stratford in 1988, directed by Adrian Noble and designed by Bob Crowley. The three parts of *Henry VI* were condensed into two plays, '*Henry VI*' and '*The Rise of Edward IV*', in an adaptation of a version by Charles Wood, the plays being performed as a trilogy along with *Richard III*.[2] The first half of *Henry VI* ran from the beginning of Shakespeare's *1 Henry VI*, the second half from the last scene of *1 Henry VI* through to the end of Act 3 of *2 Henry VI*. *The Rise of Edward IV* began with Cade (the Horner scenes having been cut), and the first half ended with the battle of Towton (*3 Henry VI*, 2.5). 'What we see is the disintegration of England as it moves from a world of medieval chivalry to become a rancid slaughterhouse under the pressure of power-mania, naked will, and hunger for the crown.'[3]

Design took a high profile in the production. A raked deep stage was used, covered with a grille from which smoke wafted up throughout most of the production, thus enhancing the elaborate lighting effects (by Chris Parry) that were deployed throughout. The costumes were elaborate and, generally, historically accurate, unlike the uniform styles devised for the earlier Stratford productions by Hall and Hands. Ralph Fiennes as the king was, unlike some of his modern predecessors in the role, no pious milksop but a firm-minded politician made politically impotent by the web of intrigue which surrounded him. His

---

[1] See MacD. P. Jackson, '*The Wars of the Roses*: The English Shakespeare Company on Tour', *SQ* 40 (1989), 208–11.
[2] '*Henry VI*' was first performed on 29 September 1988, '*The Rise of Edward IV*' on 6 October 1988, and the trilogy on one day, 22 October 1988. In the programme to the production, Alan Sinfield offers an analysis of the ideological assumptions which informed the previous RSC productions by Hall and Hands.
[3] Michael Billington, *Guardian*, 24 October 1988.

woollen shift signified not piety but probity, and yet his policy of promoting his allies was simply not enough to protect him from the forces York was able to muster. This was signified by reducing the size of the throne, which had soared heavenwards in the first half of the play, to more customary proportions. 'When he lets the lords frame David Waller's juicily-imposing Gloucester, you feel, with him, that all is lost.'[1] Irving Wardle wrote that 'Fiennes' Henry is the first I have seen who communicates the sense of a real moral alternative to his faction-riven court: without sacrificing the character's gentleness, he has moments of spectacular strength and his political irrelevance and unresisting death are not those of an ineffectual weakling.'[2] Penny Downie's gold-clad queen was a strong and subtle performance: her sexual attraction for her husband withered early, but she remained fiercely loyal throughout the political bickerings, if only to enhance her own power. Henry was at times her match: he cast her off physically in the scene in which he banishes Suffolk (3.2). 'Downie's performance makes clear that the turning point in Margaret's mental history is the barbarous slaying of her lover, Suffolk. Staggering in with his hacked off head cradled maternally at her breast, she lets you see that this same atrocity will at once turn her into a monster and preserve, at some deep core, a capacity for intense human feeling. When she is railed at by her victims, Downie's face twitches uncomfortably, as though she can dimly recall a time when she could afford to be sensitive. But then, she jerks herself back with imperious sarcasm to her chosen hardness.'[3] David Calder played a fine-voiced York with authority and clarity. He 'shrewdly sets the tone by showing the gulf between the conciliatory public face and the snarling private one'.[4]

The Cade scenes were so severely cut that there was no time for the rebels' claims to be understood by the audience, who were alienated early in the sequence by a prolonged sequence of mob torment meted out to the Clerk of Chartham before his death. The rebels' tendency to orgiastic violence was enhanced by bringing on a whole forest of aristocratic heads on spears (4.7). Oliver Cotton played Cade, and Robert Demeger was Dick the Butcher – Demeger had been Talbot in the earlier play. The rebels were reduced to the level of conspirators, emerging from stage traps: they fell back spontaneously on the entrance of Lord Say and were put down with savage efficiency by the king's henchmen. 'Mr Noble...reminds us that there is still an ancestral memory of old England: Henry V is frequently invoked and Jack Cade's rebels are disarmed by cynical arousal of the fears of French invasion.'[5]

[1] Michael Coveney, *Financial Times*, 24 October 1988.
[2] *The Times*, 24 October 1988.
[3] Paul Taylor, *Independent*, 24 October 1988.
[4] Michael Billington, *Guardian*, 24 October 1988.
[5] Michael Billington, *Guardian*, 24 October 1988; articles concerning and reviews of other modern productions may be traced through the stage history section of Judith Hinchcliffe's *King Henry VI, Parts 1, 2, and 3: An Annotated Bibliography*, 1984.

## Date and occasion

*1 Henry VI*, or a version of it, would seem to have been written and performed by 8 August 1592, the date of entry in the Stationers' Register of Thomas Nashe's *Pierce Penilesse his Supplication to the Divell*.[1] There, in the course of a defence of drama, the author offers a description of theatrical heroism as a 'reproof to these degenerate effeminate days of ours'. He continues:

How would it have joyed brave Talbot (the terror of the French) to think that after he had lain two hundred years in his tomb, he should triumph again on the stage, and have his bones new embalmed with the tears of ten thousand spectators at least (at several times), who, in the tragedian that represents his person, imagine they behold him fresh bleeding.[2]

This would seem to indicate that Nashe had seen, in a public playhouse, a play with Talbot as a central figure. It is reasonable to assume that this was a performance of the text that the compilers of the Folio present to us as being by Shakespeare, because in 1593, when Nashe wrote another pamphlet, *The Terrors of the Night*, he included a number of expressions and images found in that text.[3] (Nashe might well, indeed, have written part of the play himself.)[4]

On 2 September of the same year (1592), another pamphleteer and dramatist, Robert Greene, lay dying.[5] Later that month and shortly after his death another pamphlet was printed, *Greenes Groats-worth of Witte. . . written before his death and published at his dyeing request*,[6] which contains a famous warning to gentlemen play-makers, the so-called university wits, to distrust the fickle nature of players, especially one:

Yes, trust them not; for there is an upstart crow, beautified with our feathers that, with his 'Tiger's heart wrapped in a player's hide', supposes he is as well able to bombast out a blank verse as the best of you: and being an absolute *Iohannes fac totum*, is in his own conceit the only Shake-scene in a country.                               (sig. F1ʳ)[7]

The reference is obviously to Shakespeare, who was, as may be inferred from this mock invective, serving as a player as well as a playwright – the phrase 'beautified with our feathers' means, probably, that he appeared in plays by Greene and his fellows. (The problem is whether Greene was pillorying Shakespeare's pride or alleging plagiarism – taking 'beautified with our feathers' to mean the latter.)[8]

---

[1] Arber, II, 292.

[2] Nashe, I, 212.

[3] See C. G. Harlow, 'A source for Nashe's *Terrors of the Night* and the authorship of *1 Henry VI*', *SEL* 5 (1965), 31–47, 269–81.

[4] See my introduction to *1H6*, p. 42.

[5] The date comes from a pamphlet entitled *The Repentance of Robert Greene*, 1592, sig. D2ʳ.

[6] Entered in the Stationers' Register 20 September 1592 (Arber, II, 620).

[7] The controversies raised by this passage since Malone are reviewed by D. Allen Carroll, 'Greene's "vpstart crow" passage: a survey of commentary', *RORD* 28 (1985), 111–27.

[8] We cannot tell whether Greene was alluding to vain or ostentatious crows described in Macrobius, Martial, and Aesop or, far less likely, a thieving crow in Horace's third *Epistle*; see S. Schoenbaum, *William Shakespeare, A Compact Documentary Life*, 1977, pp. 151ff. D. Allen Carroll, '*Johannes Factotum* and Jack Cade', *SQ* 40 (1989), 491–2, argues that this is a second allusion to Shakespeare in that Cade was known as 'Mend-all'.

Moreover, the pastiche of the line from *3 Henry VI*, 'O tiger's heart wrapped in a woman's hide!' (1.4.137) indicates that the third play of the trilogy was at least written by this date, although we cannot surmise at this stage of the argument whether Greene knew the line from reading a manuscript or from hearing it in the playhouse.

As for the *terminus a quo* for the play's composition, there is very little evidence.[1] Now that the opinion of Chambers that Shakespeare made a 'late start' in his writing career has been strongly challenged,[2] it has seemed possible that Shakespeare may have begun to write plays as early as 1584, and that the *Henry VI* plays may have been written soon after the publication of the second edition of Holinshed's *Chronicles* in 1587. Honigmann is prepared to conjecture that *1 Henry VI* could have been written as early as 1589.[3] I am inclined to believe that the play was written before the other two parts of the sequence, at some date between 1589 and 1591, although recent work, based on rare-word tests, suggests that it may have been written after them.[4]

The problem of when exactly *1 Henry VI* was first *performed*, and by whom, has given rise to a vast amount of enquiry and is intricately bound up with the question of the theatrical genesis of the other two plays in the sequence. The following account is the most probable; it is based on the premise that Shakespeare wrote the whole of the trilogy, and in the order of the events it portrays.[5] (The part of the argument that follows concerning the play's theatrical provenance, however, is not invalidated by a proof that the play was written and performed after *2* and *3 Henry VI*.) It assumes that the Folio texts derive from holographic copy (see

---

[1]  For some circumstantial evidence see *1H6* 4.7.61–70 n.

[2]  See E. A. J. Honigmann, *Shakespeare's Impact on his Contemporaries*, 1982, pp. 70ff.

[3]  Honigmann, *Impact*, p. 88. Chambers argued that *1 Henry VI* 'was put together in 1592, to exploit an earlier theme which had been successful' in *2* and *3 Henry VI* (*William Shakespeare*, 2 vols., 1930, I, 292–3). Antony Hammond, the editor of the New Arden edition of the play (1981), argues that *Richard III* was written in 1591 (p. 61).

[4]  See Wells and Taylor, p. 217.

[5]  Arguments concerning the authorship of *2H6* are reviewed by Wells and Taylor, *Textual Companion*, p. 112. My findings in respect of chronology are supported by Antony Hammond, the most recent editor of *R3* (see his New Arden edition, 1981, pp. 54–61). Wilson centred his contention that *1 Henry VI* must have been written after the other two parts of the sequence on the two observations: that the six months between March and September offered Shakespeare insufficient time to write and have performed *2H6* and *3H6*, and that Talbot, the 'hero' of *Part 1*, is not mentioned in the latter plays (p. xiii). But this latter observation is predicated on a misleading literary premise, that plays must have heroes and that Talbot is here 'the' hero. It is also unlikely that Shakespeare would have conflated (as he did in *1H6*) two generations of the houses of Warwick and Somerset (see notes in the 'List of Characters'). Wells and Taylor also argue that the play was written after *2* and *3 H6*: 'Internal evidence has suggested to most editors that *Part One* assumes a familiarity with *Contention* and *Duke of York*, which in turn require no familiarity with *Part One*. Rare vocabulary in the portions most securely attributable to Shakespeare link them most strongly (in order) with *Duke of York* [i.e. *3H6*], *Richard III*, *Titus*, and *Two Gentlemen*' (p. 113). Rare vocabulary tests, however, surely point only to possible near contiguities with, say, *3H6* and *R3*, which could obviously have been as easily written soon *after 1H6* as *before*. For echoes in *1 Contention* of *1H6*, see Appendix 2, p. 237. The Taylor chronology also rests on the assumption that *2H6* and *3H6* had already been written and *performed* before March 1592.

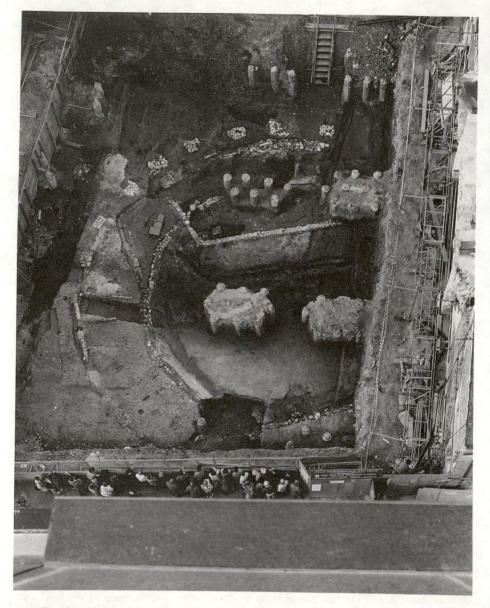

19   The foundations of the Rose playhouse, excavated in May 1989; see John Orrell and Andrew Gurr, 'What the Rose can tell us', *TLS*, 9–15 June 1989, 636, 649 and *Antiquity* 63 (1989), 421–9

Textual analysis, p. 218) and admits the possibility of some revision. It assumes that Shakespeare wrote the trilogy for performance by Lord Strange's Men.

On 3 March 1592, Philip Henslowe recorded taking £3.16s.8d. at a performance of 'harey the vj' put on by Lord Strange's Men at the Rose.[1] Ferdinando, Lord Strange, who succeeded his father as fifth Earl of Derby in 1593, was a patron of Shakespeare[2] and a descendant of the Lord Talbot who appears in the play.[3] As we know of no other play about Henry VI, it is reasonable to assume that this note refers to one of the plays from Shakespeare's sequence. Henslowe's entry bears a marginal note 'ne', but it is not certain that this designates a new play rather than one newly licensed by the Master of the Revels[4] – or else substantially revised. (It was unlikely to have been a performance of 2 Henry VI or 3 Henry VI, since Henslowe regularly registered the first parts of multi-part plays only by their main titles and indicated parts only for later plays in these sequences.)[5] There is, however, some external evidence to support the very reasonable conjecture that this entry records receipts for a play by Shakespeare. Nashe's Pierce Penilesse (which contains the passage about Talbot) is dedicated to Lord Strange, and contains an encomium of Edward Alleyn, who at the time was the leading player of Lord Strange's Men.[6] The play, moreover, may well have been newly written – or, equally plausibly, revived – for events in the play parallel recent contemporary history: in the period from 1589 until 1591, three forces of English soldiers were sent to France in support of the Huguenot Henry of Navarre.[7] From October 1591 until January 1592, Englishmen under the command of the Earl of Essex participated in another, unsuccessful, siege of Rouen.[8] (It is extremely unlikely, furthermore, that there was a rival Henry VI play performing at the same time of which no record has survived.)[9]

---

[1] Henslowe, p. 16; for the company see Chambers, II, 118–27.

[2] E. A. J. Honigmann, Shakespeare: The 'Lost Years', 1985, pp. 59ff.; Honigmann's findings contest the long-held and influential view that Shakespeare did not have anything to do with Strange's Men before 1594. For this, see Peter Alexander, Shakespeare's Henry VI and Richard III, 1929, pp. 188ff. Sidney Thomas, 'On the dating of Shakespeare's early plays', SQ 39 (1988), 187–94, contests Honigmann's findings, but Thomas does not consider the evidence that derives from a comparison of the texts of the Henry VI plays (see below, pp. 63–8).

[3] One of Talbot's titles is 'Lord Strange of Blackmere' (1H6 4.7.65).

[4] Henslowe, p. xxx; E. A. J. Honigmann, Shakespeare's Impact on his Contemporaries, 1982, 76–7, is extremely sceptical about taking 'ne' to mean 'new'. It could even be that the Privy Council Order of 12 November 1589 to the Archbishop of Canterbury, the Lord Mayor of London, and the Master of the Revels asking them to scrutinize all plays performed in and about the City of London because the players had taken 'upon them without judgement or decorum to handle in their plays matters of divinity and state' 'unfit to be suffered' (Chambers, IV, 306) made relicensing in 1592 necessary.

[5] See Roslyn L. Knutson, 'Henslowe's naming of parts', NQ 228 (1983), 157–60.

[6] Chambers, II, 120.

[7] See 1H6 4.7.61–70 n.; for a general account of possible topical interest see Bullough, III, 24–5, who on these grounds argues for composition in autumn 1591 or winter 1591–2.

[8] See J. E. Neale, Queen Elizabeth I, 1979 edn, pp. 326ff.; Bullough, III, 80–6, reprints extracts from the journal kept at the siege by Sir Thomas Coningsby. These historical analogues, however, offer no proof of the chronology of Shakespeare's early works, and there is no reason not to postulate, as Honigmann does, a date of composition and performance as early as 1589.

[9] See Hanspeter Born, 'The Date of 2, 3 Henry VI', SQ 25 (1974), 323–34, and Peter Alexander's revised opinion, Shakespeare, 1964, p. 80.

After this (first?) performance, '*harey the vj*' was performed fourteen more times until 19 June.[1] The comparatively high receipts for these performances compared with those from the plays that are not marked 'ne' in this sequence of the diary could further confirm the conjecture that the play was newly written or of topical interest. (It is worth recording that Strange's Men were performing Greene's *A Looking-Glass for London and England* and *Friar Bacon and Friar Bungay* during this same season,[2] which may explain that author's jealousy. Greene therefore could have known *3 Henry VI*, from which he parodied the 'tiger's heart' line, from performances, from manuscript, or even, if the play was newly written, from rehearsal.)

Unfortunately, these inconclusive entries are the only documentary material that would associate Shakespeare with Strange's Men, although Honigmann has recently adduced strong circumstantial evidence that would point to a long association with that company.[3] This helps to dispose of claims, made by those theatre historians who were uneasy about the Henslowe evidence, that there is a stronger probability that at this time Shakespeare was working for the rival Queen's Men, with whom Greene also had an association.[4] (A recent advocate of this theory, G. M. Pinciss, argued his case from the presence of verbal similarities between lines of Shakespeare and lines from plays known to have belonged to the Queen's Men.[5] However, an author's knowledge of a company's repertoire does not imply that the author was a member of that company. Then as now players and playwrights presumably saw each other's offerings.)

Henslowe's season came to an end in June, for on 23 June 1592 the Privy Council, because of an outbreak of the plague,[6] forbade theatrical performances until Michaelmas[7] of that year, and the players were kept out of their theatres. About July – the documents are undated – Strange's Men, supported by the Watermen of the Bankside (who ferried members of the audience across the Thames), petitioned the Privy Council for leave to return from provincial touring to the Rose: 'forasmuch...our company is great, and thereby our charge intolerable in travelling the country, and the continuance thereof will be a mean to bring us to division and separation'.[8] By 29 December, more entries in Henslowe's *Diary* indicate that they were installed in their playhouse again, and the relevant run of entries includes receipts from two more performances of '*harey the vj*' before it ceases on 1 February,[9] all theatrical performances having been again prohibited because of the plague.[10]

---

[1] Henslowe, pp. 16–19.

[2] Henslowe, pp. 16–17.

[3] E. A. J. Honigmann, *Shakespeare, the 'Lost Years'*, 1985, 59–76.

[4] See Pollard's introduction to Alexander's *Shakespeare's Henry VI and Richard III*, pp. 13–21.

[5] 'Shakespeare, Her Majesty's Players, and Pembroke's Men', *S. Sur* 27 (1974), 129–36.

[6] Chambers, IV, 347–8.

[7] Chambers, IV, 310–11.

[8] Chambers, IV, 311–12.

[9] Henslowe, pp. 19–20; the epilogue to *H5* (1599) notes that the *Henry VI* plays were 'oft' shown on the stage (line 13).

[10] Chambers, IV, 313.

The arguments of many scholars who have investigated the problems of the *Henry VI* sequence have rested on the assumption that it would have been impossible for Strange's Men to have prepared all three plays for performance in the period between February (Henslowe records his first takings from what we may now presume to have been *1 Henry VI* on 3 March) and 2 September, when Greene lay dying. (This is the nub of Dover Wilson's argument[1] and would seem to have been taken over by Cairncross, who argues that all of the plays must have been *written* before the first was *performed*.)[2] However, as Bernard Beckerman, working from Henslowe's diaries, pointed out, 'the time between final purchase of the manuscript and the first indication of production extends from three to fifty-one days, the average duration being a little over twenty days'.[3] If the plays had not been written and performed before 1592, this would still have allowed ample time for the company to have prepared, if not performed, the whole of the sequence before Greene's death – that is, between March and early September 1592. Shakespeare may well have been finishing *2* and *3 Henry VI* during the spring of that year in preparation for a summer production which had to be cancelled because of the plague.[4]

There is confirmation for both these schedules in the Folio texts, which indicate that the manuscripts from which they derive were at least prepared for performance in a London playhouse rather than for the scantier theatrical resources of a provincial tour. All three parts of the sequence demand that scenes be played 'aloft': *1 Henry VI* 1.4.21 (*on the turrets*), 1.6.0, 3.2.40, and 5.3.130 (*on the walls*), 3.2.25 (*on the top*), 4.2.2 (*aloft*); *2 Henry VI* 1.4.11 (*aloft*), 4.9.0 (*on the tarras* [terrace]); *3 Henry VI* 5.1.0 and 5.6.0 (*on the walls*). All the plays contain references to the tiring-house doors that could signify the gates to a city[5] or serve to build up a symmetrical stage image.[6]

But some time in the latter half of 1592 it seems that what Lord Strange's Men had feared did happen: while they were exiled from the Rose it appears that they divided,[7] and one group, under the patronage of the Earl of Pembroke, embarked on a provincial tour that began in October and lasted about ten months until the group had to return to London, pawn their costumes, and sell their playbooks.[8]

---

[1] J. Dover Wilson (ed.), *1 Henry VI*, 1952, p. xiv.

[2] A. S. Cairncross (ed.), *1 Henry VI*, 1962, p. xxxv; this is also the view of Bullough, III, 23–4.

[3] B. Beckerman, *Shakespeare at the Globe*, 1962, p. 10.

[4] This is also the conclusion of Born, pp. 328ff. It seems legitimate to infer from *1H6* 3.1.133 that in *1 Henry VI* the part of the king was taken by a boy player who would have surrendered his role to an adult for the later plays of the sequence. This might account for the way in which *2 Henry VI* and *3 Henry VI* were associated as a two-part 'Contention' play.

[5] *1H6* 1.3.14 and 28 ('*the Tower gates*'), 2.1.38 ('*Enter several ways*' (indicating that each character was to use a different entrance)).

[6] *2H6* 1.1.0 SD, 2.3.58 SD. 1–3; *3H6* 2.5.54 and 78.

[7] Chambers, II, 129; however, Karl P. Wentersdorf, 'The origin and personnel of the Pembroke Company', *Theatre Research International* 5 (1979–80), 45–68, argues that Pembroke's men had belonged to the Queen's Men.

[8] Chambers, II, 128; *Diary*, p. 280.

The fact that the quarto version of the play of 1594 (Q1) is entitled *The First Part of the Contention betwixt the Two Famous Houses of Yorke and Lancaster* has encouraged some scholars to endorse the view that *2 Henry VI* was the first play in the sequence to be written. However, there are various equally conjectural arguments that can be set against this. Perhaps *The First Part of the Contention* was chosen as a more interesting title and one more likely to attract an audience than '*The Second Part of King Henry VI*'. It might also have been judged uneconomical to attempt the mounting of a three-part sequence in the provinces. Given that Henry has a small part in *1 Henry VI*, and a part likely to have been taken by a boy player rather than the adult who presumably took the role in the later two plays, *Part 2* and *Part 3* might have been rehearsed together. The sources also make a thematic distinction between their account of the Hundred Years War and the Wars of the Roses, even though in chronicle terms the two overlapped. After their accounts of the death of Talbot (see *1 Henry VI* 4.7) both Hall and Holinshed make it apparent that they have finished with the wars in France and are picking up their pens to begin a new sequence: in effect, the contention of the houses of York and Lancaster.[1] There is no reason to deny that Shakespeare may well have thought of the play as *The First Part of the Contention* but equally no reason to disturb tradition and rename it for modern audiences. The title, in other words, seems to record the beginning of a sequence rather than the beginning of the trilogy. As Dr Johnson wrote: 'It is apparent that this play begins where the former ends, and continues the series of transactions, of which it presupposes the first part already known. This is a sufficient proof that the second and third parts were not written without dependence on the first, though they were printed as containing a complete period of history.'[2]

The name of Pembroke's company is on the title-page of the 'bad Quarto' of *3 Henry VI, The True Tragedy of Richard Duke of York*[3] (1595), on that of *Titus Andronicus* (1594), and *The Taming of A Shrew* (1594) – a bad quarto of *The Taming of the Shrew*[4] – as well as Marlowe's *Edward II* (1592). *The First Part of the Contention* does not bear the name of a company on its title-page, although the compilers of Q1 included in their text recollections of several plays Pembroke's Men owned, including some of the above.[5] The Shakespeare texts, moreover, all show evidence of having been shortened and adapted for a smaller number of players. The presence of three of his plays in this group would confirm Shakespeare's association with the new company as well as the association of Pembroke's Men with the parent group, Strange's Men – which confirms in turn the preliminary assumption of this argument that '*harey the vj*' was probably *1 Henry VI*. It seems, however, that Shakespeare was not acting with the new touring

---

[1] Hall, p. 231; compare Holinshed, p. 237, reprinted in Appendix 1, p. 225.
[2] Johnson, v, 3.
[3] This again suggests an attempt to disguise the fact that the play was part of a sequence.
[4] See Ann Thompson (ed.), *The Taming of the Shrew*, 1984, pp. 1–3.
[5] See Appendix 2, pp. 236–41; see also 1.4.23 n.

group, for his name does not figure among those of the six sharers of the company.[1]

Further confirmation that *2 Henry VI* and *3 Henry VI* were written for performance by Strange's Men comes from the appearance of actors' names in speech headings. (There is no way of telling whether these derive from Shakespeare or the book-keeper.) John Holland is named in *2 Henry VI* 4.2 and Sincklo in *3 Henry VI* 3.1. These in all probability were the same J. Holland and John Sincler whose names appear in the 'plot' of *2 Seven Deadly Sins*, which Greg conjectures to have been performed by Strange's Men at the Curtain, probably in 1590.[2] A third player is named in *3 Henry VI* 3.1 simply as 'Humphrey'. The only known player of the period with this name is Humphrey Jeffes, whose name occurs frequently in Henslowe's *Diary*, but only from 1597. Recently, W. Schrickx found a record of the date of Jeffes's birth (23 December 1576) and conjectures that he was abroad from 1592.[3] This small piece of evidence would push back the beginning of the period of composition to some time before that date and confirm the conjecture that, although the three plays may all have been written for Strange's Men, only the first part was performed by them for the reasons given above.

The hypothesis that would follow from this argument would be that *The First Part of the Contention* and *The True Tragedy*, which are adaptations of *2 Henry VI* and *3 Henry VI*, were designed for the provincial tour. Strange's Men would have retained ownership of the 'books' of these plays but may have allowed some of their ex-members to prepare the abridgements. David George has accumulated a list of fifteen players who could have been included in the 1592 Pembroke company;[4] the number of players required for 2.3 of *The First Part of the Contention* is eighteen, the same number as that required for 1.1 of *The True Tragedy*[5] and the quarto version of *Richard III*.[6] (This number allows for only two extras and includes two boys' parts.)[7] It is possible, then, that there were at least three more players in the group who have left no trace. This would have been a larger group than usual: texts like the 1600 Quarto of *Henry V* that derive from

---

[1] See Mary Edmond, 'Pembroke's Men', *RES* 25 (1974), 129–36. Edmond shows that two of the other sharers had earlier associations with Henslowe. See also David George, 'Shakespeare and Pembroke's Men', *SQ* 32 (1981), 305–23.

[2] W. W. Greg, *Elizabethan Dramatic Documents*, 1931, p. 113; see also B. Morris (ed.), *The Taming of the Shrew*, 1981, pp. 49–50. George Bevis, who appears in 4.2. and 4.7 of *2H6*, does not appear in this 'plot'. Andrew Gurr notes that 'There is also a "Nicke" in that list who may be the same as the "Nicke" named in the Cade scene in the pirated text of *2 Henry VI* and in *The Taming of the Shrew* (3.1.82)', *The Shakespearean Stage 1574–1642*, 1970, p. 26.

[3] W. Schrickx, 'English actors at the courts of Wolfenbüttel...', *S. Sur* 33 (1980), 153–68.

[4] George, 'Shakespeare and Pembroke's Men', p. 313.

[5] A. C. Sprague, *Shakespeare's Histories*, calculated that thirteen players were needed for *1H6* (p. 114).

[6] See A. Hammond (ed.), *R3*, p. 65.

[7] The arguments of Scott McMillin, 'Casting for Pembroke's Men: the *Henry VI* quartos and *The Taming of A Shrew*', *SQ* 23 (1972), 141–59, must be considered invalid as he inexplicably discounts 'bit' parts, 'defined as roles of [less] than ten lines altogether'. His article does contain, however, useful descriptions of the regrouping of Strange's Men as Pembroke's Men.

touring performances can be played by as few as eleven players.[1] But a large company *is* conceivable, given the fact that many players would have been driven out of the metropolis by the plague.

There is, however, some evidence in the stage directions of *1 Contention* which might suggest that the text *recalls* performance in a London playhouse:[2] two doors are stipulated in 1.1, 3.2, 4.10, and 5.1; there is a possible reference to a discovery space in 3.2; alarms are sounded 'within' in 4.1; and 1.4 demands three levels, since Dame Eleanor goes *up to the tower* (TLN 488) and exits *above* (TLN 533), while a spirit *riseth up* (TLN 507), presumably from a cellarage. Likewise, *The True Tragedy* seems to demand a tiring-house: two entrances are called for (2.4.0), a post is sounded *within* (3.3.160 SD), and a functional door is required (*The Mayor opens the door and brings the keys in his hand* (4.7.34 SD)). Other stage directions suggest a stage gallery: 'three suns' appear, presumably lowered from above (2.1.20 SD), and an upper playing area is used in 5.1 which is set *on the walls*. Unless *2* and *3 Henry VI* had in fact been performed at the Rose by June, we have to conjecture that the compilers of these texts were players recalling actions worked out in rehearsals – or that the stage directions are the relics of performances designed for halls. The recollections of *1 Henry VI* which appear in the text of the second play[3] also allow us to conjecture that this text was compiled while memories of London performances of *Part 1* were still fresh.

The conclusion must be that the whole sequence was *written* some time before March 1592. If it was written late, circumstances may have conspired to prevent the *production* in that season of the second and third parts of the play. The quartos may represent a condensation of Shakespeare texts for performance in one afternoon, either planned but not performed for London, or planned and performed in the provinces.

## Sources

In *1 Henry VI*, it could be demonstrated, Shakespeare used the 1587 edition of Holinshed as his main source, with some recourse to Hall, Fabyan, and others.[4] The material he covered ran from the funeral of Henry V in 1422 to the betrothal of his son in 1446, and adds the death of Talbot, which historically occurred seven years later in 1453.[5] In *2 Henry VI* he doubled back a little to include Eleanor's penance, which was imposed in 1442, but took the action forward from Margaret's arrival in England to York's victory at the first battle of St Albans in 1455.[6] He

---

[1] See Stanley Wells and Gary Taylor, *Modernizing Shakespeare's Text*, 1979, pp. 72ff.
[2] My arguments are confirmed by William Montgomery's Oxford D Phil thesis, '*The Contention of York and Lancaster*: a critical edition', 1985; see also Wells and Taylor, *Textual Companion*, p. 176, and William Montgomery, 'The original staging of *The First Part of the Contention* (1594)', *S. Sur.* 41 (1988), 13–22. This article also contains a detailed analysis of problems of doubling.
[3] See Appendix 2, p. 237.
[4] See my introduction to *1H6*, pp. 56–7.
[5] Holinshed, pp. 136–207, 235–6.
[6] Holinshed, pp. 203–42; R. B. McKerrow, 'A note on *2 Henry VI* and *The Contention of York and*

turned back further to the account of the reign of Richard II in order to fuse material concerning the revolt of Wat Tyler with his dramatisation of the Cade rebellion,[1] and consulted Grafton, More, or Foxe for the tale of the mock miracle at St Albans (2.1).[2] From Hall (or Grafton) he took the 'germ of Winchester's dying speech',[3] and there are some traces of Fabyan.

As Brockbank pointed out: 'Seventeen of the twenty-three scenes of *2 Henry VI* can be illustrated at choice from Holinshed, Grafton, or Hall [1.1–4, 2.3, 3.2, 4.1, 4.3–9, 5.1–3].[4] Of the other scenes, only one (2.2) offers anything like proof that Shakespeare wrote with a chronicle open before him; and here he was certainly copying from the 1587 Holinshed...The 1587 Holinshed [along with Foxe], moreover, is...the only relevant chronicle that both mentions the taper carried by the penitent Duchess and misnames Stanley "Sir John"[5]...The drunken armourer's duel [is] more likely to be adapted from Holinshed than from Hall or Grafton.[6] Shakespeare makes no use of the extra detail in Hall, and he had a good dramatic motive for departing from all the chronicles to make the servant innocent.'[7] Shakespeare may have had recourse to *The Mirror for Magistrates* generally and specifically for the detail that Dame Eleanor was guilty of prophesying (see Appendix 1 and 1.4). He may also have been thinking of Plutarch's *Life of Caesar*.[8] In 4.2 and 4.7, which draw upon accounts of the two rebellions, Cade's and Tyler's, most of the details come from Holinshed's accounts (see Appendix 1), although Shakespeare may have also read of them in Grafton.[9] There is, therefore, enough evidence, it seems, for us to conclude that Holinshed served as Shakespeare's principal source for the events, although he had recourse to Hall – as he did in *1 Henry VI* – for some details and for 'Characters' of the main personages of the play, which tend to be fuller than those in Holinshed.[10]

---

Lancaster', *RES* 9 (1933), 157–69 and 315–16, proved that the F text derives from the 1587 edition of Holinshed.

[1] See Appendix 1, pp. 227–9. This may have been suggested by the anonymous *Life and Death of Jack Straw*, printed in 1593 but probably acted a couple of years before – by whom is unknown. Bullough prints part of that play as an 'analogue' of *2H6* as well as a 'device' for the Lord Mayor's Pageant of 1590, by T. Nelson, which portrays Jack Straw (pp. 133–50).

[2] I offer Foxe's account in Appendix 1, p. 224. Karl Schmidt, *Palaestra* 54 (1906), p. 246 gives an account of the transmission of the episode through the chronicles.

[3] Brockbank, p. 31; see Appendix 1, p. 226.

[4] Brockbank adds, 'The seventeen scenes are reduced to fourteen, however, if we insist on the dependence of the Cade scenes on Holinshed's (rather than Grafton's) account of the Tyler rebellion, as I do' (p. 309 n.).

[5] Holinshed, p. 203; Hall, p. 202.

[6] See Appendix 1, p. 222.

[7] Brockbank, pp. 30–1.

[8] For suggestive analogies with Plutarch and a discussion of *Mirror* as a source, see Robinson.

[9] See 4.2.62, 4.7.1, 2 notes.

[10] See, for example, 1.3, which shows evidence of familiarity with Hall's portrait of Margaret compare Appendix 1, p. 223). David Bevington (ed.), *1H4*, 1987, p. 10, notes that Shakespeare need not have consulted Hall for that play and G. Melchiori (ed.), *2H4*, 1989, p. 7, indicates no recourse to Hall for its sequel.

# NOTE ON THE TEXT

The principal authoritative text for this play is that provided by the 1623 First Folio (F). The nature and provenance of F – it derives basically from Shakespeare's manuscript – are discussed in the Textual analysis (pp. 215–20) below. The first edition of the play, which appeared almost thirty years earlier, the quarto of 1594 (Q1), does derive from theatrical performances, but by a process of memorial reconstruction.[1] This means that when there are substantive differences between passages of dialogue in F and Q1 it is seldom possible to regard the quarto reading as being authoritative. The quarto stage directions, however, deriving as they do from performances, often help to supply F's omissions or to amplify what is unspecific in what Shakespeare probably set down in his 'study'. The 'editor' of the Second Folio (F2) made a lot of corrections, especially corrections to metre. Some of these have been accepted, although they have no special authority. The second and third quartos (1600 and 1619) derive independently from Q1 and also have therefore no special authority.

The collation in this edition (immediately below each page of text) records all significant departures from F, including variants in lineation and variants in the wording and placing of stage directions, as well as in speech headings. It does not record corrections of misprints or modernisations of spellings except where these may be of some consequence. In the format of the collation, the authority for this edition's reading follows immediately after the quotation from the text. Other readings, if any, follow in chronological order. Readings offered by previous editors are registered only if they must be considered in relationship to recent discussions of the play's textual cruces, or if they offer a challenging alternative where no certainty is possible. When, as is usually the case, the variant or emendation adopted has been used by a previous editor or suggested by a textual commentator, those authorities are cited in the abbreviated forms *Rowe* and *conj. Vaughan* respectively. *Subst.* stands for *substantively*, and indicates that I have not transcribed part of the Folio or a later emendation literally – see pp. xii–xvi above for an explanation of the abbreviations and a full list of the editions and commentaries cited. The form *Eds* is used for insignificant and obvious editorial practices (minor clarifications and expansions of stage directions or modernisations of proper names, for example, which do not need to be ascribed to one originator), and the form *This edn* is used for innovations of my own. Significant additions to the Folio stage directions are enclosed in square brackets – there is a comparatively large number of these because of the fact that the Folio text derives from an authorial manuscript and because the quarto directions provide a useful

---

[1] See Textual analysis, pp. 215–17.

quarry of information concerning early staging (see above). In the Commentary an asterisk in the lemma (the key word or phrase printed in bold type) is used to call attention to an emendation in the text; the collation should be consulted for further information.

I have, according to the convention of this edition, modernised and regularised proper names. Where past forms of verbs require an accentuation that they would not receive in modern speech, they are marked with a *grave* accent ('fixèd', 'tunèd'). Unmarked '-eds' can be assumed to have been elided.

I have tried to keep punctuation as light as is consistent with the clarification of sense, often removing line-end commas from F's text, for the reason that a line-ending can itself provide a subtle and flexible pause or break in the sense. The rhythms surpass what Nashe derided as 'the spacious volubility of a drumming decasyllabon'.[1] Previous editors who punctuated heavily gave us texts that impose rhythmic monotony for readers and actors – there is more enjambment in early Shakespeare than might be supposed from some modern editions. Any significant departure from the F punctuation, however, is recorded in the collation. I have not attempted to purge the text of half-lines or automatically to expunge metrical irregularity, believing that players can use these for special emphases or effects.[2] Consistency in this area is both impossible and undesirable: if I have regularised metre, I have done so only when I would have made the decision as an actor. Given that there is a lot of metrical irregularity in this text, however, I have recorded in the collation further regularisations that players or readers may care to adopt.

With regard to problems of verse and prose I have been conservative. Like most modern editors, I have followed Pope and restored paired half-lines to whole lines, but I have generally not attempted to reconstruct verse from prose.[3]

I have followed traditional act and scene divisions. These were determined by eighteenth-century editors – the divisions registered in F are irregular and inconsistent. I have not, however, recorded the location of any scenes, as it seems to me that all scenes in the drama of the English Renaissance 'take place' on the stage, not in 'the Duke of Gloucester's House' or 'The Coast of Kent', and that localisation encourages readers at least to impose expectations appropriate only to naturalist drama.

Headnotes to scenes in the Commentary give references to source material in both Holinshed and Hall. Headnotes also relate the action, where this is possible, to actual places and historical events.

---

[1] Epistle prefixed to Greene's *Menaphon*; see Nashe, I, 311.

[2] For the neo-Augustan regularising of the recent Oxford edition, see David Bevington, 'Determining the indeterminate', *SQ* 38 (1987), 501–19.

[3] As, for example, at 2.1.129–35 (see collation).

# The Second Part of
King Henry VI

# LIST OF CHARACTERS

KING HENRY THE SIXTH
QUEEN MARGARET OF ANJOU, *daughter of Reignier, King of Naples*
DUKE OF GLOUCESTER, *Lord Protector, and fourth son of Henry IV*
DAME ELEANOR COBHAM, *the Duchess of Gloucester*
CARDINAL WINCHESTER, *Henry Beaufort, second son of John of Gaunt*
DUKE OF SOMERSET, *Edmund Beaufort, nephew to the Cardinal*      } *Lancastrians*
MARQUESS OF SUFFOLK, *William de la Pole*
DUKE OF BUCKINGHAM, *Humphrey Stafford*
LORD CLIFFORD
YOUNG CLIFFORD, *son of Lord Clifford*
VAUX

DUKE OF YORK, *Richard Plantagenet, son of Richard, late Earl of*
    *Cambridge*
EDWARD, *Earl of March, son of York and later Edward IV*      } *Yorkists*
RICHARD, *son of York, later Duke of Gloucester and Richard III*
EARL OF SALISBURY, *Richard Neville*
EARL OF WARWICK *Richard Neville, son of Salisbury*

JOHN HUME, *a priest*
JOHN SOUTHWELL, *a priest*
MARGERY JOURDAIN, *a witch*      } *The Conjuring Sequence*
ROGER BOLINGBROKE, *a conjurer*
ASNATH, *a spirit*

THOMAS HORNER, *an armourer*      } *The Trial by*
PETER THUMP, *Horner's assistant*      } *Combat*
PETITIONERS, APPRENTICES, and NEIGHBOURS      } *Sequence*

SAUNDER SIMPCOX
SIMPCOX'S WIFE
MAYOR OF SAINT ALBANS      } *The False Miracle*
A BEADLE
CITIZENS, ATTENDANTS, and MUSICIANS

SIR JOHN STANLEY
A SHERIFF OF LONDON
A HERALD      } *Dame Eleanor's Penance*
OFFICERS, GUARDS, and SERVANTS

*TWO* MURDERERS      } *Gloucester's*
COMMONS      } *Murder*

74

LIEUTENANT
MASTER
THE MASTER'S MATE                                          *Suffolk's*
WALTER WHITMORE                                            *Murder*
TWO GENTLEMEN, *prisoners with Suffolk*
SOLDIERS

JACK CADE
GEORGE BEVIS
JOHN HOLLAND
DICK THE BUTCHER
SMITH THE WEAVER
A SAWYER
MICHAEL
REBELS                                                     *The Cade*
                                                           *Sequence*
EMMANUEL THE CLERK OF CHARTHAM
SIR HUMPHREY STAFFORD
WILLIAM STAFFORD, *brother to Sir Humphrey*
LORD SAY, *James Fiennes*
LORD SCALES
MATTHEW GOUGH
ALEXANDER IDEN
DRUMMERS, TRUMPETERS, SOLDIERS, CITIZENS

*Attendant lords, soldiers, guards, petitioners, falconers, servants, messengers*

## Notes

F does not supply a list of characters; one was first given by Rowe.

KING HENRY THE SIXTH (1421–71) Son of Henry V (1387–1422) whom he succeeded when nine months old. The part might have been taken by a boy in *1H6* (see *1H6* Introduction, p. 38 n. 9).

QUEEN MARGARET (1430–82) Daughter of Reignier, who married Henry VI by proxy at Nancy in 1445, Suffolk standing as proxy for the king. She courted unpopularity by allying herself with Suffolk and then Somerset, both of whom were held responsible for the loss of territories in France – a league that York was able to exploit.

DUKE OF GLOUCESTER (1391–1447) 'Good' Duke Humphrey of Lancaster, youngest son of Henry IV. At his brother Henry V's death he claimed the regency, but had to defer to Bedford and accept the title 'Protector of England' which he held from 1427 to 1429. He was the constant enemy of his uncle, Cardinal Beaufort, Bishop of Winchester, and, in this play, of Suffolk. After a relationship with the Lady Jaquet, wife of John of Brabant, he married Eleanor Cobham. After the death of his brother Bedford in 1435, he became heir presumptive to the crown. Images of his life can be pursued in S. M. Pratt, 'Shakespeare and Humphrey Duke of Gloucester: a study in myth', *SQ* 16 (1965), 201–16.

ELEANOR COBHAM Third daughter of Sir Reginald Cobham of Sterborough, Surrey, first the mistress then wife of Gloucester, whom she married in 1428. Her ambition caused her downfall, and she is said to have died in Peel Castle in 1454.

BISHOP OF WINCHESTER (d. 1447) Henry Beaufort, the second of Gaunt's illegitimate sons, Chancellor on the accession of Henry V and named guardian of Henry VI. He was made a Cardinal in 1426 by Pope Martin V, and led the opposition to Gloucester, although historically he could not have helped his death.

DUKE OF SOMERSET Shakespeare, like the chroniclers, conflated two historical personages, John and Edmund Beaufort. John Beaufort, first Duke of Somerset (1403–44), was still 'alive' at the time of 1.2 (1441; see 29 n.) as he was at the time of *1H6* 2.4, which alludes to the death of Mortimer in 1425. The chroniclers there draw upon an account of a quarrel in 1435 between York and John Beaufort, whom Holinshed (p. 185) and Hall (p. 179) wrongly call Edmund. This was his younger brother, Edmund Beaufort, second Duke of Somerset (1406–55), who succeeded York as Regent over France.

MARQUESS OF SUFFOLK (1396–1450) William de la Pole, fourth Earl, then Marquess, and finally Duke of Suffolk (1448), had served with success in France. He married the widowed Countess of Salisbury and emerged as an advocate of peace with France in opposition to Humphrey, Duke of Gloucester, who, after Bedford's death, led the war party. He had arranged the marriage of Henry with Margaret of Anjou, but the sexual intimacy between him and the queen has no basis in the chronicles.

BUCKINGHAM (1402–60) Humphrey Stafford, Constable of France (1430) and first Duke of Buckingham (1444); a member of the group which opposed Gloucester and supported the queen against York. He was the grandson of Thomas of Woodstock, the seventh son of Edward III. Killed at the battle of Northampton.

LORD CLIFFORD (1414–55) Thomas, twelfth Baron Clifford, of Clifford Castle in Herefordshire. His father was killed while fighting for Henry V at Meaux, and he himself served with distinction under Bedford in France. One of the most loyal supporters of Henry VI, and killed while fighting for him at the first battle of St Albans. The chroniclers call him John (Holinshed, p. 240; Hall, p. 233).

YOUNG CLIFFORD (1435–61) John, thirteenth Baron Clifford, son of the above and, like his father, a determined foe of the Duke of York. He survived the second battle of St Albans but was killed at Ferrybridge on the eve of the battle of Towton.

VAUX Probably Sir William Vaux (d. 1471) of Harrowden in Northamptonshire, a staunch Lancastrian who was attainted by Edward IV's first parliament in 1461 and who was killed at Tewkesbury.

DUKE OF YORK (1411–60) Descended through his mother from the Mortimer line, which derived from Lionel, Duke of Clarence, third son of Edward III. His father, who was descended from Edmund of Langley, fifth son of Edward III and first Duke of York, had been executed in 1415 for conspiring against Henry V. He was restored to his title of Duke of York in *1H6* 3.1.

EDWARD (1442–83) Born at Rouen, he was attainted as a Yorkist in 1459. Defeated Henry VI's forces at Northampton in 1460 and proclaimed King Edward IV in 1461. Privately married Elizabeth Woodville, widow of Sir John Grey, in 1464. Defeated at Edgecote in 1469, fled to Holland, but in 1471 returned and captured Henry VI who had just been reinstalled as king, slew Warwick at Barnet, captured Margaret at Tewkesbury, and slew her son immediately after the battle.

RICHARD (1452–85) Eleventh son of Richard, Duke of York, born at Fotheringay Castle. Created Duke of Gloucester 1461, accompanied his brother into exile but commanded the vanguard at Barnet and Tewkesbury. Murdered Henry VI and contrived to have himself proclaimed king in 1483. His nickname 'Crouchback' derived from a real but possibly minor deformity: More reports that his left shoulder was higher than his right.

EARL OF SALISBURY (1400–60) Neville was the first Earl of Salisbury. In 1431 he joined Henry VI in France and later was connected with the Beauforts in opposition to York. He persuaded York to lay down his arms at Dartford in 1452, but supported his claim to the protectorship in 1453 when Henry became insane; after Henry's recovery, however, he allied himself with the Yorkists, being one of the chief commanders at the first battle of St Albans. After York was slain at Wakefield in 1460 Salisbury was wounded, imprisoned, and then beheaded at Pontefract.

EARL OF WARWICK (1428–71) Shakespeare again conflated two personages (see 1.1.116 n. and 1.3.168–9 n.). The 'Warwick' of *1H6* was Richard de Beauchamp, Earl of Warwick (1382–1439) – who had accompanied Henry V to France, was present at his funeral in 1422 (see *1H6* 1.1), was charged with the education of the infant Henry VI in 1428, and who was dead by the time of the truce signed at Tours (see *1H6* 5.4). The 'Warwick' of this play is his son-in-law, Richard Neville, known as the 'Kingmaker'. Son of the Earl of Salisbury, he succeeded in 1449 to the title and estates of Richard de Beauchamp, whose daughter Anne he had married. He supported York, distinguished himself at the first battle of St Albans, and won the battle of Northampton in 1460, taking King Henry prisoner. At Wakefield in 1460, however, the Lancastrians regained their ascendancy when York and Warwick's father, Salisbury, were killed; Margaret recaptured her husband a year later at the second battle of St Albans. Warwick escaped, helped proclaim Edward king, and defeated the Lancastrians at Towton in 1461. His defection to the Lancastrians was caused by his annoyance at Edward's marriage with Elizabeth Woodville while he was negotiating a marriage for him with Bona of Savoy. He withdrew from the court but returned to be reconciled with Margaret, whose young son Edward was betrothed to his daughter Anne. In 1470 Henry VI was proclaimed king again, and Warwick was made Protector with Clarence. In 1471 the 'Kingmaker' was defeated and killed at Barnet.

HUME A counsellor of the Duchess of Gloucester and her fellow conspirator; reported by Hall (p. 202) and Holinshed (p. 204) in fact to have been pardoned. Foxe is the only chronicler to spell his name 'Hume': Holinshed, Hall, and Grafton name him 'Hum'.

SOUTHWELL A canon of St Stephen's, Westminster, who died in the Tower before his execution.

JOURDAIN Named the witch of Eye, she was burned at Smithfield.

BOLINGBROKE Taken to Tyburn where he was drawn and quartered, after denying that any conspiracy had taken place.

HORNER Holinshed and Hall do not name this character, but Shakespeare may have fabricated the name from one of the sheriffs for the year of the duel, Robert Horne (Fabyan p. 618). The name of the armourer given in Stow's *Survey* was William Catur (Boswell-Stone, p. 248 n.).

PETER THUMP Stow records that the servant was in fact named John David. Hall (p. 208) and Holinshed (p. 210) record that this man, a 'coward and a wretch' (Hall), was hanged at Tyburn.

SAUNDER SIMPCOX Sir Thomas More (*A Dialogue...of Images, Praying to Saints...*, 1530 edn, f. 25), Foxe (1583, 1, 704–5, see Appendix 1, p. 224) and Grafton (p. 630) tell the story of the false miracle at St Albans, but do not name the beggar who claimed he had recovered his sight. The name seems therefore to have been Shakespeare's invention. 'Saunder' may be an abbreviated form of 'Alexander'.

SIR JOHN STANLEY Shakespeare follows the error of Hall (p. 202) and Holinshed (p. 203) in sending the Duchess of Gloucester into the keeping of Sir John Stanley (1350?–1414), father of the Sir Thomas Stanley (1406?–59), who, as Stow and Fabyan record, succeeded him as Governor of the Isle of Man.

WALTER WHITMORE Hall (p. 219) and Holinshed (p. 220) do not record the name of Suffolk's murderer. 'The Whitmores of Cheshire were an ancient family, and in the play (4.1.31) Walt Whitmore claims to be a gentleman' (Thomson).

JACK CARDE Like 'Jack Straw', the name might be folkloric (see Thomas Pettitt, '"Here comes I, Jack Straw": English folk drama and social revolt', *Folklore* 95 (1984), 3–20), and Holinshed reports that some called him John Mend-all (p. 220) and that *Polychronicon* said he was an Irishman. R. A. Griffiths, *The Reign of King Henry VI*, 1981, pp. 617–18, records that he was proclaimed to have been a young Irishman in the household of Sir Thomas Dacre in Sussex. Hall (p. 220) does not have anything to say about his origins.

SIR HUMPHREY STAFFORD 'The eldest son of Sir Humphrey Stafford of Grafton, and was sheriff of the county of Gloucester in the second year of Henry VI, by whom he was knighted and made Governor of Calais. On his return to England he was slain by the rebels under Jack Cade' (Thomson).

WILLIAM STAFFORD Brother to the above, 'the manliest man of all this realm of England', according to a contemporary (Griffiths, p. 612); also slain by rebels.

LORD SAY A member of Suffolk's faction, made Chancellor in 1447 and joined the Council in 1448. Executed by the rebels in 1450.

LORD SCALES (1399?–1460) Thomas de Scales, seventh Baron Scales, fought in France with Bedford and commanded the fight on London Bridge against the rebels. A loyal Lancastrian, he was commissioned to hold London for the king in 1460, defended the Tower of London against Salisbury, and was murdered by some boatmen while going to seek sanctuary at Westminster.

MATTHEW GOUGH Had served in France under Arundel and Talbot. Was appointed a commissioner by Henry to hand the towns and fortresses of Anjou and Maine over to Charles VI.

ALEXANDER IDEN Appointed Sheriff of Kent in succession to William Crowmer, who was murdered by the rebels and whose widow, a daughter of James Fiennes, he married (Griffiths, p. 340).

# THE SECOND PART OF HENRY THE SIXTH
# WITH THE DEATH OF GOOD DUKE HUMPHREY

**1.1** *Flourish of trumpets; then hautboys.* Enter KING [HENRY], DUKE HUMPHREY [OF GLOUCESTER], SALISBURY, WARWICK, *and* BEAUFORT, [BISHOP OF WINCHESTER] *on the one side; the* QUEEN [MARGARET], SUFFOLK, YORK, SOMERSET, *and* BUCKINGHAM *on the other*

SUFFOLK  As, by your high imperial majesty,
    I had in charge at my depart for France,
    As Procurator to your excellence,
    To marry Princess Margaret for your grace;

Title] F; THE First part of the Contention betwixt the two famous Houses of Yorke and Lancaster, with the death of the good Duke Humphrey: And the banishment and death of the Duke of *Suffolke*, and the Tragicall end of the proud Cardinall of Winchester, with the notable Rebellion of *Iacke Cade: And the Duke of Yorkes first claime vnto the Crowne.* Q1
Act 1, Scene 1    1.1] *This edn; Actus Primus. Scæna Prima.* F    o SD *Flourish...other*] F; *Enter at one doore, King Henry the sixt, and* Humphrey *Duke of Gloster, the Duke of* Sommerset, *the Duke of* Buckingham, *Cardinall* Bewford, *and others. Enter at the other doore, the Duke of* Yorke, *and the Marquesse of* Suffolke, *and Queene* Margaret, *and the Earle of Salisbury and* Warwicke. Q1

**Act 1, Scene 1**
  **1.1** The action continues directly from where *1H6* concluded. At the end of that play Suffolk announced his departure for France to negotiate the marriage of Henry with Margaret of Anjou, daughter to Reignier, titular King of Sicily, Naples, and Jerusalem. Margaret's coronation took place on 30 May 1445 (see Appendix 1, p. 221).
  Margaret's arrival in England and Gloucester's objections to the Treaty signed at Tours are found in Holinshed (p. 207) and Hall (pp. 204–5), both of which texts Shakespeare seems to have consulted (see notes to 48 and 50). Suffolk's elevation to a dukedom is in Holinshed, p. 212 (Hall, p. 210). The alliance between Buckingham and Winchester (but not Somerset) against Gloucester is in Holinshed, pp. 210–11 (Hall, p. 209). For the formation of the counter-alliance against Somerset etc., see Holinshed, p. 237 (Hall, p. 231). Warwick's popularity with the commons may derive from Hall or Grafton (see 188–9 n.) For York in Ireland, see 191–2 n. Some phrases in the text are to be found in

Fabyan (111 n.) and Foxe (155–6 n.).
  o SD.1 *Flourish* a fanfare that announced a royal entrance.
  o SD.1 *hautboys* oboes; they were probably playing a 'sennet' or processional march – see Long, pp. 12 and 24.
  o SD.3–4 *on the one side...on the other* Such details could be prescriptive or descriptive, deriving from either foul papers or prompt-book copy. Neither F nor Q (see collation) divides the entrants neatly into Lancastrian and Yorkist camps. In processions the most eminent person entered last, so it is not possible to argue that either text offers a record of performance. For similar symmetrical tableau settings see Hattaway, p. 56.
  1 *imperial* Henry ruled over the empire of England, France, and Ireland.
  2 **had in charge** was commissioned (*OED* Charge *sb* 12).
  2 **depart** departure.
  3 **Procurator to** Agent or deputy of.
  4 **marry** i.e. marry by proxy.

79

So, in the famous ancient city Tours,                                     5
In presence of the Kings of France and Sicil,
The Dukes of Orléans, Calaber, Bretagne, and Alençon,
Seven earls, twelve barons, and twenty reverend bishops,
I have performed my task, and was espoused;
And humbly now upon my bended knee,                                       10
In sight of England and her lordly peers,
Deliver up my title in the queen
To your most gracious hands that are the substance
Of that great shadow I did represent;
The happiest gift that ever marquess gave,                                15
The fairest queen that ever king received.

KING HENRY  Suffolk, arise. – Welcome, Queen Margaret:
I can express no kinder sign of love
Than this kind kiss. – O Lord, that lends me life,
Lend me a heart replete with thankfulness!                                20
For Thou hast given me in this beauteous face
A world of earthly blessings to my soul,
If sympathy of love unite our thoughts.

MARGARET  Great King of England, and my gracious lord,
The mutual conference that my mind hath had                               25
By day, by night, waking, and in my dreams,
In courtly company, or at my beads,

---

8 twenty] F, Q3; then the Q1, 2

---

**5 Tours** In fact (*pace* the chroniclers) the proxy marriage took place at Nancy (Griffiths, p. 315).

**6 France** i.e. Charles VII, who had succeeded his father in 1422.

**6 Sicil** Sicily, of which Reignier, Margaret's father, was titular monarch; see 47 below.

**7 Calaber** Calabria (in southern Italy).

**9 espoused** united in (a proxy) marriage.

**11 England** i.e. Henry as king of England.

**12 title** in claim to (*OED* Title *sb* 6).

**13–14 substance...shadow** i.e. the king's 'two bodies', his body natural and body politic – a common trope, often invoked by Shakespeare. See Introduction, p. 12, and E. H. Kantorowicz, *The King's Two Bodies*, 1957; compare *1H6* 2.3.35–65, 5.4.133–5.

**15 happiest** most fortunate.

**15 marquess** the rank of peerage between a duke and an earl. Suffolk appeared as an earl in *1H6* (see 5.5.1). He was elevated to this rank

after arranging the marriage between Margaret and Henry (Holinshed, p. 207; Hall, p. 204).

**18 kinder** more natural.

**19 kind** affectionate, with a pun on 'kinder' in the previous line.

**19 lends** grants (*OED* Lend 2).

**21–2** an expansion of the proverb 'Beauty is a blessing' (Tilley B168).

**22 world** an infinite number (*OED* sv 19).

**23 sympathy** corresponding feelings.

**24–31** Q1 offers a radically different version of these lines (see Appendix 2, p. 231), but there is no need to conclude, as Oxford does, that 'Q here reflects a revised version of the speech made in the preparation of the prompt-book' (Wells and Taylor, p. 178).

**25 mutual** intimate (*OED* sv 3).

**25 conference** communing (*OED* sv 5).

**27 at my beads** while saying prayers with a rosary.

With you, mine alder-liefest sovereign,
Makes me the bolder to salute my king
With ruder terms, such as my wit affords                    30
And over-joy of heart doth minister.
KING HENRY  Her sight did ravish, but her grace in speech,
Her words yclad with wisdom's majesty,
Makes me from wond'ring fall to weeping joys,
Such is the fullness of my heart's content. –              35
Lords, with one cheerful voice welcome my love.
LORDS  [*Kneeling*] Long live Queen Margaret, England's happiness.
MARGARET  We thank you all.

                    *Flourish* [*They rise*]

SUFFOLK  My Lord Protector, so it please your grace,
Here are the articles of contracted peace                  40
Between our sovereign and the French King Charles,
For eighteen months concluded by consent.
GLOUCESTER  (*Reads*) '*Inprimis*, It is agreed between the French
King Charles and William de la Pole, Marquess of Suffolk,
Ambassador for Henry King of England, That the said Henry  45
shall espouse the Lady Margaret, daughter unto Reignier King
of Naples, Sicilia, and Jerusalem, and crown her Queen of
England, ere the thirtieth of May next ensuing.
   *Item*...That the duchy of Anjou and the county of Maine

---

37 SH] *Oxford; All* F    38 SD *They rise.*] *Oxford; not in* F    46 Reignier] F; *Raynard* Q1    49 *Item*...That] *This edn;*
Item. That F; Item. It is further agreed betweene them Q1

28 **alder-liefest** most loved of all. The expression was almost archaic in Shakespeare's day (see *OED* All, *adj* D3).

29 **salute** honour (*OED* sv 2f.).

30 **ruder** less courtly.

30 **wit** mind, intelligence.

31 **over-joy** excess of joy (see *OED* Over 29).

31 **minister** provide.

32 **Her sight** The sight of her.

33 **yclad** clad. Spenser had revived this archaic form of the past participle ('y' represents the original 'ge-' of early English).

34 **Makes** The subject of the verb is 'grace' in 32.

34 **wond'ring** admiring.

37 **England's happiness** England's good fortune. In the light of what Margaret will do, the salutation is ironic.

38 **We** Margaret's immediate adoption of the royal 'we' is significant.

39 **Protector** In fact, Gloucester had relin-

quished the office when Henry was crowned in London in 1429 (compare 1.1.163 n).

40 Henry had instructed Suffolk before his departure to 'agree to any covenants' (*1H6* 5.5.88).

43 *Inprimis* Old form of *imprimis* = first; used in formal documents such as wills.

46 **Reignier** Q1's corruption 'Raynard' (fox) may derive from performance and serve to describe the family (compare *1H6* 4.4.27 collation).

47 **Naples, Sicilia** The two comprised one kingdom.

48 **thirtieth...ensuing** Holinshed reads 'thirtieth of May next following' (p. 208).

49 *Item* Likewise.

49 *\*Item*...See collation. I have not inserted, as other editors have done, the words from Q1 that appear below (55) when Winchester reads, although F's omission of them may have been caused by a compositor's eye skipping from 'it*em*' to 'th*em*'. Gloucester may be imagined to

shall be released and delivered to the king her father – ' 50

               *[Gloucester lets it fall]*

KING HENRY Uncle, how now?

GLOUCESTER             Pardon me, gracious lord,
   Some sudden qualm hath struck me at the heart
   And dimmed mine eyes that I can read no further.

KING HENRY Uncle of Winchester, I pray read on.

WINCHESTER *Item*, It is further agreed between them…That the 55
   duchies of Anjou and Maine…*[Reading]* 'shall be released and
   delivered to the king her father, and she sent over of the king
   of England's own proper cost and charges, without having
   any dowry'.

KING HENRY They please us well. – Lord Marquess, kneel down: 60
   We here create thee the first Duke of Suffolk,
   And gird thee with the sword. – Cousin of York,
   We here discharge your grace from being regent
   I'th' parts of France, till term of eighteen months
   Be full expired. – Thanks, Uncle Winchester, 65
   Gloucester, York, Buckingham, Somerset,

---

**50** father – ] *Malone; father* F; *fa.* Q1   **50** SD] Q1; *not in* F   **56** duchies…Maine] F; duchy of Anjou and the county of Maine *Cairncross (see 49 above)*   **56** duchies] *Eds; Dutchesse* F   **56** SD] *This edn; not in* F   **57** delivered] *Cairncross;* deliuered ouer F   **60–7**] F; They…well. / Lord…thee / First…sword. / Cousin…Grace / From… France, / Till…expir'd. / Thanks…York, / Buckingham…Warwick. *Cairncross*   **60** kneel] F; kneel you *Pope*   **61** thee the] F; thee Q1   **62** gird] *Eds;* girt F   **66** Buckingham] F; Buckingham and F2

---

be skimming on to the important part of the document.

  **50 released…father** The phrase is found in Hall (p. 204), whereas Holinshed reads 'delivered to the king' (p. 206).

  **50 released** made over (*OED* Release *vb* 4b).

  **50 father –** Q1's 'fa.[ – ]' may well record what Shakespeare indicated for performance, the word being corrected by F's compositor.

  *****50 SD** This is adapted from the SD in Q which presumably records the action of early performances.

  **52 qualm** feeling of sickness (*OED sb*$^3$1); but also 'fit of misgiving' (*OED sb*$^3$2a).

  **53 that** so that.

  **54 Uncle** As half-brother to Henry IV, the cardinal was actually great-uncle to the king. Henry's turning to the cardinal, Gloucester's enemy, is either tactless or an indication of how little he understands or respects Gloucester's misgivings.

  **56 duchies** F and Q3 read 'Dutchesse', but this does not prove that this part of F derives from Q3.

*****56 SD** If Winchester actually starts reading here, the difference between 49 and 55–6 may be accounted for.

  **57 *delivered** F's 'delivered over' differs from what we heard in 50, and is probably the consequence of the compositor's eye skipping to 'sent over' in 57.

  **57 of** at (Abbott 168).

  **58 own…charges** a legal formula (see Hart for further examples).

  **58 proper** personal.

  **60–1** See 40 n. above. Henry's elevation of Suffolk to a dukedom can be read as a mark of gratitude to that lord or of defiance to the surrounding peers.

  **61 the…Suffolk** In fact, Suffolk was not elevated to a dukedom until three years later in 1448 (Holinshed, p. 212, Hall, p. 207).

  **62 *gird** invest (by fastening on a sword by means of a belt).

  **62 Cousin** The form of address used by a monarch to a nobleman (*OED* sv 5a).

  **64 parts** regions (*OED* Part *sb* III.13), i.e.all of France owned by England.

Salisbury, and Warwick.
We thank you all for this great favour done
In entertainment to my princely queen.
Come, let us in, and with all speed provide                          70
To see her coronation be performed.

*Exit King Henry, Margaret, and Suffolk*
[*Gloucester stays all*] *the rest*

GLOUCESTER Brave peers of England, pillars of the state,
To you Duke Humphrey must unload his grief –
Your grief, the common grief of all the land.
What, did my brother Henry spend his youth,                          75
His valour, coin, and people in the wars?
Did he so often lodge in open field,
In winter's cold and summer's parching heat,
To conquer France, his true inheritance?
And did my brother Bedford toil his wits                             80
To keep by policy what Henry got?
Have you yourselves, Somerset, Buckingham,
Brave York, Salisbury, and victorious Warwick,
Received deep scars in France and Normandy?
Or hath mine Uncle Beaufort and myself,                             85
With all the learnèd counsel of the realm,
Studied so long, sat in the council-house
Early and late, debating to and fro
How France and Frenchmen might be kept in awe,

---

71 SD *Gloucester...rest*] Q1; *Manet the rest* F    86 counsel] F; council F3

**69 entertainment** welcome.
**69 princely** royal.
**71 SD** It is significant that no flourish accompanies this exit (Long, pp. 24–5).
**72 peers** punning on 'piers' = pillars (*OED* records 'piers' in this sense only from 1611 (3f.), but see James Sledd, 'A note on the use of renaissance dictionaries', *MP* 49 (1951–2), 10).
**72 pillars...state** proverbial (Dent PP10).
**75 Henry** Henry V.
**75 spend** waste, use pointlessly (*OED* sv¹, 10b).
**77 lodge** encamp (*OED* sv *v* 6).
**79 his true inheritance** The English claimed the French throne by virtue of the marriage of Edward III with Isabella, daughter of Philip IV of France. The Treaty of Troyes (1420) had

secured the title for Henry V although his father-in-law, Charles VI – Henry married his daughter, Catherine of Valois – wore the crown.
**80 Bedford** John of Lancaster (1389–1435), third son of Henry IV, created Duke of Bedford in 1415. During Henry V's absence in France, Bedford was appointed Lieutenant of England, and on his death-bed Henry made him Regent of France. His death is depicted in *1H6*, 3.2.
**80 toil** exert.
**81 policy** skilful contrivance.
**85 Beaufort** The cardinal.
**86 counsel** F's form of the word could designate not only a body of legal advisers (*OED* sv 8) but the Privy Council (*OED* sv 7).
**88 to and fro** for and against.
**89 awe** obedience.

And had his highness in his infancy                                   90
Crowned in Paris in despite of foes?
And shall these labours and these honours die?
Shall Henry's conquest, Bedford's vigilance,
Your deeds of war, and all our counsel die?
O peers of England, shameful is this league,                          95
Fatal this marriage, cancelling your fame,
Blotting your names from books of memory,
Razing the characters of your renown,
Defacing monuments of conquered France,
Undoing all, as all had never been!                                  100

WINCHESTER Nephew, what means this passionate discourse,
This peroration with such circumstance?
For France, 'tis ours; and we will keep it still.

GLOUCESTER Ay, uncle, we will keep it if we can;
But now it is impossible we should.                                  105
Suffolk, the new-made duke that rules the roast,
Hath given the duchy of Anjou and Maine
Unto the poor King Reignier, whose large style
Agrees not with the leanness of his purse.

SALISBURY Now, by the death of Him that died for all,               110
These counties were the keys of Normandy. –
But wherefore weeps Warwick, my valiant son?

WARWICK For grief that they are past recovery.
For were there hope to conquer them again,
My sword should shed hot blood, mine eyes no tears.                  115

---

**90** had] *White;* hath F; was *Rowe*    **98** Razing] Racing F    **102** peroration] *Eds;* preroration F    **106** roast] Q1; rost F

**90** *had F's 'hath' might just stand, with its subject 'Beaufort and myself' in 85, but the construction is very awkward. 'An original "hat" (for "had") might easily have been miscorrected to "hath"' (McKerrow, in Wells and Taylor, p. 179).

**90 in his infancy** Henry was crowned King of England in 1429 and King of France in 1431; i.e. at the ages of eight and ten.

**91** This is depicted in *1H6* 4.1.

**91 despite** defiance.

**94 counsel** plans.

**96 Fatal** Fraught with destiny (*OED* sv 5).

**97 memory** history (*OED* sv 9).

**98 Razing the characters** Erasing the written records.

**99 monuments** (1) refers to the provinces of Anjou and Maine, which serve as reminders of the conquest of France (Montgomery), (2) written records (*OED* Monument 2).

**102 peroration** rhetorical speech (*OED* sv 2).

**102 such circumstance** so many adjuncts or details.

**103 For** As for.

**103 still** always.

**106 rules the roast** occupies the head of the table (Tilley R144).

**108 large style** grandiose title.

**109 Agrees** Accords.

**110 by…all** Compare 2 Cor. 5.15: 'And he died for all.'

**111 keys of Normandy** The phrase is found in Fabyan, p. 617 (Boswell-Stone, p. 260).

Anjou and Maine? Myself did win them both:
Those provinces, these arms of mine did conquer.
And are the cities that I got with wounds
Delivered up again with peaceful words?
*Mort Dieu!*                                                                   120

YORK For Suffolk's duke, may he be suffocate,
That dims the honour of this warlike isle!
France should have torn and rent my very heart
Before I would have yielded to this league.
I never read but England's kings have had                                      125
Large sums of gold and dowries with their wives:
And our King Henry gives away his own
To match with her that brings no vantages.

GLOUCESTER A proper jest, and never heard before,
That Suffolk should demand a whole fifteenth                                    130
For costs and charges in transporting her!
She should have stayed in France, and starved in France,
Before –

WINCHESTER My Lord of Gloucester, now ye grow too hot:
It was the pleasure of my lord the king.                                        135

GLOUCESTER My Lord of Winchester, I know your mind.
'Tis not my speeches that you do mislike,
But 'tis my presence that doth trouble ye.
Rancour will out: proud prelate, in thy face
I see thy fury. If I longer stay                                                140
We shall begin our ancient bickerings. –
Lordings, farewell; and say when I am gone,
I prophesied France will be lost ere long.                              *Exit*

WINCHESTER So, there goes our Protector in a rage.

---

118 wounds] F; swords *conj. Collier (following* Q1)

116 **Myself...win** To the speaker, Richard
Neville, 1428–71 – the 'Kingmaker' – who
became Duke of Warwick in 1449, Shakespeare
attributes the conquests of his father-in-law,
Richard de Beauchamp (1382–1439), who appears in *1H6*; compare 1.3.168–9.
120 *Mort Dieu* compare 5.2.28; Peele noted
'And rife was French those days with Englishmen' (*The Honour of the Garter*, 124, in D. H.
Horne ed., *The Life and Minor Works of George
Peele*, 1952, p. 250).
121 **suffocate** Compare the pun on 'Maine'
in 209 below.

128 **match with** wed.
128 **vantages** profits or gains; i.e. a dowry.
129 **proper** real, true
130 **fifteenth** a tax of a fifteenth part of a profit or property; in *1H6* (5.5.93) Suffolk was
promised a tenth.
132 **starved** died (*OED* Starve 1).
141 **ancient bickerings** Dramatised in *1H6*
3.1.
142 **Lordings** My lords (with some suggestion
of contempt).

'Tis known to you he is mine enemy;                                    145
Nay more, an enemy unto you all,
And no great friend, I fear me, to the king.
Consider, lords, he is the next of blood
And heir apparent to the English crown:
Had Henry got an empire by his marriage                               150
And all the wealthy kingdoms of the west,
There's reason he should be displeased at it:
Look to it, lords; let not his smoothing words
Bewitch your hearts; be wise and circumspect.
What though the common people favour him,                             155
Calling him, 'Humphrey, the good Duke of Gloucester',
Clapping their hands, and crying with loud voice,
'Jesu maintain your royal excellence!'
With 'God preserve the good Duke Humphrey!' –
I fear me, lords, for all this flattering gloss,                      160
He will be found a dangerous Protector.

BUCKINGHAM Why should he then protect our sovereign,
He being of age to govern of himself?
Cousin of Somerset, join you with me,
And all together, with the Duke of Suffolk,                           165
We'll quickly hoise Duke Humphrey from his seat.

WINCHESTER This weighty business will not brook delay:
I'll to the Duke of Suffolk presently.                            *Exit*

SOMERSET Cousin of Buckingham, though Humphrey's pride
And greatness of his place be grief to us,                            170
Yet let us watch the haughty cardinal;
His insolence is more intolerable

165 all together] *Rowe;* altogether F

148 **next of blood** Henry VI had no children, so, as Henry V's sole surviving brother, Gloucester was next in line to the throne.

149 **heir apparent** technically 'heir presumptive' (see *OED* Heir 1b).

151 **all…west** an anachronistic allusion to Spanish possessions in the Americas.

152 **he** Gloucester.

153 **smoothing** plausible, flattering (*OED* sv 2).

155–6 **common…Gloucester** Compare Foxe: 'he was loved of the poor commons and well spoken of all men, and no less deserving the same, being called the "good" Duke of Gloucester': *Acts and Monuments*, 1844 edn, III, 713 (cited Sanders).

160 **gloss** fair semblance (*OED* Gloss $sb^2$ 1b).

163 **of age** At this time Henry was in fact twenty-four, and Gloucester was no longer Protector (see 1.1.39 n.); but Shakespeare retains him in that office to make his fall the greater.

166 **hoise** remove (*OED* sv 4) – an archaic form of 'hoist'.

167 **brook** tolerate.

168 **presently** immediately.

170 **place** position.

170 **grief** a trouble (*OED* sv 2).

172 **insolence** overbearing pride (*OED* sv 1b).

Than all the princes in the land beside:
If Gloucester be displaced, he'll be Protector.

BUCKINGHAM  Or thou or I, Somerset, will be Protector,                      175
Despite Duke Humphrey or the cardinal.

                                        *Exeunt Buckingham and Somerset*

SALISBURY  Pride went before, Ambition follows him.
While these do labour for their own preferment
Behoves it us to labour for the realm.
I never saw but Humphrey, Duke of Gloucester,                              180
Did bear him like a noble gentleman.
Oft have I seen the haughty cardinal –
More like a soldier than a man o'th' church,
As stout and proud as he were lord of all –
Swear like a ruffian, and demean himself                                  185
Unlike the ruler of a commonweal. –
Warwick, my son, the comfort of my age,
Thy deeds, thy plainness, and thy housekeeping
Hath won the greatest favour of the commons,
Excepting none but good Duke Humphrey. –                                   190
And, brother York, thy acts in Ireland
In bringing them to civil discipline,
Thy late exploits done in the heart of France
When thou wert regent for our sovereign,
Have made thee feared and honoured of the people. –                       195
Join we together for the public good,

173 princes] F; princes' *conj. Vaughan*    175 Protector] Q1; Protectors F    176 SD *Exeunt*] Eds; *Exit* F    195] F; Hath
wonne thee credit amongst the common sort, / The reuerence of mine age, and *Neuels* name, / Is of no litle force if I
command, Q1

174 **displaced** removed from office.
175 **Or...or** Either...or.
177 A variation on the proverb 'Pride goes before and Shame comes after' (Tilley P576). Salisbury refers to the cardinal and to the Buckingham-Somerset partnership respectively.
178 **preferment** advancement.
179 **Behoves** As F's spelling indicates, it could rhyme with 'proves' (Cercignani, p. 184).
180 **never saw but** have always seen that.
184 **stout** haughty (*OED* sv 1).
185 **demean** behave (*OED* vb¹ 6).
188–9 Compare Hall, 'he obtained great love, much favour...[amongst the common people] which things daily more increased by his abundant liberality and plentiful housekeeping than

by his riches, authority, or high parentage' (pp. 231–2; Grafton, p. 652)
188 **housekeeping** hospitality (*OED* sv 2) – as praised in Jonson's poem 'To Penshurst'.
191 **brother** York was in fact Salisbury's brother-in-law as he had married Cecily Neville, Salisbury's sister.
191–2 **acts...discipline** an anachronism, since York suppressed a rebellion in 1449, four years after this scene. (Holinshed, p. 215; Hall, p. 213, and see Boswell-Stone, p. 248 n.)
193 **late** recent.
193 **exploits** military feats.
195 Q1 (see collation) may well record the substance of lines that originally followed this.

In what we can, to bridle and suppress
The pride of Suffolk and the cardinal
With Somerset's and Buckingham's ambition;
And, as we may, cherish Duke Humphrey's deeds,                    200
While they do tend the profit of the land.

WARWICK So God help Warwick, as he loves the land
And common profit of his country.

YORK And so says York – [*Aside*] for he hath greatest cause.

SALISBURY Then let's make haste away and look unto the main.    205

WARWICK Unto the main? O, father, Maine is lost,
That Maine, which by main force Warwick did win
And would have kept, so long as breath did last.
Main chance, father, you meant, but I meant Maine,
Which I will win from France, or else be slain.                  210

*Exeunt Warwick and Salisbury*

YORK Anjou and Maine are given to the French,
Paris is lost, the state of Normandy
Stands on a tickle point now they are gone.
Suffolk concluded on the articles,
The peers agreed, and Henry was well pleased,                    215
To change two dukedoms for a duke's fair daughter.
I cannot blame them all – what is't to them?
'Tis thine they give away and not their own.
Pirates may make cheap pennyworths of their pillage,
And purchase friends and give to courtesans,                     220
Still revelling like lords till all be gone,

---

204] *Pope;* And...Yorke / For...cause F    204 SD] *Alexander; before* And *Theobald; not in* F    205] *Pope (omitting* 'away');* Then...away, / And...maine F    205 let's make haste] F *subst.;* let's Oxford    206] *Pope;* Vnto...maine? / Oh...lost, F    207 Warwick did] F; did Warwick *Collier MS*    209 Main] *Theobald²;* Main- F    210 SD *Exeunt*] *Eds; Exit* F    219 pennyworths] F; penn'worths *Pope*

**200 cherish** encourage (*OED* sv 7).

**201 tend** promote.

**205 make haste** The Oxford editors might well be right in their conjecture that these words were inserted by Compositor B to eke out his copy at the foot of an imperfectly cast-off page.

**205 look...main** a proverb (Tilley E235) deriving from the gambling game of hazard = have an eye to the main chance.

**207 main** sheer (*OED adj* 1b).

**211–32** These lines have left no trace in Q. This means they may have been cut in performance or, conceivably, that they represent an undeleted early draft that remained in the foul papers.

**213 tickle** unstable, tottering (*OED* sv 6; Dent TT14).

**214 concluded** determined (*OED* Conclude 13).

**216 change** exchange.

**218 thine** York is addressing himself, referring to his inheritance as rightful king.

**219 make...pennyworths** give away for a robber's price. Pope's emendation 'penn'worths' improves the metre.

**221 Still** Continuously.

While as the silly owner of the goods
Weeps over them, and wrings his hapless hands,
And shakes his head, and trembling stands aloof,
While all is shared and all is borne away,                          225
Ready to starve, and dare not touch his own.
So York must sit and fret and bite his tongue,
While his own lands are bargained for and sold:
Methinks the realms of England, France, and Ireland
Bare that proportion to my flesh and blood                          230
As did the fatal brand Althaea burnt
Unto the prince's heart of Calydon.
Anjou and Maine both given unto the French!
Cold news for me, for I had hope of France
Even as I have of fertile England's soil:                           235
A day will come when York shall claim his own.
And therefore I will take the Nevilles' parts
And make a show of love to proud Duke Humphrey,
And, when I spy advantage, claim the crown –
For that's the golden mark I seek to hit.                            240
Nor shall proud Lancaster usurp my right,
Nor hold the sceptre in his childish fist,
Nor wear the diadem upon his head,
Whose church-like humours fits not for a crown.
Then, York, be still awhile till time do serve:                     245
Watch thou and wake, when others be asleep,
To pry into the secrets of the state,

---

225, 226] F; *226, 225 Hudson*    226 darc] F; dares *Theobald*

222 **While as** While (Abbott 116).
222 **silly** poor, helpless.
224 **aloof** at a distance (*OED* sv 3).
227 **bite his tongue** keep silence (Dent T400.1).
230 **proportion** relation (*OED* sv 3).
231–2 Ovid tells in *Metamorphoses* VIII, 593ff. how Meleager, Prince of Calydon, was destined to live only as long as a brand burning in the fire at the time of his birth. His mother Althaea snatched it out, but years later, after he had killed her brothers, cast it back into the flames.
232 **Unto** Against (*OED* sv 23).
232 **prince's...Calydon** the heart of the Prince of Calydon.
234–5 The lines are repeated almost verbatim at 3.1.87–8. Their appearance in Q might be due

to anticipation of the later passage, and in turn this suggests that F's copy here derives in some way from Q (see Textual analysis).
234 **Cold** Chilling (*OED* sv 10).
234 **hope** expectation.
237 **take...parts** ally myself with Salisbury and Warwick.
239 **advantage** an opportunity (*OED* sv 4).
240 **mark** target (as in archery).
241 **Lancaster** Henry VI.
244 **church-like humours** pious temperament.
244 **fits** For the singular inflection see Abbott 333 – although 'humours', the subject of this verb, may have been thought of as singular.
245 **still** silent.
246 **Watch** Be alert.

Till Henry surfeit in the joys of love
With his new bride and England's dear-bought queen,
And Humphrey with the peers be fall'n at jars.                    250
Then will I raise aloft the milk-white rose
With whose sweet smell the air shall be perfumed,
And in my standard bear the arms of York
To grapple with the house of Lancaster;
And force perforce I'll make him yield the crown,                 255
Whose bookish rule hath pulled fair England down.      *Exit*

[1.2] *Enter* DUKE HUMPHREY [OF GLOUCESTER] *and his wife*
ELEANOR

ELEANOR Why droops my lord like over-ripened corn
Hanging the head at Ceres' plenteous load?
Why doth the great Duke Humphrey knit his brows,
As frowning at the favours of the world?
Why are thine eyes fixed to the sullen earth,                     5
Gazing on that which seems to dim thy sight?
What seest thou there? King Henry's diadem
Enchased with all the honours of the world?
If so, gaze on, and grovel on thy face
Until thy head be circled with the same.                          10
Put forth thy hand, reach at the glorious gold.

---

248 surfeit in the] *Hanmer;* surfetting in F, Q1      253 in] Q1; in in F      254 grapple] F, Q3; graffle Q1; wrassle (wrestle)
*conj.* Wells and Taylor      Act 1, Scene 2      1.2] Capell; not in F

---

**248** *surfeit** becomes cloyed or sick with
excess. F's 'surfeiting' may indicate the beginning
of a participial clause, so Capell's conjecture that
a line is missing after 249 may be correct.
  **250 at jars** into dissension.
  **251 the...rose** the badge of the Yorkists –
see *1H6* 2.4.
  **253 arms** armorial bearings (with a quibble
engendered by 'grapple' in the next line).
  **254 grapple with** wrestle with, fight (*OED*
Grapple *v* 8c, the first recorded use of the idiom).
  **255 force perforce** by strength of numbers
(see *OED* Force *sb* 5b).
  **256 bookish** refers to Henry's predilection for
religious texts.

**Act 1, Scene 2.**
  ***1.2** Shakespeare backtracks to events before
Margaret's arrival in England in 1445 – Eleanor

was exiled in 1441 (see the headnote to 1.4) for
her attempt to destroy the king by witchcraft.
Accordingly, Shakespeare invented the enmity
between her and the queen (see 1.3), as well as
inventing the role of Hume as *agent provocateur*
in the pay of Winchester and Suffolk – it is
merely hinted at in the chroniclers (Holinshed,
p. 203; Hall, p. 202).
  **2 Ceres'** Ceres was a goddess who represented the generative power of nature, manifest
particularly at harvest time; see Ovid, *Metamorphoses* V, 434ff.
  **3 knit his brows** proverbial (Dent KK4).
  **5 sullen** dark.
  **8 Enchased** Adorned.
  **9 grovel** (perhaps in order to conjure spirits –
compare 1.4.10).
  **11 reach at** take hold of.

What, is't too short? I'll lengthen it with mine
And, having both together heaved it up,
We'll both together lift our heads to heaven,
And never more abase our sight so low                          15
As to vouchsafe one glance unto the ground.

GLOUCESTER  O Nell, sweet Nell, if thou dost love thy lord,
Banish the canker of ambitious thoughts;
And may that thought, when I imagine ill
Against my king and nephew, virtuous Henry,                    20
Be my last breathing in this mortal world.
My troublous dream this night doth make me sad.

ELEANOR  What dreamed my lord? Tell me, and I'll requite it
With sweet rehearsal of my morning's dream.

GLOUCESTER  Methought this staff, mine office-badge in court,    25
Was broke in twain; by whom I have forgot,
But, as I think, it was by th' cardinal;
And on the pieces of the broken wand
Were placed the heads of Edmund, Duke of Somerset,
And William de la Pole, first Duke of Suffolk.                  30
This was my dream: what it doth bode, God knows.

ELEANOR  Tut, this was nothing but an argument
That he that breaks a stick of Gloucester's grove
Shall lose his head for his presumption.
But list to me, my Humphrey, my sweet duke:                     35
Methought I sat in seat of majesty

---

19 thought] F; hour *Cairncross (conj. Vaughan)*    22 dream] *Capell;* dreams F *subst.*    36 seat] F; state *conj. Vaughan*

13 **heaved** raised (*OED* Heave v 1a).
18 **canker** spreading sore, ulcer.
19 **thought** This, F's reading, may have been caught from 'thoughts' in the previous line, but there is no need to emend to 'hour' if we take 'breathing' in 21 below in the sense given.
19 **imagine ill** form evil designs (*OED* Imagine 7).
21 **breathing** inspiration (*OED* sv 1d).
22 ***dream...doth** Emendation of F's 'dreames' would not be justified by the singular verb alone, since a plural subject could be followed by a 'th' termination (Abbott, 334), but it also accords with 'dream' at 31.
22 **this night** last night.
24 **rehearsal** telling, description.
24 **morning's dream** These were reputed to contain truths – see Horace, *Sat.* I.x.33; 'Post

mediam noctem visus cum somnia vera', and Jonson, *Love Restored*, 299–300 (Jonson, VII, 395).
28 **wand** staff.
29–30 Gloucester's prognostication is proved well founded when Hume reveals in his soliloquy at the end of the scene that he is in the pay of Suffolk and Winchester.
29 **Edmund...Somerset** In fact, John Beaufort (1403–44), first Duke of Somerset and older brother of Edmund (died 1455), held the title at this time.
30 **first...Suffolk** Gloucester is grimly remembering what happened at 1.1.60–2.
32 **argument** piece of evidence (*OED* sv 1).
33 The metaphor aligns itself with the 'staff' and 'wand' of 25 and 28. There may be an allusion to biblical accounts of groves being cut down: Exod. 34.13, Deut. 7.5 etc.

In the cathedral church of Westminster;
And in that chair where kings and queens are crowned,
Where Henry and Dame Margaret kneeled to me
And on my head did set the diadem –                             40
GLOUCESTER Nay, Eleanor, then must I chide outright:
Presumptuous dame, ill-nurtured Eleanor!
Art thou not second woman in the realm
And the Protector's wife, beloved of him?
Hast thou not worldly pleasure at command                       45
Above the reach or compass of thy thought?
And wilt thou still be hammering treachery
To tumble down thy husband and thyself
From top of honour to disgrace's feet?
Away from me, and let me hear no more!                          50
ELEANOR What, what, my lord? Are you so choleric
With Eleanor for telling but her dream?
Next time I'll keep my dreams unto myself
And not be checked.
GLOUCESTER Nay, be not angry; I am pleased again.               55

*Enter [a]* MESSENGER

MESSENGER My Lord Protector, 'tis his highness' pleasure
You do prepare to ride unto Saint Albans
Where as the king and queen do mean to hawk.
GLOUCESTER I go. – Come, Nell, thou wilt ride with us?
ELEANOR Yes, my good lord, I'll follow presently.              60

                                  *Exit Gloucester [with Messenger]*
Follow I must: I cannot go before

---

37 Westminster;] *Pelican;* Westminster, F    38 are] Q1; wer F    39 Where] F; There *Dyce*²    40 diadem – ] *Pelican;* Diadem. F    59] F *subst.;* thou'lt ride with us, I'm sure] *Dyce², following* Q1    60 SD] *Capell subst.; Ex.Hum.* F (*after line 59*)

38 **chair** the coronation throne.

38 ***are*** F's unusual 'wer' may be due to the compositor anticipating 'Where' in the next line.

42 **ill-nurtured** ill-bred.

43 **second woman** since her husband was heir presumptive – see 1.1.149.

46 **compass** limits.

47 **hammering** (1) contriving, (2) insisting upon (*OED* Hammer *v* 2 and 4).

48 **tumble** Hulme (p. 330) conjectures that the word may have been suggested by 'hammering' in the line before. Hammers and tumblers were both part of gun-locks.

49 **From...honour** The phase is found in *Mirror*, 'from top of honours high' ('Suffolk', p. 162, line 4).

54 **checked** rebuked (*OED* Check *v* 10).

58 **Where as** where (Abbott 116).

59 Dyce's emendation (see collation) restores the metre, but the imperfect line might serve well as an index of Gloucester's perturbation.

61 Compare Tilley G156, 'They that cannot go before must come behind'.

61 **go before** claim precedence over the queen.

While Gloucester bears this base and humble mind.
Were I a man, a duke, and next of blood,
I would remove these tedious stumbling-blocks
And smooth my way upon their headless necks.                    65
And, being a woman, I will not be slack
To play my part in Fortune's pageant. –
Where are you there? Sir John! Nay, fear not, man,
We are alone; here's none but thee and I.

*Enter* HUME

HUME  Jesus preserve your royal majesty!                         70
ELEANOR  What say'st thou? Majesty? I am but grace.
HUME  But by the grace of God and Hume's advice
    Your grace's title shall be multiplied.
ELEANOR  What say'st thou, man? Hast thou as yet conferred
    With Margery Jourdain the cunning witch,                  75
    With Roger Bolingbroke the conjurer,
    And will they undertake to do me good?
HUME  This they have promised to show your highness:
    A spirit raised from depth of underground
    That shall make answer to such questions                  80
    As by your grace shall be propounded him.
ELEANOR  It is enough; I'll think upon the questions.
    When from Saint Albans we do make return
    We'll see these things effected to the full.
    Here, Hume, take this reward; make merry, man,           85
    With thy confederates in this weighty cause.    *Exit*

68 Where] F; What, *conj. this edn*     68 there? Sir John!] *Hanmer*; there? Sir *Iohn*; F     70 Jesus] F; Jesu *Cairncross*
75 etc. Jourdain] *Capell (following Hall)*; *Iordane* F     75–6] F; With Margery Jourdain, the witch of Eie, / With
Bolingbroke, the cunning conjurer, *Cairncross (following Q1's 'with Margery Iordaine, the cunning Witch of Ely')*
76 With] F; And *Pope*     76 etc. Bolingbroke] *Eds*; *Bollingbrooke* F

66 **being** since I am (Abbott 378). Eleanor
claims affinity with the female figure of Fortune.
68 **Where** It is possible that 'What' is the
correct reading, the text being compositorially
contaminated by the following 'there'.
68 **Sir John** a customary Elizabethan designation for a clerk of the church.
69 **thee** For the use of 'thee' for 'thou' see
Abbott 213.
70 **Jesus** Cairncross's emendation to 'Jesu'
might be supported on the grounds that it appears twenty-one times in Shakespeare's works,
and 'Jesus' only four times.

71 **grace** the title for a duchess.
73 Alluding to 1 Pet. 1.2: 'Grace and peace be
multiplied unto you'.
75 **cunning** skilful.
76 **conjurer** magician.
77 **do me good** bring me prosperity.
79 **spirit** 1.4 makes it apparent that the 'spirit'
had the appearance of a devil; see Thomas,
pp. 318–9.
79 **depth** the innermost parts (*OED* sv 10).
'Depth of underground' is a phrase used by Kyd
(*Spanish Tragedy* 1.5.1).
81 **propounded** put to.

HUME   Hume must make merry with the duchess' gold;
        Marry, and shall. But how now, Sir John Hume?
        Seal up your lips and give no words but mum:
        The business asketh silent secrecy.                          90
        Dame Eleanor gives gold to bring the witch:
        Gold cannot come amiss, were she a devil.
        Yet have I gold flies from another coast:
        I dare not say from the rich cardinal
        And from the great and new-made Duke of Suffolk;             95
        Yet I do find it so: for, to be plain,
        They (knowing Dame Eleanor's aspiring humour)
        Have hired me to undermine the duchess
        And buzz these conjurations in her brain.
        They say, 'A crafty knave does need no broker':             100
        Yet am I Suffolk and the cardinal's broker.
        Hume, if you take not heed, you shall go near
        To call them both a pair of crafty knaves.
        Well, so it stands: and thus, I fear, at last
        Hume's knavery will be the duchess' wrack,                  105
        And her attainture will be Humphrey's fall.
        Sort how it will, I shall have gold for all.          *Exit*

[**1.3**] *Enter three or four* PETITIONERS, [PETER] *the Armourer's Man
being one*

I PETITIONER   My masters, let's stand close; my Lord Protector will
        come this way by and by, and then we may deliver our
        supplications in the quill.

97 Eleanor's aspiring] F; Eleanor's F3 *subst.*    **Act 1, Scene 3    1.3**] *Capell; not in* F    0 SD PETER] *Theobald; not in*
F    3 in the quill] F; in quill *Hanmer;* in sequel *Collier²;* in the coil *conj. Singer*

87ff. Hume was pardoned according to the
chroniclers (Holinshed, p. 204; Hall, p. 202)
who, however, do not mention the bribe from
Winchester and Suffolk. At 2.3.8 Hume is sentenced to hang.
   88 **Marry, and shall** proverbial (Dent M699.1).
   89 **no...mum** proverbial (Tilley w767). As
Hume was spelled 'Hum' in Hall (p. 202), there
may have been a rhyme here.
   90 **asketh** demands (*OED* Ask 19).
   93 **coast** quarter (*OED* sv 8).
   97 **aspiring humour** ambitious nature.
   99 **buzz** whisper, implant.

99 **conjurations** incantations, spells.
100 **A...broker** proverbial (Tilley K122).
100 **broker** agent, middleman.
105 **wrack** destruction.
106 **attainture** attaintment, conviction,
disgrace.
107 **Sort...will** Whatever happens.

**Act 1, Scene 3**
*1.3 · Shakespeare invents the detail that the
armourer's treason was to support York's claim
to the crown: see Holinshed, p. 210, and Appendix 1, p. 222 (compare Hall, p. 206). The

2 PETITIONER Marry, the Lord protect him, for he's a good man, Jesu bless him.        5

*Enter* SUFFOLK *and* QUEEN [MARGARET, *and they take him for Duke Humphrey and give him their writings*]

PETER Here a comes, methinks, and the queen with him. I'll be the first, sure.

2 PETITIONER Come back, fool! This is the Duke of Suffolk and not my Lord Protector.

SUFFOLK How now, fellow; would'st anything with me?       10

1 PETITIONER I pray my lord pardon me: I took ye for my Lord Protector.

MARGARET 'For my Lord Protector'? Are your supplications to his lordship? Let me see them: what is thine?

1 PETITIONER Mine is, and't please your grace, against John   15 Goodman, my lord cardinal's man, for keeping my house and lands and wife and all from me.

SUFFOLK Thy wife too? That's some wrong indeed. – What's yours? What's here! [*Reads*] 'Against the Duke of Suffolk, for enclosing the commons of Melford.' How now, sir knave!     20

---

5 SD.1–2 MARGARET...*writings*] *This edn (following Q1); not in* F    6 SH] F; 1 Pet. F4    13 'For] *Capell;* To F; [*Reading*] 'To *Rowe*²    19 SD] *Rowe; not in* F

---

growing intimacy between Suffolk and Margaret is also Shakespeare's invention; it began when Suffolk captured Margaret in *1H6* 5.3. Shakespeare seems to have used Hall's portrait of Margaret (Appendix 1, p. 223) for some details (see 41–2 n. and 125–6 n.), although the charges against Gloucester are found in both chroniclers (Holinshed, p. 211; Hall, p. 209). Only Holinshed (p. 209) records both that it was Suffolk who aided Somerset to obtain the regency (compare 159–60 n.) and that York was suspicious that Somerset would again thwart his request for resources (162–7; Holinshed, pp. 208–9); compare the account of similar events in 1436 when York was appointed to succeed Bedford (Holinshed, p. 185; Hall, p. 179).

1 **close** free from observation and quiet.

2 **by and by** immediately.

3 **supplications** petitions.

3 **in the quill** as a group (*OED* Quill *sb*²2) – unless we accept Singer's conjecture and read 'in the coil' (tumult), 'quile' being a possible variant of that word (see *OED*). Pelican suggests an 'illiterate error for "in sequel"(?)' (compare *H5* 5.2.333).

4 **protect** the pun alludes to Gloucester's office.

6 SH I follow F's assignation of this speech to Peter; editors usually follow F4 and reassign it to 1 Petitioner – the designations (see collation) are easily confused. Peter eagerly pushes forward and retires somewhat abashed after he has learned of his mistake.

10 **fellow** the customary form of address to a servant or inferior.

13 ***For** Sisson (*New Readings*, II, 75) supports Capell's emendation of F's 'To' on the grounds that the compositor might have anticipated the 'to' that comes later in the line. 'To' could stand if we assumed that Margaret reads from a visible heading to the supplication.

15–17 As in *1H6* 3.1, aristocratic factionalism has infected the lower orders. The lines are also ironic, given the nature of Suffolk's relationship with Queen Margaret.

16 **Goodman** Perhaps the name suggests that he is phallically impressive.

16 **man** agent, retainer.

19–20 **enclosing the commons** The landowners' practice of fencing in and thereby appro-

2 PETITIONER Alas, sir, I am but a poor petitioner of our whole
   township.
PETER [*Giving his petitions*] Against my master Thomas Horner, for
   saying that the Duke of York was rightful heir to the crown.
MARGARET What say'st thou? Did the Duke of York say he was    25
   rightful heir to the crown?
PETER That my master was? No, forsooth: my master said that he
   was, and that the king was an usurper.
SUFFOLK Who is there?

*Enter* SERVANT

Take this fellow in, and send for his master with a pursuivant    30
presently. – We'll hear more of your matter before the king.
                                        *Exit* [*Servant with Peter*]
MARGARET And as for you that love to be protected
   Under the wings of our Protector's grace,
   Begin your suits anew, and sue to him. [*Tears the
      supplication*]
   Away, base cullions! – Suffolk, let them go.                 35
ALL [PETITIONERS] Come, let's be gone.            *Exeunt*
MARGARET My Lord of Suffolk, say, is this the guise,
   Is this the fashions in the court of England?

---

23 SD] *Capell; not in* F    27 That my master] *Warburton;* That my Mistresse F    28 usurper] F *subst.;* vsurer. / *Queene.*
An vsurper thou wouldst say. / *Peter.* I forsooth an vsurper. Q1    31 SD *Servant with Peter*] *Cam.* (*following* Q1); *not in*
F    34 SD *Tears*] *Eds; Teare* F    38 fashions] F; fashion *Rowe*

---

priating common lands had been a cause of
popular discontent and the cause of anti-enclosure
legislation – which Parliament repealed in 1593.
Enclosure was one of the grievances of Cade's
rebels – see 4.2.56–7 and critical introduction,
p. 26. Suffolk's oppression of the poor is set out
by the chroniclers (Holinshed, p. 215; Hall p.
212), although there is no mention of enclosure.
   **20 Melford** Long Melford in Suffolk.
   **20 sir knave** Suffolk ironically combines a
courtesy title with a term of abuse.
   **21 of** for (Abbott 174).
   **23 Horner** See note in 'Characters'. The
name may have been associated in Shakespeare's
mind with Suffolk's role – compare 16 n. above.
   **27 *That my master** F reads 'my Mistresse',
which may indicate a Freudian slip on the part of
Peter, overawed by the domineering Margaret –
or that he was a simpleton as indicated by the
'usurer' joke recorded in Q (see collation). If
there was a compositorial error, it could have

derived from a M$^r$:M$^{rs}$ misreading. But it is easier
to assume that Peter thinks that Margaret has
understood him to say that York said that Horner
was heir to the crown.
   **28 usurper** Q adds some characteristic 'gag'
(see collation and Hattaway, p. 90). Oxford
include it in their text on the grounds of 'compositorial eyeskip from "an vsurper" to "an
usurper"' (Wells and Taylor, p. 180).
   **30 pursuivant** a state messenger with power
to execute warrants (*OED* sv 2).
   **33** Compare Ruth 2.12, 'The Lord recom-
pense thy work and a full reward be given thee of
the Lord God of Israel, under whose wings thou
are come to trust'.
   **35 base cullions** low-born knaves (cullions
meant testicles).
   **37 guise** custom of the country (*OED* sv 2).
   **38 Is** For the singular see Abbott 335.
   **38 fashions** manners and customs (*OED*
Fashion *sb* 8b).

Is this the government of Britain's isle?
And this the royalty of Albion's king?                              40
What, shall King Henry be a pupil still
Under the surly Gloucester's governance?
Am I a queen in title and in style
And must be made a subject to a duke?
I tell thee, Pole, when in the city Tours                           45
Thou ran'st a-tilt in honour of my love
And stol'st away the ladies' hearts of France,
I thought King Henry had resembled thee
In courage, courtship, and proportion.
But all his mind is bent to holiness,                               50
To number Ave-Maries on his beads;
His champions are the prophets and apostles,
His weapons holy saws of sacred writ,
His study is his tilt-yard, and his loves
Are brazen images of canonised saints.                             55
I would the College of the Cardinals
Would choose him Pope and carry him to Rome
And set the triple crown upon his head:
That were a state fit for his holiness.
SUFFOLK Madam, be patient: as I was cause                          60
          Your highness came to England, so will I
          In England work your grace's full content.
MARGARET Beside the haught Protector, have we Beaufort

---

63 haught] F2; haughty F

40 **royalty** sovereign power (*OED* sv 1c).
40 **Albion's** England's.
41–2 There seems to be a reminiscence of Hall here: the king 'passed not much on the authority and governance of the realm…like a young scholar or innocent pupil…governed by the disposition of another man' (p. 208). Holinshed (p. 210) uses the simile but does not use the word 'governance'.
41 **still** for ever.
43 **style** form of address.
46 **a-tilt** in a jousting contest on horseback. Hall (p. 205) reports that 'triumphant jousts' took place at Margaret's marriage in Tours.
47 **ladies…France** (compare the construction at 1.1.232).
49 **courtship** courtliness of manners (*OED* sv 1) and, possibly, wooing.
49 **proportion** figure (*OED* sv 7).

50 **bent** inclined.
51 **number…beads** count his prayers to the Virgin on his rosary.
52–3 The metaphor derives from the description of the Christian as God's warrior in Eph. 6.10ff. Compare also Eph. 2.20: 'the foundation of the apostles and prophets'. The king's champion stood in for him at jousts and tournaments.
53 **saws** texts, sayings.
55 **canonised** accented on the second syllable (Cercignani, p. 41).
58 **triple crown** the papal diadem.
59 **state** (1) status, (2) dominion.
59 **his holiness** (1) his piety, (2) the title of the pope.
62 **work** strive to effect.
63 ***haught** haughty (F). This, F2's reading (which appears also in *3H6* 2.1.169), improves the metre.

The imperious churchman; Somerset, Buckingham,
And grumbling York; and not the least of these                         65
But can do more in England than the king.
SUFFOLK And he of these, that can do most of all,
    Cannot do more in England than the Nevilles:
    Salisbury and Warwick are no simple peers.
MARGARET Not all these lords do vex me half so much              70
    As that proud dame, the Lord Protector's wife:
    She sweeps it through the court with troops of ladies
    More like an empress than Duke Humphrey's wife.
    Strangers in court do take her for the queen:
    She bears a duke's revenues on her back                        75
    And in her heart she scorns our poverty.
    Shall I not live to be avenged on her?
    Contemptuous base-borne callet as she is,
    She vaunted 'mongst her minions t'other day
    The very train of her worst wearing gown                      80
    Was better worth than all my father's lands,
    Till Suffolk gave two dukedoms for his daughter.
SUFFOLK Madam, myself have limed a bush for her
    And placed a choir of such enticing birds
    That she will light to listen to their lays                     85
    And never mount to trouble you again.
    So let her rest; and, madam, list to me,
    For I am bold to counsel you in this:
    Although we fancy not the cardinal,

85 their] *Rowe;* the F

65 **grumbling** discontented.

69 **simple** ordinary; Salisbury was a grandson of John of Gaunt.

70–86 Historically Eleanor had been disgraced in 1441, four years before Margaret became queen.

72 **sweeps it** For the construction, see Abbott 226.

74 **Strangers** Foreigners.

75 Compare the proverb (first cited in 1576), 'He wears a whole lordship on his back' (Dent L452), and Marlowe, *Edward II*, 704; 'He wears a lord's revenue on his back'. 'Revenues' was stressed on the second syllable (Cercignani, p. 42). This line appears in Q3 but not Q1–2.

78 **Contemptuous** Contemptible (*OED* sv 3)

78 **callet** strumpet.

79 **minions** favourites, lovers.

80 **worst wearing** least fashionable, oldest, cheapest.

81 **better worth** worth more.

82 See 1.1.214–16.

83 **limed a bush** set a trap (as fowlers did by smearing twigs with bird-lime, which was made from the bark of holm-oaks).

84 **choir** (1) chorus, (2) group (*OED* sv 6).

84 **enticing birds** decoys (?).

85–6 **light...mount** land...fly up (continuing the birding metaphor).

85 *their Sisson (*New Readings*, II, 75) argues for the emendation from F's 'the' on the basis of a y$^r$/y$^e$ confusion.

85 **lays** songs.

89 **fancy** love.

Yet must we join with him and with the lords                 90
Till we have brought Duke Humphrey in disgrace.
As for the Duke of York, this late complaint
Will make but little for his benefit:
So one by one we'll weed them all at last,
And you yourself shall steer the happy helm.                 95

*Sound a sennet. Enter the* KING [*with* YORK *and* SOMERSET *on either*
*side of him, whispering with him; and enter*] DUKE HUMPHREY,
[WINCHESTER,] BUCKINGHAM, SALISBURY, WARWICK, *and the*
DUCHESS [ELEANOR]

KING HENRY For my part, noble lords, I care not which:
    Or Somerset or York, all's one to me.
YORK If York have ill demeaned himself in France,
    Then let him be denied the regentship.
SOMERSET If Somerset be unworthy of the place,                100
    Let York be regent: I will yield to him.
WARWICK Whether your grace be worthy, yea or no,
    Dispute not that: York is the worthier.
WINCHESTER Ambitious Warwick, let thy betters speak.
WARWICK The cardinal's not my better in the field.           105
BUCKINGHAM All in this presence are thy betters, Warwick.
WARWICK Warwick may live to be the best of all.
SALISBURY Peace, son, and show some reason, Buckingham,
    Why Somerset should be preferred in this.
MARGARET Because the king, forsooth, will have it so.        110
GLOUCESTER Madam, the king is old enough himself
    To give his censure. These are no women's matters.
MARGARET If he be old enough, what needs your grace

95 helm.] *Rowe ( following* Q1); *Helme. Exit.* F; *Realm. Theobald*   96 SD.1–2 *with. . .enter*] *This edn ( following* Q1); *not*
*in* F 99 denied] F4; *denay'd* F

92 **late** recent (see 23–4 above).
94 **weed** uproot, destroy
95 **happy** fortunate
95 **helm** of the ship of state; the phrase,
however, seems not to have been used by seamen
(*Shakespeare's England*, I, 162), which makes
Theobald's emendation (see collation) attractive.
*95 At the end of the line, F marks an exit for
Suffolk, which must be removed, given that he
has an important role in the rest of the scene.
There is no way of telling whether this is a compositorial error or whether it derives from the
manuscript.

95 SD **sennet** see 1.1.0.1 SD n.
97 **Or. . .York** for the rivalry between the two
see 3.1 and 5.1; compare *1H6* 2.4. 'Or' =
'either'.
104 **betters** superiors in rank.
105 **in the field** in armed combat.
106 **presence** presence-chamber, a room for
royal reception (*OED* sv 2c).
106 **thy betters** morally superior to you.
112 **censure** formal judgement or opinion
(*OED* sv 2).

To be Protector of his excellence?
GLOUCESTER Madam, I am Protector of the realm,                           115
   And at his pleasure will resign my place.
SUFFOLK Resign it then, and leave thine insolence.
   Since thou wert king – as who is king, but thou? –
   The commonwealth hath daily run to wrack,
   The dauphin hath prevailed beyond the seas,                        120
   And all the peers and nobles of the realm
   Have been as bondmen to thy sovereignty.
WINCHESTER The commons hast thou racked: the clergy's bags
   Are lank and lean with thy extortions.
SOMERSET Thy sumptuous buildings and thy wife's attire                   125
   Have cost a mass of public treasury.
BUCKINGHAM Thy cruelty in execution
   Upon offenders hath exceeded law,
   And left thee to the mercy of the law.
MARGARET Thy sale of offices and towns in France,                       130
   If they were known, as the suspect is great,
   Would make thee quickly hop without thy head.
             *Exit Gloucester. [Margaret drops her fan]*
   Give me my fan; what, minion, can ye not?
        *She gives the duchess a box on the ear*
   I cry you mercy, madam; was it you?
ELEANOR Was't I! Yea, I it was, proud Frenchwoman;                      135
   Could I come near your beauty with my nails

---

126 treasury] F; Treasure F2   132 SD *Margaret...fan*] *Johnson subst. (following* Q1's 'The Queene lets fall her glouc'); *not in* F

---

**114–5** Gloucester was ordained 'Protector of England' but not custodian of the infant prince Henry VI; this role was assigned to Exeter and Winchester (Holinshed, p. 136).

**117 insolence** overbearing conduct (*OED sv* 1).

**120 dauphin** F's customary spelling 'dolphin' makes the pun clear. 'Charles VII is so called here because the English considered Henry VI the rightful king of France' (Riverside).

**120 prevailed** gained in strength (*OED* Prevail 1).

**122 bondmen** slaves.

**123 racked** reduced to poverty by extortionate levies (*OED* Rack *v* 4).

**123 bags** purses.

**125–6** Hall (pp. 208–9) and not Holinshed mentions Gloucester's extravagance (see Appendix 1, p. 223).

**125 sumptuous buildings** Somerset refers to Gloucester's palace at Greenwich, which he had had enlarged in Renaissance style.

**126 treasury** treasure, wealth (*OED sv* 5).

**130** This in fact was one of the charges brought against Winchester by Gloucester himself (Holinshed, p. 203; Hall, p. 201). It is not mentioned as a charge against Gloucester by the chroniclers; compare 3.1.60–3 n.

**131 suspect** ground of suspicion (*OED sv* 1f).

**132 hop...head** be executed – proverbial (Dent HH11).

**133 minion** hussy (*OED sv* 1e (b)).

**134 I...mercy** I beg your pardon (sarcastic).

I'd set my ten commandments in your face.

KING HENRY Sweet aunt, be quiet; 'twas against her will.

ELEANOR Against her will! – Good king, look to't in time:
　　　　She'll hamper thee and dandle thee like a baby.                    140
　　　　Though in this place most master wear no breeches,
　　　　She shall not strike Dame Eleanor unrevenged.        *Exit*

BUCKINGHAM Lord Cardinal, I will follow Eleanor,
　　　　And listen after Humphrey how he proceeds:
　　　　She's tickled now, her fury needs no spurs,                       145
　　　　She'll gallop far enough to her destruction.          *Exit*

*Enter* GLOUCESTER

GLOUCESTER Now, lords, my choler being overblown
　　　　With walking once about the quadrangle,
　　　　I come to talk of commonwealth affairs.
　　　　As for your spiteful false objections,                            150
　　　　Prove them, and I lie open to the law;
　　　　But God in mercy so deal with my soul
　　　　As I in duty love my king and country.
　　　　But to the matter that we have in hand:
　　　　I say, my sovereign, York is meetest man                         155
　　　　To be your regent in the realm of France.

SUFFOLK Before we make election, give me leave

---

**137** I'd] Q1; I could F   **139** will! – Good king,] *Johnson;* will, good King? F   **140** hamper] F; pamper *Oxford* (*conj.*
*McKerrow*)   **143** I will] F; I'll *Pope*   **145** fury] *White;* Fume F   **146** far] F; fast *Pope*

**137** *I'd** The emendation from F's 'I could' is justified on the grounds that 'could' was caught by the compositor from the line above.

**137 ten commandments** the marks of my fingernails (*OED* Commandment 3). This proverbial slang (Tilley C553) derived from a legend that God scratched the Ten Commandments on the Tables with His nails (see Exod. 31.18 and Deut. 9.10).

**138 quiet** calm (*OED* sv 3b).

**138 against her will** unintentional (*OED* Will sb 14).

**140 hamper** 'perhaps with a back-sense of the cradle [i.e. 'swaddle']' (Hart). Oxford's emendation 'pamper' is attractive.

**141 most...breeches** a proverbial saying (Tilley M727) meaning that women rule the house.

**141 most master** the greatest master (*OED* Most 1h). i.e. the queen.

**141 wear** a subjunctive form.

**144 listen after** endeavour to hear of (*OED* Listen 2c).

**145 tickled** provoked (*OED* Tickle v 7).

**145 *fury** F's 'fume' = 'rage' (compare *Ven.* 316) makes sense, but is a likely misreading of 'furie' (Sisson, *New Readings*, II, 76), which better suits the metre and aligns itself with the proverb 'Do not spur a free (willing) horse' (Tilley H638). Norman Blake, 'Fume/Fury in *2 Henry VI*', *NQ* (forthcoming) defends 'fume', arguing that 'tickled' here means intoxicated or besotted.

**147 overblown** passed away.

**148 quadrangle** court of a royal palace where the scene may be supposed to be set; the first recorded use of the word in *OED*.

**150 objections** accusations (*OED* Objection 1b).

**153 duty** reverence (*OED* sv 1).

**155 meetest** most suitable.

**157 election** choice.

>    To show some reason, of no little force,
>    That York is most unmeet of any man.

YORK  I'll tell thee, Suffolk, why I am unmeet:                    160
>    First, for I cannot flatter thee in pride;
>    Next, if I be appointed for the place,
>    My Lord of Somerset will keep me here
>    Without discharge, money, or furniture,
>    Till France be won into the dauphin's hands:               165
>    Last time I danced attendance on his will
>    Till Paris was besieged, famished, and lost.

WARWICK  That can I witness, and a fouler fact
>    Did never traitor in the land commit.

SUFFOLK  Peace, headstrong Warwick!                                170

WARWICK  Image of pride, why should I hold my peace?

*Enter* [HORNER *the*] *Armourer, and his Man* [PETER *guarded*]

SUFFOLK  Because here is a man accused of treason:
>    Pray God the Duke of York excuse himself!

YORK  Doth anyone accuse York for a traitor?

KING HENRY  What mean'st thou, Suffolk? Tell me, what are these?  175

SUFFOLK  Please it, your majesty, this is the man
>                    [*Pointing to Peter*]
>    That doth accuse his master of high treason;
>    His words were these: that Richard, Duke of York,
>    Was rightful heir unto the English crown
>    And that your majesty was an usurper.                      180

KING HENRY  Say, man, were these thy words?

HORNER  And't shall please your majesty, I never said nor thought
>    any such matter. God is my witness, I am falsely accused by the
>    villain.

---

163 here] F; *there Collier*[2]    171 SD] *Theobald; Enter Armorer and his Man* F    176 SD] *This edn; not in* F    182 etc.
SH HORNER] *Malone; Armorer* F

**159–60** These might contain an echo of lines found only in Holinshed: 'the Duke of York was...(as a man most meet...) appointed...as Regent of France' (p. 208).
**161 for** because.
**161 in pride** without losing my self-respect.
**164 discharge** payment (*OED* sv 5).
**164 furniture** military equipment (*OED* sv 4b).
**166 Last time** See *1H6* 4.3.9–11.

**166 danced attendance** proverbial (Tilley A392).
**168–9** Again Shakespeare confuses Richard Neville with his father-in-law; see 1.1.116 n.
**168 fact** crime (*OED* sv 1c).
**171 Image** Embodiment (*OED* sv 4c).
**174 for** as.
**175 what** who (Abbott 254).
**183 God...witness** Rom. 1.9.

PETER [*Holding up his hands*] By these ten bones, my lords, he did   185
    speak them to me in the garret one night, as we were scouring
    my Lord of York's armour.

YORK Base dunghill villain and mechanical,
    I'll have thy head for this thy traitor's speech. –
    I do beseech your royal majesty,                                   190
    Let him have all the rigour of the law.

HORNER Alas, my lord, hang me if ever I spake the words! My
    accuser is my prentice, and when I did correct him for his fault
    the other day, he did vow upon his knees he would be even with
    me, I have good witness of this. Therefore, I beseech your   195
    majesty, do not cast away an honest man for a villain's
    accusation.

KING HENRY Uncle, what shall we say to this in law?

GLOUCESTER This doom, my lord, if I may judge:
    Let Somerset be regent o'er the French,                            200
    Because in York this breeds suspicion;
    And let these have a day appointed them
    For single combat in convenient place;
    For he hath witness of his servant's malice.
    This is the law, and this Duke Humphrey's doom.                    205
            [*King Henry nods assent*]

SOMERSET I humbly thank your royal majesty.

HORNER And I accept the combat willingly.

PETER Alas, my lord, I cannot fight; for God's sake pity my case!

185 SD] *Steevens; not in* F   199 my] F; *my gracious Collier*²   199 judge:] F *subst.; judge by case Cairncross* (*following*
Q1)   205 doom.] F; *doom. /* KING HENRY *Then be it so.* (*To Somerset*) *My lord of Somerset, / We make you regent
o'er the realm of France / There to defend our rights 'gainst foreign foes. Theobald subst.* (*omitting* There…foes)
(*following* Q1)   205 SD]*This edn; not in* F

185 **bones** fingers – an ancient asseveration
(*OED* Bone 1c; Dent TT7).

  186 **garret** watch-tower (*OED* sv 1).

  188 **mechanical** menial, manual labourer.

  193 **correct** chastise (*OED* Correct *v* 4).

  193 **his fault** an improper act he had committed.

  196 **cast away** ruin.

  196 **for** on account of.

  199 Various suggestions have been made to
supply two extra syllables for this line (see
collation). However, Shakespeare often begins a
declarative speech of this kind with a metrically
irregular line.

  199 **doom** judgement.

201 Because this case casts doubts on York's
loyalty.

  203 **convenient** an appropriate (*OED* sv 4).

  203 **single combat** Q supplies the details:
'With *Eben* staues, and *Standbags* [i.e. sandbags
attached to one end of the staves] combatting /
In Smythfield, before your Royall Maiestie' (TLN,
432–3).

  206 **your…majesty** Editors, having noted
that Somerset responds to the king rather than to
Gloucester, have either made up a preceding line
for the king (Cairncross) or supplied lines from Q
(Oxford). But the problem may be solved by the
simple stage direction I have supplied after 205.

The spite of man prevaileth against me. O Lord, have mercy
upon me! I shall never be able to fight a blow. O Lord, my heart!  210
GLOUCESTER  Sirrah, or you must fight or else be hanged.
KING HENRY  Away with them to prison; and the day of combat shall
be the last of the next month. – Come, Somerset, we'll see thee
sent away.                                                   *Flourish. Exeunt*

[1.4]  *Enter the witch* [MARGERY JOURDAIN], *the two priests* [HUME
*and* SOUTHWELL], *and* BOLINGBROKE

HUME  Come, my masters, the duchess I tell you expects performance of your promises.
BOLINGBROKE  Master Hume, we are therefore provided. Will her
ladyship behold and hear our exorcisms?
HUME  Ay, what else. Fear you not her courage.                        5
BOLINGROKE  I have heard her reported to be a woman of an
invincible spirit; but it shall be convenient, Master Hume, that
you be by her aloft, while we be busy below; and so, I pray you,
go in God's name, and leave us.

                                                           *Exit Hume*
Mother Jourdain, be you prostrate, and grovel on the earth.          10
             [*She lies down upon her face*]

209 man] F; *my master* F4; *many conj.* Vaughan    212–14 Away...away] F *subst.;* Away...day / Of...month. –
/Come...away. *Capell*    212–13 shall be] F; *be* Cairncross    **Act 1, Scene 4**    1.4] *Capell; not in* F    0 SD.1
MARGERY JOURDAIN] *Eds* (*following* Hall 'Margerie Iourdayne'); *not in* F    0 SD.2 BOLINGBROKE] *Eds; Bullingbrooke*
F    10 SD] Q1; *not in* F

209 **The...me!** Compare Ps. 65.3, 'Wicked
deeds have prevailed against me: but thou wilt be
merciful unto our transgressions'.
210 **my heart!** An ellipsis for 'bless my heart!'.
211 **Sirrah** a contemptuous form of address.

**Act 1, Scene 4**
*1.4  See 1.2 headnote. The details of the
conjuring and Eleanor's arrest are Shakespeare's
invention. The sources (Holinshed, p. 204; Hall,
p. 202) record that they made a wax image of the
king, for which Shakespeare, perhaps following
the poem about Eleanor in *Mirror* (p. 435 – see Appendix 1, pp. 221–2 and 41 n. below), substituted
the political crime of prophesying. For an account
of the political uses to which prophecies were put
throughout the sixteenth century and the acts that
were passed to suppress them, see Thomas, pp.
470–86.

3 **provided** i.e. with magic book, etc.; see
Thomas, pp. 272ff.
4 **exorcisms** conjurations of spirits (*OED*
Exorcism 1b), an improper but common use of
the word.
5 **what else** certainly.
8 **aloft** i.e. on the tiring-house balcony.
10 The hocus-pocus is described in lines from
Q: '*Witch.* Then *Roger Bullinbrooke* about thy taske
/ And frame a Cirkle here upon the earth, /
Whilst I thereon all prostrate on my face, / Do
talke and whisper with the divels be low / And
coniure them for to obey my will.' (TLN 492–6)
See W. H. Hart, 'Observations on some documents relating to magic...', *Archaeologia* 40
(1866), 397 for a description of the apparatus left
when some magicians were surprised at their
conjuring in 1590; for contemporary attitudes to
fortune-telling and divination, see Thomas, pp.
282ff.

John Southwell, read you; and let us to our work.

*Enter* ELEANOR *aloft,* [*Hume following*]

ELEANOR Well said, my masters, and welcome all. To this gear, the
    sooner the better.
BOLINGBROKE Patience, good lady; wizards know their times. –
    Deep night, dark night, the silent of the night,                    15
    The time of night when Troy was set on fire,
    The time when screech-owls cry, and bandogs howl,
    And spirits walk, and ghosts break up their graves;
    That time best fits the work we have in hand.
    Madam, sit you and fear not. Whom we raise                    20
    We will make fast within a hallowed verge.

*Here* [*they*] *do the ceremonies belonging and make the circle; Bolingbroke or*
*Southwell reads, 'Coniuro te', etc. It thunders and lightens terribly; then the*
SPIRIT *riseth.*

SPIRIT *Adsum.*
JOURDAIN Asmath,

11 SD] *Hume following*] *Dyce subst.; not in* F    12 gear] *Eds;* geere F; gyre *conj. this edn*    15 silent] F; silence Q1    18
up] F; ope *Collier MS*    23–6] *Capell; Asmath . . . God, / Whose . . . at, / Answere . . . speake, / Thou . . . hence.* F
23 SH] *Eds; Witch* F    23 Asmath] F; Asnath *Cairncross*

11 SD Q here reads '[Eleanor] goes vp to the
Tower'. (TLN 488) 'Tower' here describes the
place signified by the tiring-house gallery and not
part of the playhouse.
    12 **Well said** Eleanor either enters to hear the
previous line or uses the phrase to mean 'well
done', as at 3.2.8 and *Tit.* 4.3.63.
    12 *To this gear Let's get down to business
(see *OED* Gear 11c). F, in fact, reads 'geere',
which is a possible variant of 'gyre', i.e. the magic
circle. This word, however, is not found elsewhere in Shakespeare.
    12–13 the sooner . . . better proverbial (Tilley
s641).
    15 silent For adjectives used as nouns see
Abbott 5; Sisson, however, argues for Q's 'silence', conjecturing that the compositor read
'silenc' as 'silent' (*New Readings*, II, 76).
    16 The account of the sacking of Troy is to be
found in Virgil, *Aeneid* II.
    17–8 For similar prodigies see *Metamorphoses*
XV, 887–895.
    17 screech-owls from classical times had
been regarded as harbingers of death.
    17 bandogs tied-up fierce watchdogs.
    18 break up burst open (*OED* Break 56j).
    21 verge circle (*OED* sv 13b).

21 SD Compare the conjuring scenes in *Dr
Faustus* (iii, iv) and see also Thomas, p. 273. The
circle may very well have been marked out by a
circle of lighted candles (see A.C. Kors and
E. Peters, *Witchcraft in Europe*, 1973, p. 138).
Lightning and thunder effects were also common
in such scenes (*The Old Wives Tale*, 435 SD;
Hattaway, pp. 114–15). Spirits customarily
entered through the stage trap (Hattaway, p.
115). The permissive nature of the SD indicates
foul paper copy; compare 4.10.53 SD n.
    21 SD.1–2 or Southwell Compare 11 and 28.
Southwell is cut from Q1's version of the play and
has no other lines in F.
    21 SD.2 *Coniuro te* I conjure you. An
extended spell is to be found in *Dr Faustus*
iii.16ff.
    22 Adsum I am here.
    23 Asmath The name is unknown; the closest
devils' names are 'Asmenoth, guider of the
North' in Greene's *Friar Bacon* (ix.144) or
Asmodeus from the apocryphal Tobit 3.8–17.
Cairncross emends to 'Asnath', considering the
name to be an anagram of 'Sathan'. Q1 offers
'Askalon', the name of a spirit in the plot of *1
Tamar Cham*, a play owned by Strange's Men.

By the eternal God, whose name and power
Thou tremblest at, answer that I shall ask; 25
For till thou speak, thou shalt not pass from hence.
SPIRIT Ask what thou wilt. That I had said and done!
BOLINGBROKE [*Reading from a scroll*] 'First, of the king: what shall
of him become?'
SPIRIT The duke yet lives that Henry shall depose:
But him outlive and die a violent death. 30
[*As the spirit speaks, Southwell writes the answer*]
BOLINGBROKE 'What fates await the Duke of Suffolk?'
SPIRIT By water shall he die and take his end.
BOLINGBROKE 'What shall betide the Duke of Somerset?'
SPIRIT Let him shun castles:
Safer shall he be upon the sandy plains 35
Than where castles mounted stand. –
Have done, for more I hardly can endure.
BOLINGBROKE Descend to darkness and the burning lake!
False fiend, avoid!
*Thunder and Lightening. Exit spirit* [*sinking down again*]

*Enter the* DUKE OF YORK *and the* DUKE OF BUCKINGHAM *with their*
GUARD [SIR HUMPHREY STAFFORD *as Captain*], *and break in* [*and
seize the papers*]

27 That] F *subst.; Aside.* That *conj. this edn*　28 SD] *This edn* (*following* Q1 1.4.1: Here sir Iohn, take this scrole of paper here); *not in* F　30 SD] *Capell subst.; not in* F　31 What] F; Tell me what *Pope* (*following* 62)　31 fates await] F *subst.;* fate awaits Q2; fates awaiteth then *conj.* Vaughan　33 betide] Q1; befall F (see 64)　39 SD.1 *sinking. . .again*] Pelican (*following* Q1 He sinkes downe againe.); *not in* F　39 SD.3 SIR. . .Captain] *Riverside* (see 51); *not in* F　39 SD.3–4 *and. . .papers*] *This edn; not in* F

24–5 God. . .at Compare James 2.19: 'the devils also believe [there is one God]. . .and tremble'.
25 that that which.
27 That Would that.
27 That. . .done The tradition was that some spirits were reluctant to answer questions because they were in torment (compare *Mac.* 4.1.72). Perhaps the sentence could be played as an aside.
28 SH Shakespeare may have forgotten that at 11 he allocated the reading to Southwell – compare 21 SD.1–2 n. But perhaps there was some comedy here, with Southwell scared witless by the apparition of the devil.
29–30 The prognostication refers to York, who dies wretchedly in *3H6* 1.4. In the manner of oracles, the syntax is ambiguous: either 'the duke' or 'Henry' can be taken as the subject of the

following verbs (compare 1.4.60).
*33 betide F's 'befall' (compare 64) is presumably due to contamination by 'shall' at 32 and 33.
34 castles see 5.2.67–9.
36 mounted on elevated situations (*OED sv vbl adj* 2).
37 Have done Finish quickly.
38 burning lake compare Rev. 19.20: 'a lake of fire, burning with brimstone'.
39 False Treacherous.
39 avoid depart; compare Matt. 4.10: 'Avoid, Satan'.
39 SD.2 SIR. . .Captain Line 51 would suggest that Stafford, who appears in 4.2, is on stage as captain of the guard. Some editors have suggested that as Buckingham's family name was Stafford, Buckingham is there addressing himself.

YORK Lay hands upon these traitors and their trash.                    40
        Beldam, I think we watched you at an inch. –
        What, madam, are you there? The king and commonweal
        Are deep indebted for this piece of pains.
        My Lord Protector will, I doubt it not,
        See you well guerdoned for these good deserts.             45
ELEANOR Not half so bad as thine to England's king,
        Injurious duke, that threatest where's no cause.
BUCKINGHAM True, madam, none at all. [*Showing her the papers*]
        What call you this? –
        Away with them, let them be clapped up close
        And kept asunder. You, madam, shall with us. –           50
        Stafford, take her to thee. –
                [*Exeunt aloft Eleanor and Hume, guarded*]
        We'll see your trinkets here all forthcoming.
        All away!
        [*Exeunt Guard with Jourdain, Southwell, and Bolingbroke*]
YORK Lord Buckingham, methinks you watched her well:
        A pretty plot, well chosen to build upon!                55
        Now pray, my lord, let's see the devil's writ.
                [*Buckingham hands him the papers*]
        What have we here? *Reads*
        'The duke yet lives that Henry shall depose;
        But him outlive, and die a violent death.'

---

42 commonweal] F; realm *Pope*     43 deep indebted] *Rowe*; deeply indebted F; deeply debted *conj. anon. in Oxford*
48 SD] *Capell; not in* F     51 SD] *Dyce subst. (following* Q1 *Exet Elnor abouc.); not in* F     53 All, away F; Away *Dyce*
53 SD] *Rowe; Exit* F     56 SD] *This edn; not in* F     58–67] F *subst.; transposed to follow* 2.1.178 Q1, *Oxford*

40 **trash** doxy or worthless woman, i.e.,
Margery Jourdain (*OED* sv 4, and compare *Oth.*
5.1.85).
    41 **Beldam** Hag, witch (*OED* sv 3); the word
occurs in *Mirror*, 93.
    41 **at an inch** close at hand (*OED* Inch *sb* 3a;
Dent 112).
    43 ***deep** F's 'deeply' spoils the metre, unless it
is elided with 'indebted'.
    43 **this...pains** the trouble you have taken
(sarcastic).
    45 **guerdoned** rewarded.
    47 **Injurious** Insulting (*OED* sv 2).
    49 **clapped up close** securely locked up.
    50 **shall** must go.
    52 **your trinkets** the tools of your trade (*OED*
Trinket 1).

52 **forthcoming** safe and ready to be produced
as evidence in court (*OED* sv *ppl adj* 1).
    55 **plot** (1) trick, (2) piece of ground.
    57 Dent (w280.2) traces the phrase back to
1553.
    58–67 Q1 transposes these lines into the next
scene, where they are read out by the king after
175. It may be that this records a change made for
performance, but there is as much dramatic effect
in watching the embarrassment of Eleanor and
her crew as the reactions of Henry and Suffolk to
these prophecies, and therefore no way of decid-
ing whether the copy which may derive ultimately
from a prompt-book is more 'authentic' than that
which derives from foul papers. I therefore print
F's version of the scene.

Why this is just, '*Aio te, Æacida, Romanos vincere posse*'.                60
Well, to the rest:
Tell me 'What fate awaits the Duke of Suffolk?'
'By water shall he die and take his end.'
'What shall betide the Duke of Somerset?'
'Let him shun castles:                                                      65
Safer shall he be upon the sandy plains
Than where castles mounted stand.'
Come, come, my lord, these oracles
Are hardly attained and hardly understood.
The king is now in progress towards Saint Albans,                          70
With him the husband of this lovely lady.
Thither go these news as fast as horse can carry them:
A sorry breakfast for my Lord Protector.
BUCKINGHAM Your grace shall give me leave, my Lord of York,
To be the post in hope of his reward.                                       75
YORK At your pleasure, my good lord. – Who's within there, ho?

*Enter a* SERVINGMAN

Invite my Lords of Salisbury and Warwick
To sup with me tomorrow night. Away!   *Exeunt* [*severally*]

60 *Aio te*] *Pope; Aio* F   60 *Æacida*] F *subst.; Æacidam Oxford*   64 betide] F; *befall Capell* (*see 33*)   68–9] *Capell* (*printing* 'Come, come away' *at 68*); Come...Lords / These...attain'd, / And...vnderstood. F; These oracles are hardily attained / And hardly vndertsood. Come, come, my lord, *Oxford*; Come, come, my Lords, these oracles are hard, / Hardly attained and hardly understood. *conj. G. R. Hibbard in NQ* 210 (1965), 332   68 lord] *Oxford;* lords F   69 hardly attained] F; hardily attain'd *Theobald*   72] *Pope subst.*; Thither...Newes, / As...them: F   76] *Capell subst.*; At...Lord. / Who's...hoe? F   78 SD *severally*] Q1; *not in* F

60 **just** exactly.
60 ***Aio...posse*** When Pyrrhus visited the Pythian Apollo to ask whether he would conquer Rome, the oracle gave this classic reply, which can be construed as either 'I tell you that you, a descendant of Aeneas, can conquer the Romans', or vice versa. See Cicero, *De Divin.* II.56 and Puttenham, *The Arte of English Poesie*, 1589, p. 218.
68 ***lord*** F's 'lords' is inappropriate, for York is addressing only Buckingham.

69 Are obtained with difficulty and scarcely comprehended (but see collation).
70 **in progress** on a state journey (*OED* Progress *sb* 2).
71 **lovely** loveable (ironic).
72 **goes these news** for the singular verb see Abbott 335; 'news' was often treated as a plural in the period.
73 **A...breakfast** Compare the proverb (?) 'To give a hot breakfast' (Dent B636.1).
75 **post** messenger.

**[2.1]** *Enter the* KING, QUEEN [MARGARET *with her hawk on her fist*],
*Protector* [GLOUCESTER], *Cardinal* [WINCHESTER], *and* SUFFOLK,
*with* FALCONERS *hallooing*

MARGARET Believe me, lords, for flying at the brook,
    I saw not better sport these seven years' day;
    Yet, by your leave, the wind was very high
    And, ten to one, old Joan had not gone out.
KING HENRY But what a point, my lord, your falcon made,        5
    And what a pitch she flew above the rest!
    To see how God in all his creatures works!
    Yea, man and birds are fain of climbing high.
SUFFOLK No marvel, and it like your majesty,
    My Lord Protector's hawks do tower so well:        10
    They know their master loves to be aloft
    And bears his thoughts above his falcon's pitch.
GLOUCESTER My lord, 'tis but a base ignoble mind

Act 2, Scene 1    2.1] *Pope; not in* F    0 SD.1 *with...fist*] Q1; *not in* F    9 and it] F; *an it* Pope

**Act 2, Scene 1**
  **\*2.1** The mock miracle is not found in Hall or Holinshed, but in Sir Thomas More's *Dialogue...of Images and Relics*, 1530 edn., fo. 25. This was copied by Grafton, p. 630, and Foxe, *Acts and Monuments*, 1583, I, 704–5 (see Appendix 1, p. 224). Shakespeare adds feigned lameness to Simpcox's feigned blindness.
  Gloucester engages in a verbal duel with the cardinal; it could be that his exposure of Simpcox stands as a discovery of 'the crafty working of false miracles in the clergy' (Foxe, *Acts and Monuments*, 1583, I, 704; compare Thomas, pp. 78–9 and 87–8). In this scene the king reveals himself both blind to the practical and unorthodox manner whereby Gloucester exposes the fraud of Simpcox and his wife and oblivious to the possibility that the charges against the Protector's wife may be a covert attack on himself – unless he subconsciously welcomes the chastening of Gloucester (see Introduction, p. 35).
  **0 SD.3** *hallooing* calling up the dogs.
  **1** *flying...brook* 'A stream was chosen with sedge or bushes along the banks and, preferably, with open ground for the horses on either side. Duck, and perhaps other minor wildfowl, were roused out of the cover with the help of spaniels and beaters with poles...the quarry might return again to the safety of the cover or plunge into the

stream' (T. R. Henn, *The Living Image*, 1972, p. 31); compare *Shakespeare's England*, II, 359–60.
  **2** *these...day* for the last seven years – an approximation (*OED* Day 18; Dent Y25).
  **4** *ten...out* the odds were against my hawk (old Joan, although she may be speaking jocularly of herself) flying. Dr Johnson, however, reports that 'the meaning, however expressed, is that, the wind being high, it was ten to one that the old hawk had flown away; a trick which hawks often play their masters in windy weather'.
  **5** *what a point* to what a great height (*OED* Point C4, which records the term only from 1651); compare *Shakespeare's England*, II, 360.
  **5–6** These lines could be addressed to either Suffolk or Gloucester. Suffolk's device was a falcon, an emblem used by Drayton: 'Our falcon's kind cannot the cage endure, / Nor buzzard-like doth stoop to every lure' ('William de la Pole... to Queen Margaret', *Works*, II, 230). If the lines are directed to Suffolk, they suggest that the king is already aware of Suffolk's relationship with his wife. Gloucester's badge was a falcon with a maiden's head.
  **6** *pitch* height (to which a falcon flies) (*OED* sv *sb* 18).
  **9** *and it like* if it please.
  **10** *tower* mount up – a term from falconry (*OED* sv *v* 3).

That mounts no higher than a bird can soar.

WINCHESTER I thought as much: he would be above the clouds.                    15

GLOUCESTER Ay, my lord cardinal, how think you by that?

Were it not good your grace could fly to heaven?

KING HENRY The treasury of everlasting joy.

WINCHESTER Thy heaven is on earth, thine eyes and thoughts

Beat on a crown, the treasure of thy heart;                                  20

Pernicious Protector, dangerous peer,

That smooth'st it so with king and commonweal!

GLOUCESTER What, cardinal?

Is your priest-hood grown peremptory?

*Tantaene animis coelestibus irae?*                                          25

Churchmen so hot? Good uncle, hide such malice:

With such holiness, can you do it?

SUFFOLK No malice, sir, no more than well becomes

So good a quarrel and so bad a peer.

GLOUCESTER As who, my lord?

SUFFOLK                           Why, as you, my lord,                       30

An't like your lordly Lord Protectorship.

GLOUCESTER Why, Suffolk, England knows thine insolence.

MARGARET And thy ambition, Gloucester.

KING HENRY I prithee peace, good queen,

And whet not on these furious peers;                                         35

---

15 he would] F; he'd *Pope*    20 Beat] F, Q1; Bent *Johnson*; Bate *Johnson Var. subst.*    25–6] *Theobald; Tantaene…* hot? / Good…mallice: F    26–7 hide…it?] F *subst.*; can you dote, / To hide such malice with such holiness? *Cairn-cross;* hide…With such holiness can you do it. *Pelican*    31 Lord Protectorship] F4; Lords Protectorship F    34–5] F; KING…peace, / Good…peers; *Malone subst.*

**16 how…you** what do you mean.

**18–20** Compare Matt. 6.19–20: 'Lay not up treasures for yourselves upon the earth…But lay up treasures for yourselves in heaven…For where your treasure is, there will your heart be also.'

**20 Beat on** Dwell upon (*OED* Beat 9). Johnson (Var.) might well be right in suggesting that the text should read 'Bate on', since 'bate' is a term in falconry' meaning to beat the wings impatiently (*OED* Bate $v^1$ 2; compare *Shr.* 4.1.196). 'Beat' and 'bate' may have been pronounced similarly (but see Cercignani, pp. 14, 158).

**21 dangerous** injurious (*OED* sv 5).

**22 smooth'st…with** is so flattering to.

**24 grown** Probably two syllables (Cercignani,

p. 220), which means that 'What, cardinal', constitutes a half-line.

**24 peremptory** overbearing – here accented on the second syllable (Cercignani, p. 43).

**25 *Tantaene…irae?*** Virgil, *Aeneid* I, 11: '[Can there be] so much anger in minds of heavenly creatures?'

**26 Churchmen…hot** A verb is omitted in imitation of the Virgilian construction in the previous line.

**26–7** Various emendations have been proposed for these unmetrical lines (see collation). Pelican may be right in arguing that 'can you' = 'you can' and, by implication, that the final question mark represents an exclamation.

**35 whet not on** do not encourage.

For blessèd are the peacemakers on earth.
WINCHESTER Let me be blessèd for the peace I make
      Against this proud Protector with my sword!
GLOUCESTER [*Aside to Winchester*] Faith, holy uncle, would't were
      come to that!
WINCHESTER [*Aside to Gloucester*] Marry, when thou dar'st.                40
GLOUCESTER [*Aside to Winchester*] Make up no factious numbers for
      the matter;
      In thine own person answer thy abuse.
WINCHESTER [*Aside to Gloucester*] Ay, where thou dar'st not peep:
      and if thou dar'st,
      This evening, on the east side of the grove.
KING HENRY How now, my lords?
WINCHESTER                        Believe me, cousin Gloucester,        45
      Had not your man put up the fowl so suddenly,
      We had had more sport. [*Aside to Gloucester*] Come with thy
      two-hand sword.
GLOUCESTER True, uncle. [*Aside to Winchester*] Are ye advised? The
      east side of the grove?
WINCHESTER [*Aside to Gloucester*] I am with you.
KING HENRY                        Why how now,
      Uncle Gloucester?
GLOUCESTER Talking of hawking; nothing else, my lord.                  50

---

39–52 SDD] *Rowe subst.; not in* F   43–5] *Theobald subst.;* I...peepe: / And...Euening, / On...Grouc. / How...
Lords? / Beleeue...Gloster, F   47–8] *Rowe subst.;* We...sport. / Come...Sword. / Truc...aduis'd? / The...
Grouc: F   48] F *subst.;* GLOUCESTER...uncle. / WINCHESTER Arc...grove. *Theobald subst.*   49 WINCHESTER I]
*Cairncross;* Cardinall, I F; GLOUCESTER Cardinal, I *Theobald subst.*

---

36 blessed...peacemakers from Matt. 5.9
(Tilley P155).

37–8 Compare Matt. 10.34: 'I came not to
send peace, but the sword.' The sentence plays
on the phrase 'make war against'.

40 Q1 adds some lines in which Gloucester
taunts Winchester with bastardy (see Appendix
2, p. 230). Cairncross argues (p. xxvii) that they
might have been censored from the MS after performance, and Oxford includes them on the
grounds that they contain historical material
unlikely to be known to a reporter. However,
Gloucester had made the same charge against
Winchester at *1H6* 3.1.42. As the lines also make
play with the word 'dare', they could be actor's
'gag', and I therefore exclude them.

41 Do not assemble members of your faction to
abet the quarrel.

42 answer pay for.

42 abuse wrong-doing (*OED* sv *sb* 5).

43 peep appear (*OED* sv *v*² 2).

46 your man a disrespectful designation for
the king himself.

46 put...fowl started the game.

47 two-hand sword the long two-handed
sword was obsolescent by Shakespeare's time; see
*Shakespeare's England*, II, 391–4.

48 Are ye advised? Do you understand?
(Schmidt). If, however, Theobald's emendation
of giving the phrase to Winchester is followed,
the words mean 'Are you sure?'

*49 Cairncross's emendation, that of assuming
that F's 'Cardinall' should be a speech heading, is
the simplest of those proposed (see collation).

49 am with you (1) understand (Dent WW22),
(2) will be even with you (*OED* With 22d).

[*Aside to Winchester*] Now by God's mother, priest, I'll shave
   your crown for this,
Or all my fence shall fail.
WINCHESTER [*Aside to Gloucester*] *Medice, teipsum.* –
   Protector see to't well, protect yourself.
KING HENRY The winds grow high; so do your stomachs, lords –
   How irksome is this music to my heart!                                       55
   When such strings jar, what hope of harmony?
   I pray, my lords, let me compound this strife.

*Enter* [*a* CITIZEN] *crying* 'A miracle!'

GLOUCESTER What means this noise?
   Fellow, what miracle dost thou proclaim?
CITIZEN A miracle! A miracle!                                                    60
SUFFOLK Come to the king and tell him what miracle.
CITIZEN Forsooth, a blind man at Saint Alban's shrine
   Within this half hour hath received his sight:
   A man that ne'er saw in his life before.
KING HENRY Now God be praised, that to believing souls                          65
   Gives light in darkness, comfort in despair.

*Enter the* MAYOR OF SAINT ALBANS, *and his* BRETHREN [*with music*],
   *bearing the man* [SIMPCOX] *between two in a chair;* [*his* WIFE *and*
   TOWNSPEOPLE *following*]

51] *Pope;* Now...Priest, / Ile...this, F    **51** Now...mother] F *subst.;* Faith Q1; Gods Mother Priest Q3    **52–4**]
*Theobald subst.;* Or...fayle. / Medice...selfe. / The...high, / So...Lords: F    **52** *teipsum.* – ] *Eds; teipsum,* F    **57**
SD *a* CITIZEN] *This edn; one* F    **60, 62** SHH CITIZEN] *This edn; One* F    **66** SD.1] *with music*] Q1; *not in* F    **66**
SD.2–3 *his* WIFE...*following*] *Eds; not in* F

**51 by...mother** Q1 records a milder oath,
'Faith', probably as a consequence of moves to
restrict profanity (see Chambers, I, 277–307, and
IV, 306–19).
**51 crown** his cardinal's tonsure.
**52 Or** my skill at fencing is all for nothing.
**52 Medice, teipsum** From Luke 4.23 in the
Vulgate, *Medice, cura teipsum* ('Physician, heal
thyself'; Tilley P267).
**54 stomachs** angry tempers.
**55–6** For related images see J. E. Hankins,
*Backgrounds of Shakespeare's Thought*, 1978, pp.
201–9; compare the proverb 'Discords make
harmony' (Dent D351.1).
**57 compound** settle (*OED* sv v 6).
**62ff.** The episode is a kind of parody of
Christ's gift of sight to the blind man narrated in

John 9. For Protestant discrediting of Catholic
miracles, see Thomas, pp. 87–8.
**62 Saint Alban's shrine** Alban was executed
at Verulam (later renamed St Albans), c. 304, for
protecting converts.
**66 light in darkness** Compare Ps. 112.4:
'Unto the righteous ariseth light in darkness.'
**66 SD.1 BRETHREN** fellow members of the
Mayor's guild or the town corporation (*OED*
Brother 4).
**66 SD.1 with music** This detail from Q1 is
given by Sir Thomas More's report that a *Te
Deum* was sung after the miracle (see Appendix 1,
p. 224; compare 2.1 headnote). However, this
false miracle does not bring the harmony Henry
craved above (see 55–6; Long, pp. 25–6).

WINCHESTER Here comes the townsmen on procession
  To present your highness with the man.
KING HENRY Great is his comfort in this earthly vale,
  Although by sight his sin be multiplied.      70
GLOUCESTER Stand by, my masters, bring him near the king:
  His highness' pleasure is to talk with him.
KING HENRY Good fellow, tell us here the circumstance,
  That we for thee may glorify the Lord.
  What, hast thou been long blind, and now restored?  75
SIMPCOX Born blind, and't please your grace.
WIFE Ay, indeed was he.
SUFFOLK What woman is this?
WIFE His wife, and't like your worship.
GLOUCESTER Hadst thou been his mother, thou couldst have better 80
 told.
KING HENRY Where wert thou born?
SIMPCOX At Berwick in the north, and't like your grace.
KING HENRY Poor soul, God's goodness hath been great to thee;
  Let never day nor night unhallowed pass,     85
  But still remember what the Lord hath done.
MARGARET Tell me, good fellow, cam'st thou here by chance,
  Or of devotion, to this holy shrine?
SIMPCOX God knows, of pure devotion: being called
  A hundred times and oft'ner in my sleep     90
  By good Saint Alban, who said, 'Simon, come;
  Come offer at my shrine, and I will help thee'.
WIFE Most true, forsooth; and many time and oft

---

70 by sight] *Wilson* (*conj. Lloyd*); by his sight F  83 Berwick] *Rowe*; Barwick F  84] *Capell subst.*; Poore Soule, / Gods...thee: F  87–8] *Capell subst.*; Tell...good-fellow, / Cam'st...Deuotion, / To...Shrine F  91 Simon] F *subst*; Simpcox *Theobald subst.*  92 help] F; heal *conj. Walker*

**67 on procession** obs. construction for 'in procession'.

**69 earthly vale** Vaguely biblical. Compare the *Homily against Wilful Rebellion*, p. 490: 'This wretched earth and vale of all misery'.

**70** Compare John 9.41: 'If ye were blind, ye should not have sin: but now ye say, "We see": therefore your sin remaineth.'

**70 \*by sight** The unmetrical 'his' in F's 'by his sight' was probably caught by the compositor from the adjacent incidences of the word.

**70 his...multiplied** he will be subject to more temptation.

**74 glorify the Lord** Compare Matt. 5.16: 'glorify your Father which is in heaven'.

**82 Berwick** A town on the Scottish border at the mouth of the Tweed.

**85 unhallowed** unblessed.

**86 still** always.

**91 Simon** Simpcox's first name is Saunder (see 128), so it would seem that the saint addressed him by the name from which Simpcox derives.

**92 offer** make an offering (*OED* sv 1).

Myself have heard a voice to call him so.

WINCHESTER What, art thou lame? 95

SIMPCOX Ay, God Almighty help me!

SUFFOLK How cam'st thou so?

SIMPCOX A fall off of a tree.

WIFE A plum-tree, master.

GLOUCESTER How long hast thou been blind? 100

SIMPCOX O, born so, master.

GLOUCESTER What, and wouldst climb a tree?

SIMPCOX But that in all my life, when I was a youth.

WIFE Too true, and bought his climbing very dear.

GLOUCESTER 'Mass, thou lov'dst plums well, that wouldst venture 105
so.

SIMPCOX Alas, good master, my wife desired some damsons, and
made me climb, with danger of my life.

GLOUCESTER A subtle knave, but yet it shall not serve: –
Let me see thine eyes: wink now; now open them. 110
In my opinion, yet thou seest not well.

SIMPCOX Yes, master, clear as day, I thank God and Saint Albones.

GLOUCESTER Sayst thou me so? What colour is this cloak of?

SIMPCOX Red, master, red as blood.

GLOUCESTER Why that's well said. What colour is my gown of? 115

SIMPCOX Black, forsooth, coal-black as jet.

KING HENRY Why then, thou know'st what colour jet is of?

SUFFOLK And yet I think jet did he never see.

GLOUCESTER But cloaks and gowns, before this day, a many.

WIFE Never before this day, in all his life. 120

GLOUCESTER Tell me, sirrah, what's my name?

SIMPCOX Alas, master, I know not.

GLOUCESTER What's his name?

SIMPCOX I know not.

GLOUCESTER Nor his? 125

95–107] F; *as verse Eds*    98 off of] F; off F3

95 The cardinal's exclamation suggests that Simpcox might rise from his chair here.

100ff. Gloucester's questioning turns the scene into a 'trial upon examination', a controversial procedure recently introduced in Shakespeare's day; see Introduction, p. oo, and compare Cade's 'trial' of Lord Say in 4.7.

103 **But** Only (Abbott 128).

104–7 Simpcox constructs a figure of blind ambition, driven on by a domineering wife, which may describe Gloucester as well as himself.

107 **damsons** slang for testicles (Partridge, p. 164).

110 **wink** close your eyes (*OED sv* 1).

112 **clear as day** proverbial (Tilley D56).

114 **red as blood** proverbial (Tilley B455).

116 **Black...as jet** proverbial (Tilley J49).

119 **a many** (Abbott 87).

SIMPCOX No indeed, master.

GLOUCESTER What's thine own name?

SIMPCOX Saunder Simpcox, and if it please you, master.

GLOUCESTER Then, Saunder, sit there the lying'st knave in
Christendom. If thou hadst been born blind, thou mightst as well    130
have known all our names as thus to name the several colours we
do wear. Sight may distinguish of colours, but suddenly to
nominate them all, it is impossible. – My lords, Saint Alban here
hath done a miracle; and would ye not think his cunning to be
great that could restore this cripple to his legs again?    135

SIMPCOX O master, that you could!

GLOUCESTER My masters of Saint Albans, have you not beadles in
your town, and things called whips?

MAYOR Yes, my lord, if it please your grace.

GLOUCESTER Then send for one presently.    140

MAYOR Sirrah, go fetch the beadle hither straight.

*Exit [an Attendant]*

GLOUCESTER Now fetch me a stool hither by and by. – Now, sirrah,
if you mean to save yourself from whipping, leap me over this
stool and run away.

SIMPCOX Alas, master, I am not able to stand alone: you go about to    145
torture me in vain.

*Enter a* BEADLE *with whips*

128 Saunder] F; Sander *conj. this edn;* Simon *Oxford*    129–35] *as prose* Q1; Then...there, / The...Christendome.
/ If...blinde, / Thou...Names, / As...weare. / Sight...Colours: / But...all, / It is impossible. / My...Miracle: /
And...great, / That...againe. F    134 his] Q1; it, F    137–8] *This edn;* My...Albones / Haue...Towne, / And...
Whippes? F    141 SD *an Attendant*] Capell; *not in* F    142–6] F *subst.;* Bring me...mean / To...o'er / This...
master, / I...alone. / You...vain. *Oxford*    146 SD] F; *placed after* 144 *in* Q1

**128 Saunder** The Oxford editors (following
McMillin) argue that Sander (a shortened form
of Alexander?) was the name of an actor in
Pembroke's Men, that his name got into Q1, and
that F was set up here from an annotated copy of
Q. However, the name may equally derive from
the association of 'sand' with blindness (compare
*MV.* 2.2.36).

**129 sit there** there you are (Hart).

**129–35, 145–6, 157–8** F sets these lines as
verse, but almost certainly to eke out imperfectly
cast-off copy. Editors who follow suit are compelled to make a lot of consequent emendations
to establish metrical regularity.

**130–2 If...wear** Compare the proverb 'A
blind man can judge no colours' (Tilley M80).

**132 suddenly** without premeditation (Wilson).

**133 nominate** name (*OED* sv 1).

**134 cunning** skill.

**137 beadles** inferior parish officers appointed
to keep order and act as parish constables.

**138 things called whips** This became a catch-
phrase (Dent W306.1) and occurs in Jonson's
addition to *The Spanish Tragedy* 3.9. It may derive
ultimately from the old *Hamlet*. See Kyd, *The
Spanish Tragedy*, ed. Philip Edwards, 1959, p. 126
n. 42. This whipping was added by Shakespeare to
the account of the false miracle in Grafton and
Foxe, perhaps to indicate that the charges that
Gloucester, as his accusers allege, devised 'strange
tortures for offenders' (3.1.122).

**140 presently** immediately.

**142 by and by** immediately (*OED* By and by 3).

**143–4 leap...stool** an indoor sport; see
Jonson, *Epicoene* 5.1.44–5 (Jonson, x, 42).

**143 me** for me (Abbott 220).

GLOUCESTER Well, sir, we must have you find your legs. – Sirrah
beadle, whip him till he leap over that same stool.

BEADLE I will, my lord. – Come on, sirrah, off with your doublet
quickly.                                                                                     150

SIMPCOX Alas, master, what shall I do? I am not able to stand.

*After the Beadle hath hit him once, he leaps over the stool and runs away;*
*and they follow and cry, 'A Miracle!'*

KING HENRY O God, seest thou this, and bearest so long?

MARGARET It made me laugh to see the villain run.

GLOUCESTER [*To the Beadle*] Follow the knave, and take this drab
away.                                                                                        155

WIFE Alas, sir, we did it for pure need.

GLOUCESTER [*To the Mayor*] Let them be whipped through every
market-town till they come to Berwick, from whence they came.

[*Exeunt Wife, Beadle, Mayor, etc.*]

WINCHESTER Duke Humphrey has done a miracle today.

SUFFOLK True: made the lame to leap and fly away.                   160

GLOUCESTER But you have done more miracles than I:
You made in a day, my lord, whole towns to fly.

*Enter* BUCKINGHAM

KING HENRY What tidings with our cousin Buckingham?

BUCKINGHAM Such as my heart doth tremble to unfold:
A sort of naughty persons, lewdly bent,                                    165
Under the countenance and confederacy
Of Lady Eleanor, the Protector's wife,
The ringleader and head of all this rout,
Have practised dangerously against your state,
Dealing with witches and with conjurers,                                 170
Whom we have apprehended in the fact,

---

154, 157 SDD] *Oxford; not in* F    157–8] *Pope;* Let…Towne, / Till…came. F    157 them] *Eds;* the F    158 SD]
*Capell; Exit* F

---

147 **sir** sarcastic, given that inferiors are
generally addressed as 'sirrah'.

154 **drab** slut.

156 **pure need** utter poverty.

157–8 In 1576 an act was passed which
stipulated that 'sturdy beggars' should be whipped
and sent back to their native place.

160 **lame to leap** Compare Isa. 35.6: 'Then
should the lame man leap as an hart.'

162 **fly** referring to Suffolk's bargaining over
Margaret's dowry whereby French towns were
surrendered to the French – see 1.1.49ff. and
4.1.86ff. The king pointedly ignores Gloucester's
jibe (compare 1.1.54n.).

165–6 A crew of wicked people intent on evil
with the moral support and complicity.

169 **practised** conspired (*OED* Practise 9).

171 **in the fact** in the very act (*OED* Fact 2).

Raising up wicked spirits from under ground,
Demanding of King Henry's life and death,
And other of your highness' Privy Council,
As more at large your grace shall understand.　　　175

WINCHESTER And so, my Lord Protector, by this means
Your lady is forthcoming yet at London.
This news, I think, hath turned your weapon's edge;
'Tis like, my lord, you will not keep your hour.

GLOUCESTER Ambitious churchman, leave to afflict my heart:　　180
Sorrow and grief have vanquished all my powers;
And, vanquished as I am, I yield to thee,
Or to the meanest groom.

KING HENRY O God, what mischiefs work the wicked ones,
Heaping confusion on their own heads thereby.　　　185

MARGARET Gloucester, see here the tainture of thy nest;
And look thyself be faultless, thou wert best.

GLOUCESTER Madam, for myself, to heaven I do appeal,
How I have loved my king and commonweal;
And for my wife, I know not how it stands.　　　190
Sorry I am to hear what I have heard:
Noble she is; but if she have forgot
Honour and virtue and conversed with such
As, like to pitch, defile nobility,
I banish her my bed and company　　　195
And give her as a prey to law and shame
That hath dishonoured Gloucester's honest name.

KING HENRY Well, for this night we will repose us here;

---

181 vanquished] F; languished *conj. Walker;* banished *conj. Vaughan*

---

**173 Demanding of** Making enquiries about (*OED* Demand *v* 12).

**174** Following this line Q1 prints a version, read out by the king, of the prophecies that were seized in the last scene (see 1.4.58–67 n.).

**175 at large** in full.

**176–9** Rowe suggested an aside for this speech.

**177–8 forthcoming...weapon's** There is possibly a sexual pun embedded here.

**177 forthcoming** arrested awaiting her court appearance (compare 1.4.52 n.).

**178 turned** bent back (*OED* Turn *v* 9b).

**179 hour** set for the duel – see 40ff. above.

**180 leave** cease.

**181 vanquished** The compositor's eye may

well have caught this word from the next line (see collation).

**183 meanest** lowest.

**184–5** Compare Ps. 7.16 'His mischief shall return upon his own head, and his cruelty shall fall upon his own pate.'

**186 tainture** defilement (*OED* sv 2); compare the proverb 'It is a foul bird that defiles his own nest' (Tilley B377).

**193 conversed** consorted (*OED* Converse *v* 2).

**194 like...nobility** Compare Ecclus. 13.1: 'He that toucheth pitch, shall be defiled with it' and Tilley P358.

**196 prey** recalls the falconry imagery of 1ff.

Tomorrow toward London, back again,
To look into this business thoroughly                          200
And call these foul offenders to their answers;
And poise the cause in Justice' equal scales,
Whose beam stands sure, whose rightful cause prevails.

*Flourish. Exeunt*


[2.2] *Enter* YORK, SALISBURY, *and* WARWICK


YORK  Now, my good lords of Salisbury and Warwick,
     Our simple supper ended, give me leave
     In this close walk to satisfy myself
     In craving your opinion of my title,
     Which is infallible, to England's crown.                  5
SALISBURY  My lord, I long to hear it at full.
WARWICK  Sweet York, begin: and if thy claim be good,
     The Nevilles are thy subjects to command.
YORK  Then thus:
     Edward the Third, my lords, had seven sons:               10
     The first, Edward the Black Prince, Prince of Wales;
     The second, William of Hatfield; and the third,
     Lionel, Duke of Clarence; next to whom
     Was John of Gaunt, the Duke of Lancaster;
     The fifth was Edmund Langley, Duke of York;               15
     The sixth was Thomas of Woodstock, Duke of Gloucester;

---

202 cause] F; case *conj. Vaughan*     **Act 2, Scene 2**     2.2] *Capell; not in* F     6 it] F; it out *Oxford (conj. McKerrow)*
16 sixth was] F, Q1 *subst.;* sixth F3

---

**201 answers** defence against charges (*OED* Answer *sb* 1).

**202 poise the cause** weigh the case.

**203 beam stands sure** bar (from which the pans are hung) lies level.

**Act 2, Scene 2**

*2.2 The scene derives from the chroniclers' account of how, in 1448, York, 'perceiving the king to be no ruler but the whole burden of the realm to rest in direction of the queen and the Duke of Suffolk, began secretly to allure his friends of the nobility, and privily declared unto them his title and right to the crown' (Holinshed, p. 212; Hall, p. 210). York's genealogy probably derives from Holinshed's account, taken from Stow's *Annals* (pp. 679–80), of Articles between King Henry and the Duke of York (Holinshed, pp. 265–6; see Appendixes 1 and 2, pp. 225–6 and 234–5), although certain phrases (see notes to 20, 38, 42) could have come from a reading of Hall (pp. 2 and 23) who, at the beginning of his account of the reign of Henry IV, prints the equivalent text.

**2 supper** to which they were invited in 1.4.77–8.

**3 close** secluded, private.

**4–5** 'I know not well whether he means the "opinion" or the "title" is "infallible"' (Johnson).

William of Windsor was the seventh and last.
Edward the Black Prince died before his father
And left behind him Richard, his only son,
Who, after Edward the Third's death, reigned as king,                    20
Till Henry Bullingbrook, Duke of Lancaster,
The eldest son and heir of John of Gaunt,
Crowned by the name of Henry the Fourth,
Seized on the realm, deposed the rightful king,
Sent his poor queen to France from whence she came,                      25
And him to Pomfret where, as all you know,
Harmless Richard was murdered traitorously.

WARWICK  Father, the Duke of York hath told the truth:
Thus got the house of Lancaster the crown.

YORK  Which now they hold by force and not by right:                     30
For Richard, the first son's heir, being dead,
The issue of the next son should have reigned.

SALISBURY  But William of Hatfield died without an heir.

YORK  The third son, Duke of Clarence, from whose line
I claim the crown, had issue Philippe, a daughter,                       35
Who married Edmund Mortimer, Earl of March;
Edmund had issue, Roger, Earl of March;
Roger had issue, Edmund, Anne, and Eleanor.

SALISBURY  This Edmund, in the reign of Bullingbrook,
As I have read, laid claim unto the crown,                               40
And, but for Owen Glendower, had been king,

26 all] F; both Q1; well *Oxford*   28 Duke of York] *Cairncross*; Duke F   34–5] *Pope*; The. . .Clarence, / From. . .
Crowne, / Had. . .Daughter, F   35 Philippe] *Hanmer*; Phillip F

20 **after. . .death** Hall (p.2) reads 'after the death of King Edward the III'.

**21–4** These lines contain what was common knowledge. York noted the facts in an oration to Parliament in 1460 (Holinshed, p. 263; Hall, p. 246), but there is no need to conjecture that Shakespeare had recourse to that report here.

**26 Pomfret** Pontefract in Yorkshire.

**26 all** For a similar use of the word referring to only two people see *2H4* 3.1.35.

**27 Harmless** Innocent.

**28 *Duke of York** I accept the emendation of Cairncross for F's 'Duke' on the grounds that it was probably caused by eyeskip from '−ke', to '-ke', that it regularises the metre, and that it balances 'Lancaster' in the next line.

**38 Edmund. . .Eleanor** Holinshed reads 'Edmund, Earl of March, Roger Mortimer, Anne, Eleanor', where Hall is a little closer to

Shakespeare: 'Edmund Mortimer, Anne and Eleanor' (p. 2).

**38 Edmund** Fifth Earl of March, 1391–1425; Richard II declared him heir presumptive in 1398.

**38–42** Salisbury, like the chroniclers (Holinshed, p. 263; Hall, p. 246), confuses the fifth Earl of March with his uncle, Sir Edmund Mortimer (1374–1409). This Mortimer was captured by Glendower, but after Bullingbrook had made no effort to ransom him, joined the side of Glendower whose daughter he married (see Thomson, pp. 207–10). The 'Mortimer' of *1H6* 2.5 is the fifth Earl, depicted as dying as a prisoner in the Tower of London, the fate in fact of his cousin, Sir John Mortimer. See Gillian West, 'Shakespeare's Edmund Mortimer', *NQ* 223 (1988), 463–5.

Who kept him in captivity till he died.
But to the rest.
YORK                          His eldest sister, Anne,
My mother, being heir unto the crown,
Married Richard, Earl of Cambridge, who was son              45
To Edmund Langley, Edward the Third's fifth son.
By her I claim the kingdom: she was heir
To Roger, Earl of March, who was the son
Of Edmund Mortimer, who married Philippe,
Sole daughter unto Lionel, Duke of Clarence.                50
So, if the issue of the elder son
Succeed before the younger, I am king.
WARWICK What plain proceedings is more plain than this?
Henry doth claim the crown from John of Gaunt,
The fourth son; York claims it from the third.             55
Till Lionel's issue fails, his should not reign;
It fails not yet, but flourishes in thee
And in thy sons, fair slips of such a stock.
Then, father Salisbury, kneel we together,
And in this private plot be we the first                   60
That shall salute our rightful sovereign
With honour of his birthright to the crown.
BOTH Long live our sovereign Richard, England's king!
YORK We thank you, lords; but I am not your king
Till I be crowned and that my sword be stained             65
With heart-blood of the house of Lancaster;
And that's not suddenly to be performed

---

**45–6**] *Theobald²; Marryed...Cambridge, / Who was to...Langley / Edward...fift Sonnes Sonne;* F   **47–50**]
*Theobald subst.; By...Kingdome: / She...March, / Who...Mortimer, / Who...Daughter / Vnto...Clarence.* F
**53 proceedings**] F; *proceeding* F2   **55 son;**] *This edn; son,* F   **56 his**] F; *John's Oxford*   **64–5**] *Pope subst.; We...*
*Lords: / But...Crown'd, / And...stayn'd* F

---

**42 Who** Glendower.
**42 in...died** Boswell-Stone (p.258) points
out that this phrase is used by Hall (p. 23) of Lord
Grey of Ruthin, who was, with Mortimer, a
prisoner of Glendower. However, this does not
seem evidence sufficient to prove that Shakespeare was consulting Hall rather than Holinshed.
**\*45–6** F's text is, anomalously, historically
incoherent and unmetrical here (see collation), so
emendation is necessary. It is impossible to guess
when the errors were introduced.
**53 proceedings** 'The word refers to the...
pedigree not to the narration' (Hart). Warwick's
tone here is equivocal, perhaps jocular.

**56 his** Gaunt's. It is tempting to substitute
'John's' or 'Gaunt's' for 'his'.
**57–60 flourishes...slips...stock...plot** an
extended metaphor deriving from the notion of
the family tree.
**58 slips** cuttings.
**60 plot** ground.
**62 birthright** 'specifically used of the special
rights of the first-born' (*OED*).
**64 We** Richard immediately adopts the royal
'we'; compare *R2* 2.3.162, 4.1.319, etc.
**65 that** till.
**67 suddenly** immediately.

But with advice and silent secrecy.
Do you as I do in these dangerous days:
Wink at the Duke of Suffolk's insolence,                    70
At Beaufort's pride, at Somerset's ambition,
At Buckingham, and all the crew of them,
Till they have snared the shepherd of the flock,
That virtuous prince, the good Duke Humphrey:
'Tis that they seek; and they, in seeking that,            75
Shall find their deaths, if York can prophesy.

SALISBURY My lord, break we off; we know your mind at full.

WARWICK My heart assures me that the Earl of Warwick
Shall one day make the Duke of York a king.

YORK And, Neville, this I do assure myself:                  80
Richard shall live to make the Earl of Warwick
The greatest man in England but the king.

*Exeunt*

**[2.3]** *Sound trumpets. Enter the* KING *and State:* [MARGARET,
GLOUCESTER, SUFFOLK, BUCKINGHAM, WINCHESTER. *Enter
guarded* ELEANOR, MARGERY JOURDAIN, SOUTHWELL, HUME *and*
BOLINGBROKE, *and then enter to them* YORK, SALISBURY, *and*
WARWICK]

KING HENRY Stand forth, Dame Eleanor Cobham, Gloucester's
wife:
In sight of God, and us, your guilt is great:
Receive the sentence of the law for sins
Such as by God's book are adjudged to death. –

---

77] *as prose in* F    77 break we] F; break *Capell*    **Act 2, Scene 3**    2.3] *Capell; not in* F    0 SD.1–5 *State:*
MARGARET...WARWICK] *This edn (following* Q1); *State, with Guard, to banish the Duchess* F    1] *Rome*; Stand...
*Cobham, / Gloster's* Wife: F    3 sins] *Theobald; sinne* F

**68 advice** deliberation (*OED* sv 4).

**70 Wink** Close your eyes to.

**71** For similar sentiments, compare 1.1.177.

**73 the...flock** Compare Hall on Henry V:
'This captain was a shepherd whom his flock
loved and lovingly obeyed' (p.112).

**Act 2, Scene 3**
\*2.3 The scene combines two 'trials', the
conclusion of that of Dame Eleanor and the trial
by combat between Horner and his man Peter –
see headnotes to 1.4 and 1.3.

**0 SD.1 State** 'Persons of state' or rank who
participated in the government of the realm (*OED*
sv *sb* 22).

**0 SD.2–5 BUCKINGHAM, WINCHESTER...**
WARWICK None of these characters speaks or is
spoken to in this scene, but their presence is
indicated in both F and Q1.

**3–4 \*sins...death** The most quoted text was
Exod. 22.18: 'Thou shalt not suffer a witch to
live'; compare Deut. 18.10–12, Lev. 20.6.

**4 adjudged to** deemed to be demanding of
(*OED* Adjudged 2). 'Adjudged' could also be

You four, from hence to prison back again;                                   5
From thence unto the place of execution:
The witch in Smithfield shall be burnt to ashes,
And you three shall be strangled on the gallows. –
You, madam, for you are more nobly born,
Despoilèd of your honour in your life,                                       10
Shall, after three days' open penance done,
Live in your country here in banishment
With Sir John Stanley in the Isle of Man.

ELEANOR  Welcome is banishment, welcome were my death.

GLOUCESTER  Eleanor, the law, thou see'st, hath judged thee:               15
I cannot justify whom the law condemns.

> [*Exeunt Eleanor and other prisoners, guarded*]

Mine eyes are full of tears, my heart of grief.
Ah, Humphrey, this dishonour in thine age
Will bring thy head with sorrow to the ground. –
I beseech your majesty, give me leave to go;                                20
Sorrow would solace and mine age would ease.

KING HENRY  Stay, Humphrey, Duke of Gloucester. Ere thou go,
Give up thy staff: Henry will to himself
Protector be; and God shall be my hope,
My stay, my guide, and lantern to my feet.                                  25

---

16 SD] *Theobald subst.; not in* F    19 ground] F; grave *Cairncross*    22–5] *Pope;* Stay…Gloster, / Ere…Staffe, / Henry…be, / And…guide, / And…feete: F    25 lantern] *Malone;* Lanthorne F

---

construed as meaning 'sentenced' (*OED* 3), but this would entail restoring F's 'sinne' for Theobald's emendation 'sins' in 3.

**7 Smithfield** the place of execution for heretics in London.

**8 strangled on the gallows** Shakespeare simplifies the various fates of the conspirators: Hume was pardoned, and Southwell died in the Tower before his execution (Holinshed, p. 204; Hall p. 202).

**8 strangled** hanged.

**9 for** because.

**12 here** during your lifetime (*OED* sv 4).

**13 Sir John Stanley** So in Holinshed (p. 203) and Hall (p. 202), although Eleanor was in fact given into the custody of Sir Thomas Stanley, as only Fabyan and Stow (*The Annals of England*, 1592) record. See R. B. McKerrow, '*2 Henry VI* and *The Contention* – A Correction', *RES* 9 (1933), 315–16. Sir William Stanley appears in *3H6* 4.5.

**14 were** would be.

**15–16** Compare Rom. 2.12–13: 'As many as have sinned in the law shall be judged by the law…but the doers of the law shall be justified'.

**16 justify** absolve (*OED* sv 4).

**19** Compare Gen. 42.38: 'ye shall bring my gray head with sorrow unto the grave'. In view of the fact that at *Ham.* 4.5.39, Q1 and F read 'graue' and Q2 reads 'ground', Cairncross's emendation of 'ground' to 'grave' may be acceptable.

**21 would** requires.

**21 ease** rest, retirement from duty (*OED* sv *sb* 4).

**23 staff** badge of the Protector; compare 1.2.25.

**24 God…hope** Compare Ps. 71.5: 'for thou art mine hope, O Lord God'.

**25 My stay, my guide** Compare Ps. 49.9 (Sternhold and Hopkins), 'my guide and stay'.

**25 lantern…feet** Compare Ps. 119.105: 'Thy word is a lantern unto my feet'.

And go in peace, Humphrey, no less beloved
Than when thou wert Protector to thy king.

MARGARET I see no reason why a king of years
Should be to be protected like a child.
God and King Henry govern England's helm:                    30
Give up your staff, sir, and the king his realm.

GLOUCESTER My staff? Here, noble Henry, is my staff:
As willingly do I the same resign
As e'er thy father Henry made it mine;
And even as willingly at thy feet I leave it                  35
As others would ambitiously receive it.
Farewell, good king: when I am dead and gone,
May honourable peace attend thy throne.              *Exit*

MARGARET Why, now is Henry king and Margaret queen,
And Humphrey, Duke of Gloucester scarce himself,             40
That bears so shrewd a maim: two pulls at once –
His lady banished, and a limb lopped off.
[*Picks up the staff and places it in the king's hand*]
This staff of honour raught, there let it stand
Where it best fits to be, in Henry's hand.

SUFFOLK Thus droops this lofty pine, and hangs his sprays;   45
Thus Eleanor's pride dies in her youngest days.

YORK Lords, let him go. – Please it your majesty,
This is the day appointed for the combat,

---

30 helm:] *Steevens (conj. Johnson)*; Realme: F; helm! *Dyce*   34 e'er] F *subst.*; crst Q1   35 willingly] F; willing Q1
42 SD] *This edn; not in* F

26 **go in peace** Perhaps alluding to Simeon's words in Luke 2.29.
28–9 **king...child** Compare *Mirror*, p. 455: 'A king of years, still governed to be like a pupil' (320–1).
28 **of years** who is of age (*OED* Year 5b).
30 **govern** steer (*OED* sv 7).
30 ***helm** F's 'realm' probably derives from the compositor's sighting of 'realm' in the next line; compare 1.3.95.
31 **king his** king's (Abbott 217).
35 **willingly** See collation. F's reading may derive from the compositor's memory of this word two lines before.
37 **dead and gone** a catch-phrase (Dent DD9).
41 **so...maim** so grievous a wound.
41 **pulls** wrenches. Compare Marlowe, *1*

*Tamburlaine* 1.1.31–33: 'a fox...doth mean to pull my plumes' (= dishonour me). Or perhaps the word means a wrestling bout (*OED* Pull *sb* 3).
43 **raught** seized, snatched from (him) (*OED* Reach 4c).
45 **this lofty pine** Compare *Ant.* 4.12.23, although the phrase may derive from the rebus of the stock of a tree used by the Duke's father, Henry IV, and adopted from Thomas of Woodstock (G. C. Rothery, *The Heraldry of Shakespeare*, 1930, p.47).
45 **sprays** slender shoots (*OED* Spray *sb* 2), i.e. dependants.
46 **pride** prime, highest glory (*OED* sv 9).
46 **her** its (Abbott 229). (Eleanor is not a young woman.)
47 **let him go** think no more of him.

And ready are the appellant and defendant,
The armourer and his man, to enter the lists,                    50
So please your highness to behold the fight.
MARGARET Ay, good my lord; for purposely therefore
Left I the court to see this quarrel tried.
KING HENRY A God's name, see the lists and all things fit:
Here let them end it, and God defend the right!                 55
YORK I never saw a fellow worse bestead
Or more afraid to fight than is the appellant,
The servant of this armourer, my lords.

*Enter at one door* [HORNER] *the armourer and his* NEIGHBOURS,
*drinking to him so much that he is drunk; and he enters with a* DRUM
*before him, and his staff, with a sandbag fastened to it; and at the other door*
[PETER] *his man, with a* DRUM *and sandbag, and* PRENTICES *drinking*
*to him*

1 NEIGHBOUR Here, neighbour Horner, I drink to you in a cup of
sack; and fear not, neighbour, you shall do well enough.         60
2 NEIGHBOUR And here, neighbour, here's a cup of charneco.
3 NEIGHBOUR And here's a pot of good double beer, neighbour:
drink, and fear not your man.
[*Horner drinks with them*]
HORNER Let it come, i'faith, and I'll pledge you all; and a fig for
Peter.                                                           65

---

56 bestead] F; bested *Eds*    59 SH] *Pope subst.*; Neighbour F    62 And here's] F; Here's Q1    63, 68 SDD] *This edn;*
*not in* F    64 etc. SHH] *Eds;* Armorer F

**49–50** (York is mocking the mechanicals'
inability to employ the forms of knightly combat.)
**49 appellant and defendant** challenger and
defender in a trial by combat.
**50 lists** place designated for a duel (*OED* List
*sb*², 9).
**52 therefore** for that reason.
**53 quarrel** accusation (*OED* sv *sb* 1).
**56 bestead** placed, prepared (*OED* Bestead *pa.*
*pple* 5).
**58 SD HORNER** Possibly played by 'Bevis' (see
4.2.0 SD n.)
**58 SD.2 DRUM** drummer.
**58 SD.3 staff. . . sand-bag** Since this weapon
could be used both as a real weapon (as illustrated
in Hans Burgkmair, *The Triumph of Maximilian*,
ed. S. Applebaum, 1964, pp. 7 and 33) and in
mock duels (*OED* Sand-bag 2c) there is no need
to infer that the sequence that follows was

intended as a travesty of a chivalric combat
(from information supplied privately by Ronald
Knowles).
**60 sack** the generic name for Spanish and
Canary wines (*Shakespeare's England*, II, 136).
**61 charneco** a kind of port, possibly named
after a region of that name near Lisbon (*charneca*
means 'heath' in Portuguese); see Sugden, p.
111.
**62 double beer** extra strong ale, produced for
festive wassailing.
**64 Let it come** Let the pot go round – a
drinking catch-phrase; compare *2H4* 5.3.52.
**64 a fig for** (Tilley F210 – probably accompanied by an obscene gesture made by poking the
thumb between two of the closed fingers or into
the mouth.) 'An anecdote in Rabelais (trans. J. M.
Cohen, 1955, p. 544) throws some light on its
lewd implications. The story is that after putting

1 PRENTICE Here, Peter, I drink to thee, and be not afraid.

2 PRENTICE Be merry, Peter, and fear not thy master. Fight for
   credit of the prentices.
   *[Peter rejects what they offer him]*

PETER I thank you all. Drink and pray for me, I pray you, for I think I
   have taken my last draught in this world. – Here, Robin, and if I    70
   die, I give thee my apron; and, Will, thou shalt have my hammer;
   and here, Tom, take all the money that I have. – O Lord bless
   me, I pray God, for I am never able to deal with my master: he
   hath learnt so much fence already.

SALISBURY *[To Horner]* Come, leave your drinking, and fall to blows.    75
   – Sirrah, what's thy name?

PETER Peter, forsooth.

SALISBURY Peter! What more?

PETER Thump.

SALISBURY Thump? Then see thou thump thy master well.                    80

HORNER Masters, I am come hither, as it were upon my man's
   instigation, to prove him a knave, and myself an honest man; and
   touching the Duke of York, I will take my death I never meant
   him any ill, nor the king, nor the queen; and therefore, Peter,
   have at thee with a downright blow!                                   85

YORK Dispatch! This knave's tongue begins to double. – Sound,
   trumpets, alarum to the combatants!

---

67–8 Be...prentices] F *subst.;* Here Peter, here's a pinte of Claret-wine for thee. / 3. *Pren.* And here's a quart for me,
and be merry Peter, / And feare not thy maister, fight for credit of the Prentices. Q1      75 SD] *This edn; not in* F      85
blow!] F; blowes, as Beuys of South-hampton fell vpon Askapart Q1      86 Sound,] *Collier;* Sound F

down a revolt in Milan, the Emperor Barbarossa
(*c.* 1123–90) forced all his prisoners to choose
between being hanged and undertaking to extract
and replace, by means of their teeth, a fig
specially inserted for the purpose in the vulva of a
mule. Half-way through this feat, each candidate
had to announce *Ecco lo fico,* "Behold the fig.'"
(Colman, p. 193).

**67–8** Q1 adds a part for a third prentice here
(see collation), presumably to make the sequence
symmetrical with that involving the neighbours.
But there is no way of telling whether it has any
authorial authority.

**68 credit** reputation (*OED* sv *sb* 5).

**\*68 SD** That Peter does not drink is indicated
by Q1's line, 'I thanke you all, but ile drinke no
more' (TLN 863). Differences between the two
texts' versions of the episode are set out by Arthur

Freeman, 'Notes on the text of *2 Henry VI* and the
"Upstart Crow"', *NQ* 213 (1968), 128–9.

**74 fence** fencing (*OED* sv *sb* 2).

**83 take my death** stake my life on it (*OED*
Take *v* 40b).

**85 with...blow** see collation. As Bevis was
probably one of the original players (see 4.2.0 SD),
Q may well record an 'in joke' in this piece of gag.

**85 downright** vertically downwards (*OED* sv
1).

**86 double** reiterate his cause (*OED* sv *v* 3b) or
stutter (see *OED* Doubling *pple adj* 1 (1621)).

**86–7 Sound...combatants** These words
(omitted from Q) may have stood in the compositor's MS as a stage direction (see Freeman, 68 SD
n. above).

**87 alarum** the call to arms.

*[Alarums.] They fight, and Peter strikes Horner down [by hitting him on the head]*

HORNER  Hold, Peter, hold! I confess, I confess treason.        *[Dies]*

YORK  Take away his weapon. – Fellow, thank God, and the good
    wine in thy master's way.                                          90

PETER  *[He kneels down]*  O God, have I overcome enemies in this
    presence? O Peter, thou hast prevailed in right!

KING HENRY  Go, take hence that traitor from our sight,
    For by his death we do perceive his guilt;
    And God in justice hath revealed to us                         95
    The truth and innocence of this poor fellow,
    Which he had thought to have murdered wrongfully.
    Come, fellow, follow us for thy reward.

                          *Sound a flourish. Exeunt*

**[2.4]** *Enter* DUKE HUMPHREY [OF GLOUCESTER] *and his* MEN *in mourning cloaks*

GLOUCESTER  Thus sometimes hath the brightest day a cloud;
    And after summer evermore succeeds
    Barren winter with his wrathful nipping cold:
    So cares and joys abound, as seasons fleet. –
    Sirs, what's o'clock?

SERVANT                Ten, my lord.                     5

GLOUCESTER  Ten is the hour that was appointed me
    To watch the coming of my punished duchess;
    Uneath may she endure the flinty streets,

---

87 SD.1 *Alaums*] Q1; *not in* F    87 SD.1–2 *by...head*] This edn (*following* Q1); *not in* F    88 SD] Q1; *not in* F    90
way] F; *wame* Oxford    91 SD] Q1; *not in* F    91 enemies] F; *enemy* F2    **Act 2, Scene 4**    2.4] Capell; *not in* F    4
abound] F; *rebound conj.* Oxford    5 Ten] F *subst.*; *Almost ten* Q1

*88 SD The chroniclers report that after his
defeat Horner was taken off to execution, but
Q1's direction that he dies on stage (see collation)
is confirmed by 94.
  **90 in...way** which prevented your master
from fighting properly. Oxford's emendation
'wame' (= belly) does not seem likely.
  **91–2 in this presence** before the king (*OED*
Presence 2b).
  **97 Which** Whom.

**Act 2, Scene 4**
*2.4   See headnotes to 1.4 and 2.3. Holinshed

(p. 203), quoting the *Polychronicon*, notes that the
duchess 'was enjoined to go through Cheapside
with a taper in her hand'; the detail is also in Foxe
and *Mirror* (p. 436 line 139), but not in Hall. The
parliament at Bury (see 71 below) did not in fact
meet until 1447, six years after Eleanor's disgrace
(Holinshed, p. 211; Hall, p. 209).
  **0 SD.2 mourning cloaks** hooded cloaks, as
worn at funerals; see *1H6* 1.1.0 SD. 1n.
  **1 sometimes...cloud** Compare the proverb,
'No day so clear but has dark clouds' (Dent D92).
  **4 fleet** slip away.
  **8 Uneath** With difficulty.

> To tread them with her tender-feeling feet.
> Sweet Nell, ill can thy noble mind abrook                    10
> The abject people gazing on thy face,
> With envious looks laughing at thy shame,
> That erst did follow thy proud chariot-wheels
> When thou didst ride in triumph through the streets.
> But soft, I think she comes; and I'll prepare              15
> My tear-stained eyes to see her miseries.

*Enter the* DUCHESS [ELEANOR *barefoot*] *in a white sheet,* [*and verses written on her back and pinned on,*] *and a taper burning in her hand, with* [SIR JOHN STANLEY,] *the* SHERIFF, *and* OFFICERS [*with bills and halberds*]

SERVANT  So please your grace, we'll take her from the sheriff.
GLOUCESTER  No, stir not for your lives: let her pass by.
ELEANOR  Come you, my lord, to see my open shame?
> Now thou dost penance too. Look how they gaze!            20
> See how the giddy multitude do point,
> And nod their heads, and throw their eyes on thee.
> Ah, Gloucester, hide thee from their hateful looks
> And, in thy closet pent up, rue my shame,
> And ban thine enemies, both mine and thine.              25
GLOUCESTER  Be patient, gentle Nell, forget this grief.
ELEANOR  Ah, Gloucester, teach me to forget myself:
> For whilst I think I am thy married wife

---

12 looks] F; looks still F2   16 SD.1–4 ELEANOR *barefoot and...on* SIR...STANLEY *with...halberts*] Q1; *not in* F
16 SD.3 SHERIFF] F; the Sheriffes of London Q1

10 **abrook** brook, endure.
11 **abject** lowly (*OED* sv 2).
12 **envious** spiteful.
13 **erst** formerly.
13–14 Compare Marlowe, *2 Tamburlaine* 2532–4: 'And as thou rid'st in triumph through the streets, / The pavement underneath thy chariot wheels / With Turkey carpets shall be coverèd.'
15 **soft** stay, wait.
16 SD A form of public penance where the malefactor wore a white sheet and went bareheaded and barefooted holding a white rod through the market place was imposed still in Shakespeare's time: see E. R. C. Brinkford, *Shakespeare and the Bawdy Court of Stratford*, 1972, p. 15; Thomas, p. 312.
16 SD.2 **taper** see headnote above.

16 SD.3 **bills** long-handed weapons 'having at one end a blade or axe-shaped head' (Onions).
16 SD.4 **halberds** weapons 'consisting of a sharp-edged blade ending in a point and a spearhead mounted on a handle five to seven feet long' (Onions).
19 **open shame** public disgrace; the phrase occurs in *Mirror*, p. 436 line 133.
20 **they** Presumably the officers and servant, unless we postulate that commoners – the 'abject people' of 11 – entered with the procession.
23 **hateful** full of hate (*OED* sv 1).
24 **closet** study, private chamber.
24 **rue** pity.
25 **ban** curse.
27 **forget myself** lose remembrance of my station (Dent FF9).

And thou a prince, Protector of this land,
Methinks I should not thus be led along,                          30
Mailed up in shame, with papers on my back,
And followed with a rabble that rejoice
To see my tears and hear my deep-fet groans.
The ruthless flint doth cut my tender feet,
And when I start, the envious people laugh,                        35
And bid me be advisèd how I tread.
Ah, Humphrey, can I bear this shameful yoke?
Trowest thou, that e'er I'll look upon the world
Or count them happy that enjoys the sun?
No: dark shall be my light and night my day;                      40
To think upon my pomp shall be my hell.
Sometime I'll say I am Duke Humphrey's wife,
And he a prince and ruler of the land:
Yet so he ruled and such a prince he was
As he stood by whilst I, his forlorn duchess,                     45
Was made a wonder and a pointing-stock
To every idle rascal follower.
But be thou mild and blush not at my shame,
Nor stir at nothing till the axe of death
Hang over thee, as sure it shortly will.                          50
For Suffolk, he that can do all in all
With her that hateth thee and hates us all,
And York, and impious Beaufort, that false priest,
Have all limed bushes to betray thy wings,
And, fly thou how thou canst, they'll tangle thee.                55
But fear not thou until thy foot be snared,
Nor never seek prevention of thy foes.
GLOUCESTER Ah, Nell, forbear; thou aimest all awry:
    I must offend before I be attainted:

31 **Mailed up** Enveloped, a term used also in falconry. (*OED* Mail *v*³ 1).
31 **papers...back** describing her offences – see 16SD.1–2.
33 **deep-fet** fetched from deep inside me.
35 **start** flinch with pain.
35 **envious** malicious, spiteful (*OED* sv 2).
36 **be advisèd** consider (*OED* Advised 1).
39 **enjoys** For the termination see Abbott 247.
45 **As** That (Abbott 109).
45 **forlorn** abandoned, desolate (*OED* sv 4).
46 **pointing-stock** object of derision.

47 **rascal** low-born (*OED* sv *adj.* 2).
49 **nothing** anything (Abbott 406).
52 **her** Margaret.
54 **limed** smeared with bird-lime (see 1.3.83 n.).
55 **fly...canst** no matter how strongly you fly.
56–7 Eleanor is being sarcastic.
57 **seek...prevention** try to anticipate the actions.
58 **aimest** conjecture (*OED* Aim *v* 3).
59 **attainted** subjected to attainder = condemned for treason (see Williams, pp. 378–80).

And had I twenty times so many foes,                                60
And each of them had twenty times their power,
All these could not procure me any scathe
So long as I am loyal, true, and crimeless.
Wouldst have me rescue thee from this reproach,
Why yet thy scandal were not wiped away,                            65
But I in danger for the breach of law.
Thy greatest help is quiet, gentle Nell:
I pray thee sort thy heart to patience;
These few days' wonder will be quickly worn.

*Enter a* HERALD

HERALD  I summon your grace to his majesty's parliament,            70
    Holden at Bury, the first of this next month.
GLOUCESTER  And my consent ne'er asked herein before?
    This is close dealing. Well, I will be there.

                                                      *[Exit Herald]*

    My Nell, I take my leave: and, Master Sheriff,
    Let not her penance exceed the king's commission.               75
SHERIFF  And't please your grace, here my commission stays;
    And Sir John Stanley is appointed now
    To take her with him to the Isle of Man.
GLOUCESTER  Must you, Sir John, protect my lady here?
STANLEY  So am I given in charge, may't please your grace.          80
GLOUCESTER  Entreat her not the worse, in that I pray
    You use her well: the world may laugh again,
    And I may live to do you kindness, if you do it her.
    And so, Sir John, farewell.
              *[Gloucester turns to go]*

---

**64** reproach,] *This edn;* reproach? F     **73** SD] Q1; *not in* F     **79** here] F; there *conj. Walker*     **83–4]** *Pope subst.;*
And...her. / And...farewell. F     **84** SD] *This edn; not in* F

**62 scathe** harm.
**64 Wouldst** Even if you would.
**65 were not** would not be.
**67** 'The poet has not endeavoured to raise much compassion for the duchess, who indeed suffers but what she had deserved' (Johnson).
**68 sort** fit, adapt (*OED* sv *v* 1b).
**69 These...wonder** Compare the proverb 'A wonder lasts but nine days' (Tilley W728).
**69 worn** worn out, i.e. forgotten.
**71 Holden** To be held.
**71 Bury** Bury St Edmunds in Suffolk.

**73 close dealing** underhand plotting.
**75 the king's commission** what is contained in the royal warrant.
**79 protect** act as protector or guardian of; Gloucester is ruefully thinking of his own former office.
**81 Entreat** Treat (*OED* sv 1).
**81 in that** because.
**82 the...again** proverbial (but not in Tilley), meaning 'the world may look again favourably upon me' (Johnson).

ELEANOR What, gone, my lord, and bid me not farewell?                    85
GLOUCESTER Witness my tears, I cannot stay to speak.

*Exeunt Gloucester [and his men]*

ELEANOR Art thou gone too? All comfort go with thee,
　　　　　For none abides with me: my joy is death –
　　　　　Death, at whose name I oft have been afeared
　　　　　Because I wished this world's eternity. –                    90
　　　　　Stanley, I prithee go, and take me hence:
　　　　　I care not whither, for I beg no favour;
　　　　　Only convey me where thou art commanded.
STANLEY Why, madam, that is to the Isle of Man,
　　　　　There to be used according to your state.                    95
ELEANOR That's bad enough, for I am but reproach:
　　　　　And shall I then be used reproachfully?
STANLEY Like to a duchess and Duke Humphrey's lady:
　　　　　According to that state you shall be used.
ELEANOR Sheriff, farewell, and, better than I, fare,                    100
　　　　　Although thou hast been conduct of my shame.
SHERIFF It is my office, and, madam, pardon me.
ELEANOR Ay, ay, farewell: thy office is discharged. –
　　　　　Come, Stanley, shall we go?
STANLEY Madam, your penance done, throw off this sheet                    105
　　　　　And go we to attire you for our journey.
ELEANOR My shame will not be shifted with my sheet:
　　　　　No, it will hang upon my richest robes
　　　　　And show itself, attire me how I can.
　　　　　Go, lead the way: I long to see my prison.          *Exeunt*  110

---

86 SD] Q1 *subst.; Exit Gloster* F    87 too] F2; *to* F    105] *Pope;* Madame...done, / Throw...Sheet, F

87 **too** alas (*OED* sv 2c).
95 **state** (1) rank, (2) condition.
95, 97, 99 **used** Possibly with a sinister meaning. Stow records that Stanley's 'pride, false covetise, and lechery were cause of her confusion' (Boswell-Stone, p. 262).

96 **but reproach** in complete disgrace.
101 **conduct** guide, conductor (*OED* sv *sb* 3).
103 **is discharged** has been performed.
107 **shifted** altered, removed (with a pun on 'shifted' = changed like an undergarment or smock).

[3.1] *Sound a sennet. Enter* [*two* HERALDS *before, then the* DUKE OF
BUCKINGHAM *and the* DUKE OF SUFFOLK, *and then the* DUKE OF
YORK *and the* CARDINAL OF WINCHESTER, *and then the* KING *and*
QUEEN, *and then the* EARL OF SALISBURY *and the* EARL OF WARWICK,
*with* ATTENDANTS] *to the Parliament*

KING HENRY I muse my Lord of Gloucester is not come:
    'Tis not his wont to be the hindmost man,
    Whate'er occasion keeps him from us now.
MARGARET Can you not see or will ye not observe
    The strangeness of his altered countenance?       5
    With what a majesty he bears himself,
    How insolent of late he is become,
    How proud, how peremptory, and unlike himself?
    We know the time since he was mild and affable,
    And if we did but glance a far-off look,       10
    Immediately he was upon his knee,
    That all the court admired him for submission.
    But meet him now, and be it in the morn,
    When everyone will give the time of day,
    He knits his brow and shows an angry eye       15
    And passeth by with stiff unbowèd knee,
    Disdaining duty that to us belongs.
    Small curs are not regarded when they grin,

---

Act 3, Scene 1   3.1] *Pope; not in* F   0 SD.1–5 *two*...WARWICK] Q1; *King, Queene, Cardinall, Suffolke, Yorke,
Buckingham, Salisbury, and Warwicke,* F   0 SD.5] *with* ATTENDANTS] *Eds; not in* F   8 himself?] *Johnson;* himselfe. F

---

**Act 3, Scene 1**
*3.1 The plots laid by the queen, Suffolk,
Buckingham, Winchester, and York against
Gloucester before and during the parliament at
Bury in 1447–8 are found in Holinshed, pp.
210–11 (Hall, pp. 208–9) – see Appendix 1, p.
223. The loss of territories in France, reported at
84–5 below, took place two years later and was
due, according to the chroniclers, to the cowar-
dice of Somerset and not the corruption of
Gloucester (Holinshed, p. 217; Hall, pp. 215–
16). York's trumped-up charge that the latter had
taken bribes from the King of France (104–6)
resembles the articles brought by the commons
against Suffolk in 1450 (Holinshed p. 219; Hall,
p. 218). The rebellion in Ireland took place in
1448, and the chroniclers report the despatching
of York to quell it (Holinshed, p. 215; Hall, p.

213). Details of York's subornation of Cade
derive from both Hall (pp. 219–20 – see 349–54
n.) and Holinshed (p. 220 – see 360 n.).
  1 **muse** am astonished (*OED* sv v 3).
  5 **strangeness** aloofness (*OED* sv 2). The
queen does not attempt to explain the change in
Humphrey's demeanour: it may have been
caused by the betrayal of his wife or by his loss of
office.
  7 **insolent** disdainful (*OED* sv 1).
  9 **since** when (Abbott 132).
  10 **glance** cast.
  10 **far-off** indistinct (Hart), ambiguous.
  12 **That** So that.
  12 **admired** wondered at (*OED* sv 1).
  14 **give...day** exchange greetings.
  17 **duty** the respect (*OED* sv 1).
  18 **grin** bare their teeth (*OED* sv v 1).

But great men tremble when the lion roars:
And Humphrey is no little man in England.                                   20
First note that he is near you in descent,
And, should you fall, he is the next will mount.
Me seemeth then it is no policy,
Respecting what a rancorous mind he bears
And his advantage following your decease,                                   25
That he should come about your royal person
Or be admitted to your highness' council.
By flattery hath he won the commons' hearts,
And when he please to make commotion,
'Tis to be feared they all will follow him.                                 30
Now 'tis the spring and weeds are shallow-rooted;
Suffer them now, and they'll o'er-grow the garden
And choke the herbs for want of husbandry.
The reverent care I bear unto my lord
Made me collect these dangers in the duke.                                  35
If it be fond, call it a woman's fear;
Which fear, if better reasons can supplant,
I will subscribe, and say I wronged the duke. –
My Lord of Suffolk, Buckingham, and York,
Reprove my allegation, if you can,                                          40
Or else conclude my words effectual.

SUFFOLK Well hath your highness seen into this duke;
And, had I first been put to speak my mind,
I think I should have told your grace's tale.
The duchess, by his subornation,                                           45

**19 lion** symbolised both England and the king, whose power scarcely exceeded that of Gloucester.
**21** See 1.1.148 n.
**23 no policy** not prudent.
**24 Respecting** Considering.
**28–30** Shakespeare may be indebted to Hall here: 'his capital enemies...fearing that some ...commotion might arise, if a prince so well beloved of the people should be openly executed...determined to trap...him, ere he therof should have knowledge' (p. 209).
**29 make commotion** sir up insurrection (*OED* Commotion 4).
**31–33** Shakespeare often compares states with gardens: see, in particular, *R2* 3.4.
**32 Suffer** Tolerate.

**35 collect** gather, infer (*OED* sv *v* 5b).
**36 fond** foolish.
**37 supplant** remove, uproot (*OED* sv *v* 4, 5) – like 'gather' a metaphor that relates to the garden imagery at 31–3.
**38 subscribe** confess my error (*OED* sv 8c).
**40 Reprove** Disprove (*OED* sv 5).
**40 allegation** assertion (*OED* sv 3).
**41 effectual** to the point, pertinent (*OED* sv 6).
**42–4 highness...grace's** 'Suffolk uses "highness" and "grace" promiscuously to the Queen. "Majesty" was not the settled title till the time of King James the First' (Johnson).
**43 put** set, assigned (*OED* sv *v* 51b).
**45 subornation** procuring, instigation (*OED* sv 1).

Upon my life, began her devilish practices;
Or if he were not privy to those faults,
Yet by reputing of his high descent
As next the king he was successive heir,
And such high vaunts of his nobility,                                    50
Did instigate the bedlam brain-sick duchess
By wicked means to frame our sovereign's fall.
Smooth runs the water where the brook is deep,
And in his simple show he harbours treason.
The fox barks not when he would steal the lamb. –                       55
No, no, my sovereign: Gloucester is a man
Unsounded yet, and full of deep deceit.
WINCHESTER Did he not, contrary to form of law,
   Devise strange deaths for small offences done?
YORK And did he not, in his protectorship,                              60
   Levy great sums of money through the realm
   For soldiers' pay in France, and never sent it?
   By means whereof the towns each day revolted?
BUCKINGHAM Tut, these are petty faults to faults unknown
   Which time will bring to light in smooth Duke Humphrey.    65
KING HENRY My lords, at once: the care you have of us
   To mow down thorns that would annoy our foot
   Is worthy praise; but, shall I speak my conscience,

---

46 life,] *Pope;* life F

**46 \*Upon…life,** Suffolk's phrase is an asseveration: there is no evidence that the duchess plotted his death, and therefore editors are correct to insert the comma – see collation.
**46 practices** plots.
**48 reputing of** considering highly (*OED* Repute 5).
**50–1** Shakespeare in fact has already shown Gloucester *rebuking* his wife for her ambition (1.2.1–60).
**51 bedlam** frantic.
**52 frame** contrive (*OED* sv v 8a).
**53** proverbial: 'Water runs smoothest where it is deepest' (Tilley W123).
**54 simple show** artless appearance.
**55** Not a proverb found in Tilley. Greene has 'The fox wins the favour of the lambs by play, and then devours them' (*Works*, ed. Grosart, II, 27, cited Hart).
**57 Unsounded** Unfathomed (continuing the metaphors from 53–4).

**59 Devise** Order (*OED* sv 5).
**59 strange** cruel and illegal.
**60–3** Shakespeare may be recalling here a passage in Hall, who suggested that the loss of Normandy may have been caused by the fact that the Duke of Somerset, 'for his own peculiar profit, kept not half his number of soldiers and put their wages in his purse' (p. 216); compare 1.3.130 n.
**64 to** compared with.
**65 time…light** Compare the proverb 'Time brings the truth to light' (Tilley T324).
**65 smooth** plausible.
**66 at once** either Henry is addressing all the lords, or he means 'without more ado'.
**67 annoy** injure, hurt (*OED* sv v 4).
**68 shall…conscience** if I were to utter what I am convinced is true (*OED* Conscience 1).

Our kinsman Gloucester is as innocent
From meaning treason to our royal person                      70
As is the sucking lamb or harmless dove:
The duke is virtuous, mild, and too well given
To dream on evil or to work my downfall.

MARGARET Ah, what's more dangerous than this fond affiance?
Seems he a dove? His feathers are but borrowed,              75
For he's disposèd as the hateful raven.
Is he a lamb? His skin is surely lent him,
For he's inclined as is the ravenous wolves.
Who cannot steal a shape that means deceit?
Take heed, my lord, the welfare of us all                    80
Hangs on the cutting short that fraudful man.

*Enter* SOMERSET

SOMERSET All health unto my gracious sovereign.
KING HENRY Welcome, Lord Somerset. What news from France?
SOMERSET That all your interest in those territories
Is utterly bereft you: all is lost.                          85
KING HENRY Cold news, Lord Somerset; but God's will be done.
YORK [*Aside*] Cold news for me: for I had hope of France
As firmly as I hope for fertile England.
Thus are my blossoms blasted in the bud
And caterpillars eat my leaves away;                         90
But I will remedy this gear ere long,
Or sell my title for a glorious grave.

---

78 wolves] F; wolf *Rowe*     87 SD] *Rowe; not in* F

**69–71 as...lamb** Compare the proverb 'As innocent as a lamb' (Dent L34.1).

**71 sucking lamb** 1 Sam. 7.9.

**71 harmless dove** proverbial (Tilley D572), from Matt. 10.16: 'be ye...as innocent as doves' (Geneva); 'harmless as the...doves' (Bishops').

**72 given** disposed.

**74 fond affiance** foolish confidence (*OED* Affiance 2).

**76 he's disposèd** he has the disposition of.

**77–8** Compare the proverbial designation 'A wolf in a lamb's (sheep's) skin' (Tilley W614), from Matt. 7.15: 'Beware of false prophets, which come to you in sheep's clothing, but inwardly they are ravening wolves'.

**78 is...wolves** Rowe's emendation 'wolf' reinforces the pattern of the comparisons.

However, the original could stand on the grounds that it may be a biblical quotation (see previous note), and that a singular verb sometimes appears if it precedes a plural subject (see Abbott 335).

**79 shape** (theatrical) costume (*OED* sv *sb* 8).

**79 that** The antecedent is 'Who'.

**79 means** intends.

**81 cutting short** (1) forestalling, (2) beheading (compare the proverb 'shorten by the head', Dent SS10).

**81 fraudful** treacherous.

**87–8** Compare the almost identical words at 1.1.234–5.

**89** Compare the proverb 'To nip in the bud (blossom)' (Tilley B702).

**91 gear** matter.

*Enter* GLOUCESTER

GLOUCESTER All happiness unto my lord the king!
    Pardon, my liege, that I have stayed so long.

SUFFOLK Nay, Gloucester, know that thou art come too soon,    95
    Unless thou wert more loyal than thou art:
    I do arrest thee of high treason here.

GLOUCESTER Well, Suffolk, thou shalt not see me blush
    Nor change my countenance for this arrest:
    A heart unspotted is not easily daunted;    100
    The purest spring is not so free from mud
    As I am clear from treason to my sovereign.
    Who can accuse me? Wherein am I guilty?

YORK 'Tis thought, my lord, that you took bribes of France,
    And, being Protector, stayed the soldiers' pay;    105
    By means whereof his highness hath lost France.

GLOUCESTER Is it but thought so? What are they that think it?
    I never robbed the soldiers of their pay,
    Nor ever had one penny bribe from France.
    So help me God, as I have watched the night –    110
    Ay, night by night, in studying good for England!
    That doit that e'er I wrested from the king,
    Or any groat I hoarded to my use,
    Be brought against me at my trial day!
    No: many a pound of mine own proper store,    115
    Because I would not tax the needy commons,
    Have I dispursèd to the garrisons
    And never asked for restitution.

WINCHESTER It serves you well, my lord, to say so much.

GLOUCESTER I say no more than truth, so help me God!    120

---

98 Suffolk] F; Suffolkes Duke Q1    104] *Pope;* 'Tis...Lord, / That...France, F    107] *Pope;* Is...so? / What...it?
F    114 my trial] F; the iudgement Q1

94 **stayed** delayed.
104 **of** from (Abbott 166).
104 **France** The King of France (see head-note).
105 **Protector** Somerset in fact was appointed Regent of France at 1.3.200.
105 **stayed** held back.
107 **What** Whoever (Abbott 254).
110 **watched the night** kept awake all night (*OED* Watch *v* 1).

112 **That** May any.
112 **doit** small Dutch coin worth half a farthing.
113 **groat** coin worth four pence.
114 **trial day** Q1's reading (see collation) suggests that what may have been intended was a reference to the Day of Judgement.
115 **proper store** personal wealth (*OED* Store *sb* 5).
117 **dispursèd** disbursed, paid out.

YORK  In your protectorship you did devise
       Strange tortures for offenders, never heard of,
       That England was defamed by tyranny.
GLOUCESTER  Why 'tis well known that, whiles I was Protector,
       Pity was all the fault that was in me:                                      125
       For I should melt at an offender's tears,
       And lowly words were ransom for their fault.
       Unless it were a bloody murderer
       Or foul felonious thief that fleeced poor passengers,
       I never gave them condign punishment.                                       130
       Murder indeed, that bloody sin, I tortured
       Above the felon or what trespass else.
SUFFOLK  My lord, these faults are easy, quickly answered;
       But mightier crimes are laid unto your charge
       Whereof you cannot easily purge yourself.                                   135
       I do arrest you in his highness' name,
       And here commit you to my Lord Cardinal
       To keep until your further time of trial.
KING HENRY  My Lord of Gloucester, 'tis my special hope
       That you will clear yourself from all suspense:                            140
       My conscience tells me you are innocent.
GLOUCESTER  Ah, gracious lord, these days are dangerous:
       Virtue is choked with foul ambition
       And charity chased hence by rancour's hand;
       Foul subornation is predominant                                            145
       And equity exiled your highness' land.
       I know their complot is to have my life

137 commit you] F; commit *Capell*    140 suspense] F *subst.*; suspect *Capell*

122 **Strange** Barbarous (because foreign). Gloucester did call for whips to hasten the confession of Simpcox and his wife (see 2.1.137 ff.).

123 **was defamed by** became infamous for.

126 **should** would, was accustomed to (Abbott 326).

127 **for their fault** for the offences of those that spoke them.

129 **felonious** wicked (*OED* sv 1).

129 **passengers** wayfarers (*OED* Passenger 1). 'Only the poor travelled on foot' (Wilson).

130 **condign** well deserved, fitting.

132 More than the doers of wicked deeds or any other crime – 'felon' here is an obs. form of 'felony' (*OED* sv 4).

133 **easy** insignificant, slight (*OED* sv 15).

140 **suspense** doubt (*OED* sv 2d).

143–6 The lines bear some resemblance to the beginning of Ovid's description of the age of iron (*Metamorphoses* I, 146–8).

145 **predominant** in the ascendant (a term from astrology).

146 **equity** 'a system of law existing side by side with the common and statute law...and superseding these when they conflict with it' (*OED* sv 4).

146 **exiled** accented on the second syllable (Cercignani, p. 38).

147 **complot** conspiracy.

And, if my death might make this island happy
And prove the period of their tyranny,
I would expend it with all willingness;                        150
But mine is made the prologue to their play:
For thousands more, that yet suspect no peril,
Will not conclude their plotted tragedy.
Beaufort's red sparkling eyes blab his heart's malice,
And Suffolk's cloudy brow his stormy hate;                     155
Sharp Buckingham unburdens with his tongue
The envious load that lies upon his heart;
And dogged York, that reaches at the moon,
Whose overweening arm I have plucked back,
By false accuse doth level at my life. –                       160
And you, my sovereign lady, with the rest,
Causeless have laid disgraces on my head
And with your best endeavour have stirred up
My liefest liege to be mine enemy:
Ay, all of you have laid your heads together –                 165
Myself had notice of your conventicles –
And all to make away my guiltless life.
I shall not want false witness to condemn me
Nor store of treasons to augment my guilt;
The ancient proverb will be well effected:                     170
A staff is quickly found to beat a dog.
WINCHESTER My liege, his railing is intolerable:
If those that care to keep your royal person
From treason's secret knife and traitor's rage
Be thus upbraided, chid, and rated at,                         175
And the offender granted scope of speech,

166 notice] F; note *conj. Vaughan*    169 treasons] F; reasons *conj. Walker*

**149 period** end.
**150 expend it** pay the price of my death.
**154–5** These lines are to be echoed later: see 4.1.1–7 n.
**158 dogged** (1) currish, (2) stubborn.
**158 that...moon** compare the proverb 'He casts beyond the moon' (Tilley M1114).
**160 accuse** accusation (Abbott 451).
**160 level** aim as with a weapon (*OED* sv *v* 6d).
**162 Causeless** Adjectives were freely used as adverbs (Abbott 1).
**164 liefest** dearest.

**165 laid...together** proverbial (Tilley H280).
**166 conventicles** clandestine meetings (*OED* Conventicle 3).
**167 make away** put an end to (*OED* Make *v* 84).
**168 want** lack.
**170 effected** fulfilled (*OED* Effect *v* 2).
**170–1** Compare the proverb 'It is an easy thing to find a staff to beat a dog' (Dent T138).
**173 care** trouble themselves (*OED* sv *v* 2b).
**175 rated at** scolded.
**176 scope** license.

'Twill make them cool in zeal unto your grace.
SUFFOLK  Hath he not twit our sovereign lady here
    With ignominious words, though clerkly couched?
    As if she had subornèd some to swear                                    180
    False allegations to o'erthrow his state?
MARGARET  But I can give the loser leave to chide.
GLOUCESTER  Far truer spoke than meant: I lose indeed;
    Beshrew the winners, for they played me false!
    And well such losers may have leave to speak.                   185
BUCKINGHAM  He'll wrest the sense and hold us here all day.
    Lord Cardinal, he is your prisoner.
WINCHESTER  [*To his attendants*] Sirs, take away the duke and guard
      him sure.
GLOUCESTER  Ah, thus King Henry throws away his crutch
    Before his legs be firm to bear his body.                              190
    Thus is the shepherd beaten from thy side
    And wolves are gnarling who shall gnaw thee first.
    Ah, that my fear were false; ah, that it were!
    For, good King Henry, thy decay I fear.
                  *Exit Gloucester* [*with the cardinal's men*]
KING HENRY  My lords, what to your wisdoms seemeth best          195
    [*Rising*] Do or undo, as if ourself were here.
MARGARET  What, will your highness leave the parliament?
KING HENRY  Ay, Margaret: my heart is drowned with grief,
    Whose flood begins to flow within mine eyes;
    My body round engirt with misery:                                        200
    For what's more miserable than discontent? –
    Ah, Uncle Humphrey, in thy face I see
    The map of honour, truth, and loyalty,
    And yet, good Humphrey, is the hour to come
    That e'er I proved thee false or feared thy faith.              205

188 SD] *This edn; not in* F    194 SD *with...men*] Q1; *not in* F    196 SD] *Collier²; not in* F

178 **twit** twitted (Abbott 342).
179 **clerkly couched** phrased in learned style.
182 Compare the proverb 'Give losers leave to speak' (Tilley L458).
184 **Beshrew** Curse.
186 **wrest the sense** distort the meaning.
189 **crutch** here used of a device to help a child to walk – as perhaps at *Ado* 2.1.356–7: 'Time goes on crutches till love have all his rites.'

191–2 Compare Matt. 26.31, 'I will smite the shepherd, and the sheep of the flock shall be scattered', and Ezek. 34.8, 'my sheep were devoured of all the beasts of the field, having no shepherd'.
192 **gnarling** snarling.
194 **decay** downfall, ruin (*OED sv* 1b).
203 **map** incarnation, image (*OED sv sb* 2b).
204 **yet** now as always.

What louring star now envies thy estate
That these great lords and Margaret our queen
Do seek subversion of thy harmless life?
Thou never didst them wrong nor no man wrong.
And as the butcher takes away the calf                           210
And binds the wretch and beats it when it strains,
Bearing it to the bloody slaughter-house,
Even so remorseless have they borne him hence;
And, as the dam runs lowing up and down,
Looking the way her harmless young one went                      215
And can do nought but wail her darling's loss,
Even so myself bewails good Gloucester's case
With sad unhelpful tears and, with dimmed eyes,
Look after him and cannot do him good;
So mighty are his vowèd enemies.                                 220
His fortunes I will weep and, 'twixt each groan,
Say, 'Who's a traitor, Gloucester he is none'.
            *Exit* [*with Buckingham, Salisbury, and Warwick*]
MARGARET Free lords, cold snow melts with the sun's hot beams.
Henry my lord is cold in great affairs,
Too full of foolish pity; and Gloucester's show                  225
Beguiles him, as the mournful crocodile
With sorrow snares relenting passengers,
Or as the snake, rolled in a flowering bank

---

206 louring] *Eds;* lowring F    211 strains] *Cairncross;* strayes F; strives *Theobald*    218 cyes,] *Rowe;* cyes; F    219
Look] F; Looks *conj. Vaughan*    222 SD *with...Warwick*] *Riverside; Salsbury,* and *Warwicke.* Q1; *not in* F    223] *Pope;*
Free Lords: / Cold...Beames: F    223 Free] F; *See Hanmer; Fair Collier*

**206 envies thy estate** feels malice towards
your position (*OED* Envy 2).
   **208 subversion** overthrow (*OED* sv 1).
   **211 *strains** F's 'strayes' is probably a misreading of 'strayes'. Compositor A made the same
mistake in Folio *H5* 3.1.32. Johnson noted that
'there is a confusion of ideas...the poet had at
once before him a butcher carrying a calf bound,
and a butcher driving a calf to the slaughter, and
beating him when he did not keep the path. Part
of the line was suggested by one image, and part
by another, so that "strive" [see collation] is the
best word, but "stray" is the right.'
   **217 bewails** The third-person inflection was
probably generated by 'myself' (F's 'my selfe')
   **221 weep** lament.
   **222 Who's** Whoever may be.

**222 SD** As at 1.1.71 SD, it is significant that no
flourish marks the king's exit.
   **223 Free** Noble.
   **223 cold...beams** Compare the proverb 'To
melt like snow before the sun' (Dent S593.1).
   **224 cold...affairs** indifferent to matters of
state.
   **225 foolish pity** Compare the proverb 'Foolish pity mars a city' (Tilley P366).
   **225 show** outward appearance.
   **226–7** The reference is to 'crocodile tears'
(Tilley C831). The crocodile was reputed to weep
either to attract or when devouring its prey;
compare *FQ*, I, v, 18.
   **227 relenting** pitying (*OED* Relent 5c).
   **228** Compare the proverb of the 'snake in the
grass' (Tilley S585).

With shining chequered slough, doth sting a child
That for the beauty thinks it excellent.                               230
Believe me, lords, were none more wise than I –
And yet herein I judge mine own wit good –
This Gloucester should be quickly rid the world
To rid us from the fear we have of him.
WINCHESTER That he should die is worthy policy;                        235
But yet we want a colour for his death:
'Tis meet he be condemned by course of law.
SUFFOLK But, in my mind, that were no policy:
The king will labour still to save his life;
The commons haply rise to save his life;                              240
And yet we have but trivial argument,
More than mistrust, that shows him worthy death.
YORK So that, by this, you would not have him die.
SUFFOLK Ah, York, no man alive so fain as I.
YORK 'Tis York that hath more reason for his death. –                  245
But, my Lord Cardinal – and you, my Lord of Suffolk,
Say as you think, and speak it from your souls:
Were't not all one an empty eagle were set
To guard the chicken from a hungry kite,
As place Duke Humphrey for the king's Protector?                      250
MARGARET So, the poor chicken should be sure of death.
SUFFOLK Madam, 'tis true: and were't not madness then
To make the fox surveyor of the fold
Who, being accused a crafty murderer,

244 Ah] F; *Aside* Ah *conj. Walker*

229 **slough** skin.
233 **rid the world** killed (*OED* Rid *v* 6c).
235 **is worthy policy** is a sensible aim.
236 **colour** (1) plausible reason (*OED* sv *sb* 12)
– with a quibble on 'die' (dye) in the previous line,
(2) noose or 'collar' (compare *2H4* 5.5.91–3, and
see Cercignani, p. 121).
237 **course** regular process.
239 **still** always.
241 **trivial argument** insubstantial evidence
(*OED* Argument 1).
243 **by this** according to this reasoning.
245 The line might be played as an aside.
Johnson noted 'Why York had more reason than
the rest for desiring Humphrey's death is not very
clear; he had only decided the deliberation about
the regency of France in favour of Somerset.'
However, York might be remembering 1.3.201

where Gloucester obviously thought that Peter's
accusation against Horner was significant.
247 Compare the proverb 'To speak as one
thinks' (Tilley S725).
248 **Were't…one** Would it not be as if.
248 **empty** hungry (*OED* sv 3b).
249 **kite** a bird of prey, notable for its
scavenging, which was difficult to train for
falconry.
251 **So** If in this way.
253 Compare the proverb 'Give not the wolf
(fox) the wether (sheep) to keep' (Tilley W602).
253 **surveyor** overseer (*OED* sv 1).
254–6 Whose guilt, if he were accused of
cunning murder, would be foolishly passed over,
simply because he had not implemented his
plans.

His guilt should be but idly posted over                                       255
Because his purpose is not executed?
No: let him die, in that he is a fox
(By nature proved an enemy to the flock)
Before his chaps be stained with crimson blood –
As Humphrey proved by reasons to my liege.                                     260
And do not stand on quillets how to slay him:
Be it by gins, by snares, by subtlety,
Sleeping, or waking, 'tis no matter how,
So he be dead: for that is good deceit
Which mates him first that first intends deceit.                               265

MARGARET Thrice noble Suffolk, 'tis resolutely spoke.

SUFFOLK Not resolute, except so much were done:
For things are often spoke and seldom meant:
But that my heart accordeth with my tongue –
Seeing the deed is meritorious –                                               270
And, to preserve my sovereign from his foe,
Say but the word, and I will be his priest.

WINCHESTER But I would have him dead, my Lord of Suffolk,
Ere you can take due orders for a priest:
Say you consent and censure well the deed                                      275
And I'll provide his executioner –
I tender so the safety of my liege.

SUFFOLK Here is my hand, the deed is worthy doing.

MARGARET And so say I.

---

260 Humphrey...reasons] F *subst.;* Humphrey,...reasons, *Eds*   260 Humphrey] F; Humphrey's. *Hanmer*   260
reasons] F; treasons *Hudson*   264 deceit] F; conceit *Delius*²

259 **chaps** chops, jaws.

260 **reasons** Some editors emend to
'treasons', but Suffolk is referring back to
Gloucester's own plea to the king at 142 ff. 'The
drift of the argument is to show that there may be
"reason" to kill him before any "treason" has
broken out' (Johnson).

261 **stand on quillets** insist on subtle legal
arguments.

262 **gins** traps.

264–5 **for...deceit** Compare the proverb 'To
deceive the deceiver is no deceit' (Tilley D182).

264 **deceit** Delius' emendation, 'conceit', is
tempting, in that 'deceit' could have been caught
from the next line. However, the threefold

repetition of 'deceit' in the proverb (see previous
note) inclines me to accept F's reading.

265 **mates** checkmates, kills off (*OED* sv *v* 1
and 2b).

267 **except so** unless as.

269 **that** in order that.

269 **my heart...tongue** Compare the
proverb 'What the heart thinks the tongue speaks'
(Tilley H334).

270 **meritorious** applied to works that were
deserving of reward by God.

272 **I will...priest** Compare the saying 'To be
one's priest' (Tilley P587), i.e. to kill someone.

275 **censure well** approve (Johnson).

277 **tender so** am so concerned for.

YORK And I; and now we three have spoke it,                          280
    It skills not greatly who impugns our doom.

*Enter a* POST

POST Great lords, from Ireland am I come amain
    To signify that rebels there are up
    And put the Englishmen unto the sword.
    Send succours, lords, and stop the rage betime     285
    Before the wound do grow uncurable:
    For, being green, there is great hope of help.

WINCHESTER A breach that craves a quick expedient stop! –
    What counsel give you in this weighty cause?

YORK That Somerset be sent as regent thither:                       290
    'Tis meet that lucky ruler be employed –
    Witness the fortune he hath had in France.

SOMERSET If York, with all his far-fet policy,
    Had been the regent there instead of me,
    He never would have stayed in France so long.      295

YORK No, not to lose it all, as thou hast done:
    I rather would have lost my life betimes
    Than bring a burden of dishonour home
    By staying there so long till all were lost.
    Show me one scar charactered on thy skin:          300
    Men's flesh preserved so whole do seldom win.

MARGARET Nay, then, this spark will prove a raging fire
    If wind and fuel be brought to feed it with.
    No more, good York. – Sweet Somerset, be still. –
    Thy fortune, York, hadst thou been regent there,    305

301 flesh preserved] F; flesh-preserved *conj. Vaughan*

280 **spoke** For the curtailed form of the participle, see Abbott 343.

281 **It...greatly** It makes little difference (*OED* Skill *v* 2b).

281 **impugns our doom** calls our judgement into question.

282 **amain** with full speed.

283 **signify** announce (*OED sv* 3).

283 **up** up in arms (*OED sv adj* 10).

285–7 **stop...help** Compare the proverb 'A green wound is soon healed' (Tilley w927).

285 **rage** rabies (*OED sv* 1c).

285 **betime** in good time.

287 **green** fresh (*OED sv adj* 10).

288 **expedient** expeditious (*OED sv* 1).

291 **lucky** successful (*OED sv* 1); York is being savagely ironic (see 83 ff.).

293 **far-fet** far-fetched, devious.

297 **betimes** speedily.

299 **staying** delaying.

300 **charactered** inscribed – accented on the second syllable (Cercignani, p. 41).

302 **this...fire** Compare the proverb 'Of little spark a great fire' (Tilley s714).

304 **still** quiet.

Might happily have proved far worse than his.

YORK What, worse than nought? Nay then, a shame take all!

SOMERSET And in the number thee that wishest shame!

WINCHESTER My Lord of York, try what your fortune is:
　　　　　Th'uncivil kerns of Ireland are in arms　　　　　　　310
　　　　　And temper clay with blood of Englishmen.
　　　　　To Ireland will you lead a band of men
　　　　　Collected choicely, from each county some,
　　　　　And try your hap against the Irishmen?

YORK I will, my lord, so please his majesty.　　　　　　　315

SUFFOLK Why, our authority is his consent,
　　　　　And what we do establish he confirms:
　　　　　Then, noble York, take thou this task in hand.

YORK I am content. Provide me soldiers, lords,
　　　　　Whiles I take order for mine own affairs.　　　　　320

SUFFOLK A charge, Lord York, that I will see performed.
　　　　　But now return we to the false Duke Humphrey.

WINCHESTER No more of him; for I will deal with him
　　　　　That henceforth he shall trouble us no more.
　　　　　And so break off, the day is almost spent –　　　325
　　　　　[*Aside*] Lord Suffolk, you and I must talk of that event.

YORK My Lord of Suffolk, within fourteen days
　　　　　At Bristol I expect my soldiers;
　　　　　For there I'll ship them all for Ireland.

SUFFOLK I'll see it truly done, my Lord of York.　　　　330
　　　　　　　　　　　　　　　*Exeunt* [*all but*] *York*

YORK Now, York, or never, steel thy fearful thoughts
　　　　　And change misdoubt to resolution:

---

307 nought] *Pope*; naught F　　326] F; *Suf.* Lord, you and I must talk of that event. *Cairncross*; QUEENE Lord Suffolke
...*conj. Taylor in* Oxford; SUFFOLKE *(aside to the Cardinall) conj.* Oxford　　326 SD] *This edn; not in* F　　328 Bristol]
*Rowe*; Bristow F　　330 SD] F *subst. (Exeunt. Manet Yorke)*

**306 happily** perhaps.

**309–14** This and the references to the Irish rebellion at 1.1.191–2 and 360 below 'refer confusedly to the same rebellion' (Hart).

**310 uncivil** uncivilised.

**310 kerns** lightly armed Irish foot soldiers; see also Appendix 2, p. 231.

**311 temper** moisten (like mortar) (*OED* sv *v* 10).

**317 establish** enact (*OED* sv 2).

**319 ff.** Q1 provides an additional sequence here (see Appendix 2, p. 231) which provides

some lines for Buckingham who has been silent since 65. These may be part of an authorial revision.

**320 take order for** make arrangements (*OED* Order *sb* 14).

***326** Various conjectures have been made concerning the assignation of this line (see collation). The addition of an 'aside' provides a simple and plausible reading.

**331 Now...never** Proverbial (Tilley N351).

**332 misdoubt** apprehension.

Be that thou hop'st to be, or what thou art
Resign to death – it is not worth th'enjoying.
Let pale-faced fear keep with the mean-born man                    335
And find no harbour in a royal heart.
Faster than spring-time showers comes thought on thought,
And not a thought but thinks on dignity.
My brain, more busy than the labouring spider,
Weaves tedious snares to trap mine enemies.                        340
Well, nobles, well: 'tis politicly done
To send me packing with an host of men;
I fear me you but warm the starvèd snake
Who, cherished in your breasts, will sting your hearts.
'Twas men I lacked, and you will give them me:                     345
I take it kindly, yet be well assured
You put sharp weapons in a madman's hands.
Whiles I in Ireland nurse a mighty band,
I will stir up in England some black storm
Shall blow ten thousand souls to heaven, or hell;                 350
And this fell tempest shall not cease to rage
Until the golden circuit on my head,
Like to the glorious sun's transparent beams,
Do calm the fury of this mad-bred flaw.
And, for a minister of my intent,                                 355
I have seduced a headstrong Kentishman,
John Cade of Ashford,
To make commotion, as full well he can,

---

333 art] F4; art; F    348 nurse] F (nourish)    354 mad-bred] F; mad-brain'd *Rowe*

---

335 **keep** dwell (*OED* sv *v* 37).
335 **mean-born** of humble origin.
338 **dignity** high estate (*OED* sv 2).
340 **tedious** laborious.
343–4 Compare the proverb 'To nourish a viper (snake) in one's bosom' (Tilley v68).
343 **starvèd** stiff from cold (*OED* sv *pple adj* 4).
347 Compare the proverb 'ill putting (put not) a naked sword in a madman's hand' (Tilley P669).
348 *****nurse** F's reading 'nourish' is simply a variant of 'nurse' (*OED* sv *v*) – the word in any case would have been pronounced as a monosyllable (Cercignani, p. 281).
349–54 Compare Hall: 'And to set open the flood-gates of these devices, it was thought

necessary to cause some great commotion and rising of people to be made against the king, so that if they prevailed, then had the Duke of York and his complices their appetite and desire' (p. 219).
351 **fell** deadly.
352 **circuit** crown.
353 **transparent** penetrating (*OED* sv 1c).
354 **mad-bred** i.e. by Henry's incompetent rule.
354 **flaw** squall.
355 **minister** agent.
357 **Ashford** A town in east Kent.
358 **make commotion** raise an insurrection (*OED* Commotion 4).

Under the title of John Mortimer.
In Ireland have I seen this stubborn Cade                    360
Oppose himself against a troop of kerns
And fought so long till that his thighs with darts
Were almost like a sharp-quilled porpentine;
And in the end, being rescued, I have seen
Him caper upright, like a wild Morisco,                      365
Shaking the bloody darts as he his bells.
Full often, like a shag-haired crafty kern,
Hath he conversèd with the enemy
And, undiscovered, come to me again
And given me notice of their villainies.                     370
This devil here shall be my substitute;
For that John Mortimer, which now is dead,
In face, in gait, in speech, he doth resemble:
By this, I shall perceive the commons' mind,
How they affect the house and claim of York.                375
Say he be taken, racked, and tortured,
I know no pain they can inflict upon him
Will make him say I moved him to those arms.
Say that he thrive, as 'tis great like he will,
Why, then from Ireland come I with my strength              380
And reap the harvest which that rascal sowed.
For Humphrey being dead, as he shall be,
And Henry put apart, the next for me.                       *Exit*

378 arms] F; aims *conj. Dyce*    381 rascal] F; coystrill Q1

359 Compare 4.2.115–25.
**360 Ireland** Holinshed (but not Hall) notes that Cade was an Irishman (p. 220).
**360 stubborn** implacable, fierce (*OED* sv 1).
**362 till that** until (Abbott 287).
**362 darts** light spears or arrows.
**363 porpentine** porcupine.
**365 Morisco** morris-dancer. For the etymology from the Spanish word for 'Moor', see François Laroque, *Shakespeare et la fête*, 1988, pp. 130–4. Manly, a character in William Cavendish's *The Varietie* (1641), remembers Elizabeth's court: 'There was a musick then, and a Heaven and Earth beyond your branles, or your Mountague, with a la, la, la, like a Bachanalian dancing the Spanish Morisco, with knackers [castanets] at his fingers' (3.42–5). The dancers also bore weapons and mimed the battles of the Christians with the 'Moors' – see Peter Burke, *Popular Culture in Early Modern Europe*, 1978, p. 117.
**366 bells** tied to the legs of morris-dancers.
**370 notice** information (*OED* sv 1).
**371 substitute** deputy (*OED* sv 1).
**372 For that** Because.
**372 John Mortimer** executed in 1424 (Hall, p. 128); see *1H6* 2.5 n.
**375 affect** favour.
**378 moved** instigated.
**379 great like** very likely.
381 Compare Luke 19.21–2 and the proverb 'One sows, another reaps' (Tilley S691).
**381 rascal** low-born knave.

**[3.2]** *Enter two or three* [MURDERERS] *running over the stage from the murder of Duke Humphrey*

1 MURDERER   Run to my Lord of Suffolk; let him know
            We have dispatched the duke, as he commanded.
2 MURDERER   O, that it were to do! What have we done?
            Didst ever hear a man so penitent?

*Enter* SUFFOLK

1 MURDERER   Here comes my lord.                                              5
SUFFOLK   Now, sirs, have you dispatched this thing?
1 MURDERER   Ay, my good lord, he's dead.
SUFFOLK   Why, that's well said. Go, get you to my house;
            I will reward you for this venturous deed.
            The king and all the peers are here at hand.                      10
            Have you laid fair the bed? Is all things well,
            According as I gave directions?
1 MURDERER   'Tis, my good lord.
SUFFOLK   Away! Be gone.

*Exeunt* [*Murderers*]

Act 3, Scene 2   3.2] *Capell; not in* F   0 SD] F; Then the Curtaines being drawne, Duke *Humphrey* is discouered in his bed, and two men lying on his brest and smothering him in his bed. And then enter the Duke of *Suffolke* to them. Q1   1 SH 1 MURDERER] *Capell subst.;* 1 F (*throughout scene*)   14] F *subst.;* Then draw the Curtaines againe and get you gone, Q1   14 SD.1 *Murderers*] Q1; *not in* F

## Act 3, Scene 2

*3.2 Both Holinshed (p. 211) and Hall report that all 'indifferent persons' knew that Gloucester died in 1447 not 'of a palsy or impostume...but of some violent force' (p. 209) – see Appendix 1, p. 223. The popular uprising consequent on his death (see 125–7) is recorded only by Hall (p. 210). The plaints of the commons against Suffolk (242 ff.) were made after the queen had adjourned to Leicester a parliament held at Blackfriars in 1450 (Holinshed, p. 218; Hall, p. 217). For Suffolk's banishment see Holinshed, p. 220 (Hall, p. 219), an account which may have been supplemented by memories from Ovid (see 339–42 n., 350 n.).

0 SD Q's stage direction (see collation) presumably records details of the staging of the scene's opening in a London playhouse. Claire Saunders, '"Dead in his bed": Shakespeare's staging of the death of the Duke of Gloucester in *2 Henry VI*', *RES* 36 (1985), 19–34, argues that Q's staging may have been influenced by the staging of 5.1 of the anonymous play *Woodstock*. F's stage direction is ambiguous in that it does not allow us to infer

whether or not Shakespeare intended the violent deed to be shown. (Arthur Freeman, 'Notes on the text of *2 Henry VI*', *NQ* 213 (1968), 129 argues that F could have been played in a playhouse without a discovery space.) After the killing, the murderers would have run downstage from the discovery space. On the grounds that F includes Suffolk among those entering at 14 (he is already on the stage), Wilson (p. 159) suggests that 1–14 are 'a later insertion'.

2 **as he commanded** Suffolk was responsible jointly with Winchester for Gloucester's death – see 3.1.275–6.

3 **to do** yet to be done (so that it might be undone).

8 **well said** well done (compare 1.4.12 n.).

9 **venturous** hazardous (*OED* sv 2).

11 **laid fair** remade (see 0 SD n.).

11 **bed** The chroniclers did not know how Gloucester met his end (see Appendix 1, p. 223).

*14 SD F has Suffolk entering here – see 0 SD n. Winchester and Somerset have only one speech each: 31–2, 34. See 202 SD n. below.

*Sound trumpets. Enter the* KING, *the* QUEEN, CARDINAL
[WINCHESTER], SOMERSET, *with* ATTENDANTS

KING HENRY [*To Suffolk*] Go, call our uncle to our presence straight:    15
        Say we intend to try his grace today
        If he be guilty, as 'tis publishèd.
SUFFOLK I'll call him presently, my noble lord.                    *Exit*
KING HENRY Lords, take your places; and, I pray you all,
        Proceed no straiter 'gainst our Uncle Gloucester           20
        Than from true evidence of good esteem
        He be approved in practice culpable.
MARGARET God forbid any malice should prevail
        That faultless may condemn a noble man:
        Pray God he may acquit him of suspicion!                   25
KING HENRY I thank thee, Meg: these words content me much. –

*Enter* SUFFOLK

        How now? Why look'st thou pale? Why tremblest thou?
        Where is our uncle? What's the matter, Suffolk?
SUFFOLK Dead in his bed, my lord: Gloucester is dead.
MARGARET Marry, God forfend!                                      30
WINCHESTER God's secret judgment: I did dream tonight
        The duke was dumb and could not speak a word.
*The king swoons*
MARGARET How fares my lord? – Help, lords, the king is dead!
SOMERSET Rear up his body; wring him by the nose.
MARGARET Run, go, help, help! [*Exit attendant*] – O Henry, ope
        thine eyes!                                               35
SUFFOLK He doth revive again: madam, be patient.

---

14 SD.2−3] CARDINALL WINCHESTER] *This edn; Cardinall, Suffolke* F; *the Duke of Buckingham*...*and the Cardinall* Q1
15 SD] *This edn (following* Q1)    26 Meg] *Capell; Nell* F; *Well, Theobald*    31 WINCHESTER...judgment:] F *subst.;*
WINCHESTER *Aside*...*judgment. − conj. this edn*    32 SD] F4 *subst.; King sounds* F    35 SD] *This edn; not in* F

17 **If** Whether.
17 **publishèd** proclaimed.
18 **presently** immediately.
20 **straiter** more rigorously.
22 **approved...culpable** proved guilty of
ill-doing.
25 **him** himself.
26 ***Meg** Here, and at 79, 100, 120, F reads
'*Nell*' or '*Elianor*'. The error doubtless derives
from Shakespeare's foul papers, being caused by
the presence of Gloucester's name, and would
not have survived transcription into a prompt-
book.

30 **forfend** forbid.
31 **God's...judgement** These words could
be effectively delivered as an aside, showing
Winchester touched by conscience and prophesying his own death in 3.3.
31 **tonight** last night.
34 **wring...nose** to restore circulation; compare *Ven.* 475.
***35** SD Either an attendant could obey the
queen here or, as Joseph Ritson conjectured
(*Remarks, Critical and Illustrative, on...*
*Shakespeare*, 1783), Winchester and Somerset
could exit here rather than at 202.

KING HENRY O heavenly God!
MARGARET                 How fares my gracious lord?
SUFFOLK Comfort, my sovereign! Gracious Henry, comfort!
KING HENRY What, doth my Lord of Suffolk comfort me?
    Came he right now to sing a raven's note,         40
    Whose dismal tune bereft my vital powers;
    And thinks he that the chirping of a wren,
    By crying comfort from a hollow breast,
    Can chase away the first-conceivèd sound?
    Hide not thy poison with such sugared words;      45
    Lay not thy hands on me – forbear, I say,
    Their touch affrights me as a serpent's sting.
    Thou baleful messenger, out of my sight!
    Upon thy eye-balls murderous tyranny
    Sits in grim majesty, to fright the world.        50
    Look not upon me, for thine eyes are wounding:
    Yet do not go away. Come, basilisk,
    And kill the innocent gazer with thy sight:
    For in the shade of death I shall find joy;
    In life, but double death, now Gloucester's dead.    55
MARGARET Why do you rate my Lord of Suffolk thus?
    Although the duke was enemy to him,
    Yet he most Christian-like laments his death;
    And for myself, foe as he was to me,
    Might liquid tears or heart-offending groans      60
    Or blood-consuming sighs recall his life,
    I would be blind with weeping, sick with groans,
    Look pale as primrose with blood-drinking sighs,
    And all to have the noble duke alive.
    What know I how the world may deem of me?     65

---

**40 raven's note** the croaking of the raven portended death; compare *Mac.* 1.5.38–40 and Tilley R33.

**41 dismal** malign, sinister (*OED* sv 2).

**42 wren** It seems that Henry refers to his wife.

**43 hollow** deceitful.

**44 first-conceivèd** previously perceived (see *OED* Conceive 10).

**45** Compare the catch-phrases 'poison under sugar' (Dent P458.1) and 'sugared words' (Dent SS27).

**52 basilisk** 'a fabulous reptile, also called a *cockatrice*, alleged to be hatched by a serpent from a cock's egg..., [whose] breath, and even its

look, was fatal' (*OED*); compare Tilley B99 and Dent B99.1: 'To kill like a basilisk'.

**54 shade** shadow; 'shadow of death' was proverbial (Dent SS5).

**56 rate** chide.

**58 most Christian-like** (compare Matt. 5.44: 'Love your enemies').

**60–3 tears...primrose** For the recurrent clustering of these images see E. A. Armstrong, *Shakespeare's Imagination*, 1963 edn, p. 80.

**60 offending** wounding (*OED* Offend 6).

**61–3 blood-consuming...sighs** Every sigh was supposed to draw a drop of blood from the heart (compare *3H6* 4.4.22 and *Ham.* 4.7.123).

For it is known we were but hollow friends
It may be judged I made the duke away:
So shall my name with slander's tongue be wounded,
And princes' courts be filled with my reproach:
This get I by his death. Ay, me unhappy!                    70
To be a queen and crowned with infamy.

KING HENRY Ah, woe is me for Gloucester, wretched man!
MARGARET Be woe for me, more wretched than he is.
          What, dost thou turn away and hide thy face?
          I am no loathsome leper: look on me.               75
          What? Art thou, like the adder, waxen deaf?
          Be poisonous too and kill thy forlorn queen.
          Is all thy comfort shut in Gloucester's tomb?
          Why then, Dame Margaret was ne'er thy joy.
          Erect his statua and worship it,                   80
          And make my image but an alehouse sign.
          Was I for this nigh wracked upon the sea
          And twice by awkward wind from England's bank
          Drove back again unto my native clime?
          What boded this, but well forewarning wind          85
          Did seem to say, 'Seek not a scorpion's nest
          Nor set no footing on this unkind shore'?
          What did I then but cursed the gentle gusts
          And he that loosed them forth their brazen caves
          And bid them blow towards England's blessed shore   90
          Or turn our stern upon a dreadful rock?

79 Dame] F; Queen *Oxford*    **79, 100, 120** Margaret] *Rowe*; Eleanor F *subst.*    80 statua] *Dyce*; Statue F    83 wind]
F; winds Q1    88 gentle] F; ungentle *Singer*[2]    90 them] F; him *conj. Vaughan*

**69 my reproach** reproach of me.
**72 woe…for** I am sorrowful on account of.
**73 woe** sorry (*OED* sv *adj* 2).
**76 adder, waxen deaf** see Ps. 58.4–5 for the belief that the adder placed its tail in its ear and the other ear on the ground to resist attempts to charm it, and Tilley A32.
**79, 100, 120** *Margaret See 26 n.
**80** *statua The metre demands the three-syllable form of the word.
**83 awkward** adverse (*OED* sv 1).
**83 bank** sea-coast (*OED* sv *sb* 9).
**84 clime** region (*OED* sv 2).
**85 well forewarning** truthfully predicting.
**87 unkind** rough, unnatural.
**89 he** Aeolus, to whom Zeus had given dominion over the winds.

**89 brazen caves** strong (as brass) (*OED* Brazen 1b); compare *3H6* 2.4.4. The claim that Shakespeare displays a capacity to read the Greek description of Aeolus' island in *Odyssey* x.3–4 is tenuous, as Homer refers to bronze walls and not brazen caves. Shakespeare is more likely to have drawn on Ovid: 'Aeoliis Aquilonem claudit in antris' (*Metamorphoses* I, 262–3). Compare Nashe, *Summer's Last Will and Testament*, 1793–4: 'imprison him…with the winds in bellowing caves of brass' (Nashe, III, 289); see also G. Bush, 'Notes on Shakespeare's classical mythology', *PQ* 6 (1927), 295.
**91 turn…rock** i.e., cause me to drown.

Yet Aeolus would not be a murderer,
But left that hateful office unto thee:
The pretty vaulting sea refused to drown me,
Knowing that thou wouldst have me drowned on shore    95
With tears as salt as sea, through thy unkindness;
The splitting rocks cow'red in the sinking sands
And would not dash me with their ragged sides
Because thy flinty heart, more hard than they,
Might in thy palace perish Margaret.    100
As far as I could ken thy chalky cliffs,
When from thy shore the tempest beat us back,
I stood upon the hatches in the storm;
And when the dusky sky began to rob
My earnest-gaping sight of thy land's view,    105
I took a costly jewel from my neck –
A heart it was, bound in with diamonds –
And threw it towards thy land. The sea received it,
And so I wished thy body might my heart:
And, even with this, I lost fair England's view    110
And bid mine eyes be packing with my heart,
And called them blind and dusky spectacles
For losing ken of Albion's wishèd coast.
How often have I tempted Suffolk's tongue –
The agent of thy foul inconstancy –    115
To sit and witch me as Ascanius did
When he to madding Dido would unfold
His father's acts commenced in burning Troy?
Am I not witched like her, or thou not false like him?

96 sea] F; he *conj. Vaughan*    101 thy] F; the *Pope*    105 earnest-gaping sight] *Eds;* earnest-gaping-sight F    107
heart] *Eds;* Hart F    116 witch] *Theobald;* watch F

94 **vaulting** (1) rising and falling, (2) referring to the vault-like form of a curling wave.
96 **as salt...sea** proverbial (Dent S170.1).
97 **splitting** strong enough to split a ship.
97 **sinking** able to sink a ship.
99 **flinty...hard** Compare the proverb 'A heart as hard as a flint' (Tilley H311).
100 **perish** destroy (*OED* sv 3).
101 **ken** descry (*OED* sv 6).
103 **hatches** deck (*OED* Hatch 3).
106 **jewel** ornament (*OED* sv 1).
110 **with** by (Abbott 193).
111 **be...heart** be gone with my heart (the ornament).

112 **spectacles** instruments of sight (*OED* Spectacle 5).
115 Margaret refers to the part played by Suffolk in arranging her marriage.
116–18 **Ascanius...Troy** Venus gave Cupid the semblance of Aeneas' son Ascanius so that he could bewitch Dido Queen of Carthage with tales of his father's deeds at Troy; see *Aeneid* I, 657 ff.
116 ***witch** Virgil's tale (see 116–18 n.) gives support to Theobald's emendation of F's 'watch'.
117 **madding** made frantic by love.

Ay me, I can no more! Die, Margaret,                    120
For Henry weeps that thou dost live so long!

*Noise within. Enter* WARWICK, [SALISBURY,] *and many* COMMONS

WARWICK It is reported, mighty sovereign,
    That good Duke Humphrey traitorously is murdered
    By Suffolk and the Cardinal Beaufort's means.
    The commons, like an angry hive of bees                125
    That want their leader, scatter up and down
    And care not who they sting in his revenge.
    Myself have calmed their spleenful mutiny,
    Until they hear the order of his death.

KING HENRY That he is dead, good Warwick, 'tis too true;    130
    But how he died, God knows, not Henry.
    Enter his chamber, view his breathless corpse,
    And comment then upon his sudden death.

WARWICK That shall I do, my liege. – Stay, Salisbury,
    With the rude multitude till I return.                 135

        [*Exeunt Warwick, then Salisbury with the commons*]

KING HENRY O Thou that judgest all things, stay my thoughts,
    My thoughts that labour to persuade my soul
    Some violent hands were laid on Humphrey's life.
    If my suspect be false, forgive me, God,
    For judgement only doth belong to thee.                140
    Fain would I go to chafe his paly lips
    With twenty thousand kisses and to drain
    Upon his face an ocean of salt tears,

---

121 SD SALISBURY] *Theobald (following* Q1)*; not in* F    135 SD] *Alexander (following Theobald); Exet Salbury* Q1*; not in*
F

120 I...more my strength fails me.
120 *Margaret F's 'Elinor' again must clearly
be emended. Perhaps the name crept in to the
text here because of the 'witched' in the line
before, which may have recalled Humphrey's
wife.
126 want lack.
127 his revenge in revenge for him.
128 spleenful passionately angry.
128 mutiny uprising.
129 order sequence of events.
131 God...Henry Compare the proverb
'God he knows, not I' (Dent G189.1).
132 breathless lifeless (*OED* sv 1b).
133 comment report (*OED* sv *v* 4) or ponder
(*OED* 5) as at *R3* 4.3.51.

135 rude barbarous, uncivilised.
*135 SD It may be felt that an exit for Salisbury
and the commons (see collation) is not called for
until 202; they could simply retire to another part
of the stage.
136 judgest all things compare Abraham's
plea in Gen. 18.25 to 'the judge of all the world'.
136 stay (1) strengthen, (2) stop. The ambiguous words 'unintentionally give away his confused feelings' (Mahood, p. 34).
139 suspect suspicion (Abbott 451).
141 chafe warm (*OED* sv 1).
142 drain let fall (*OED* sv *v* 2b).
143 ocean...tears proverbial (Dent T82.1).

To tell my love unto his dumb deaf trunk,
And with my fingers feel his hand unfeeling:                                145
But all in vain are these mean obsequies,
                    *Bed put forth*
And to survey his dead and earthy image,
What were it but to make my sorrow greater?

[WARWICK *enters and draws the curtains, and shows* DUKE HUMPHREY
                    *in his bed*]

WARWICK  Come hither, gracious sovereign, view this body.

KING HENRY  [*Averting his gaze*] That is to see how deep my grave is
        made;                                                              150
    For with his soul fled all my worldly solace;
    For, seeing him, I see my life in death.

WARWICK  As surely as my soul intends to live
    With that dread King that took our state upon Him
    To free us from his Father's wrathful curse,                          155
    I do believe that violent hands were laid
    Upon the life of this thrice-famèd duke.

SUFFOLK  A dreadful oath, sworn with a solemn tongue!
    What instance gives Lord Warwick for his vow?

WARWICK  See how the blood is settled in his face.                        160

---

146 mean] F; meant *conj. Vaughan*     148 SD] Q1 *subst. (omitting 'enters and'); not in* F     150 SD] *This edn; not in* F
152 For] F; And *Capell* 152 life in death] F *subst.; death in life conj. Johnson*

---

146 SD Although this anticipates the discovery, suggesting that it derives from a prompter, two lines would not be sufficient to place the bed in position. Either, therefore, the SD was displaced by the compositor, or it may derive from a note by Shakespeare himself in his MS. This may mean not that the bed was simply to be prepared in the discovery space but that it was to be 'thrust out' onto the stage (see Hattaway, pp. 36–7 and Plate 4(a), p. 25). Alternatively, Warwick could draw the curtains from within the discovery space (see 148 SD) at this point, thus creating a tableau which ironically fulfills the forebodings Henry expresses in the next two lines.

147 **earthy** cold and lifeless (Schmidt).

148 SD **\*curtains** concealing the discovery space at the rear of the stage.

152 **seeing him** were I to see him (Abbott 377).

152 **my...death** death as the future condition of my life; compare the Order for the Burial of

the Dead: 'In the midst of life we be in death.'

153–77 Holinshed (p. 211) and Hall (p. 209) report that although Gloucester's body was shown to the lords and commons, no cause of death could be perceived (see Appendix 1, p. 223). Given that Warwick is the only one on stage able to see the corpse, it may be that he is speaking for effect, arousing horror in order to point the finger of suspicion at Suffolk. There is no need, in other words, for the body to resemble Warwick's description of it.

154 **King** Christ.

154 **took...Him** Compare the Collect for Christmas Day: 'which hast given us thy only begotten son to take our nature upon him'.

155 Compare Gal. 3.13: 'Christ hath redeemed us from the curse of the law.'

157 **thrice-famèd** very famous (*OED* Thrice 3b).

159 **instance** fact, evidence (*OED* sv 6).

160 **settled** coagulated (*OED* sv *pple adj* 6).

Oft have I seen a timely-parted ghost,
Of ashy semblance, meagre, pale, and bloodless,
Being all descended to the labouring heart
Who, in the conflict that it holds with death,
Attracts the same for aidance 'gainst the enemy,          165
Which with the heart there cools and ne'er returneth
To blush and beautify the cheek again.
But see, his face is black and full of blood,
His eye-balls further out than when he lived,
Staring full ghastly like a strangled man;               170
His hair upreared, his nostrils stretched with struggling;
His hands abroad displayed, as one that grasped
And tugged for life, and was by strength subdued.
Look, on the sheets his hair, you see, is sticking;
His well-proportioned beard made rough and rugged,        175
Like to the summer's corn by tempest lodged.
It cannot be but he was murdered here:
The least of all these signs were probable.

SUFFOLK Why, Warwick, who should do the duke to death?
    Myself and Beaufort had him in protection         180
    And we, I hope, sir, are no murderers.

WARWICK But both of you were vowed Duke Humphrey's foes,
    And you, forsooth, had the good duke to keep:
    'Tis like you would not feast him like a friend,
    And 'tis well seen he found an enemy.               185

MARGARET Then you, belike, suspect these noblemen
    As guilty of Duke Humphrey's timeless death?

WARWICK Who finds the heifer dead and bleeding fresh
    And sees fast by a butcher with an axe,
    But will suspect 'twas he that made the slaughter?  190
    Who finds the partridge in the puttock's nest,

---

186 Then] *Eds;* Than F     189 fast by] *Eds;* fast-by F

---

**161 timely-parted ghost** the body of one who
has died in a natural manner (ghost = person
(*OED* sv 4)).

**162 meagre** emaciated (*OED* sv 1).

**163 Being** (The blood) having.

**163 labouring** palpitating (*OED* Labour *v* 3).

**165 same** (blood).

**165 aidance** assistance.

**166 Which** The blood.

**172 abroad displayed** spread widely apart
(*OED* Abroad 1c).

**175 well-proportioned** well-shaped.

**176 lodged** beaten flat (*OED* Lodge *v* 5).

**178 were probable** would offer sufficient
evidence.

**183 keep** protect, guard.

**184 'Tis like** It is probable.

**187 timeless** untimely (*OED* sv 1).

**191 puttock's** kite's. Kites often stole par-
tridges – see Armstrong, *Shakespeare's Imagination*, pp. 11, 15 on this and on the association in
other passages of kites with sheets (see 174
above).

But may imagine how the bird was dead,
Although the kite soar with unbloodied beak?
Even so suspicious is this tragedy.

MARGARET Are you the butcher, Suffolk? Where's your knife?          195
Is Beaufort termed a kite? Where are his talons?

SUFFOLK I wear no knife to slaughter sleeping men;
But here's a vengeful sword, rusted with ease,
That shall be scourèd in his rancorous heart
That slanders me with murder's crimson badge.                        200
Say, if thou dar'st, proud Lord of Warwickshire,
That I am faulty in Duke Humphrey's death.

                    [*Exeunt Cardinal, Somerset, and others*]

WARWICK What dares not Warwick, if false Suffolk dare him?

MARGARET He dares not calm his contumelious spirit
Nor cease to be an arrogant controller,                              205
Though Suffolk dare him twenty thousand times.

WARWICK Madam, be still, with reverence may I say;
For every word you speak in his behalf
Is slander to your royal dignity.

SUFFOLK Blunt-witted lord, ignoble in demeanour,                     210
If ever lady wronged her lord so much,
Thy mother took into her blameful bed
Some stern untutored churl, and noble stock
Was graft with crab-tree slip, whose fruit thou art
And never of the Nevilles' noble race.                               215

WARWICK But that the guilt of murder bucklers thee,
And I should rob the deathsman of his fee,
Quitting thee thereby of ten thousand shames,

---

202 SD] *Capell subst.; Exet Cardinall* Q1; *the Cardinal closes the curtains and goes out* / Wilson; *not in* F

198 **with ease** from lack of use.
200 **slanders** unlawfully attributes to.
200 **badge** a device to identify a knight to his followers, but here metaphorical.
202 **faulty in** guilty of (*OED* Faulty 3a).
*202 SD See 35 and 135 SDD n. The stage direction has been adapted from Q, as F marks no exit for the cardinal. Perhaps he leaves, assisted by Somerset and 'displaying signs of incipient sickness and guilt after seeing Gloucester's corpse' (Sanders). Wilson's suggestion (see collation) that the cardinal should draw the curtains as he leaves solves the problem of disposing of the corpse. His exit is also a theatrical necessity – he

must be prepared and made up for his death scene, which comes next.
204 **contumelious** insolent (*OED* sv 1).
205 **controller** critic (*OED* sv 3).
207 **still** silent.
209 **slander** a disgrace.
210 **ignoble** not noble, common.
213 **stern** bold (*OED* sv *adj* 2).
213 **untutored** ignorant, unmannered.
214 **slip** (1) cutting, (2) moral lapse (*OED* sv *sb²* and *sb³*).
216 **bucklers** shields, protects.
217 **deathsman** executioner.
218 **Quitting** Ridding.

And that my sovereign's presence makes me mild,
I would, false murderous coward, on thy knee                    220
Make thee beg pardon for thy passèd speech,
And say it was thy mother that thou meant'st,
That thou thyself wast born in bastardy;
And, after all this fearful homage done,
Give thee thy hire and send thy soul to hell,                   225
Pernicious blood-sucker of sleeping men!
SUFFOLK Thou shalt be waking while I shed thy blood,
If from this presence thou dar'st go with me.
WARWICK Away even now, or I will drag thee hence:
Unworthy though thou art, I'll cope with thee                   230
And do some service to Duke Humphrey's ghost.
                          *Exeunt [Suffolk and Warwick]*
KING HENRY What stronger breast-plate than a heart untainted?
Thrice is he armed that hath his quarrel just,
And he but naked, though locked up in steel,
Whose conscience with injustice is corrupted.                   235
        *A noise within: [cries of* 'Down with Suffolk!']
MARGARET What noise is this?

*Enter* SUFFOLK *and* WARWICK *with their weapons drawn*

KING HENRY Why, how now, lords! Your wrathful weapons drawn
Here in our presence? Dare you be so bold?
Why what tumultuous clamour have we here?
SUFFOLK The traitorous Warwick with the men of Bury            240
Set all upon me, mighty sovereign.

[*The commons again cry,* 'Down with Suffolk! Down with Suffolk!' *And
then*] enter [*from them the* EARL OF] SALISBURY

---

223 born] *Eds*; borne F      231 SD] *Hanmer; Exeunt* F; Warwicke puls him out. *Exet Warwicke and Suffolke,* and then all
the Commons within, cries, downe with *Suffolke,* downe with *Suffolk,* And then enter againe, the Duke of *Suffolke* and
*Warwicke,* with their weapons drawne. Q1      235 SD *cries...Suffolk!*] *This edn (following Q1); not in* F      237] *Pope;*
Why...Lords? / Your...drawne, F      241 SD.1–2 *The...then from...*OF] Q1; *not in* F

---

221 **passèd** uttered.
224 **fearful homage** craven submission
(Wilson).
225 **Give...hire** Compare the proverb 'To
give one his hire' (Dent H474.1), i.e. kill him.
225 **hire** just payment.
228 **presence** royal presence.
230 **cope** fight (*OED* sv $v^2$ 2).
232–5 Compare the proverb 'Innocence bears
its defence with it' (Tilley 182).

232 **breast-plate** compare Eph. 6.14: 'the
breast-plate of righteousness'.
234 Even if completely unarmed and encircled
by strongly armed opponents.
*235 SD The vagueness of what constitutes the
'noise' is typical of foul paper texts like F.
237–8 Drawing a weapon in the monarch's
presence was an offence; compare *1H6* 1.3.46.
240 **Bury** This parliament was held at the
Abbey of Bury St Edmunds in Suffolk.

SALISBURY  Sirs, stand apart: the king shall know your mind. –
　　　　　 Dread lord, the commons send you word by me,
　　　　　 Unless Lord Suffolk straight be done to death
　　　　　 Or banishèd fair England's territories,　　　　　　　　　245
　　　　　 They will by violence tear him from your palace
　　　　　 And torture him with grievous lingering death.
　　　　　 They say, by him the good Duke Humphrey died;
　　　　　 They say, in him they fear your highness' death;
　　　　　 And mere instinct of love and loyalty,　　　　　　　　　250
　　　　　 Free from a stubborn opposite intent,
　　　　　 As being thought to contradict your liking,
　　　　　 Makes them thus forward in his banishment.
　　　　　 They say, in care of your most royal person,
　　　　　 That if your highness should intend to sleep　　　　　255
　　　　　 And charge that no man should disturb your rest
　　　　　 In pain of your dislike or pain of death,
　　　　　 Yet not withstanding such a strait edict,
　　　　　 Were there a serpent seen, with forkèd tongue,
　　　　　 That slyly glided towards your majesty,　　　　　　　　260
　　　　　 It were but necessary you were waked,
　　　　　 Lest, being suffered in that harmful slumber,
　　　　　 The mortal worm might make the sleep eternal.
　　　　　 And therefore do they cry, though you forbid,
　　　　　 That they will guard you, whe'r you will or no　　　　265
　　　　　 From such fell serpents as false Suffolk is,
　　　　　 With whose envenomèd and fatal sting
　　　　　 Your loving uncle, twenty times his worth,
　　　　　 They say is shamefully bereft of life.
COMMONS  *Within* An answer from the king, my Lord of Salisbury.  270

---

244 Lord] F; false Q1, *Dyce*　　252, 253] F *subst.*; 253, 252 *conj. this edn*　　252 As being] F; Albeit *conj. McKerrow in Oxford*　　262 harmful] F; harmless F2 *subst.*　　263 the] F; thy *conj. Vaughan*　　265 whe'r] F4 *subst.*; where F

249 **in** by (Abbott 162).
250 **mere instinct of** pure impulse toward (*OED* Instinct 2); 'instinct' was accented on the second syllable (Cercignani, p. 37).
251 **opposite** antagonistic (*OED* sv 4).
252 Which might be thought to be contrary to your pleasure. However, the line may qualify 'Suffolk' (understood) rather than 'intent' in 251. The sense would then be clearer if 252 and 253 were reversed.
252 **contradict** oppose (*OED* sv 1).

253 **forward** zealous for.
257 **In** On (see *OED* Pain *sb* 1b).
257 **dislike** displeasure (*OED* sv *sb* 1).
258 **strait** strict.
262 **suffered** allowed to remain.
263 **mortal worm** deadly serpent.
265 **whe'r...no** Compare the catch-phrase 'Whether one will or no' (Dent w400.1).
265 **whe'r** whether.
266 **fell** cruel.
268 **his** Suffolk's.

SUFFOLK 'Tis like the commons, rude unpolished hinds,
   Could send such message to their sovereign:
   But you, my lord, were glad to be employed
   To show how quaint an orator you are.
   But all the honour Salisbury hath won     275
   Is that he was the lord ambassador
   Sent from a sort of tinkers to the king.
[COMMONS] *Within* An answer from the king, or we will all break in.
KING HENRY Go, Salisbury, and tell them all from me
   I thank them for their tender loving care;   280
   And had I not been cited so by them,
   Yet did I purpose as they do entreat:
   For, sure, my thoughts do hourly prophesy
   Mischance unto my state by Suffolk's means;
   And therefore, by His Majesty I swear,   285
   Whose far unworthy deputy I am,
   He shall not breathe infection in this air
   But three days longer, on the pain of death.
           [*Exit Salisbury*]
MARGARET O Henry, let me plead for gentle Suffolk.
KING HENRY Ungentle queen to call him gentle Suffolk.  290
   No more I say: if thou dost plead for him,
   Thou wilt but add increase unto my wrath.
   Had I but said, I would have kept my word;
   But when I swear, it is irrevocable. –
   If after three days' space thou here be'st found  295
   On any ground that I am ruler of,
   The world shall not be ransom for thy life. –
   Come, Warwick, come, good Warwick, go with me;
   I have great matters to impart to thee.
      [*Exeunt all but Margaret and Suffolk*]
MARGARET Mischance and sorrow go along with you!  300

---

278 SH] Q1 *subst.; not in* F 288 SD] Q1 *subst.; not in* F  298 Come, Warwick] F *subst.;* Come, Margaret *conj. this edn*
299 SD] Eds; Exit F

271 **like** probable (ironical).
271 **hinds** boors.
274 **quaint** clever (*OED* sv *adj* 1).
277 **sort** gang.
277 **tinkers** vagabonds (*OED* Tinker 1b).
281 **cited** called, aroused (*OED* Cite 2).
284 **Mischance** Disaster (*OED* sv 1).
285 **His** God's.
287 **breathe infection in** contaminate.

289 **gentle** noble.
290 **Ungentle** Discourteous (*OED* sv 2).
\*299 SD Again, as at 1.1.71SD, the king departs without the usual flourish, an index of his loss of authority (Long, p. 27). Presumably it is here that Gloucester's body is removed or the curtains drawn – in the latter case so that the discovery of the bed-ridden Winchester could be prepared in time for the next scene.

Heart's discontent and sour affliction
Be playfellows to keep you company!
There's two of you, the devil make a third,
And threefold vengeance tend upon your steps!

SUFFOLK  Cease, gentle queen, these execrations                            305
And let thy Suffolk take his heavy leave.

MARGARET  Fie, coward woman and soft-hearted wretch!
Hast thou not spirit to curse thine enemies?

SUFFOLK  A plague upon them! Wherefore should I curse them?
Could curses kill as doth the mandrake's groan,                            310
I would invent as bitter-searching terms,
As curst, as harsh, and horrible to hear,
Delivered strongly through my fixèd teeth,
With full as many signs of deadly hate,
As lean-faced Envy in her loathsome cave.                                  315
My tongue should stumble in mine earnest words,
Mine eyes should sparkle like the beaten flint,
Mine hair be fixed an end, as one distract;
Ay, every joint should seem to curse and ban:
And even now my burdened heart would break                                 320
Should I not curse them. Poison be their drink!
Gall – worse than gall – the daintiest that they taste;
Their sweetest shade, a grove of cypress trees;
Their chiefest prospect, murdering basilisks;
Their softest touch, as smart as lizards' stings;                         325
Their music, frightful as the serpent's hiss,

308 enemies] Q1; enemy] F    310 Could] Q1; Would F    311 bitter-searching] *Steevens*; bitter searching F    318
an] F; on Q1

303 Compare *MV* 3.1.77–8: 'Here comes another...a third cannot be match'd, unless the devil himself turn Jew'. Tilley offers the version 'There cannot lightly come a worse except the devil come himself' (w910). Perhaps the triadic paradigm derives from the three tempters of man: the world, the flesh, and the devil.

306 heavy sorrowful (*OED* sv 27).

308 *enemies Q1's reading (for F's 'enemy') accords with 'them' in the next line.

310 *Could F's 'Would' may well have been caught from the next line.

310 mandrake's groan The forked root of this poisonous plant was supposed to emit a groan when pulled from the ground, the hearing of which made men run mad or die.

311 *bitter-searching keenly piercing.

312 curst malignant (*OED* sv 4).

313 fixèd clenched.

315 Envy appears as an emaciated hag in Ovid: see *Metamorphoses* II, 949 ff.

316 earnest ardent, violent (*OED* sv 1).

317 beaten repeatedly struck so as to produce a spark.

318 an on (*OED* An *prep*).

319 ban utter curses.

323 cypress trees planted in graveyards.

324 prospect view.

324 basilisks see 52 n.

325 smart sharp, painful (*OED* sv *adj* 1).

325 lizards' stings From medieval times, lizards were popularly confused with snakes.

And boding screech-owls make the consort full!
All the foul terrors in dark-seated hell –

MARGARET  Enough, sweet Suffolk; thou torment'st thyself,
    And these dread curses, like the sun 'gainst glass      330
    Or like an over-chargèd gun, recoil
    And turn the force of them upon thyself.

SUFFOLK  You bade me ban, and will you bid me leave?
    Now, by the ground that I am banished from,
    Well could I curse away a winter's night      335
    Though standing naked on a mountain top
    Where biting cold would never let grass grow,
    And think it but a minute spent in sport.

MARGARET  O, let me entreat thee cease. Give me thy hand
    That I may dew it with my mournful tears;      340
              [*Kisses his hand*]
    Nor let the rain of heaven wet this place
    To wash away my woeful monuments.
    O, could this kiss be printed in thy hand,
    That thou mightst think upon these by the seal,
    Through whom a thousand sighs are breathed for thee.  345
    So get thee gone that I may know my grief:
    'Tis but surmised whiles thou art standing by,
    As one that surfeits thinking on a want.
    I will repeal thee or, be well assured,
    Adventure to be banishèd myself:      350

---

332 turn] F *subst.*; turns *Rowe*    340 SD] *This edn; not in* F

**327 boding** ominous.
**327 consort** group of musicians.
**328 dark-seated** situated in the dark.
**329–32** 'This inconsistency is very common in real life. Those who are vexed to impatience are angry to see others less disturbed than themselves, but when others begin to rave, they immediately see in them what they could not find in themselves, the deformity and folly of useless rage' (Johnson).
**331 over-chargèd** overloaded.
**332 turn** Rowe's emendation produces consistency but is not grammatically necessary, as plural subjects ('curses') could be followed by verbs with singular terminations (Abbott 330).
**333 leave** cease (*OED* sv 10).
**339–402** Passages from this sequence are strongly reminiscent of Ovid, *Tristia* 1.3, where the poet's wife laments his being driven into exile by Caesar's wrath.
**340 dew...tears** proverbial (Dent DD13).
**342 woeful monuments** i.e. her tears.
**344–5** 'That by the impression [as of a seal on wax] of my kiss forever remaining on thy hand, thou mightest think of those lips through which a thousand sighs will be breathed for thee' (Johnson).
**346 know** fully realise.
**347 surmised** imagined.
**348 want** famine (*OED* sv *sb* 3).
**349 repeal thee** call you back from exile (*OED* Repeal *v* 3b).
**350** Compare *Tristia* 1.3.82: 'te sequar et coniunx exulis exul ero'.
**350 Adventure** Dare (*OED* sv *v* 5).

And banishèd I am, if but from thee.
Go; speak not to me; even now be gone.
O go not yet! Even thus two friends condemned
Embrace and kiss and take ten thousand leaves,
Loather a hundred times to part than die;                          355
Yet now farewell; and farewell life with thee.
SUFFOLK Thus is poor Suffolk ten times banished:
Once by the king and three times thrice by thee.
'Tis not the land I care for, were't thou thence:
A wilderness is populous enough                                    360
So Suffolk had thy heavenly company.
For where thou art, there is the world itself,
With every several pleasure in the world;
And where thou art not, desolation.
I can no more: live thou to joy thy life,                          365
Myself to joy in nought but that thou liv'st.

*Enter* VAUX

MARGARET Whither goes Vaux so fast? What news I prithee?
VAUX To signify unto his majesty
That Cardinal Beaufort is at point of death;
For suddenly a grievous sickness took him                          370
That makes him gasp and stare and catch the air,
Blaspheming God and cursing men on earth.
Sometime he talks as if Duke Humphrey's ghost
Were by his side; sometime he calls the king
And whispers to his pillow as to him                               375
The secrets of his overchargèd soul.
And I am sent to tell his majesty
That even now he cries aloud for him.
MARGARET Go tell this heavy message to the king.        *Exit* [*Vaux*]
Ay me! What is this world? What news are these?                    380
But wherefore grieve I at an hour's poor loss,
Omitting Suffolk's exile, my soul's treasure?

366 to] *Singer²; no F; now conj.* Oxford      379 SD] Q1 *subst.; Exit* F

358 **three...thrice** proverbial (Dent TT11).
363 **several** separate, individual.
366 SD VAUX Q's *Vawse* indicates how the name was pronounced.
366 ***to** Singer's emendation strengthens the repetition.
368 **signify** make known (*OED* sv 3).

376 **overchargèd** overburdened (with guilt).
379 **heavy** sad.
380 **What...world?** Compare the proverb 'What a world is this' (Dent W889.1).
381 **an...loss** the loss of the short time the old cardinal might otherwise have lived.
382 **Omitting** Disregarding (*OED* Omit 2c).

Why only, Suffolk, mourn I not for thee
And with the southern clouds contend in tears,
Theirs for the earth's increase, mine for my sorrow's?          385
Now get thee hence: the king, thou knowst, is coming;
If thou be found by me, thou art but dead.

SUFFOLK  If I depart from thee, I cannot live;
And in thy sight to die, what were it else
But like a pleasant slumber in thy lap?                        390
Here could I breathe my soul into the air,
As mild and gentle as the cradle-babe
Dying with mother's dug between its lips:
Where, from thy sight, I should be raging mad
And cry out for thee to close up mine eyes,                    395
To have thee with thy lips to stop my mouth;
So shouldst thou either turn my flying soul,
                    [*He kisses her*]
Or I should breathe it, so, into thy body,
And then it lived in sweet Elysium.
To die by thee were but to die in jest:                        400
From thee to die were torture more than death.
O let me stay, befall what may befall!

MARGARET  Away!
                    [*He turns to go*]
          Though parting be a fretful corrosive,

---

385 sorrow's] *Pelican* (*conj. Vaughan*); sorrows F   393 its] F *subst.;* his Q1   397 SD] *This edn; not in* F   403 Away!
...Though] F; Though *Cairncross*   403 SD] *This edn; not in* F

---

**383** (On the other hand) why don't I mourn, Suffolk, for you alone.

**384 southern** rain was believed to come from the south; compare *FQ*, III, IV, 13; *Metamorphoses* I, 314 ff.

**385 increase** fruition.

**387 by me** at my side.

**387 but dead** as good as dead.

**388–402** The speech is derived from Ovid's *Tristia* III.3.43–4, 61–2.

**393 dug** nipple.

**393 its** Oxford points out that 'its' as a possessive is not found in Shakespeare before *WT* and emends to 'his'.

**394 Where, from** Whereas, out of.

**396** Compare the proverb 'To stop one's mouth with a kiss' (Dent M1264.1).

**397 turn** turn back (*OED* sv v 19); the soul of a

dying man was believed to fly out from his mouth; compare *3H6* 5.2.35.

**398** Compare '[Kissing] is the opening of an entry to the souls, which...pour themselves by turn the one into the other's body' (Castiglione, *The Book of the Courtier*, trans. T. Hoby, 1928 edn, p. 315).

**399 lived** would live (Abbott 361).

**399 Elysium** The Islands of the Blest, a classical paradise for heroes and patriots.

**400 but...jest** not to die at all.

**402 befall...befall** Compare the proverb 'Come (befall) what come (befall) may' (Tilley C529).

**\*403 SD** The dialogue indicates that Suffolk is twice about to exit, only to be held back by Margaret.

**403 fretful** irritating (*OED* sv 1).

**403 corrosive** a caustic medication (*OED* sv *sb* B2).

It is applièd to a deathful wound.
To France, sweet Suffolk: let me hear from thee. 405
For wheresoe'er thou art in this world's globe,
I'll have an Iris that shall find thee out.
SUFFOLK I go.
MARGARET    And take my heart with thee.
                    [*She kisses him*]
SUFFOLK A jewel locked into the woefullest cask
That ever did contain a thing of worth. 410
Even as a splitted bark, so sunder we:
This way fall I to death.
MARGARET                    This way for me.
                                *Exeunt* [*severally*]


[3.3] *Enter the* KING, SALISBURY, *and* WARWICK: [*and then the
curtains be drawn and the* CARDINAL WINCHESTER *is discovered in his
bed, raving and starting as if he were mad*]


KING HENRY How fares my lord? Speak, Beaufort, to thy sovereign.
WINCHESTER If thou be'st Death, I'll give thee England's treasure,
        Enough to purchase such another island,
        So thou wilt let me live and feel no pain.
KING HENRY Ah, what a sign it is of evil life 5
        Where death's approach is seen so terrible.

---

407 out.] F; out. / Away! *Cairncross*    408 And] F; And going *conj. Vaughan*    408 SD] Q1 *subst.; not in* F    412 SD
*severally*] Q1 *subst.; not in* F    Act 3, Scene 3    3.3] *Capell; not in* F    0 SD.1–3 *and*. . . *mad*] *This edn* (*following* Q1);
*to the Cardinal in bed* F

---

404 **applièd** suitable.
404 **deathful** mortal.
407 **Iris** Personification of the rainbow and
Juno's messenger; see *Metamorphoses* I, 321,
*Temp.* 4.1.76–7.
408 **And**. . .**thee** Compare the proverb 'The
lover is not where he lives but where he loves'
(Dent L565).
409 **into** in (Abbott 159).
409 **cask** casket.
411 **bark** ship.
411 **sunder we** do we part (*OED* Sunder 4).

**Act 3, Scene 3**
*3.3 Hall (pp. 210–11; see Appendix 1, p. 226)
but not Holinshed (p. 212) records a speech of
repentance for Winchester. Shakespeare has him

die still raging against his old enemy Gloucester.
'This is one of the scenes which have been
applauded by the critics, and which will continue
to be admired when prejudice shall cease and
bigotry give way to impartial examination. These
are beauties that rise out of nature and of truth;
the superficial reader cannot miss them, the
profound can imagine nothing beyond them'
(Johnson).
    If Henry had a subconscious desire to rid
himself of Gloucester (see Introduction, p. 35),
Warwick could play this scene in such a way as to
be a psychological attack on the king (Robinson,
p. 185).
    0 SD.2 ***curtains** See 3.2.148 SD n.
    4 **So** Provided that (Abbott 133).

WARWICK Beaufort, it is thy sovereign speaks to thee.
WINCHESTER Bring me unto my trial when you will.
    Died he not in his bed? Where should he die?
    Can I make men live, whe'r they will or no?                                     10
    O torture me no more, I will confess.
    Alive again? Then show me where he is;
    I'll give a thousand pound to look upon him.
    He hath no eyes, the dust hath blinded them.
    Comb down his hair; look, look, it stands upright                              15
    Like lime-twigs set to catch my wingèd soul!
    Give me some drink, and bid the apothecary
    Bring the strong poison that I bought of him.
KING HENRY O Thou eternal mover of the heavens,
    Look with a gentle eye upon this wretch!                                       20
    O beat away the busy meddling fiend
    That lays strong siege unto this wretch's soul
    And from his bosom purge this black despair!
WARWICK See how the pangs of death do make him grin.
SALISBURY Disturb him not, let him pass peaceably.                                       25
KING HENRY Peace to his soul, if God's good pleasure be.
    Lord Cardinal, if thou thinkst on heaven's bliss,
    Hold up thy hand, make signal of thy hope –
             *[Winchester dies]*
    He dies and makes no sign. O God, forgive him.
WARWICK So bad a death argues a monstrous life.                                          30
KING HENRY Forbear to judge, for we are sinners all.

---

10 whe'r] *Pope subst.;* where F    28 SD] Q1 *subst.; not in* F

9 **he** Gloucester.
10 **whe'r** whether.
13 **thousand pound** a proverbial hyperbole
(Dent T428.1).
14 **dust** i.e. that to which all things return in
death.
16 **lime-twigs** see 1.3.83 n.
18 Winchester apparently wishes to dispatch
Gloucester finally, or to kill himself.
19 **eternal mover** According to Aristotle
(*Physics* VIII, etc.), the attribute of God who,
himself unmoved, moved the universe; compare
Richard Hooker, *Of the Laws of Ecclesiastical
Polity*, I.i.1–2.
24 Robinson suggests that Warwick should
here demonically 'lift up the dying man's head for
Henry to look at' (p. 184).
24 **pangs of death** taken from 2 Sam. 22.5.

24 **grin** grimace, bare his teeth (*OED* sv *v* 1).
25 **pass** die.
28 **Hold...hand** 'A sign (as for an act of
solemn attestation in a court of law) commonly
asked of the dying at this time...See...the
death of King John in *2 Troublesome Reign* 8.136,
146' (Wilson).
30 **argues** evinces, indicates (*OED* Argue 3).
31 Compare Matt. 7.1: 'Judge not, that ye be
not judged'. Johnson offers as a gloss 'Peccantes
culpare cave, nam labimur omnes, / Aut sumus,
aut fuimus, vel possumus esse quod hic est', a
proverb to be found in Bodleian Digby MS 53
and Harleian MS 3362, beginning 'Peccantem
damnare' (*Johnson on Shakespeare*, ed. A. Sherbo,
1968, II, 590). See the headnote above.
31 **for...all** Compare Matt. 3.23: 'for all have
sinned'.

Close up his eyes and draw the curtain close;
And let us all to meditation.

*Exeunt*

[4.1] *Alarum. Fight at sea. Ordnance goes off. Enter* [*a*] LIEUTENANT[, *a*
MASTER, *a* MASTER'S MATE, WALTER WHITMORE, *and* SOLDIERS;
*with*] SUFFOLK, [*disguised, and two* GENTLEMEN, *prisoners*]

LIEUTENANT The gaudy, blabbing, and remorseful day
Is crept into the bosom of the sea;
And now loud-howling wolves arouse the jades
That drag the tragic melancholy night,
Who, with their drowsy, slow, and flagging wings,                   5
Clip dead men's graves, and from their misty jaws
Breathe foul contagious darkness in the air.

Act 4, Scene 1    4.1] *Pope; not in* F    0 SD] *This edn; Alarmes with, and the chambers be discharged, like as it were a fight at sea. And then enter the Captaine of the ship and the Maister, and the Maisters Mate, & the Duke of Suffolke disguised, and others with him, and Water Whickmore* Q1    6 Clip] *Theobald; Cleape* F; *Clepe conj. Wilson*

32 **Close...eyes** The last rite of death, a mark of respect and affection.

**Act 4, Scene 1**
*4.1 Suffolk's death in 1450 at the hands of the captain of a ship of war, the *Nicholas of the Tower*, which belonged to the Duke of Exeter, is narrated by Holinshed, p. 220 (Hall, p. 219). For Holinshed's report of the way the populace detested Suffolk, see Appendix 1, p. 227. Shakespeare seems to have invented the figure of Whitmore.

0 SD.1 **Fight at sea** This descriptive note suggests holograph copy; compare 4.2.25 SD.2 n.

0 SD.1 **Ordnance goes off** Q's SD (see collation) reveals that 'chambers' (small cannon used for sound effects.

0 SD.1 LIEUTENANT ('Captaine' in Q), the military commander of the pirates' ship. Holinshed (p. 220) and Hall (p. 219) designate him as a captain.

0 SD.2 WALTER WHITMORE A gentleman volunteer serving on the ship (compare *H5* 4.1.39).

1–7 The fustian style of these lines suggested to Hart and other editors that they might be an interpolation. There is, however, a strange echo of Gloucester's description of Winchester, who has just died, and of Suffolk, who is about to die:

'Beaufort's red sparkling eyes blab his heart's malice, / And Suffolk's cloudy brow his stormy hate' (3.1.154–5). Perhaps the lines serve as a prologue to the uprising of the people in Act 4, a sea-change in the action (see Robinson, p. 183).

1 **gaudy** (1) bright, (2) full of trickery (?) (*OED* sv 2).

1 **blabbing** 'The epithet "blabbing" applied to the day by a man about to commit murder is exquisitely beautiful. Guilt is afraid of light, considers darkness as a natural shelter, and makes night the confidante of those actions which cannot be trusted to the "tell-tale" day' (Johnson).

1 **remorseful** penitent (*OED* sv 1).

2 Compare the proverb 'He will creep into your bosom' (Tilley B546).

3 **jades** worthless horses; here a derogatory term for the dragons that drew Night's chariot; compare *MND* 3.2.379, Marlowe, *Hero and Leander* 1, 107–8.

5 **flagging wings** drooping wings (of Night's dragons).

6 *Clip Embrace; see collation and *Cor.* 4.5.110 n. (New Arden). F's 'Cleape' may, however, be a spelling of 'clepe' = summon (*OED* sv 2).

Therefore bring forth the soldiers of our prize;
For, whilst our pinnace anchors in the Downs,
Here shall they make their ransom on the sand                      10
Or with their blood stain this discoloured shore.
Master, [*He points to 1 Gentleman*] this prisoner freely give I
    thee;
And thou that art his mate, [*He points to 2 Gentleman*] make
    boot of this;
The other, [*He points to Suffolk*] Walter Whitmore, is thy
    share.

1 GENTLEMAN What is my ransom, master? Let me know.          15
MASTER A thousand crowns, or else lay down your head.
MATE And so much shall you give, or off goes yours.
LIEUTENANT What, think you much to pay two thousand crowns,
    And bear the name and port of gentlemen? –
WHITMORE Cut both the villains' throats – for die you shall –     20
    The lives of those which we have lost in fight
    Be counterpoised with such a petty sum!
1 GENTLEMAN I'll give it, sir, and therefore spare my life.
2 GENTLEMAN And so will I, and write home for it straight.
WHITMORE I lost mine eye in laying the prize aboard,              25
                    [*To Suffolk*]
    And therefore, to revenge it, shalt thou die,
    And so should these, if I might have my will.
LIEUTENANT Be not so rash; take ransom, let him live.
SUFFOLK Look on my George: I am a gentleman.
    Rate me at what thou wilt, thou shalt be paid.               30

---

12–14 SDD] *This edn; not in* F    20 WHITMORE Cut] *Oxford (conj. Malone²); Cut* F    21 The] F; *Can Collier²*    22
sum!] *White; summe* F    25 SD] *Rowe; not in* F    29 George] F; *ring* Q1

---

**8 Therefore** That being so.
**8 of our prize** from this ship we have captured.
**9 pinnace** a small two-masted vessel.
**9 Downs** An anchorage off the termination of the North Downs in Kent and protected by the Goodwin Sands.
**10 make** draw up (*OED* sv v 5d).
**11 discoloured** used proleptically, i.e. which will be discoloured.
**13 make...this** take your profit from this second gentleman.
**19 port** demeanour, style.
*****20 SH** I accept Malone's conjecture that a SH

has been lost here (see collation). Whitmore is the bloodthirsty one: the lieutenant, to whom F continues the speech, urges him to be 'not so rash' (28).
**22 counterpoised** compensated (*OED* Counterpoise v 2b).
**25 laying...aboard** manoeuvring my ship next to the prize vessel (*OED* Aboard 2c).
**28 rash** hasty (*OED* sv 2).
**29 George** A badge showing St George slaying the dragon, the insignia of the Order of the Garter with which Suffolk had been invested by Henry V.
**30 Rate me** Set my ransom.

WHITMORE And so am I; my name is Walter Whitmore.
　　　　　How now? Why starts thou? What, doth death affright?

SUFFOLK Thy name affrights me, in whose sound is death:
　　　　　A cunning man did calculate my birth
　　　　　And told me that by water I should die: 35
　　　　　Yet let not this make thee be bloody-minded,
　　　　　Thy name is Gualtier, being rightly sounded.

WHITMORE Gualtier or Walter, which it is I care not;
　　　　　Never yet did base dishonour blur our name
　　　　　But with our sword we wiped away the blot; 40
　　　　　Therefore, when merchant-like I sell revenge,
　　　　　Broke be my sword, my arms torn and defaced,
　　　　　And I proclaimed a coward through the world.
　　　　　*[Laying hands on Suffolk to bear him off]*

SUFFOLK Stay, Whitmore, for thy prisoner is a prince,
　　　　　The Duke of Suffolk, William de la Pole. 45

WHITMORE The Duke of Suffolk, muffled up in rags?

SUFFOLK Ay, but these rags are no part of the duke.
　　　　　Jove sometime went disguised, and why not I?

LIEUTENANT But Jove was never slain as thou shalt be.

SUFFOLK Obscure and lousy swain, King Henry's blood, 50
　　　　　The honourable blood of Lancaster,
　　　　　Must not be shed by such a jaded groom.
　　　　　Hast thou not kissed thy hand, and held my stirrup,
　　　　　And bare-head plodded by my foot-cloth mule,

---

32 death] F; *thee Cairncross*　39 Never] F; *Ne'er Rowe*　43 SD] *Capell subst.; not in* F　48] *Pope (following* Q1); *not in* F　49–50 be. / SUFFOLK Obscure] *Pope (following* Q1); be, / Obscure F　50 lousy] F; *lowly Pope*　51 The] *Pope; Suf.* The F　54 And bare-head] Q1; Bare-headed F

**32 starts** For this second-person-singular inflection on verbs ending in 't' see Abbott 340.

**33 Thy name** Walter, which was pronounced 'water' (Cercignani, p. 88).

**33 death** The one-eyed Whitmore (see 25) appears as a personification of Death.

**34 cunning** skilled.

**34 calculate my birth** cast my horoscope – in fact, Bolingbroke received the prophecy from a spirit: see 1.4.31–2.

**36 make...bloody-minded** turn your thoughts to murder.

**37 Gualtier** The French version of the name.

**37 sounded** pronounced.

**41 sell revenge** i.e. for ransom.

**42 arms** coat of arms.

**42 torn and defaced** a mark of disgrace – see *R2* 3.1.24–5.

**\*48** The adoption of this line from Q is justified by 49. Stories of Jove in disguise are recapitulated in *Metamorphoses* VI, 126 ff.

**\*50 SH** In F the line is given to the lieutenant. It is clear from 66 that Suffolk is addressing the lieutenant and not Whitmore.

**50 lousy** dirty, contemptible (*OED* sv 2).

**50–1 King...Lancaster** In fact, Suffolk's mother was merely a distant cousin of Henry VI.

**52 jaded** contemptible (*OED* sv 3).

**52 groom** fellow.

**53 kissed thy hand** a courtier's gesture of obsequious respect; see *LLL* 5.2.324.

**54 \*bare-head** Footmen of the great wore no hats as a sign of respect for their masters; see Jonson, *The New Inn* 4.1.17. F's 'bare-headed' was probably due to contamination by 'plodded'.

**54 foot-cloth mule** mule used to transport the

And thought thee happy when I shook my head?                                55
How often hast thou waited at my cup,
Fed from my trencher, kneeled down at the board
When I have feasted with Queen Margaret?
Remember it, and let it make thee crest-fall'n,
Ay, and allay thus thy abortive pride;                                      60
How in our voiding lobby hast thou stood
And duly waited for my coming forth?
This hand of mine hath writ in thy behalf
And therefore shall it charm thy riotous tongue.

WHITMORE  Speak, Captain, shall I stab the forlorn swain?                   65
LIEUTENANT  First let my words stab him, as he hath me.
SUFFOLK  Base slave, thy words are blunt and so art thou.
LIEUTENANT  Convey him hence, and on our long-boat's side
    Strike off his head.
SUFFOLK                          Thou dar'st not, for thy own.
LIEUTENANT  Yes, Pole.
SUFFOLK                  Pole!
LIEUTENANT              Pool! Sir Pool! Lord!                                70
    Ay, kennel, puddle, sink; whose filth and dirt
    Troubles the silver spring where England drinks.
    Now will I dam up this thy yawning mouth

---

70 LIEUTENANT...Pole!] *Capell subst. following* Q1 (*Cap. for* LIEUTENANT); LIEUTENANT Pole – / SUFFOLK Pole? *Alexander; not in* F

large ornamental cloths that were hung over horses (extending to their feet) on ceremonial occasions.

**55 shook my head** a gesture of scorn or pity – see *R3* 2.2.5.

**57 trencher** plate.

**57 kneeled...board** served at table.

**59 crest-fall'n** humble, abashed, punning on the crest which formed part of armorial bearings.

**60 abortive pride** 'pride issuing before its time' (Johnson), although *OED* cites the passage and glosses 'abortive' as 'useless, unsuccessful' (*OED* sv 2).

**61 voiding lobby** a passage or ante-room in which the great would congregate before departure.

**63 hath...behalf** has furnished you with testimonials.

**64 charm** silence (*OED* sv *v* 4; Dent CC9).

**65 captain** See 0 SD.1n.

**65 forlorn** wretched.

**65 swain** (1) fellow, (2) lover (of the queen).

**67 blunt** not pointed, stupid.

**68 long-boat's side** the side of the longest boat carried on the ship.

**70–103** This long speech enumerates all the actions that made Suffolk hated by the people.

*\*70* See collation. This edition follows the tradition of conflating the two texts here. Q indicates that the lieutenant compounds the insult of addressing Suffolk without title by punning on his name. The compositor of F missed the first part of the exchange (see Sisson, *New Readings*, II, 80). Alternatively, we could assume that the compositor misread the SHH 'S[uffolk]' as 'Sir' and 'Lieu' as 'Lord'. The puns are (1) pole on which a head was placed after execution, (2) pool, (3) Sir Pol (parrot), (4) poll (head) (Cercignani, pp. 190, 222).

**71 kennel** the open drain of a street (*OED* sv *sb²*).

**71 sink** cess-pool (*OED* sv *sb* 1).

**72 Troubles** Makes filthy or cloudy (*OED* Trouble *v* 1).

For swallowing the treasure of the realm.
Thy lips that kissed the queen shall sweep the ground;        75
And thou that smiledst at good Duke Humphrey's death
Against the senseless winds shalt grin in vain,
Who in contempt shall hiss at thee again;
And wedded be thou to the hags of hell
For daring to affy a mighty lord                             80
Unto the daughter of a worthless king,
Having neither subject, wealth, nor diadem.
By devilish policy art thou grown great
And, like ambitious Sulla, overgorged
With gobbets of thy mother's bleeding heart.                 85
By thee Anjou and Maine were sold to France,
The false revolting Normans thorough thee
Disdain to call us lord, and Picardy
Hath slain their governors, surprised our forts,
And sent the ragged soldiers wounded home.                   90
The princely Warwick and the Nevilles all,
Whose dreadful swords were never drawn in vain,
As hating thee, are rising up in arms.
And now the house of York, thrust from the crown
By shameful murder of a guiltless king                       95
And lofty proud encroaching tyranny,
Burns with revenging fire, whose hopeful colours
Advance our half-faced sun, striving to shine,
Under the which is writ, '*Invitis nubibus*'.
The commons here in Kent are up in arms;                     100

77 shalt] F2; shall F    84 Sulla] *Eds;* Sylla F    85 mother's bleeding] *Rowe;* Mother-bleeding F    93 are] *Rowe;* and F

74 **For** To prevent it (Abbott 154).
77 **senseless** unfeeling.
78 **again** in return.
79 **hags of hell** the Furies (*OED* Hag 1).
80 **affy** betroth (*OED* sv 6).
81 **worthless** unworthy (*OED* sv 3).
83 **policy** the stratagems of a 'Machiavel'.
84 *****Sulla** Lucius Cornelius Sulla (138–78 BC), a notorious roué and leader of a civil war against Marius. Eventually Dictator of Rome when he drew up a list (*proscriptio*) of his enemies who were to be put to death.
85 **gobbets** pieces of raw flesh.
85 *****mother's** native country's (see Abbott 338).

87 **thorough** through (Abbott 478; Cercignani, p. 357).
95 The murder of Richard II by Bullingbrook established the Lancastrian dynasty.
98 **Advance** Raise (*OED* sv v 9).
98 **half-faced sun** 'Edward the Third bare for his device the rays of the sun dispersing themselves out of a cloud' (Camden, *Remaines*, 1623, p. 183). Richard II used a similar device (see *R2*, p. 26 (New Cambridge)); Edward IV's badge was to be a sun in splendour.
99 *Invitis nubibus* 'Despite the clouds' (source unknown).

        And, to conclude, reproach and beggary
        Is crept into the palace of our king,
        And all by thee. – Away! Convey him hence.

SUFFOLK  O that I were a god, to shoot forth thunder
        Upon these paltry, servile, abject drudges!          105
        Small things make base men proud: this villain here,
        Being captain of a pinnace, threatens more
        Than Bargulus the strong Illyrian pirate.
        Drones suck not eagles' blood but rob bee-hives:
        It is impossible that I should die           110
        By such a lowly vassal as thyself.
        Thy words move rage and not remorse in me:
        I go of message from the queen to France;
        I charge thee waft me safely cross the Channel.

LIEUTENANT  Walter –                      115

WHITMORE  Come, Suffolk, I must waft thee to thy death.

SUFFOLK  *Paene gelidus timor occupat artus*: it is thee I fear.

WHITMORE  Thou shalt have cause to fear before I leave thee.
        What, are ye daunted now? Now will ye stoop?

1 GENTLEMAN  My gracious lord, entreat him, speak him fair.    120

SUFFOLK  Suffolk's imperial tongue is stern and rough,

---

108] F; then mightie Abradas, / The great Masadonian Pyrate Q1    112] F; *after the equivalent of this line* Q1 *adds* Cap.
I but my deeds shall staie thy fury soone. *Oxford prints* CAPTAIN But my deeds, Suffolk, soon shall stay thy rage.
**115–16** LIEUTENANT...Come] Rowe² subst.; *Lieu.* Water: W. Come F; *Whit.* Come Cairncross    117 Paene] Eds;
Pine F; Pene / Malone; Perii! / conj. J. A. K. Thomson; Sive / Sisson (*New Readings*); Pro! / J. C. Maxell in Wilson; Prae te /
J. C. Maxwell (*NQ* 218 (1973), 133)    118, 142 SHH] Rowe subst.; Wal. F

---

**101 reproach** shame (*OED* sv *sb* 2).

**102 Is crept.** For the singular verb form see Abbott 336; for the image of a sneaking animal or thief see Armstrong, *Shakespeare's Imagination*, p. 27 and compare 109 n.

**105 abject** despicable (*OED* sv 3).

**105 drudges** slaves.

**107 captain** i.e. the lieutenant; see 0 SD.1 n.

**108 Bargulus...pirate** From Cicero, *De Officiis* II.xi.10: 'Bargulus Illyrius latro'. This work was often read in Elizabethan schools. Q1's 'Abradas' (see collation) would seem to derive from memories of Greene's *Menaphon* V, p. 197 and *Penelope's Web* VI, 77 (*Works*, ed. A. B. Grosart, 15 vols., 1881–6).

**109** The drone-beetle or dor-beetle was supposed to creep under the wings of eagles and then to suck dry their veins (see Lyly, *Endymion* 5.1.130). The drone bee was supposed to eat up the honey of bees – see Primaudaye, *French Academie* (1586), chap. 62. For this and other recurrent clusters of images see Armstrong, *Shakespeare's Imagination*, pp. 25 ff.

**112** See collation. Many editors include the line from Q, but F makes perfect sense as it stands.

**112 remorse** compassion (*OED* sv 3).

**113 of** on (Abbott 175).

**114 waft** convey (*OED* sv 2).

**\*115–16** Cairncross argues that F's 'Water: W.' (see collation) is an anomalous speech prefix to this line, '*Lieu.*' having dropped down from a missing line (see 112 n.).

**117 \*Paene...artus** A confused recollection of Virgil, *Aeneid* VII, 446: 'Subitus tremor occupat artus' and Lucan, *Pharsalia* I, 246: 'gelidos pavor occupat artus'. It means 'cold fear almost entirely seizes my limbs'. F's *Pine* makes no sense, but J. A. K. Thomson's conjecture (*Shakespeare and the Classics*, pp. 89–90) 'Perii!' is palaeographically improbable. Suffolk's terror is caused by hearing the name 'Walter' again – see 33 n.

Used to command, untaught to plead for favour.
Far be it we should honour such as these
With humble suit: no, rather let my head
Stoop to the block than these knees bow to any                    125
Save to the God of heaven and to my king;
And sooner dance upon a bloody pole
Than stand uncovered to the vulgar groom.
True nobility is exempt from fear.
More can I bear than you dare execute.                            130

LIEUTENANT  Hale him away, and let him talk no more:
SUFFOLK  Come, soldiers, show what cruelty ye can,
That this my death may never be forgot.
Great men oft die by vile Bezonians:
A Roman sworder and bandetto slave                               135
Murdered sweet Tully; Brutus' bastard hand
Stabbed Julius Caesar; savage islanders
Pompey the Great; and Suffolk dies by pirates.

> *Exit Whitmore [and others] with Suffolk*

LIEUTENANT  And as for these whose ransom we have set,
It is our pleasure one of them depart: –                         140
Therefore come you with us, and let him go.

> *[Exeunt all but 1 Gentleman]*

---

128 the] F; this *Dyce*² 　132 SUFFOLK Come] *Hanmer;* Come F 　134 vile] F4; vilde F 　137 islanders] F; inlanders
*conj. this edn* 　138 SD *and others*] Capell; *not in* F 　141 SD] Capell *subst.; Exit Lieutenant, and the rest. Manet the first*
Gent. *Enter Walter with the body* F

**123 we** He adopts the royal or 'imperial' (121) pronoun.

**127 pole** the same pun as at 70 above.

**128 uncovered** 'with hat in hand' (Sanders).

**128 vulgar groom** base-born servant.

**131 Hale** Haul.

**132–8** Like Othello, Suffolk dramatises himself in his final speech. It is for a director to decide whether this suggests he is cheering himself up or evincing true heroism.

**132–3\*** The sense of these lines makes it apparent that Hanmer was right to attribute the first to Suffolk.

**134 Bezonians** base fellows (from Sp. *bisoño* = recruit); see *Shakespeare's England*, I, 120.

**135–6** Cicero (Tully) was in fact killed by 'Herennius a centurion and Pompilius Laena, tribune of the soldiers' (North's Plutarch, *Life of Cicero*, VI, 365). But see Nashe: 'Tully by one of his own slaves was slain' (III, 272).

**135 sworder** cut-throat, gladiator (*OED* sv 1).

**136 Brutus'...hand** alludes to the legend, found in Plutarch's *Life of Brutus*, that Julius Caesar believed Brutus to be a bastard son of his by Servilia.

**137–8 savage...Great** Pompey was actually killed on the Egyptian coast by former centurions of his own (see North's Plutarch, IV, 289–91). However, in Chapman's *Caesar and Pompey* (1605?), 5.1 Pompey is murdered on Lesbos where he had been staying with Cornelia during the campaign of Pharsalia. The source may be Plutarch's note that the Egyptians were incited by 'Theodotus, that was born in the Isle of Chios'. Alternatively, we might conjecture that Shakespeare wrote 'inlanders'.

**138 pirates** In Elizabeth's time this was the designation of those who waged unofficial war against Spain. Their seizing of Spanish treasure could not be officially condoned (compare *Shakespeare's England*, I, 163).

**140** 'A lame device for getting Suffolk's head to Margaret' (Wilson).

*Enter* WHITMORE *with [Suffolk's] body*

WHITMORE There let his head and lifeless body lie
    Until the queen his mistress bury it.           *Exit*
1 GENTLEMAN O barbarous and bloody spectacle!
    His body will I bear unto the king:           145
    If he revenge it not, yet will his friends;
    So will the queen, that living held him dear.

                                   *[Exit with the body]*

[4.2] *Enter* [GEORGE] BEVIS, *and* JOHN HOLLAND, *[with long staves]*

BEVIS Come and get thee a sword, though made of a lath: they have
    been up these two days.
HOLLAND They have the more need to sleep now then.
BEVIS I tell thee, Jack Cade the clothier means to dress the

147 SD] *Capell; not in* F    **Act 4, Scene 2**    4.2] *Pope; not in* F    0 SD GEORGE] *Capell (following* Q1 *which in* SHH *designates Bevis and Holland as / George / and / Nicke); not in* F    0 SD *with long staves*] Q1; *not in* F    3 SH] F; *Nicke* Q1

142 The line indicates that the head is brought in too – and compare 4.4.0 SD.2.

**Act 4, Scene 2**
*4.2 Holinshed (pp. 220–1) and Hall (p. 220) both follow their account of Suffolk's death with the account of Cade's rebellion in Kent in 1450. The rebels came first to Blackheath and then retired to Sevenoaks, where the Staffords were slain (Holinshed, p. 224; Hall, p. 220). In Holinshed (pp. 221–4), but not in Hall, may be found the bills of complaint sent to the king's Council by the rebels. These are more specifically directed at the 'misdemeanours of...bad councillors' (Holinshed, p. 221) than the demands of Cade, which derive largely from the chroniclers' account of another rebellion, the Peasants' Revolt led by Wat Tyler against Richard II in 1381, seventy-nine years earlier (see Appendix 1, pp. 228–9) and notes to 56–7, 63, 70–90, 113, 158–62 below).
0 SD *GEORGE...HOLLAND These are almost certainly the names of the two actors whom Shakespeare had in mind when writing the scene; compare *3H6* 3.1.0 SD. Bevis may have played the Armourer in 2.3, where, at 85, Q records what is probably his 'gag' – see collation. His Christian

name is possibly given at 4.7.18 SD and in Q's SHH (see collation), while Q's 'Nicke' might be the name of a replacement for Holland. John Holland's name appears in the 'plot' of *2 Seven Deadly Sins* (c. 1590). Some editors prefer to designate them as First and Second Rebel.
1 **lath** narrow piece of wood. A 'dagger of lath' was the token property of the Vice in morality plays; see David Wiles, *Shakespeare's Clown*, 1987, pp. 121–2.
2 **up** in arms (compare 152).
3 Holland takes 'up' to mean out of bed – or in a bawdy sense(?).
4 **clothier** one who performed the operations on cloth subsequent to the weaving. On the propensity of landless rural artisans to riot and on the clothiers' riots of 1586, see B. Sharp, *In Contempt of all Authority*, 1980, pp. 3–7, 13–16, and for the London riots by clothworkers in June 1592, a time when the play was probably being performed (Introduction, pp. 61–2), see Richard Wilson, '"A mingled yarn: Shakespeare and the clothworkers', *Literature and History* 12 (1986), 164–81.
4 **dress** (1) put clothes on, (2) set in order (*OED* sv *sb* 2).

commonwealth, and turn it, and set a new nap upon it.                    5

HOLLAND  So he had need, for 'tis threadbare. Well, I say, it was
    never merry world in England since gentlemen came up.

BEVIS  O miserable age! Virtue is not regarded in handicraftsmen.

HOLLAND  The nobility think scorn to go in leather aprons.

BEVIS  Nay more, the king's council are no good workmen.             10

HOLLAND  True: and yet it is said, 'Labour in thy vocation': which is
    as much to say, as let the magistrates be labouring men; and
    therefore should we be magistrates.

BEVIS  Thou hast hit it: for there's no better sign of a brave mind than
    a hard hand.                                                         15

*[A drum heard approaching]*

HOLLAND  I see them! I see them! There's Best's son, the tanner of
    Wingham.

BEVIS  He shall have the skins of our enemies, to make dog's-leather
    of.

HOLLAND  And Dick the butcher.                                          20

BEVIS  Then is sin struck down like an ox, and iniquity's throat cut
    like a calf.

HOLLAND  And Smith the weaver.

BEVIS  Argo, their thread of life is spun.

HOLLAND  Come, come, let's fall in with them.                           25

---

15 SD] *Wilson; not in* F    23 Smith] F; *Will* Q1

---

5 **commonwealth** For the subversive associations of 'commonwealth' in Shakespeare's period – its association with benefits rather than duties – see M. R. James, 'The concept of order and the Northern Uprising of 1569', *Past and Present* 60 (1973), 59–83.

5 **turn** (1) repair (by reversing the cloth), (2) turn upside down.

5 **nap** (1) the projecting fibres on cloth, (2) sleep (?).

6–7 **it...world** proverbial (Dent w878.1).

7 **merry** For the subversive associations of the word 'merry' with egalitarian freedom, see Charles Hobday, 'Clouted shoon and leather aprons', *Renaissance and Modern Studies* 23 (1979), 68.

7 **came up** came into fashion (*OED* Come 69e).

8 **handicraftsmen** not 'rude mechanicals' but skilled craftsmen or artisans.

9 **leather aprons** worn by artisans and workmen.

11 **labour...vocation** Proverbial: 'Everyone must walk (labour) in his own calling (vocation)' (Tilley c23); compare 1 Cor. 7.20: 'Let every man abide in the same vocation wherein he was called.'

12 **magistrates** rulers.

14 **brave** fine.

16 **Best's...tanner** i.e. the son of Best the tanner (see J. C. Maxwell, *NQ* 218 (1973), 133).

17 **Wingham** a village near Canterbury in Kent.

18 **dog's-leather** used for making gloves.

24 **Argo** The current pronunciation of Latin *ergo* = therefore (Cercignani 66).

24 **their...spun** by Clotho, one of the three Fates – proverbial (Tilley T249).

25 SD The occupations of the rebels indicate that this is no 'peasants' revolt' but a group dominated by artisans or 'handicraftsmen' (8). It is therefore characteristic of the risings of the sixteenth century: see Paul Slack, *Rebellion, Popular Protest and the Social Order in Early Modern England*, 1984, p. 9. Q1 adds 'Robin the

*Drum. Enter* CADE, DICK [*the*] *butcher,* SMITH *the weaver, and a*
    SAWYER, *with infinite numbers* [*with long staves*]

CADE  We John Cade, so termed of our supposed father –

DICK  [*Aside*] Or rather of stealing a cade of herrings.

CADE  For our enemies shall fail before us, inspired with the spirit of
    putting down kings and princes – Command silence.

DICK  Silence!                                      30

CADE  My father was a Mortimer –

DICK  [*Aside*] He was an honest man, and a good bricklayer.

CADE  My mother a Plantagenet –

DICK  [*Aside*] I knew her well; she was a midwife.

CADE  My wife descended of the Lacies –                   35

DICK  [*Aside*] She was indeed a pedlar's daughter, and sold many
    laces.

SMITH  [*Aside*] But now of late, not able to travel with her furred
    pack, she washes bucks here at home.

CADE  Therefore am I of an honourable house.              40

DICK  [*Aside*] Ay, by my faith, the field is honourable; and there was

---

25 SD.1 DICK *the*] This edn; Dicke F     25 SD.2 *with long staves*] Q1; *not in* F     27 SH DICK] Rowe *(throughout act)*; But. F     27–51 SDD] Rowe; not in F     28–9 For...princes] F; *transferred by Capell to the end of* 25     28 fail] F; fall F4     29 princes – ] Malone; Princes. F     38 etc. SHH] Steevens; Weauer F

Sadler, and Will that came a-wooing to our Nan last Sunday, and Harry and Tom, and Gregory that should have your parnill [mistress or whore]' (TLN, 1560–2).

**25 SD.2 *infinite*** great (*OED* sv 2); the permissive SD is evidence of authorial copy.

**27 cade** a barrel of 500 herrings (*OED* sv sb¹ 2).

**28 For** Probably introduced to give the following words a biblical resonance (but see collation).

**28 fail** Some editors adopt F4's 'fall' on the grounds that Cade puns on his name (Latin *cadere* = to fall). This could be supported (see previous note) by citing Lev. 26.8: 'ye shall chase your enemies, and they shall fall before you upon the sword'. But 'fail' is also biblical: 'the Lord shall stretch out his hand...and they shall altogether fail' (Isa. 31.3).

**31 Mortimer** See 3.1.359.

**32 bricklayer** evokes a semi-pun, 'mortar-man'.

**33 Plantagenet** The context suggests an obscene pun, probably from the 'jennet-[lance]' used by a 'Jennet' or (Spanish) light horseman (see *OED* Jennet sb¹ 2). Alternatively, 'jennet' was used simply to evoke virility (compare *Oth.* 1.1.113).

**34 midwife** The jibe suggests contempt, as in

*WT* 2.3.160: 'With Lady Margery, your midwife there' – or even sexual deviance, as in Drayton, *Mortimeriados*, 2866–7: 'No apish fan-bearing hermaphrodite, / Coach-carried midwife, weak, effeminate' (*Works*, I, 391). Marvin Spevack sees the pun linked to 'Plantagenet', i.e. a 'producer of "early pippins" (i.e. babies); see *jennetings*...a kind of early apple' ('Satirical devices in Shakespeare', in J. E. Peters and T. M. Stein, eds., *Scholastic Midwifery: Studien zum Satirischen in der englischen Literatur 1600–1800*, 1989, p. 3).

**35 Lacies** Lacy was the family name of the Earls of Lincoln.

**36 laces** punning on 'Lacies'.

**38–9 travel...pack** (1) travel with a pedlar's pack trimmed with fur or made with the fur outside, (2) labour as a prostitute. For a lewd riddle involving a 'furred glove' see Puttenham, *English Poesie*, p. 157.

**39 she...home** For the reputation of laundresses see Nashe, III, 214.

**39 washes bucks** (1) launders the quantity of clothes that could be washed in a 'buck' or tub (*OED* sv sb³ 2), (2) absolves cuckolds, men with horns (Partridge, p. 73) by 'making them "even" with their wives' (Freeman).

**41 field** possibly a pun on the heraldic term, 'the surface of an escutcheon' (*OED* sv 13a).

he born under a hedge, for his father had never a house but the
cage.

CADE Valiant I am.

SMITH [*Aside*] 'A must needs, for beggary is valiant. 45

CADE I am able to endure much.

DICK [*Aside*] No question of that: for I have seen him whipped three
market-days together.

CADE I fear neither sword nor fire.

WEAVER [*Aside*] He need not fear the sword, for his coat is of proof. 50

DICK [*Aside*] But methinks he should stand in fear of fire, being
burnt i'th'hand for stealing of sheep.

CADE Be brave then, for your captain is brave, and vows reformation.
There shall be in England seven halfpenny loaves sold for a
penny; the three-hooped pot shall have ten hoops, and I will 55
make it felony to drink small beer; all the realm shall be in
common; and in Cheapside shall my palfrey go to grass; and
when I am king, as king I will be –

ALL God save your majesty!

CADE I thank you, good people. There shall be no money, all shall eat 60

---

58 be – ] *Rowe;* be. F

---

**42 born...hedge** a proverbial attribute of the
lowly born (Dent H361.1); compare the 'hedge-
born swain' of *1H6* 4.1.43.

**43 cage** a lock-up or prison for petty malefactors (*OED* sv 2).

**45 beggary is valiant** an allusion to the lore
summed up in the proverb 'The beggar may sing
before the thief' (Dent B229), i.e. has nothing to
lose.

**47 whipped** the punishment for rogues and
vagabonds.

**49 neither...fire** Perhaps an ironic allusion
to Ovid's peroration that his poem is one that
'Nor sword, nor fire, nor fretting age with all the
force it hath / Are able to abolish quite'
(*Metamorphoses* XV, 986–7).

**50 of proof** impenetrable (*OED* Proof 10) – by
virtue of being so filthy.

**52 burnt...hand** branded with a 'T' for
'thief'.

**53 reformation** a reconstitution of the state as
radical as that performed in early Tudor times on
the church.

**54–5 There...hoops** Inflation in the Elizabethan period was much discussed but little
understood (see D. M. Palliser, *The Age of*

*Elizabeth*, 1983, pp. 130–60). Local authorities
had been entrusted with the Assize of Bread and
Ale, which served to regulate disputes between
consumers and producers (*Shakespeare's England*,
I, 317).

**55 the...hoops** wooden drinking vessels had
bands on them by which their contents could be
measured. Cade means that 'beer, like bread,
shall be three and a half times as cheap' (Wilson).

**56 felony** a capital crime.

**56–7 all...common** Grafton reports that Ball
told the people that 'matters go not well...in
England in these days nor shall not do until
everything be in common' (Grafton, I, 417–18).
Fear of enclosures was widespread, and the
anti-enclosure legislation was to be repealed in
1593 (Palliser, *Elizabeth*, p. 27); compare 1.3.19–
20 n.

**57 Cheapside...grass** London's chief market area will be given back to the people for my
horse to graze on.

**57 palfrey** a riding-horse.

**60 There...money** Abolition of money was
part of the programme of the anabaptists at
Münster in 1534: see N. Cohn, *The Pursuit of the
Millennium*, 1970 edn, p. 265.

and drink on my score; and I will apparel them all in one livery
that they may agree like brothers, and worship me their lord.

DICK  The first thing we do, let's kill all the lawyers.

CADE  Nay, that I mean to do. Is not this a lamentable thing, that of
the skin of an innocent lamb should be made parchment, that      65
parchment, being scribbled o'er, should undo a man? Some say
the bee stings, but I say, 'tis the bee's wax; for I did but seal once
to a thing, and I was never mine own man since. How now?
Who's there?

*Enter [some, bringing forward the]* CLERK [OF CHARTHAM]

SMITH  The clerk of Chartham: he can write and read, and cast      70
accompt.

CADE  O monstrous.

SMITH  We took him setting of boys' copies.

CADE  Here's a villain!

SMITH  H'as a book in his pocket with red letters in't.              75

CADE  Nay then, he is a conjurer.

DICK  Nay, he can make obligations and write court-hand.

CADE  I am sorry for't. The man is a proper man, of mine honour:

**69** SD *Enter...*CLERK] *Capell; Enter a Clearke* F; *Enter Will* with the Clarke...Q1    **69** SD Chartham] *Eds; Chartam* F;
*Chattam* Q1, F2; *Chatham Rowe²*    **75** H'as] *Rowe²; Ha's* F

**61 on my score** on my account, at my expense.

**61–2 I...brothers** This would have been a
defiance of Elizabethan sumptuary laws; see N.
B. Harte, 'State control of dress and social
change in pre-industrial England', in D. C.
Coleman and A. H. John, eds., *Trade, Government
and Economy in Pre-Industrial England*, 1976, pp.
132–65. It might also be related to the habit of
the Lord of Misrule, who invested his followers
with 'liveries of green, yellow or some other light
wanton colour' (Philip Stubbes, *The Anatomie of
Abuses*, 1583, sig. M2ʳ).

**63 kill...lawyers** For Shakespeare's attitudes
to lawyers see A. Harbage, 'Shakespeare and the
professions', in M. Crane, ed., *Shakespeare's Art*,
1973, pp. 20–2. This was one of Wat Tyler's
demands – see Holinshed, II, 740 (Appendix 1, p.
228; Grafton I, 419).

**65 innocent lamb** proverbially so (Dent
L34.1).

**67 'tis...wax** it is the sealing wax on parchment documents (that does harm).

**68 mine own man** my own master.

**69** SD CLERK the parish clerk who had charge

of the church and its precincts, and often served
as a schoolmaster.

**69** SD CHARTHAM Like Wingham (17), a
village near Canterbury. Q1 gives the more
familiar Chatham (also in Kent) and has been
followed by some editors.

**70–90** See Appendix 1, p. 228 for Holinshed's
account of the attack by Tyler's rebels on
'teachers of children in grammar schools'.

**70–1 cast accompt** do calculations (*OED*
Account *sb* 1).

**73 copies** specimens of penmanship to be
copied (*OED* Copy *sb* 8b).

**75 a...in't** Either an almanac with the saints'
days printed in red (see Thomas, pp. 352 ff.) or a
school primer with capitals so printed.

**76 conjurer** witch or magician – because he
consulted almanacs.

**77 make obligations** draw up legal bonds
(*OED* Obligation 2).

**77 court-hand** the scripts used for drawing up
charters and legal documents. Secretary hand
was used for private and business purposes (see
*Shakespeare's England*, I, 291).

unless I find him guilty, he shall not die. Come hither, sirrah, I
must examine thee: what is thy name?                                    80

CLERK  Emmanuel.

DICK  They use to write it on the top of letters. – 'Twill go hard with
you.

CADE  Let me alone. – Dost thou use to write thy name? Or hast thou
a mark to thyself, like an honest plain-dealing man?                    85

CLERK  Sir, I thank God, I have been so well brought up that I can
write my name.

ALL  He hath confessed: away with him! He's a villain and a traitor.

CADE  Away with him, I say! Hang him with his pen and inkhorn
about his neck.                                                        90

*Exit one with the clerk*

*Enter* MICHAEL

MICHAEL  Where's our general?

CADE  Here I am, thou particular fellow.

MICHAEL  Fly, fly, fly! Sir Humphrey Stafford and his brother are
hard by, with the king's forces.

CADE  Stand, villain, stand, or I'll fell thee down. He shall be       95
encountered with a man as good as himself: he is but a knight,
is 'a?

MICHAEL  No.

CADE  To equal him, I will make myself a knight presently. [*Kneels*]
Rise up, Sir John Mortimer. [*Rises*] Now have at him.                 100

*Enter* SIR HUMPHREY STAFFORD, *and his* BROTHER, *with* DRUM, [*a*
HERALD] *and* SOLDIERS

STAFFORD  Rebellious hinds, the filth and scum of Kent,
Marked for the gallows, lay your weapons down;

---

82 They] F; Thy *conj. this edn*    82 it] F; y' (that) Q1    85 an] F2; a F    90 SD.2 MICHAEL] F; *Tom* Q1    99 SD]
*Collier; not in* F    100 SD] *Dyce; not in* F    100 SD.2 *a* HERALD] *This edn; not in* F

82 They...letters Emmanuel, meaning 'God
with us', was 'formerly prefixed to letters, deeds,
etc., to convey the impression of piety' (Hart).

84 write thy name The literate could claim
the privilege of 'benefit of clergy' to avoid
hanging, a procedure which had become an
abuse; see Introduction, pp. 29–30, and compare
4.7.35–6 n.

85 mark i.e. an 'X'.

90 SD MICHAEL probably an actor's name.

92 particular private (*OED* sv 3b), punning on
'general' in 91.

97 'a he (Abbott 402).

98 No i.e. only a knight.

99 presently immediately.

100 Qq add a knighting of Dick Butcher at this
point, a characteristic piece of 'gag'.

100 SD BROTHER Sir William Stafford.

101 hinds peasants, rustics.

102 Marked Destined (*OED* Mark *v* 6);
compare the proverb 'Wedding and hanging go
by destiny' (Dent w232). Stafford's resort to the
cliché, however, may suggest to the rebels that
they have nothing to lose.

> Home to your cottages, forsake this groom;
> The king is merciful if you revolt.

BROTHER But angry, wrathful, and inclined to blood     105
> If you go forward: therefore yield, or die.

CADE As for these silken-coated slaves, I pass not:
> It is to you, good people, that I speak,
> Over whom, in time to come, I hope to reign –
> For I am rightful heir unto the crown.     110

STAFFORD Villain, thy father was a plasterer;
> And thou thyself a shearman, art thou not?

CADE And Adam was a gardener.

BROTHER And what of that?

CADE Marry, this: Edmund Mortimer, Earl of March, married  115
the Duke of Clarence' daughter, did he not?

STAFFORD Ay, sir.

CADE By her he had two children at one birth.

BROTHER That's false.

CADE Ay, there's the question; but I say, 'tis true:     120
> The elder of them, being put to nurse,
> Was by a beggar-woman stolen away;
> And, ignorant of his birth and parentage,
> Became a bricklayer when he came to age.
> His son am I: deny it if you can.     125

DICK Nay, 'tis too true, therefore he shall be king.

WEAVER Sir, he made a chimney in my father's house, and the bricks
are alive at this day to testify it; therefore deny it not.

STAFFORD And will you credit this base drudge's words,
> That speaks he knows not what?     130

---

115 this: – ] *Theobald;* this F     115 Edmund] F; Roger QI     129–30] *Pope; as prose in* F

**104 revolt** return to your allegiance (*OED* sv *v* 2b).

**107 silken-coated slaves** Only the gentry were allowed to wear silk according to the Elizabethan sumptuary laws (see 61–2 n.). Cade's oxymoron implies that Stafford and his brother have relinquished their liberty by not wearing the livery of free men.

**107 pass** care (*OED* sv *v* 23).

**112 shearman** one who cut off the superfluous nap in the process of cloth making (see 5 n.).

**113 Adam...gardener** Alluding to John Ball's slogan in the Peasants' Revolt, 'When Adam delv'd, and Eve span, / Who was then a gentleman' (Holinshed, II, 749; compare Tilley A30).

**120 question** problem (*OED* sv *sb* 3).

**125 deny...can** a catch-phrase (Dent D202.1).

**129 drudge's** slave's, hack's.

**130** Compare Hall: 'to th'intent it should not be known that the Duke of York or his friends were the cause of the sudden rising...[Cade was] not only suborned by teachers but also enforced by privy schoolmasters' (p. 220; not in Holinshed).

ALL  Ay, marry, will we; therefore get ye gone.

BROTHER  Jack Cade, the Duke of York hath taught you this.

CADE  [*Aside*] He lies, for I invented it myself. – Go to, sirrah, tell the
king from me that for his father's sake, Henry the Fifth, in
whose time boys went to span-counter for French crowns, I am   135
content he shall reign, but I'll be Protector over him.

DICK  And, furthermore, we'll have the Lord Say's head, for selling
the dukedom of Maine.

CADE  And good reason, for thereby is England mained and fain to go
with a staff, but that my puissance holds it up. Fellow kings, I tell   140
you that that Lord Say hath gelded the commonwealth and made
it an eunuch; and more than that, he can speak French; and
therefore he is a traitor.

STAFFORD  O gross and miserable ignorance!

CADE  Nay, answer if you can: the Frenchmen are our enemies; go to   145
then – I ask but this: can he that speaks with the tongue of an
enemy be a good councillor, or no?

ALL  No, no, and therefore we'll have his head.

BROTHER  Well, seeing gentle words will not prevail,
Assail them with the army of the king.                                   150

STAFFORD  Herald, away, and throughout every town
Proclaim them traitors that are up with Cade;
That those which fly before the battle ends
May, even in their wives' and children's sight,
Be hanged up for example at their doors: –                               155
And you that be the king's friends follow me.

                            [*Exeunt the two Staffords and forces*]

CADE  And you that love the commons, follow me.
Now show yourselves men; 'tis for liberty.
We will not leave one lord, one gentleman:

---

133 SD] *Capell subst.; not in* F    133, 145 to] *Theobald; too* F    140 kings] F; knight *conj. Vaughan*    156 SD] *Theobald*
*subst.; Exit* F

---

135 **span-counter** 'A game in which the
object of one player was to throw his counter so
close to those of his opponent that the distance
between them could be spanned with the hand'
(*OED*).

135 **French crowns** (1) French coins, *écus*, (2)
bald pates, the symptoms of venereal disease, (3)
the crowns of France – referring to Henry V's
successful reconquest of France.

139 **mained** an archaic form of 'maimed', with
a pun on 'Maine'.

139 **go** walk.

141 **gelded the commonwealth** 'This reflects
Cicero, *De Oratore* III, 41, "Nolo dici morte
Africani castratam esse rem publicam", which is
quoted in Talaeus's *Rhetorica*, a sixteenth-century
textbook for schools' (Wilson).

152 **up** in arms.

158–62 **'tis...parts** See Appendix 1, pp.
228–9 for Holinshed's report of how Ball exhorted the rebels to revolution.

159 **leave** let live.

> Spare none but such as go in clouted shoon,                     160
> For they are thrifty honest men and such
> As would, but that they dare not, take our parts.

DICK They are all in order and march toward us.

CADE But then are we in order when we are most out of order.
Come, march forward.                                                    165

*[Exeunt]*


**[4.3]** *Alarums to the fight, wherein both the* STAFFORDS *are slain. Enter*
CADE *and the rest*


CADE Where's Dick, the butcher of Ashford?

DICK Here, sir.

CADE They fell before thee like sheep and oxen, and thou behaved'st
thyself as if thou hadst been in thine own slaughter-house;
therefore thus will I reward thee: the Lent shall be as long again          5
as it is; and thou shalt have a licence to kill for a hundred lacking
one.

DICK I desire no more.

CADE And, to speak truth, thou deserv'st no less. This monument of
the victory will I bear [*putting on Sir Humphrey's brigandine*], and        10

---

165 SD] *Theobald; not in* F    **Act 4, Scene 3**    4.3] *Capell; not in* F    10 SD] *Cam. (following Holinshed); not in* F

**160 clouted shoon** nailed (or patched) shoes; a 'clout-shoe' became the sobriquet of a country bumpkin (*OED* sv 2), and 'clubs and clouted shoon' became a proverbial phrase for a riot or revolt in the sixteenth century (see Thomas, p. 478 and Hobday, cited at 4.2.7 n. above).

**161 thrifty** respectable (*OED* sv 2).

**163 in order** in formation (*OED* Order sb 27).

**164 out of order** against 'public order' (*OED* Order sb 19).

**Act 4, Scene 3**
**\*4.3** See 4.2 headnote. The account of the slaying of the Staffords on 18 June 1450 is given by Holinshed, p. 224 (Hall, p. 220) – see Appendix 1, p. 228. The freeing of prisoners (13–14) is narrated by Holinshed, p. 226 (Hall, p. 222).

**0 SD** In the theatre there may be no need to clear the stage here and thus create a new scene. Perhaps Cade and his men exited by the door

used by the Staffords at 4.2.156, driving them back out onto the stage by another door, thus giving the impression of having flushed them out.

**6 licence to kill** Laws of 1549–1563 enforced abstinence from flesh during the whole of Lent. 'The object aimed at in this legislation was the strengthening of the navy through the encouragement of the fisheries' (*Shakespeare's England*, I, 319). Cade aims to reward the Butcher with a larger licence than those of his rivals.

**6–7 a hundred lacking one** a stock phrase in leases. Q reads 'foure score & one a week', which suggests that the reference is to either the number of beasts that might be slaughtered or to a specific number of customers.

**9 monument** memorial (*OED* sv 4).

**10 SD \*brigandine** body armour consisting of rings or small plates sewn on to cloth or leather. Stafford's was 'set full of gilt nails' (Holinshed, p. 224).

the bodies shall be dragged at my horse heels till I do come to
London, where we will have the mayor's sword borne before us.

DICK  If we mean to thrive and do good, break open the gaols and let
out the prisoners.

CADE  Fear not that, I warrant thee. Come, let's march towards    15
London.

*Exeunt*


[4.4]  *Enter the* KING [*reading*] *a supplication, and the* QUEEN *with
Suffolk's head, the* DUKE OF BUCKINGHAM, *and the* LORD SAY [*with
others*]

MARGARET [*Aside*] Oft have I heard that grief softens the mind
        And makes it fearful and degenerate;
        Think therefore on revenge and cease to weep.
        But who can cease to weep and look on this?
        Here may his head lie on my throbbing breast:               5
        But where's the body that I should embrace?

BUCKINGHAM What answer makes your grace to the rebels'
        supplication?

KING HENRY I'll send some holy bishop to entreat:
        For God forbid so many simple souls                         10
        Should perish by the sword. And I myself,
        Rather than bloody war shall cut them short,
        Will parley with Jack Cade their general.
        But stay, I'll read it over once again.

MARGARET [*Aside*] Ah, barbarous villains! Hath this lovely face     15

Act 4, Scene 4    4.4] *Pope; not in* F    0 SD.1 *reading*] Q1; *with* F    0 SD.2–3 *with others*] Q1; *not in* F    1, 15, 56
SDD] *Collier MS; not in* F

12 **mayor's sword** Perhaps looking forward to
Cade's rout of London, a kind of revenge for
another rebel, Tyler. The chroniclers do not
mention the detail, but Tyler was killed by the
Mayor of London with his sword, 'and for this the
City giveth a sword in their arms' (Grafton, 1,
425).

13 **do good** (1) act rightly, (2) prosper (*OED*
Good c *sb.* 5a).

**Act 4, Scene 4**
*4.4 Holinshed reports Cade's supplication
(pp. 221–4) before narrating how the Staffords
were sent to the rebels.

0 SD.1 **supplication** petition.

0 SD.2 **Suffolk's head** The chroniclers report
that after Suffolk had been decapitated, his body
was found by his chaplain and conveyed to
Wingfield College in Suffolk for burial (Holinshed, p. 220; Hall, p. 219).

2 **fearful** full of fears.

9 In the event Henry has the sense to send
Buckingham and Clifford (see 4.8.6).

9 **entreat** negotiate (*OED sv* 4).

11 **perish...sword** Compare Matt. 26.52: 'all
that take the sword, shall perish with the sword'.

Ruled, like a wandering planet, over me,
And could it not enforce them to relent,
That were unworthy to behold the same?
KING HENRY Lord Say, Jack Cade hath sworn to have thy head.
SAY Ay, but I hope your highness shall have his.                    20
KING HENRY How now, madam!
    Still lamenting and mourning for Suffolk's death?
    I fear me, love, if that I had been dead,
    Thou wouldest not have mourned so much for me.
MARGARET No, my love, I should not mourn but die for thee.        25

*Enter a* MESSENGER

KING HENRY How now! What news? Why com'st thou in such haste?
MESSENGER The rebels are in Southwark; fly, my lord!
    Jack Cade proclaims himself Lord Mortimer,
    Descended from the Duke of Clarence' house,
    And calls your grace usurper openly                        30
    And vows to crown himself in Westminster.
    His army is a ragged multitude
    Of hinds and peasants, rude and merciless:
    Sir Humphrey Stafford and his brother's death
    Hath given them heart and courage to proceed.              35
    All scholars, lawyers, courtiers, gentlemen,
    They call false caterpillars, and intend their death.
KING HENRY Oh graceless men! They know not what they do.
BUCKINGHAM My gracious lord, retire to Killingworth
    Until a power be raised to put them down.                  40
MARGARET Ah, were the Duke of Suffolk now alive,
    These Kentish rebels would be soon appeased.

---

22 Still lamenting] F; Lamenting still, *Pope*    24 wouldest] *Theobald;* would'st F    25 No, my] F *subst.;* My *Pope*

16 **planet** that would control the dispositions of those born under it (*Shakespeare's England*, I, 459–60).

19 Compare Holinshed: 'And because the Kentishmen cried out against Lord Say the king's chamberlain, he was by the king committed to the Tower of London' (p. 224; Hall, p. 220).

27 **Southwark** A 'liberty' on the south bank of the Thames on the threshold of London to which both Tyler and Cade brought their rebels. It was also where some of the playhouses were situated and where brothels and sites for popular preachers were to be found. See Jean-Christophe Agnew, *Worlds Apart*, 1986, p. 55.

37 **false caterpillars** treacherous extortioners (*OED* Caterpillar 2); 'caterpillar' was 'frequently used as a term of abuse for those regarded as parasites upon society' (Hobday, cited at 4.2.7 n); compare the passage from Holinshed on Tyler (Appendix 1, p. 228).

38 **They...do** Compare Luke 23.24: 'Then said Jesus, "Father, forgive them: for they know not what they do."'

39 **Killingworth** Kenilworth, four miles from Warwick.

42 **appeased** pacified (*OED* Appease 1).

KING HENRY Lord Say, the traitors hate thee;
　　　　　Therefore away with us to Killingworth.
SAY So might your grace's person be in danger. 45
　　　The sight of me is odious in their eyes;
　　　And therefore in this city will I stay,
　　　And live alone as secret as I may.

*Enter another* MESSENGER

2 MESSENGER Jack Cade hath gotten London Bridge:
　　　　　The citizens fly and forsake their houses; 50
　　　　　The rascal people, thirsting after prey,
　　　　　Join with the traitor, and they jointly swear
　　　　　To spoil the city and your royal court.
BUCKINGHAM Then linger not, my lord: away, take horse.
KING HENRY Come, Margaret; God our hope will succour us. 55
MARGARET [*Aside*] My hope is gone, now Suffolk is deceased.
KING HENRY [*To Say*] Farewell, my lord: trust not the Kentish
　　　　　rebels.
BUCKINGHAM Trust nobody, for fear you be betrayed.
SAY The trust I have is in mine innocence,
　　　And therefore am I bold and resolute. 60

*Exeunt*

[**4.5**] *Enter* LORD SCALES *upon the Tower walking. Then enters two or*
*three* CITIZENS *below*

SCALES How now! Is Jack Cade slain?
1 CITIZEN No, my lord, nor likely to be slain; for they have won the

---

43 traitors] F; trait'rous rabble *Oxford*　49 SH] *Rowe subst.; Mess.* F　49 hath] F; hath almost Q1　50 fly] F; fly him
F2　57 SD] *Malone subst.; not in* F　58 you be] F2; you F　**Act 4, Scene 5**　4.5] *Pope; not in* F　2–5] *as prose /*
*Pope;* No...slaine: / For...Bridge, / Killing...them: / The...Tower / To...Rebels F　2 lord] F; Lord Scales
*Oxford*　2 they] F; he and his men *Oxford*

---

**43 hate** For the third-person plural in '-th',
see Abbott 334.
**51 rascal people** rabble (*OED* Rascal *adj* B1).
**53 spoil** plunder.
**59–60** Compare the proverb 'Innocence is
bold' (Tilley 182).

**Act 4, Scene 5**
*4.5 There is textual evidence that this scene

and the first five lines of the next may have been
censored (see Textual analysis, pp. 219–20). For
Holinshed's account of these events (pp. 224–5;
Hall, p. 221), see Appendix 1, p. 227.
　**0 SD** For an account of the variants in this SD
between Q1–3 and F, see Textual analysis, p. 220
n. 1.
　**0 SD.1 the Tower** The Tower of London; the
tiring-house balcony would have been used.

bridge, killing all those that withstand them: the Lord Mayor
craves aid of your honour from the Tower to defend the city
from the rebels.                                                      5
SCALES  Such aid as I can spare you shall command;
        But I am troubled here with them myself:
        The rebels have assayed to win the Tower.
        But get you to Smithfield and gather head,
        And thither I will send you Matthew Gough;            10
        Fight for your king, your country, and your lives;
        And so farewell, for I must hence again.

*Exeunt*

[4.6]  *Enter* JACK CADE *and the rest, and strikes his staff on London Stone*

CADE  Now is Mortimer lord of this city. And here, sitting upon
      London Stone, I charge and command that of the city's cost the
      Pissing Conduit run nothing but claret wine this first year of our
      reign. And now henceforward it shall be treason for any that calls
      me other than Lord Mortimer.                                   5

*Enter a* SOLDIER *running*

SOLDIER  Jack Cade! Jack Cade!

9 But...and] F; Get you to Smithfield, there to *Oxford*    9 to] F; into F2    10 I will] F; will I F2    10 Gough] *Capell*
(*following Hall*); *Goffe* F    **Act 4, Scene 6**    4.6] *Capell; not in* F    0 SD *staff*] F; sword Q1    1–5] *as prose /* Pope;
Now...City, / And...Stone, / I...cost / The...Wine / This...raigne. / And...any, /That...Mortimer. F

**3–6 the Lord...command** Holinshed gives
these details *after* Cade had entered London (p.
225; Hall, p. 221).
  **8 assayed** attempted.
  **9 Smithfield** 'The scene of the encounter
between Richard II and the rebels and of the
slaying of Wat Tyler...not mentioned by the
chroniclers in connection with Cade' (Wilson).
There were open fields there.
  **9 gather head** muster your forces.
  **10 Gough** see 4.7.0 SD.1.

**Act 4, Scene 6**
*4.6 See 4.5 headnote; for Holinshed's account
of these events see Appendix 1, p. 000.
  **0 SD** Perhaps a parody of Moses smiting the
rock so that water came out of it (Exod. 17.5–6);
see François Laroque, 'Shakespeare et la fête
populaire: le carnaval sanglant de Jack Cade',

*Réforme, Humanisme, et Renaissance* 11 (1979),
126–30. Moses used a rod, which is a reason for
preferring F's 'staff' to Q1's 'sword' (compare
4.8.58 SD ).
  **0 SD London Stone** 'Camden considered it to
have been the central milestone of the town,
similar to that in the forum at Rome. It is
now...built into the...street wall...of St
Swithin, in Cannon Street' (*Shakespeare's England*, II, 165).
  **2–4 city's...reign** A parody, as Ronald
Knowles points out to me privately, of Henry VI's
return to London after his Paris coronation when
the conduits of Cheapside ran with wine (Fabyan,
p. 605).
  **3 Pissing Conduit** The popular name of a
conduit near the Royal Exchange, which ran with
a small stream.
  **6 Jack Cade** an insult to the 'knight'.

CADE Knock him down there. *They kill him*

DICK If this fellow be wise, he'll never call ye Jack Cade more: I think he hath a very fair warning.

[*Dick takes a paper from the soldier's body and reads it*]

My lord, there's an army gathered together in Smithfield. 10

CADE Come, then, let's go fight with them; but first, go and set London Bridge on fire; and, if you can, burn down the Tower too. Come, let's away.

*Exeunt*

[4.7] *Alarums.* MATTHEW GOUGH *is slain, and all the rest [of his followers with him]. Then enter* JACK CADE *with his company*

CADE So, sirs. Now go some and pull down the Savoy; others to th'Inns of Court; down with them all!

DICK I have a suit unto your lordship.

CADE Be it a lordship, thou shalt have it for that word.

DICK Only that the laws of England may come out of your mouth. 5

HOLLAND [*Aside*] Mass, 'twill be sore law then, for he was thrust in

7 Knock] F; Sounes, knocke Q1　8 SH] *Rowe; But.* F　9 SD] *Oxford subst.; not in* F　10 My] F; *Dicke.* My F
11–13] *As prose Pope;* Come...them: / But...fire, / And...too. / Come...away F　13 SD] *Eds; Exeunt Omnes* F
Act 4, Scene 7　4.7] *Capell; not in* F　0 SD.1–2 *of...him*] *This edn (following* Q1 *with him); of his followers flye /
Capell MS; not in* F　3, 5 SHH] Q1; *But.* F　6, 13 SHH] *Eds; Iohn* F

7 **Knock** Q1's 'Zounds, knock' might record an oath suppressed from the Folio text (compare 4.10.22 n.); see Gary Taylor, 'Zounds revisited: theatrical, editorial, and literary expurgation', in Gary Taylor and John Jowett, *Shakespeare Reshaped, 1606–1623* (forthcoming).

*9 SD The soldier would seem to be a messenger, and the only way for Dick to learn of his message is by some such piece of business.

*10 F prefixes the SH 'Dicke' to this line, having assigned 8–9 to But[cher], the same character. This suggests some omission, perhaps another entrance or a SD (see previous note).

**Act 4, Scene 7**

*4.7 Matthew Gough's death is reported in Holinshed p. 225 (Hall, p. 222); for Holinshed's account of the deaths of Say and Cromer, see Appendix 1, p. 228. Some details are again taken from the events of 1381 (see notes 1, 2 below).

0 SD.1 MATTHEW GOUGH He is merely mentioned at 4.5.10 and was presumably recognizable to an audience by virtue of a livery which associated him with Lord Scales; see Roger

Warren, 'Contrarieties Agree', *S. Sur.* 37 (1984), 75–83.

0 SD.1–2 *of...him* Q1 (see collation) indicates that they were killed; Capell suggests they flee off the stage.

1 **Savoy** The London house of the Duke of Lancaster. The reference is anachronistic; Tyler's rebels had burnt it down in 1381 (see Holinshed, II, 738; Grafton, I, 421), and it was not rebuilt until 1505.

2 **Inns of Court** Where London's lawyers worked and resided (Grafton, I, 421).

4 **lordship** a lord's domain (*OED* sv 2).

5 Wat Tyler made a similar boast: 'putting his hand to his lips, that within four days all the laws of England should come forth of his mouth' (Holinshed, II, 740); see Williams, pp. 36–7.

6 **SH** It seems legitimate to identify F's '*Iohn*' with the John Holland of 4.2. Q1 assigns Holland's speeches to '*Nicke*' and confuses the issue by giving two of Dick's lines (108–9) to Nick (TLN 1781–2).

6 **sore** (1) oppressive, harsh (*OED* sv 5), (2) painful.

the mouth with a spear, and 'tis not whole yet.

SMITH [*Aside*] Nay, John, it will be stinking law, for his breath stinks
with eating toasted cheese.

CADE I have thought upon it, it shall be so. Away, burn all the    10
records of the realm; my mouth shall be the parliament of
England.

HOLLAND [*Aside*] Then we are like to have biting statutes, unless his
teeth be pulled out.

CADE And henceforward all things shall be in common.    15

*Enter a* MESSENGER

MESSENGER My lord, a prize, a prize! Here's the Lord Say which
sold the towns in France; he that made us pay one and twenty
fifteens, and one shilling to the pound, the last subsidy.

*Enter* GEORGE [BEVIS], *with the* LORD SAY

CADE Well, he shall be beheaded for it ten times. Ah, thou say, thou
serge, nay, thou buckram lord! Now art thou within point-blank    20
of our jurisdiction regal. What canst thou answer to my majesty
for giving up of Normandy unto Mounsieur Basimecu, the
dauphin of France? Be it known into thee by these presence,
even the presence of Lord Mortimer, that I am the besom that
must sweep the court clean of such filth as thou art. Thou hast    25

---

6, 8, 13 SDD] *Capell subst.; not in* F    18 SD BEVIS] *Steevens; not in* F    22 Mounsicur] F; Monsicur F4

---

**10–11** For the rebels' desire to destroy all
written law, see Appendix 1, p. 228.

**13 biting** punning on 'biting' = severe.

**17–18 one...fifteens** a comic exaggeration,
i.e. a tax of 140% of their wealth; see 1.1.129 n.

**18 subsidy** money granted by parliament to
the sovereign to meet special needs (*OED* sv 2).

**18 SD BEVIS** See 4.2.0 SD n.

**19–102** Like Gloucester in 2.1, Cade conducts
a 'trial upon examination' (see Introduction, pp.
14–15).

**19–20 say...buckram** For the sumptuary
laws of the Elizabethan period see 4.2.61–2 n.

**19 say** punning on 'say' = a fine textured cloth
containing silk (*OED* sv $sb^1$, 1, 2).

**20 serge** a durable woollen fabric.

**20 buckram** coarse gummed linen used for
linings, hence = 'starched', 'stuckup' (*OED* sv
3b). As it was widely used for stage costumes, it
also means 'false'.

**20 within point-blank** 'range' is understood.

**22 Basimecu** from French '*baisez mon cul*' =
kiss my arse; see *Shakespeare's England*, II, 572.

**23 ff.** Lord Campbell, *Shakespeare's Legal
Acquirements Considered*, 1859, pp. 75–6, says of
the indictment against Lord Say that it shows an
experienced hand: it is 'quite certain that the
drawer of this indictment must have had some
acquaintance with *The Crown Circuit Companion*,
and must have had a full and accurate knowledge
of that rather obscure and intricate subject,
Felony and Benefit of Clergy'.

**23 Be...presence** The standard opening
formula for a proclamation or legal document;
Cade confuses 'presents' (*per has literas presentes*)
with (the king's) presence.

**24–5 besom...filth** compare Isa. 14.23: 'I
will sweep it with the besom of destruction' and
the proverb 'a new besom sweeps clean' (Tilley
B682).

**24 besom** broom.

most traitorously corrupted the youth of the realm in erecting a grammar school: and whereas, before, our forefathers had no other books but the score and the tally, thou hast caused printing to be used, and, contrary to the king, his crown, and dignity, thou hast built a paper-mill. It will be proved to thy face that thou hast men about thee that usually talk of a noun and a verb, and such abominable words as no Christian ear can endure to hear. Thou hast appointed justices of peace, to call poor men before them about matters they were not able to answer. Moreover, thou hast put them in prison; and, because they could not read, thou hast hanged them; when indeed, only for that cause, they have been most worthy to live. Thou dost ride on a foot-cloth, dost thou not?                                                                 30

                                                                          35

SAY What of that?

CADE Marry, thou ought'st not to let thy horse wear a cloak when   40
honester men than thou go in their hose and doublets.

DICK And work in their shirt too – as myself, for example, that am a butcher.

SAY You men of Kent –

DICK What say you of Kent?                                            45

SAY Nothing but this: 'tis *bona terra, mala gens*.

CADE Away with him! Away with him! He speaks Latin.

---

37 on] Q1; in F

---

**28 the score...tally** Debts were recorded by notching or 'scoring' a thin piece of wood which was then split down the middle, one half for the debtor, the other for the creditor. The two halves were called tallies. For the suspicion in which written records of financial transactions were held until the seventeenth century, see Jean-Christophe Agnew, *Worlds Apart*, p. 29.

**27–8 hast...used** An anachronism: Caxton established printing in England only from 1476 – Holinshed (p. 250) gives 1477.

**29 the king...dignity** a standard legal formula.

**30 paper-mill** Another anachronism, as the first paper-mill in England was established only in 1495: see D. C. Coleman, *The British Paper Industry 1495–1860*, 1958.

**31 usually** regularly (*OED* sv 2).

**34 answer** rebut (*OED* sv *v* 1).

**35–6 because...them** Those who could read could escape hanging by claiming 'benefit of clergy'. This was established by a test to see whether the 'neck-verse' (usually the beginning

of Ps. 51) could be recited; benefit of clergy became a social privilege – see Williams, pp. 221–2, 226–7 and Christopher Hill, *Collected Essays*, 1986, II, 45; compare 4.2.84.

**36–7 only...cause** for that reason alone.

**37–8 \*on a foot-cloth** F's 'in' does not make sense, given that the garment covered a horse and not a man – see 4.1.54 n.

**40 let...cloak** 'Nothing gives so much offence to the lower ranks of mankind as the sight of superfluities merely ostentatious' (Johnson).

**41 hose and doublets** breeches and (inadequate) coats, i.e. not warmly dressed.

**46 bona...gens** 'A good land, a bad people'. 'Compare Andrew Borde, *The First Booke of the Introduction of Knowledge* (c. 1548), I.ii, "The Italian and the Lombard say *Anglia terra bona terra, mala gent* [sic]"' (Cairncross); the phrase was proverbial (Dent L49.1; Tilley E146).

**47** The comedy of this line is expanded by what is presumably 'gag' in Q1 (rather than, as the Oxford editors argue, lines supplied to give 'something for the other rebels to say' [Wells and

SAY Hear me but speak, and bear me where you will.
      Kent, in the *Commentaries* Caesar writ,
      Is termed the civil'st place of all this isle:          50
      Sweet is the country because full of riches,
      The people liberal, valiant, active, wealthy;
      Which makes me hope you are not void of pity.
      I sold not Maine, I lost not Normandy,
      Yet, to recover them, would lose my life.          55
      Justice with favour have I always done;
      Prayers and tears have moved me, gifts could never.
      When have I aught exacted at your hands,
      Kent to maintain, the king, the realm, and you?
      Large gifts have I bestowed on learnèd clerks      60
      Because my book preferred me to the king.
      And seeing ignorance is the curse of God,
      Knowledge the wing wherewith we fly to heaven,
      Unless you be possessed with devilish spirits,
      You cannot but forbear to murder me.          65
      This tongue hath parleyed unto foreign kings
      For your behoof –
CADE Tut, when struck'st thou one blow in the field?
SAY Great men have reaching hands: oft have I struck
      Those that I never saw and struck them dead.      70
GEORGE O monstrous coward! What, to come behind folks?
SAY These cheeks are pale for watching for your good.
CADE Give him a box o'th' ear, and that will make 'em red again.

---

48 where] F3; wher'e F    51 because] F; beauteous, *Hanmer*    52 wealthy] F; worthy *Hanmer*    55 Yet] F; Yea *conj. Malone in Cam.*    58 aught] *Theobald*[2]; ought F    58–9 hands, / Kent] *Sisson (New Readings)*; hands? / Kent F; hands, / But *conj. Johnson*    59 Kent] F; Bent *conj. Steevens*    67 behoof – ] *Capell subst.*; behoofe. F    72 for] F; with F2

Taylor, p. 190]): CADE *Bonum terrum.* Zounds, what's that? / DICK He speaks French. / WILL No, 'tis Dutch. / NICK No, 'tis Outalian: I know it well enough. (TLN 1811–4). However, there may be a further allusion to the 'benefit of clergy' (see 35–6 n.).

**49–50** 'Compare *De Bello Gallico*, v. chap. 14, and Golding's translation therefrom (1564), "Of all the inhabitants of this isle the civillest are the Kentish folk"' (Wilson).

**49 Commentaries** Julius Caesar's *Commentarii de Bello Gallico*, concerned with his campaigns from 58 to 52 BC.

**52 liberal** bountiful (*OED* sv 2).

**56 favour** lenity, mildness (*OED* sv 3b).

**58 exacted** raised in taxes.

**59 Kent** As Sisson (*New Readings*, II, p. 81) suggests, Say is making a distinction between the county and the mob from that county; there is, therefore, no need to follow Johnson and emend 'Kent' to 'But'.

**61 book** learning (*OED* sv *sb* 6).

**61 preferred me** recommended me for promotion.

**67 behoof** benefit, advantage.

**69 Great...hands** A translation of a line from Ovid (*Heroides* XVII, 166) that had become a proverb, 'Kings have long arms' (Tilley K87).

**72 for watching** from working through the night. 'For' here means 'because of' (*OED* sv 24b).

SAY  Long sitting to determine poor men's causes

    Hath made me full of sickness and diseases.                                    75

CADE  Ye shall have a hempen caudle, then, and the help of hatchet.

DICK  Why dost thou quiver, man?

SAY  The palsy, and not fear, provokes me.

CADE  Nay, he nods at us, as who should say, 'I'll be even with you'.

    I'll see if his head will stand steadier on a pole, or no. Take him       80

    away, and behead him.

SAY  Tell me, wherein have I offended most?

    Have I affected wealth or honour? Speak.

    Are my chests filled up with extorted gold?

    Is my apparel sumptuous to behold?                                            85

    Whom have I injured, that ye seek my death?

    These hands are free from guiltless blood-shedding,

    This breast from harbouring foul deceitful thoughts.

    O let me live!

CADE  [*Aside*] I feel remorse in myself with his words; but I'll bridle it:       90

he shall die, an it be but for pleading so well for his life. – Away

with him! He has a familiar under his tongue; he speaks not a

God's name. Go, take him away, I say, and strike off his head

presently; and then break into his son-in-law's house, Sir James

Cromer, and strike off his head, and bring them both upon two            95

poles hither.

---

76 caudle] F4; candle F    76 the...of] F; pap with a *conj. Farmer;* the health o'th' *Oxford*    90 SD] *Capell subst.; not in*
F    93 away, I say] F *subst.;* to the standerd in Cheapeside Q1    94 break into] F *subst.;* go to milende-greene, to Q1

**74 sitting** as a judge.

**76 hempen caudle** a cant term for the hangman's rope – caudle was a warm cordial of gruel mixed with wine or ale.

**76 help** cure (*OED* sv *sb* 5). See collation: offering 'pap with a hatchet' was proverbial (Tilley P45) for being cruel to be kind. Oxford's 'health' is unnecessary, given the meaning of 'help'.

**78 palsy** shaking palsy, *paralysis agitans* (*Shakespeare's England*, I, 436).

**78 provokes** induces (my trembling) (*OED* Provoke 6b).

**83 affected** aimed at (*OED* Affect 1).

**85 sumptuous** Ronald Knowles cites (privately) Elizabeth's proclamation that people might be temporarily detained to prove their sumptuary correctness 'because there are many persons that percase shall be found...more sumptuous in their apparel than by common intendment'. See Paul Hughes and James Larkin, eds., *The Tudor Proclamations*, 1969, no. 646 (1580).

**87 guiltless blood-shedding** the spilling of innocent blood.

**90 remorse** compunction.

**91 an** if.

**92 familiar** a devil at his command.

**92 a** obs. form of 'in' (*OED* sv *prep.* 4).

**93 say** Q1's addition of the historical detail 'to the Standard [conduit] in Cheapside' (TLN 1823; Holinshed, p. 225; Hall, p. 221) may be a report of a phrase omitted by F's compositor, or, less probably, due to authorial revision.

**94 presently** immediately.

**94 break into** Q1 again adds a historical detail (see collation), noting that Cromer lived at Mile End (TLN 1824; Holinshed, p. 225; Hall, p. 221); see 93 n.

**94–5 his...Cromer** Holinshed (p. 225) and Hall (p. 221) describe him as Say's son-in-law, but other historians differ (see Thomson, p. 81).

**95–6 strike...poles** Ronald Knowles suggests (privately) an analogy with the Jack o'Lent figures that were placed on poles or lances and ritually abused; a 'jack' was made by the Tyler

ALL  It shall be done.

SAY  Ah, countrymen! If, when you make your prayers,
　　　God should be so obdurate as yourselves,
　　　How would it fare with your departed souls?　　　　100
　　　And therefore yet relent, and save my life.

CADE  Away with him, and do as I command ye.

*[Exeunt one or two with the Lord Say]*

The proudest peer in the realm shall not wear a head on his
shoulders, unless he pay me tribute; there shall not a maid be
married, but she shall pay to me her maiden-head ere they have　105
it; men shall hold of me *in capite*; and we charge and command
that their wives be as free as heart can wish or tongue can tell.

DICK  My lord, when shall we go to Cheapside and take up
commodities upon our bills?

CADE  Marry, presently.　　　　　　　　　　　　　　　　　110

ALL  O, brave!

*Enter one with the heads [of the Says upon poles]*

CADE  But is not this braver? Let them kiss one another, for they

---

102 SD] QI *subst.; not in* F　　105 her] F; *for her conj.* Vaughan　　111 SD *upon poles] This edn (following* QI*); not in* F
112–17] *as prose / Theobald;* But...brauer? / Let...well / When...againe, / Lease...vp / Of...Soldiers, /
Deferre...night: / For...Maces, / Will...Corner / Haue...Away. F

rebels when they sacked the Savoy (see 4.7.1),
house of John of Gaunt (see Thomas Pettitt,
'"Here comes I, Jack Straw": English folk drama
and social revolt', *Folklore* 95 (1984), 3–20).

　*102 SD *one or two* Dick the Butcher would
make a good executioner.

　105 pay...maiden-head Cade would revive
the supposed feudal *droit de seigneur*, the lord's
right to spend the marriage night with the bride of
a vassal.

　106 hold...*capite* have tenure by direct grant
from the crown (the 'head' of the state) – with a
pun linked to 'maidenhead'.

　107 free accessible.

　107 as heart...tell proverbial (Dent H300.1);
compare Ps. 73.7: 'they have more than heart can
wish'. For the promiscuous eroticism of the
heresy of the Free Spirit which emerged in
various subversive movements from the middle
ages until the time of the Ranters in the
seventeenth century, see N. Cohn, *The Pursuit of
the Millennium*, 1970 edn, pp. 179 ff.

　107 QI here adds a passage of 17 lines (see
Appendix 2, p. 232) reporting the setting on fire
of London Bridge (4.6.12) and bringing in a
Sergeant who accuses Dick of ravishing his wife.

It may have been added to allow theatrical time
for the execution of Lord Say to take place.

　108–9 take...bills (1) 'Taking up a commodity' refers to the practice (which enabled money-
lenders to evade usury laws) of selling trash on
credit to a needy person who immediately raised
some cash by reselling it to the usurer. (2) A bill
was also an axe-like weapon, so the suggestion is
that they will use threats to obtain a lower rate of
interest. (3) Fall to fornication (see Partridge
'commodity', and compare *John* 2.1.573, 'That
smooth-faced gentleman, tickling commodity').

　110 QI substitutes for this line 'Marry, he that
will lustily stand to it, / Shall go with me and take
up these commodities following: / Item, a gown, a
kirtle, a petticoat, and a smock' (TLN 1783–5).
Were it not for the facts that Compositor B was
*short* of copy for this column (see 113–17 n.) and
that QI displaces this sequence (a memorial
error?) to just before the entrance of Lord Say
(TLN 1786), it would be tempting – on the
grounds that the next line might effectively
celebrate Cade's wit as well as his command – to
conclude that he had inadvertently omitted these
lines.

　111 brave splendid.

loved well when they were alive. Now part them again, lest they
consult about the giving up of some more towns in France.
Soldiers, defer the spoil of the city until night: for with these  115
borne before us, instead of maces, will we ride through the
streets, and at every corner have them kiss. Away!

*Exeunt*

[4.8] *Alarum and retreat. Enter again* CADE *and all his rabblement*

CADE  Up Fish Street! Down Saint Magnus' Corner! Kill and knock
down! Throw them into Thames!

*Sound a parley*

What noise is this I hear? Dare any be so bold to sound retreat or
parley when I command them kill?

*Enter* BUCKINGHAM *and* OLD CLIFFORD [, *attended*]

BUCKINGHAM  Ay, here they be that dare and will disturb thee!          5
    Know, Cade, we come ambassadors from the king
    Unto the commons whom thou hast misled;
    And here pronounce free pardon to them all
    That will forsake thee and go home in peace.

---

117 SD] *Rowe; Exit* F    **Act 4, Scene 8    4.8]** *Capell; not in* F *or Oxford*    1 Magnus'] *Warburton; Magnes* F    3–4]
*as prose / Hanmer; What...heare? / Dare...Parley / When...kill?* F    4 SD] F *subst.; after* 2 SD *conj. this edn*    4 SD]
*attended*] *Theobald; not in* F    5 Ay, here] *Rowe;* I heere F

---

112–17 Compositor B set the lines as verse,
presumably to fill out the column with copy that
had been imperfectly cast off.

116 **maces** symbols of the office of magistrate.

**Act 4, Scene 8**

*4.8 There seems little need for a new scene
here, in that Cade re-enters immediately.
However, Shakespeare was picking up details
from the chronicles, having reversed the order of
the deaths of Say and Gough (Holinshed, pp.
225–6; Hall, pp. 221–2). Now we read 'the
Londoners were beaten back to Saint Magnus'
corner, and suddenly again the rebels were
repelled to the stoops in Southwark so that both
parts, being faint and weary, agreed to leave off
fighting till the next day' (Holinshed, p. 225;
Hall, p. 222). This suggests a pattern for stage
action here, and validates F's indications of a
retreat and a parley (0, 2 SDD) – the former of

which Oxford inexplicably brands as 'highly
suspect' (Wells and Taylor, p. 191). Holinshed
(p. 226) and Hall (p. 222) tell of Cade's escape,
having assigned to the Archbishop of Canterbury
and the Bishop of Winchester the role of bringing
'a general pardon unto all the offenders' which
Shakespeare gives to Buckingham and Clifford.

0 SD **rabblement** disorderly crowd, not necessarily an object of contempt (see *OED* Rabble 2a)

1 **Fish Street** The main approach to London
Bridge from the north.

1 **Saint Magnus' Corner** Saint Magnus'
Church stood at the bottom of Fish Street, by
London Bridge. The designation of places well
known to the audience would have given the
scene an added immediacy; compare Ralph
Berry, *Shakespeare and the Awareness of the Audience*, 1985, pp. 16–29 (on *R3*).

4 SD Buckingham's response to Cade's rhetorical question indicates that the two lords overhear
line 4.

CLIFFORD  What say ye, countrymen? Will ye relent                   10
        And yield to mercy whilst 'tis offered you,
        Or let a rabble lead you to your deaths?
        Who loves the king and will embrace his pardon,
        Fling up his cap and say, 'God save his majesty!'
        Who hateth him and honours not his father,             15
        Henry the Fifth, that made all France to quake,
        Shake he his weapon at us and pass by.
        *[The rebels fling up their caps and forsake Cade]*
ALL  God save the king! God save the king!
CADE  What, Buckingham and Clifford, are ye so brave? – And you,
    base peasants, do ye believe him? Will you needs be hanged with   20
    your pardons about your necks? Hath my sword therefore broke
    through London gates that you should leave me at the White
    Hart in Southwark? I thought ye would never have given out
    these arms till you had recovered your ancient freedom: but you
    are all recreants and dastards, and delight to live in slavery to the   25
    nobility. Let them break your backs with burdens, take your
    houses over your heads, ravish your wives and daughters before
    your faces. For me, I will make shift for one! And so God's curse
    light upon you all!
                *[They run to Cade again]*
ALL  We'll follow Cade! We'll follow Cade!                           30
CLIFFORD  Is Cade the son of Henry the Fifth
        That thus you do exclaim you'll go with him?
        Will he conduct you through the heart of France
        And make the meanest of you earls and dukes?

---

12 rabble] F; rebel *Singer*² (*following* Q1)    17 SD] *This edn;* They forsake *Cade* Q1; *not in* F    22–3 White Hart] F4 *subst.;* White-heart F    23 out] F; over *conj. Walker;* up *conj. Cartwright*    29 SD] Q1 *subst.; not in* F    30] *Eds;* Wee'l......Cade, / Wee'l...Cade. F

10 **relent** yield, give up (*OED* sv 2b).

12 **rabble** By contemptuously referring to a collective leadership, Clifford insults Cade's claims to rule; there is therefore no need to emend to 'rebel'.

*17, 29, 49 SDD These SDD, derived from Q1, indicate that the mob ran backwards and forwards across the stage.

19 **brave** audacious.

21–2 **therefore...that** for that purpose.

22–3 **White Hart** punning on 'white heart', synecdoche for a coward. The White Hart stood in Borough High St, Southwark.

23 **given out** surrendered; this sense is not in *OED* – the usage may derive from the instransitive usage (*OED* Give 62e) = 'to fail' (see collation).

25 **recreants** faint-hearts (*OED* Recreant B1).

25 **dastards** cowards.

28 **make...one** fend for myself (Dent S334.1).

31 **Henry the Fifth** From the beginning of the sequence the name of the king's father has had a talismanic quality – see *1H6* 1.1.52 and 52 below.

34 **meanest** most lowly born.

Alas, he hath no home, no place to fly to;                                            35
Nor knows he how to live but by the spoil,
Unless by robbing of your friends and us.
Were't not a shame that, whilst you live at jar,
The fearful French, whom you late vanquishèd,
Should make a start o'er-seas and vanquish you?                                       40
Methinks already in this civil broil
I see them lording it in London streets,
Crying 'Villiago' unto all they meet.
Better ten thousand base-born Cades miscarry
Than you should stoop unto a Frenchman's mercy.                                       45
To France, to France, and get what you have lost!
Spare England, for it is your native coast.
Henry hath money, you are strong and manly;
God on our side, doubt not of victory.

                    *[They forsake Cade again]*

ALL  A Clifford! A Clifford! We'll follow the king and Clifford.                      50

CADE  Was ever feather so lightly blown to and fro as this multitude?
The name of Henry the Fifth hales them to an hundred
mischiefs, and makes them leave me desolate. I see them lay
their heads together to surprise me. My sword make way for me,
for here is no staying. In despite of the devils and hell, have                       55
through the very midst of you, and heavens and honour be
witness that no want of resolution in me but only my followers'
base and ignominious treasons makes me betake me to my heels!

                    *[He runs through them with his staff and flies away]*

BUCKINGHAM  What, is he fled? Go, some, and follow him;
And he that brings his head unto the king                                             60

---

49 SD] *This edn; not in* F    58 SD] Q1 *subst.; Exit* F

36 **the spoil** looting.                          51 Feathers were proverbial for lightness and
38 **at jar** in discord (*OED* Jar *sb* 5c).        for wavering (Dent F150 and F162); on this and
39 **fearful** frightened.                          related figures see C. A. Patrides, 'The beast with
40 **start** sudden invasion (*OED* sv 2c).         many heads: Renaissance views on the multi-
43 **Villiago** < It. *vigliacco* = Coward, rascal,  tude', *SQ* 16 (1965), 241–6.
villain.                                            52 **hales** draws.
44 **miscarry** perish (*OED* sv 1).                53–4 **lay…together** proverbial (Tilley H280).
48 **money** See 36–7 above.                        54 **surprise** capture (*OED* sv 2b).
49 **God** With God.                                *58 SD Q1's formula here would seem to recall
50 **A Clifford** = À Clifford, a rallying cry;     a detail of performance.
compare *1H6* 1.1.128.

Shall have a thousand crowns for his reward.

         *Exeunt some of them*

Follow me, soldiers: we'll devise a mean
To reconcile you all unto the king.     *Exeunt*


[4.9] *Sound trumpets. Enter* KING, QUEEN, *and* SOMERSET *on the*
*terrace*

KING HENRY  Was ever king that joyed an earthly throne
  And could command no more content than I?
  No sooner was I crept out of my cradle
  But I was made a king at nine months old.
  Was never subject longed to be a king     5
  As I do long and wish to be a subject?

   *Enter* BUCKINGHAM *and* [OLD] CLIFFORD

BUCKINGHAM  Health and glad tidings to your majesty!
KING HENRY  Why, Buckingham, is the traitor Cade surprised
  Or is he but retired to make him strong?

  *Enter* [*below*] *multitudes with halters about their necks*

CLIFFORD  He is fled, my lord, and all his powers do yield;  10
  And humbly thus, with halters on their necks,
  Expect your highness' doom of life or death.

---

63 SD] *Eds; Exeunt omnes* F  **Act 4, Scene 9**  4.9] *Capell; not in* F  0 SD.2 *terrace*] *Eds; Tarras* F  6 SD] F *subst.;*
*Enter the Duke of* Buckingham *and* Clifford, *with the Rebels, with halters about their necks.* Q1  6 SD OLD] *Capell;*
*not in* F  9 SD *below*] *Capell; not in* F  10 He is] F; He's *Pope*

<br>

**61 crowns** These coins could be of silver or
gold. If Buckingham meant golden crowns, the
sum would be enormous: the chroniclers mentioned marks (Holinshed, p. 227; Hall, p. 222);
compare 5.1.79.

**Act 4, Scene 9**
**\*4.9** In the chronicles the king does not sit in
judgement at Kenilworth on the rebels until after
Cade's death (portrayed in the next scene; see
Holinshed, p. 227; Hall, p. 222). York's return
from Ireland in 1450 and the plotting against
Somerset and the raising of an army (which
actually took place in 1452 – see Boswell-Stone,
p. 285) – are narrated by Holinshed (p. 229; Hall,
p. 225).

**0 SD.2 \*terrace** the tiring house balcony;
compare 1.4.11 SD and 4.5.0 SD.
 **1 joyed** enjoyed.
 **3 crept...cradle** able to crawl.
 **4 nine months old** Henry was born on 6
December 1421; his father died on 31 August
1422. Compare *3H6* 3.1.76, but also *1H6* 3.4.17,
where he remembers his father giving him advice.
 **6 SD** Q1's SDD (see collation) indicate that
Buckingham and Clifford entered below 'with the
Rebels' (TLN 1907–8).
 **8 surprised** taken.
 **9 SD multitudes** Cade's soldiers.
 **9 SD with...necks** a token of complete
submission.
 **12 Expect** Await.
 **12 doom** judgement.

KING HENRY  Then, heaven, set ope thy everlasting gates
    To entertain my vows of thanks and praise.
    Soldiers, this day have you redeemed your lives       15
    And showed how well you love your prince and country:
    Continue still in this so good a mind,
    And Henry, though he be infortunate,
    Assure yourselves will never be unkind.
    And so, with thanks and pardon to you all,       20
    I do dismiss you to your several countries.
ALL  God save the king! God save the king!

*Enter a* MESSENGER

MESSENGER  Please it your grace to be advertisèd
    The Duke of York is newly come from Ireland,
    And with a puissant and a mighty power       25
    Of galloglasses and stout kerns
    Is marching hitherward in proud array,
    And still proclaimeth, as he comes along,
    His arms are only to remove from thee
    The Duke of Somerset, whom he terms a traitor.       30
KING HENRY  Thus stands my state, 'twixt Cade and York distressed,
    Like to a ship that, having scaped a tempest,
    Is straightway calmed and boarded with a pirate.
    But now is Cade driven back, his men dispersed,
    And now is York in arms to second him.       35
    I pray thee, Buckingham, go and meet him

---

18 he] F; ye *conj. Vaughan*    18 infortunate] F; unfortunate F3    22] F; ALL...King! *Exeunt / Hanmer*    26 stout]
F; stout Irish *Collier*    29 arms] F *subst.*; aims *Singer*²    33 calmed] F4; calme F    34 dispersed] F4 *subst.*; dispierced
F    36 go] F; go thou *Dyce*²

---

13 set...gates Compare Ps. 24, 7: 'Lift up your heads ye gates, and be ye lift up ye everlasting doors.'

14 entertain receive (*OED* sv 12).

18 he...infortunate Although Henry has just given thanks to heaven for a change of fortune, he began the scene by complaining about his lot. However, Vaughan's conjecture that F's 'he' should read 'ye' may well be correct.

19 infortunate The astrological meaning, subject to evil or unlucky influences, may be intended here.

21 several countries particular regions (*OED* Country 1).

23 advertisèd informed – accented on the second syllable (Cercignani, p. 41).

26 galloglasses Irish retainers armed with poleaxes; the chroniclers state that York assembled his forces in the Marches of Wales (Holinshed, p. 230; Hall, p. 225).

26 stout valiant.

26 kerns see 3.1.310 n.

28 still continually.

33 *calmed becalmed; F's 'calme' is an e:d error.

33 with by.

34 But Just.

35 second him back him up.

And ask him what's the reason of these arms.
Tell him I'll send Duke Edmund to the Tower –
And, Somerset, we will commit thee thither,
Until his army be dismissed from him.                                    40
SOMERSET  My lord,
    I'll yield myself to prison willingly,
    Or unto death, to do my country good.
KING HENRY  In any case, be not too rough in terms;
    For he is fierce and cannot brook hard language.                 45
BUCKINGHAM  I will, my lord, and doubt not so to deal
    As all things shall redound unto your good.
KING HENRY  Come, wife, let's in, and learn to govern better;
    For yet may England curse my wretched reign.

                               *Flourish. Exeunt*

[4.10]  *Enter* CADE

CADE  Fie on ambitions! Fie on myself, that have a sword and yet am
ready to famish! These five days have I hid me in these woods
and durst not peep out, for all the country is laid for me; but now
am I so hungry that if I might have a lease of my life for a
thousand years I could stay no longer. Wherefore, o'er a brick        5
wall have I climbed into this garden to see if I can eat grass or
pick a sallet another while, which is not amiss to cool a man's
stomach this hot weather. And I think this word 'sallet' was born

---

41–2 My…myself] F *subst.;* I'ld yield, my lord, *Cairncross*    49 For] F; Or *Hudson (conj. Seymour)*    Act 4, Scene
10    4.10] *Steevens; not in* F    1 ambitions] F; ambition F2    5 o'er] *Hanmer;* on F

---

**38 Duke Edmund** Edmund Beaufort, Duke of Somerset.

**41–2 My…myself** Cairncross's emendation (see collation) assumes that 'my lord' was written above 'myself' as a correction to the MS.

**44 rough…terms** violent…language.

**45 brook** endure.

**49 yet** now as before (Abbott 76).

**Act 4, Scene 10**
***4.10** The scene derives from one sentence in the chroniclers: 'a gentleman of Kent named Alexander Eden [see 13 SD.2 note below] awaited so his time, that he took Cade in a garden in Sussex; so that there he was slain at Hothfield, and brought to London in a cart, where he was quartered, his head set on London Bridge, and his quarters sent to diverse places to be set up in the shire of Kent' (Holinshed, p. 227; Hall, p.

222). J. J. M. Tobin, *Shakespeare's Favorite Novel*, 1984, pp. 1–3, argues for similarities in situation and diction between Cade's plight and that of Lucius, newly transformed into an ass, in Apuleius' novel, *The Metamorphoses*, chap. 17–18, which Shakespeare knew in William Adlington's translation, *The Golden Asse* (1566).

**3 laid** filled with traps (*OED* 18c).

**4–5 if…years** compare the proverb 'No man has a lease of life' (Tilley M327).

**5 *o'er** F's 'on' is a likely misreading of 'or'.

**7 sallet** obs. form of 'salad', here a raw vegetable; the word may allude to the phrase 'pick a sallet' = be engaged in some trivial occupation.

**7 while** time.

**7–8 cool…stomach** (1) satisfy…hunger, (2) assuage…rage.

**8 word** punning on 'wort', a medicinal herb (?).

to do me good: for many a time, but for a sallet, my brain-pan
had been cleft with a brown bill; and many a time, when I have          10
been dry and bravely marching, it hath served me instead of a
quart-pot to drink in; and now the word 'sallet' must serve me to
feed on.

*[Lies down picking of herbs and eating them]*

*Enter* IDEN [*and his* MEN]

IDEN Lord, who would live turmoilèd in the court
        And may enjoy such quiet walks as these?                    15
        This small inheritance my father left me
        Contenteth me, and worth a monarchy.
        I seek not to wax great by others' waning
        Or gather wealth I care not with what envy:
        Sufficeth that I have maintains my state                      20
        And sends the poor well pleasèd from my gate.
CADE [*Aside*] Here's the lord of the soil come to seize me for a stray,
for entering his fee-simple without leave. – Ah, villain, thou wilt
betray me, and get a thousand crowns of the king by carrying my
head to him: but I'll make thee eat iron like an ostridge, and          25

13 SD.1] Q1; *not in* F    13 SD.2] *This edn* (*following* Q1); *Enter Iden.* F; *Enter Iacke Cade at one doore, and at the other,
maister* Alexander Eyden *and his men,* Q1    17 and] F; *and's* Rowe    18 waning] Rowe² *subst.; warning* F    22 SD]
*Dyce; not in* F    22 Here's] F; *Sounes, heres* Q1

9 **sallet** a light globular headpiece (*OED* sv 1).

10 **brown bill** halbert painted with bronze
used by watchmen (*OED* Bill *sb*¹ 2b).

13 SD.1 ***Lies...them** It may be that Cade
remains on the ground or at least kneeling until
he gets up to fight Iden – see 53.

13 SD.2 IDEN Holinshed (1577) and Hall (p.
222) read 'Iden', but the 1587 edition reads
'Eden' (p. 227). Q1's spelling 'Eyden' (TLN 1927)
probably records the pronunciation.

13 SD.2 ***and his** MEN Q1's stage directions
(see collation) as well as words inserted after the
equivalent of 49, 'Sirrah fetch me weapons, and
stand you all aside' (TLN 1950–1), indicate that,
although Iden slays Cade single-handedly, he did
not, in the performances reported on by that text,
appear in this scene alone but attended. This may
be supported by F's reference to Cade's 'five men'
at 35 (see note). An alternative would be to have
the attendants enter at 32.

14–15 The sincerity of Iden's commitment to
the happy life away from court may be judged by
the alacrity with which he grasps preferment at
5.1.81.

14 **turmoilèd** troubled, harrassed.

17 **worth** is worth (for the ellipsis, see Abbott
403).

18 ***waning** F's 'warning' is a minim misprint.

19 **envy** malice.

20 **Sufficeth that** It is enough that what (for
the ellipsis of 'it' see Abbott 404).

22 **Here's** Q1 here records another 'Zounds'
(see collation), perhaps suppressed from the MS
(compare 4.6.7 n.).

22 **lord...soil** owner of the estate (*OED* Soil
2c, 5a).

22 **stray** a wandering animal that was liable to
be impounded or forfeited.

23 **fee-simple** estate belonging to the owner
and his heirs for ever.

24 **crowns** coins worth five shillings (compare
5.1.79, where Iden is awarded a thousand marks,
the coin mentioned in the chronicles).

25 **eat...ostridge.** Proverbial (Tilley 197).
The ostridge was supposed to swallow iron for its
health. Cade means he will kill Iden.

swallow my sword like a great pin ere thou and I part.

IDEN Why, rude companion, whatsoever thou be,
   I know thee not; why, then, should I betray thee?
   Is't not enough to break into my garden
   And, like a thief, to come to rob my grounds,    30
   Climbing my walls in spite of me the owner,
   But thou wilt brave me with these saucy terms?

CADE Brave thee! Ay, by the best blood that ever was broached, and
 beard thee too. Look on me well: I have eat no meat these five
 days; yet come thou and thy five men, and if I do not leave you all  35
 as dead as a door-nail, I pray God I may never eat grass more.

IDEN Nay, it shall ne'er be said, while England stands,
   That Alexander Iden, an esquire of Kent,
   Took odds to combat a poor famished man.
   Oppose thy steadfast-gazing eyes to mine,    40
   See if thou canst outface me with thy looks.
   Set limb to limb, and thou art far the lesser;
   Thy hand is but a finger to my fist,
   Thy leg a stick comparèd with this truncheon;
   My foot shall fight with all the strength thou hast,   45
   And if mine arm be heavèd in the air,
   Thy grave is digged already in the earth.
    [*His men hand him his sword and stand aside*]
   As for words, whose greatness answers words,
   Let this my sword report what speech forbears.

CADE By my valour, the most complete champion that ever I heard! 50

---

32 terms?] F; terms? / *Enter* FIVE SERVANTS *conj. anon in* Cam.  35 five] F; fine *Collier*[2]  38 Iden, an] F; Iden,
*Cairncross*  40 steadfast-gazing] F; stedfast gazing F  47 SD] *This edn* (*following* Q1 TLN 1951 stand you all aside);
*not in* F  48–9] F *subst.*; As for more words, let this my sword report / (Whose greatness answers words) what speech
forbears. *Hanmer*  48 answers] *Eds*; answer's F

27 **companion** fellow (*OED sv* 4).

32 **brave** defy.

32 **saucy** insolent.

34 **beard** affront.

34 **meat** food.

35 **and...men** 'an insulting suggestion that this petty squire had but five men on his estate' (Wilson).

36 **dead...door-nail** proverbial (Tilley D567); the saying is discussed by Hulme, pp. 52–3.

39 **odds** advantage (*OED sv* 4b).

44 **truncheon** thick staff, i.e. Iden's leg.

46 **heavèd** raised (*OED* Heave 1).

*47 SD See 13 SD.2 n. above.

48–9 The lines seem to be corrupt. If we follow the clue left by F's 'answer's' (= answers his?) it is possible that two lines are missing after 49. Perhaps the insertion of something like 'Let him command where lesser men must fight. / I will not stoop to answer this rough churl' would clarify the passage. Alternatively, we could read 'words – whose...words' = 'which of us two in deeds best answers his words' (an indirect question after 'report'); see J. C. Maxwell, *NQ* 218 (1973), 133–4.

48 **answers** matches.

50 **complete** accomplished (*OED sv adj* 5).

50 **champion** man of valour.

Steel, if thou turn the edge or cut not out the burly-boned clown
in chines of beef ere thou sleep in thy sheath, I beseech God on
my knees thou mayst be turned to hobnails.

*Here they fight [and Cade falls down]*

O I am slain! Famine and no other hath slain me: let ten
thousand devils come against me, and give me but the ten meals    55
I have lost, and I'd defy them all. Wither, garden, and be
henceforth a burying-place to all that do dwell in this house,
because the unconquered soul of Cade is fled.

IDEN  Is't Cade that I have slain, that monstrous traitor?

    Sword, I will hallow thee for this thy deed    60
    And hang thee o'er my tomb when I am dead:
    Ne'er shall this blood be wipèd from thy point,
    But thou shalt wear it as a herald's coat
    To emblaze the honour that thy master got.

CADE  Iden, farewell, and be proud of thy victory. Tell Kent from me    65
she hath lost her best man, and exhort all the world to be
cowards; for I, that never feared any, am vanquished by famine,
not by valour.                                                    *Dies*

IDEN  How much thou wrong'st me, heaven be my judge.

    Die, damnèd wretch, the curse of her that bore thee;    70
    And as I thrust thy body in with my sword,
    So wish I I might thrust thy soul to hell.
    Hence will I drag thee headlong by the heels
    Unto a dunghill, which shall be thy grave,

---

51 the edge] F; thine edge F4    52 God] *Malone (following* Q1); Ioue F    53 SD *and...down]* Q1; *not in* F    70 bore]
Eds; bare F    71 body in] F; body *Dyce²*

**52 chines** joints (*OED* Chine *sb²* 3).

**52 *God*** F reads 'Ioue', almost certainly a
consequence of the 'Act to Restrain Abuses of the
Players' of 1606 (see Chambers, IV, 338–9); but
compare 5.1.68, 214.

**53 turned...hobnails** to become proverbial
(Dent H480.1).

**53 SD Here...fight** For this form of SD, see
*1H6*, Textual analysis, p. 191 compare 1.4.21 SD.

**59 monstrous** unnatural.

**60 hallow** consecrate (*OED* sv 2).

**61** The arms of a warrior were so displayed, as
with those of the Black Prince still in Canterbury
Cathedral.

**64 emblaze** proclaim as by a heraldic device.

**64 honour** elevation to knighthood (*OED* sv 5)
– see 5.1.78.

**67 any** anybody.

**69** 'That is in supposing that I am proud of my
victory' (Johnson). But the line is more likely to
signify that Iden is proud of his valour, given the
sentiments contained in his previous speech.

**71 thrust...sword** thrust my sword into thy
body.

**72** Johnson draws attention to 'the wickedness
of this horrid wish, with which Iden debases his
character'. The sentiment is going to be echoed
by Richard of Gloucester as he kills King Henry
(*3H6* 5.6.67); for analogous moments elsewhere
in Renaissance literature see *Hamlet*, ed. H.
Jenkins, 1982, 3.3.89–95LN. Contrast York's
benediction over the body of Clifford, whom he
has just killed (5.2.30).

**73 headlong** head downmost (*OED* sv 1).

**74 dunghill...grave** compare *Lear* 3.7.97.

And there cut off thy most ungracious head                    75
Which I will bear in triumph to the king,
Leaving thy trunk for crows to feed upon.

                       *Exit [with Cade's body]*

**[5.1]** *Enter* YORK *and his Army of Irish, with* DRUM *and colours [and*
ATTENDANTS]

YORK  From Ireland thus comes York to claim his right
      And pluck the crown from feeble Henry's head.
      Ring, bells, aloud; burn, bonfires, clear and bright
      To entertain great England's lawful king.
      Ah, *sancta majestas*, who would not buy thee dear?          5
      Let them obey that know not how to rule:
      This hand was made to handle nought but gold.
      I cannot give due action to my words
      Except a sword or sceptre balance it:

---

77 SD *with Cade's body*] Dyce; *not in* F    **Act 5, Scene 1**    5.1] *Pope; not in* F    0 SD.1–2 *and* ATTENDANTS] *This edn; not in* F    **6 know**] *Rowe;* knowcs F

**75 ungracious** wicked (*OED* sv 1).

**Act 5, Scene 1**
***5.1** Shakespeare condenses events from the time of York's return to England (see 4.9 headnote) until immediately before the first battle of St Albans in 1455. The chroniclers intersperse the narrative of events in England with accounts of battles in France, including that in which Talbot was killed, which Shakespeare had dramatised in *1H6*. York's march toward London is described in Holinshed, p. 230 (Hall, p. 226). The king sent a delegation led by the Bishops of Winchester and Ely, not Buckingham, to seek to know his purposes (Holinshed, p. 230; Hall, p. 226). For York's submission and dismissal of his army in 1452, see Holinshed, p. 233 (Hall, p. 226). The arrest of Somerset that same year and subsequent rearrest in 1455 and freeing by the queen's procurement are narrated by both chroniclers (Holinshed, pp. 233, 238; Hall, pp. 226, 232). York accused Somerset of treason in 1452 and was arrested (compare 111–13) but freed when news came that his son Edward, Earl of March, was coming toward London (Holinshed, p. 233; Hall, pp. 226–7). Richard of Gloucester who enters with his brother was, historically, not yet born. York forged an alliance with the Nevilles, Salisbury and Warwick, and marched again on London in 1455 (Holinshed, pp. 237–8; Hall, pp. 231–2). Shakespeare makes the Cliffords more prominent than do the chroniclers.

As in the final act of *Richard III*, it is possible that two tents were erected on either side of the stage, one for York, one for the king – see 55.

**0 SD.1** *Irish* See 4.9.26 n.
**0 SD.1** *colours* ensign, flag.
**1–11, 23–31** Although it is conventional to mark 23–31 as an 'aside', there is little difference in kind between those lines and York's first speech. Both could be taken as direct addresses to the audience, with the rhetorical question at 12 creating a bond between player and spectator.
**4 entertain** welcome.
**5 sancta majestas** sacred majesty. The phrase is used by Ovid, *Ars Amatoria* III, 407, to describe the honour formerly bestowed on poets.
**6** Compare the proverb 'He that has not served knows not how to command' (Tilley S246).
**7 gold** the royal regalia.
**8** 'I have not the power to carry out what I say', although 'due action' may mean 'the proper gestures of an orator' (*OED* Action 6).
**9 balance it** i.e. provide the weight my hand is accustomed to.

A sceptre shall it have, have I a soul, 10
On which I'll toss the flower-de-luce of France.

*Enter* BUCKINGHAM

Whom have we here? Buckingham to disturb me?
The king hath sent him, sure: I must dissemble.
BUCKINGHAM York, if thou meanest well, I greet thee well.
YORK Humphrey of Buckingham, I accept thy greeting. 15
Art thou a messenger, or come of pleasure?
BUCKINGHAM A messenger from Henry, our dread liege,
To know the reason of these arms in peace;
Or why thou, being a subject as I am,
Against thy oath and true allegiance sworn, 20
Should raise so great a power without his leave
Or dare to bring thy force so near the court?
YORK [*Aside*] Scarce can I speak, my choler is so great:
O, I could hew up rocks and fight with flint,
I am so angry at these abject terms; 25
And now, like Ajax Telamonius,
On sheep or oxen could I spend my fury.
I am far better born than is the king,
More like a king, more kingly in my thoughts.
But I must make fair weather yet awhile 30
Till Henry be more weak, and I more strong. –
Buckingham, I prithee pardon me
That I have given no answer all this while:
My mind was troubled with deep melancholy.

---

10 soul] F; sword *conj. Johnson*    11 toss] F; boss *conj. Vaughan*    11 flower-de-luce] *Eds*; Fleure-de-Luce F    21
Should] F; Should'st *Theobald*    23 SD] *Rowe; not in* F    32 Buckingham] F; O Buckingham F2

**10 soul** Johnson's conjecture 'sword' is attractive, but compare *H8* 4.1.44, 'As I have a soul', and *Ado* 4.1.330.

**11 toss** (1) scatter abroad like hay (*OED* sv *v* 3b), (2) carry as on the top of a pike (compare *3H6* 1.1.244). 'One of the royal sceptres shown on Henry V's seal is topped with a fleur-de-lys, perhaps in allusion to his claim to the French crown' (Scott-Giles, p. 136).

**12 Whom...here?** Dent cites examples of the phrase from 1553 (w280.2).

**16 of pleasure** voluntarily; for this use of 'of' see Abbott 175.

**23 choler** York's choleric humour emerged in *1H6* 5.4.120.

**25 abject terms** despicable words.

**26 Ajax Telamonius** After his defeat by Ulysses in the contest for Achilles' armour, Ajax, son of Telamon, fell into such a fit of madness that he slaughtered the sheep of the Greek army under the illusion that they were his enemies. He then committed suicide. G. Bush, 'Notes on Shakespeare's classical mythology', *PQ* 6 (1927), 296, lists the sixteenth-century sources for this episode that were available to Shakespeare.

**30 make...weather** pretend good will (Tilley w221).

The cause why I have brought this army hither                    35
Is to remove proud Somerset from the king,
Seditious to his grace and to the state.
BUCKINGHAM  That is too much presumption on thy part;
But if thy arms be to no other end,
The king hath yielded unto thy demand:                          40
The Duke of Somerset is in the Tower.
YORK  Upon thine honour, is he prisoner?
BUCKINGHAM  Upon mine honour, he is prisoner.
YORK  Then, Buckingham, I do dismiss my powers. –
Soldiers, I thank you all; disperse yourselves;                 45
Meet me tomorrow in Saint George's Field,
You shall have pay and everything you wish.
                                    [*Exeunt private soldiers*]
And let my sovereign, virtuous Henry,
Command my eldest son, nay, all my sons,
As pledges of my fealty and love;                               50
I'll send them all as willing as I live:
Lands, goods, horse, armour, anything I have
Is his to use, so Somerset may die.
BUCKINGHAM  York, I commend this kind submission.
We twain will go into his highness' tent.                       55

                 *Enter* KING *and* ATTENDANTS

KING HENRY  Buckingham, doth York intend no harm to us
That thus he marcheth with thee arm in arm?
YORK  In all submission and humility
York doth present himself unto your highness.
KING HENRY  Then what intends these forces thou dost bring?     60
YORK  To heave the traitor Somerset from hence

47 SD] *This edn; Exet* souldiers Q1; *not in* F

45 **Soldiers** Privates (see 109–10 n.)
46 **Saint George's Field** An open space by the church of Saint George the Martyr on the south bank of the Thames between Southwark and Lambeth, where the London militia used to drill.
*47 SD Some of York's attendants must remain, as he seems to address them at 109–10.
49 **Command** Demand (*OED* sv 7).
50 **pledges** hostages.
53 **so** provided that.

54 **kind** gracious.
55 **tent** There is a suggestion from Q that tents were erected on stage for the battle sequences: before the entrance of the king and queen (5.2.71) we read 'Alarums againe, and then enter three or foure, bearing the Duke of *Buckingham* wounded to his tent' (TLN 3294–5). Alternatively, curtains in the discovery space(s) could have been used.

And fight against that monstrous rebel Cade,
Who since I heard to be discomfited.

*Enter* IDEN *with Cade's head*

IDEN If one so rude and of so mean condition
    May pass into the presence of a king,    65
    [*Kneeling*] Lo, I present your grace a traitor's head,
    The head of Cade, whom I in combat slew.
KING HENRY The head of Cade! Great God, how just art Thou!
    O let me view his visage, being dead,
    That living wrought me such exceeding trouble.    70
    Tell me, my friend, art thou the man that slew him?
IDEN Iwis, an't like your majesty.
KING HENRY How art thou called? And what is thy degree?
IDEN Alexander Iden, that's my name;
    A poor esquire of Kent that loves his king.    75
BUCKINGHAM So please it you, my lord, 'twere not amiss
    He were created knight for his good service.
KING HENRY Iden, kneel down. [*Iden kneels*] Rise up a knight.
    We give thee for reward a thousand marks
    And will that thou henceforth attend on us.    80
IDEN May Iden live to merit such a bounty
    And never live but true unto his liege!    [*Exit*]

*Enter* QUEEN *and* SOMERSET

KING HENRY See, Buckingham, Somerset comes with th' queen.
    Go bid her hide him quickly from the duke.
MARGARET For thousand Yorks he shall not hide his head,    85
    But boldly stand and front him to his face.
YORK How now! Is Somerset at liberty?
    Then, York, unloose thy long-imprisoned thoughts
    And let thy tongue be equal with thy heart.

---

63 heard] F; hear *Capell*   66 SD] *Oxford* (*following* Q1 TLN 2015 Lo here my Lord vpon my bended knees); *not in* F
72 Iwis] *Oxford conj. Wilson;* I was F; I was the man *conj. Vaughan*   78 SD] *Johnson; not in* F   82 SD.1 *Exit*] Q1; *not in*
F   88 long-imprisoned] *Cam.;* long imprisoned F

63 **since** subsequently
63 **discomfited** routed (*OED* Discomfit 1).
64 **rude** uncourtly.
72 ***Iwis** F's 'I was' is unsatisfactory and may
represent a misreading of 'I wus' (see *OED* Iwis).
73 **degree** rank.
75 **esquire** a gentleman and, as here, a landed
proprietor, ranking immediately below a knight.

79 **marks** the amount mentioned in the
chronicles (Holinshed, p. 227; Hall, p. 222) – a
mark was two-thirds of a pound. The text has
'crowns' at 4.8.61, 4.10.24.
80 **will** command.
81 Ironic, given Iden's professed detestation of
the court at 4.10.14–15.
86 **front** confront.

Shall I endure the sight of Somerset?                              90
False king! Why hast thou broken faith with me,
Knowing how hardly I can brook abuse?
King did I call thee? No, thou art not king,
Not fit to govern and rule multitudes,
Which dar'st not, no, nor canst not rule a traitor.               95
That head of thine doth not become a crown;
Thy hand is made to grasp a palmer's staff
And not to grace an awful princely sceptre.
That gold must round engirt these brows of mine,
Whose smile and frown, like to Achilles' spear,                 100
Is able with the change to kill and cure.
Here is a hand to hold a sceptre up
And with the same to act controlling laws.
Give place! By heaven, thou shalt rule no more
O'er him whom heaven created for thy ruler.                      105

SOMERSET  O monstrous traitor! I arrest thee, York,
Of capital treason 'gainst the king and crown.
Obey, audacious traitor, kneel for grace.

YORK  Would'st have me kneel? First let me ask of these
If they can brook I bow a knee to man. –                         110
Sirrah, call in my sons to be my bail:        [*Exit an Attendant*]
I know, ere they will have me go to ward,
They'll pawn their swords for my enfranchisement.

MARGARET  Call hither Clifford; bid him come amain

---

94 govern and rule] F; rule and govern *Hudson (conj. Walker)*    95 dar'st] F; darest *Cam.*    109–10] F *subst.; not in*
*Oxford*    109 these] *Theobald;* thee F    111 F; *before* 109 / *Warburton*    111 sons] Q1; sonne F    111 SD] *Capell*
*subst.; not in* F    113 for] F2; of F

92 **how hardly** with what difficulty.

92 **brook abuse** endure deceit (*OED* Brook *v* 4); with a quibble on 'broken' in the previous line (possibly pronounced 'brooken', Cercignani, p. 184).

97 **palmer's staff** a stick carried by a pilgrim (originally a token that he had visited the Holy Land).

98 **awful** commanding fear.

100 **like…spear** According to a post-Homeric *topos*, Telephus, King of Mysia, was able to cure himself with the rust of Achilles' spear, having been wounded by it; see *Metamorphoses* XII, 121–2; XIII, 210–12. The episode became proverbial (Tilley S731).

103 **act** put into action (*OED* sv *v* 1).

109–10 Oxford cuts these lines, arguing that

Shakespeare had forgotten that York's sons were not on stage and failed to delete the lines. It is much more likely, however, that some of York's retainers or attendants remained with him after the soldiers left the stage (see 45 n. and 47 SD n.)

109 ***these** his attendants. Theobald's emendation is necessary to the sense.

110 **man** anyone.

112–13 ironic.

112 **to ward** into custody.

113 ***for** F2's reading makes more sense, unless we take F's 'of' to mean 'concerning' (Abbott 174).

113 **enfranchisement** release from prison (*OED* sv 1).

114 **amain** at full speed.

To say if that the bastard boys of York 115
Shall be the surety for their traitor father.

*[Exit Buckingham]*

YORK O blood-bespotted Neapolitan,
Outcast of Naples, England's bloody scourge!
The sons of York, thy betters in their birth,
Shall be their father's bail; and bane to those 120
That for my surety will refuse the boys!

*Enter* EDWARD *and* RICHARD [*at the one door with* DRUM *and*
SOLDIERS]

See where they come: I'll warrant they'll make it good.

*Enter* CLIFFORD [*and his son* YOUNG CLIFFORD *at the other door with*
DRUM *and* SOLDIERS]

MARGARET And here comes Clifford to deny their bail.
CLIFFORD [*Kneels*] Health and all happiness to my lord the king!
*[He rises]*
YORK I thank thee, Clifford. Say, what news with thee? 125
Nay, do not fright us with an angry look:
We are thy sovereign, Clifford, kneel again;
For thy mistaking so, we pardon thee.
CLIFFORD This is my king, York; I do not mistake;
But thou mistakes me much to think I do. – 130
To Bedlam with him! Is the man grown mad?
KING HENRY Ay, Clifford; a bedlam and ambitious humour
Makes him oppose himself against his king.
CLIFFORD He is a traitor: let him to the Tower
And chop away that factious pate of his. 135
MARGARET He is arrested but will not obey:

---

116 SD] *Capell subst. (after 114); not in* F    120 bane] F *subst.;* bale *Theobald*    121 SD.1–2 *at...soldiers*] Q1 *subst.; not in* F    122 SD.1–2 *and...soldiers*] Q1 *subst.; not in* F    124 SD *Kneels*] Q1 *subst.; not in* F    124 SD *He rises*] *Oxford; not in* F    130 mistakes] F; mistak'st F2 *subst.*

*116 SD An exit for Buckingham is necessary some time before 192, when the king summons him.

117 Neapolitan Margaret was daughter of Reignier, who laid claim to the throne of Naples. Neapolitans were held to be murderous and intriguers, and Naples the source of syphilis.

118 scourge the term was applied to Joan of Arc in *1H6* (see 1.2.129 n.).

120 bane destruction (*OED* sv 3).

124 SD *He rises* This is implied by 127.

130 mistakes For the inflection compare Abbott 340.

131 Bedlam the hospital of St Mary of Bethlehem was 'an hospital for distracted people' (Stow).

132 bedlam mad.

132 humour temperament, character.

135 factious seditious.

135 pate head (contemptuous).

   His sons, he says, shall give their words for him.
YORK Will you not, sons?
EDWARD Ay, noble father, if our words will serve.
RICHARD And if words will not, then our weapons shall.   140
CLIFFORD Why what a brood of traitors have we here?
YORK Look in a glass, and call thy image so:
   I am thy king and thou a false-heart traitor.
   Call hither to the stake my two brave bears,
   That with the very shaking of their chains   145
   They may astonish these fell-lurking curs:
   Bid Salisbury and Warwick come to me.

  *Enter the* EARLS OF WARWICK *and* SALISBURY [*with* DRUM *and*
          SOLDIERS]

CLIFFORD Are these thy bears? We'll bait thy bears to death
   And manacle the bearherd in their chains,
   If thou dar'st bring them to the baiting-place.   150
RICHARD Oft have I seen a hot o'erweening cur
   Run back and bite because he was withheld;
   Who, being suffered with the bear's fell paw,
   Hath clapped his tail between his legs and cried:
   And such a piece of service will you do,   155
   If you oppose yourselves to match Lord Warwick.
Y. CLIFFORD Hence, heap of wrath, foul indigested lump,

---

147 SD.1–2 *with...*SOLDIERS] Q1; *not in* F  149, 210 bearherd] *OED;* Berard F *subst.;* bearward *Theobald*  150
baiting-place] *This edn;* bayting place F  153 being] F; having *Collier*[2]  153 suffered] F *subst;* suffered, *conj.*
*Vaughan*  157 SH] *Capell subst.;* Clif. F

144 After this line Q1 places 192, 'Call
Buckingham, and bid him arm himself.' It then
provides another tableau of confrontation (compare 121–3) shaped by the tiring house doors:
'*Enter at one door the Earls of Salisbury and Warwick
with Drum and Soldiers, and at the other, the Duke of
Buckingham with Drum and Soldiers*' (TLN 2084–
6). This might be a memory of the earlier
symmetrical entrance and not a record of authorial revision.
 144 **two brave bears** an allusion to the
muzzled bear chained to a ragged staff that
appeared on the badge of the house of Warwick;
see 202–3 below.
 146 **astonish** terrify (*OED* sv 3).
 146 **fell-lurking** savagely waiting, treacherous
– the image is from bear-baiting.
 149 **bearherd** bear-handler (i.e. York). F's
spelling, 'berard', indicates the pronounciation
(Cercignani, p. 169).

151–2 Compare the proverb 'A man may
cause his own dog to bite him' (Tilley M258).
 151 **hot** excited.
 153 **suffered** hurt (*OED* Suffer 11); Freeman
glosses the word 'loosed' and places a comma
after the word, an interpretation I consider less
likely.
 156 **oppose yourselves** offer resistance.
 156 **match** fight (*OED* sv *v*[1] 3).
 *157 SH I have adopted Capell's assignation of
these lines to Young Clifford on the grounds that
otherwise he has to remain silent until 211. He is
also paired in contest with York's son Richard.
 157 **heap...lump** echoes Ovid's 'Chaos,
rudis indigestaque moles' (*Metamorphoses* I, 7)
and Golding's translation, 'a huge rude heap...A
heavy lump' (I, 7–8). Bear cubs were supposed to
be born formless and licked into shape by their
mothers.
 157 **indigested** improperly formed.

As crooked in thy manners as thy shape.
YORK Nay, we shall heat you thoroughly anon.
CLIFFORD Take heed lest by your heat you burn yourselves.          160
KING HENRY Why, Warwick, hath thy knee forgot to bow?
    Old Salisbury, shame to thy silver hair,
    Thou mad misleader of thy brain-sick son!
    What, wilt thou on thy death-bed play the ruffian
    And seek for sorrow with thy spectacles?                     165
    O, where is faith? O, where is loyalty?
    If it be banished from the frosty head,
    Where shall it find a harbour in the earth?
    Wilt thou go dig a grave – to find out war
    And shame thine honourable age with blood?                   170
    Why, art thou old and want'st experience?
    Or wherefore dost abuse it, if thou hast it?
    For shame! In duty bend thy knee to me,
    That bows unto the grave with mickle age.
SALISBURY My lord, I have considered with myself                    175
    The title of this most renownèd duke;
    And in my conscience do repute his grace
    The rightful heir to England's royal seat.
KING HENRY Hast thou not sworn allegiance unto me?
SALISBURY I have.                                                   180
KING HENRY Canst thou dispense with heaven for such an oath?
SALISBURY It is great sin to swear unto a sin,
    But greater sin to keep a sinful oath.
    Who can be bound by any solemn vow
    To do a murderous deed, to rob a man,                        185
    To force a spotless virgin's chastity,
    To reave the orphan of his patrimony,

---

169 dig. . .war] F; find out war to dig a grave *conj. Roderick in Cam.*   170 shame] F; stain *Dycc²* (*conj. Walker*)   173
bend. . .me] F; bend to me thy knee *conj. this edn*

158 Richard of Gloucester was supposed to have been born deformed.

165 **spectacles** indicating Salisbury's age, although the word may mean 'organs of sight' (*OED* Spectacle 6) as at 3.2.112.

169 Will you commit yourself to death and find (only) war? The sense is strained, and Roderick's conjecture (see collation) is attractive.

171 **want'st** lack.

172 **abuse** misemploy (*OED* sv *sb* 2).

177 **repute** consider (*OED* sv *sb* 1).

181–90 See the 'Homily against Swearing and Perjury': 'if a man at any time, either of ignorance or malice, swear to do anything which is either against the law of Almighty God, or not in his power to perform, let him take it for an unlawful and ungodly oath'; and compare the proverb 'An unlawful oath is better broken than kept' (Tilley O7) and *3H6* 5.1.89–90.

181 **dispense** compound (*OED* sv *sb* 9b).

187 **reave** deprive.

To wring the widow from her customed right,
And have no other reason for this wrong
But that he was bound by a solemn oath?                    190
MARGARET  A subtle traitor needs no sophister.
KING HENRY  Call Buckingham, and bid him arm himself.
YORK  Call Buckingham, and all the friends thou hast,
I am resolved for death or dignity.
CLIFFORD  The first I warrant thee, if dreams prove true.    195
WARWICK  You were best to go to bed and dream again
To keep thee from the tempest of the field.
CLIFFORD  I am resolved to bear a greater storm
Than any thou canst conjure up today;
And that I'll write upon thy burgonet,                    200
Might I but know thee by thy house's badge.
WARWICK  Now by my father's badge, old Neville's crest,
The rampant bear chained to the ragged staff,
This day I'll wear aloft my burgonet –
As on a mountain top the cedar shows                    205
That keeps his leaves in spite of any storm –
Even to affright thee with the view thereof.
CLIFFORD  And from thy burgonet I'll rend thy bear
And tread it under foot with all contempt,
Despite the bearherd that protects the bear.              210
Y. CLIFFORD  And so to arms, victorious father,
To quell the rebels and their complices.
RICHARD  Fie! Charity, for shame! Speak not in spite,
For you shall sup with Jesu Christ tonight.
Y. CLIFFORD  Foul stigmatic, that's more than thou canst tell.   215
RICHARD  If not in heaven, you'll surely sup in hell.

*Exeunt [severally]*

194 or] *Rowe²*; and F   196 You] F; Thou *Cairncross*   197 thee] F; you Q1   201 house's] F2; housed F; household Q1   207 to] Q1; io F; so F2   216 *severally*] *Theobald*; not in F

188 **customed right** the right of a widow to part of her husband's estate.
191 **sophister** specious reasoner.
200 **burgonet** a light helmet.
202 **father's** actually his father-in-law's, as he had inherited the badge from Richard Beauchamp, the Warwick of *1H6* (Scott-Giles, p. 147).
203 **ragged** with stumps and jagged outline.
204 **aloft** on high.
205 **cedar** a common symbol of royalty (compare *Cym.* 5.4.140, 5.5.453).
207 **thereof** i.e. of the burgonet.
214 Compare Luke 23.43: 'today shalt thou be with me in paradise'.
215 **stigmatic** one branded – in Richard's case, with deformity (*OED* sv 3).
215 **that's...tell** Compare the proverb 'That's more than I know' (Dent M1155.1)

**[5.2** *An inn-sign of the Castle is displayed. Alarums to the battle.]* Enter
WARWICK


WARWICK  Clifford of Cumberland, 'tis Warwick calls:
　　　　And if thou dost not hide thee from the bear,
　　　　Now, when the angry trumpet sounds alarum
　　　　And dead men's cries do fill the empty air,
　　　　Clifford, I say, come forth and fight with me:                         5
　　　　Proud northern lord, Clifford of Cumberland,
　　　　Warwick is hoarse with calling thee to arms.


*Enter* YORK

　　　　How now, my noble lord? What all afoot?
YORK  The deadly-handed Clifford slew my steed,
　　　　But match to match I have encountered him,                            10

Act 5, Scene 2    5.2] *Steevens; not in* F; 5.3 *Oxford*    o SD *An...displayed*] *This edn (following* Q1 TLN 2112–3
*Richard* kils him vnder the signe of the Castle in saint *Albones*); *not in* F    o SD *Alarums...battle*] Q1; *not in* F    8] *Eds;*
*War.* How...a-foot. F

**Act 5, Scene 2**
*5.2 The first battle of Saint Albans was fought
on 22 May 1455. York attacked the king, and the
royal forces, led by Somerset, Buckingham,
Clifford, and many others, left London, thinking
that York had too many friends there, for Saint
Albans (Holinshed, p. 238; Hall, p. 232). The
chroniclers report merely that 'John Lord Clifford' was among those slain (Holinshed, p. 240;
Hall, p. 233): that it was York who killed him
emerges only when Young Clifford kills York's
son Rutland in vengeance, he claims, for his
father's murder (Hall, p. 251; not in Holinshed;
see *3H6* 1.3). For Somerset's death see Holinshed, p. 240 (Hall, p. 233).
　Q1 places the encounter between Richard and
Somerset (65–71) at the head of this scene. The
Oxford editors follow this suggestion and treat
the sequence as a separate scene. They may well
be right, since 1–64 of the Folio text occupy an
exceptionally crowded page. The compositor may
have noticed that he had omitted the sequence
and slipped it in to the next page, which, being
the last page of the play, offered plenty of room.
　o SD.1 **\*inn-sign...Castle** This might well
have been brought in or displayed from the tiring
house balcony at the opening of the scene to serve
as a kind of locality board – and, if we accept F's
version of the scene (see previous note), to create
ironic suspense, in that Somerset is not killed
until 65. Alternatively, it might have been displayed simply for that short sequence. Q1's
version includes a line, 'What's here, the sign of
the Castle' (TLN 2115 – which suggests that a
property sign board was deployed), and its SD (see
collation) is not simply descriptive.
　1 **Clifford of Cumberland** In fact it was
Clifford's great-grandson, Henry de Clifford,
who was created first Earl of Cumberland in 1525
(*DNB*).
　4 **dead** dying (proleptic).
　*8 F prefixes the line with an additional and
superfluous SH '*War*'. Q1 at this point offers:
'*Clifford speaks within.* / Warwick stand still, and
view the way that Clifford hews with / his
murdering curtle-axe through the fainting troops
to find / thee out. / Warwick, stand still, and stir
not till I come' (TLN 2131–5). Given that the
column in which this passage appears in F is
extremely crowded, having been, presumably,
imperfectly cast off, it is tempting to assume that
Q reports something missing from the text.
Directors might want to include at least the last
line of the Q1 passage, which is metrically regular.
See Wells and Taylor, p. 193, for a discussion of
further hypotheses.
　8 **afoot** i.e. not on horseback. For an account
of the importance of horses in a chivalric world,
see Ann Lecercle, 'Epics and ethics in *1 Henry IV*'
in J. P. Teissedou ed., *Henry the Fourth...,*
*Pouvoir et musique,* 1990, pp. 191–218.
　9 **deadly-handed** murderous.

And made a prey for carrion kites and crows
Even of the bonny beast he loved so well.

*Enter* CLIFFORD

WARWICK  Of one or both of us the time is come.
YORK  Hold, Warwick, seek thee out some other chase,
    For I myself must hunt this deer to death.         15
WARWICK  Then nobly, York; 'tis for a crown thou fight'st. –
    As I intend, Clifford, to thrive today,
    It grieves my soul to leave thee unassailed.       *Exit*
CLIFFORD  What seest thou in me, York? Why dost thou pause?
YORK  With thy brave bearing should I be in love,      20
    But that thou art so fast mine enemy.
CLIFFORD  Nor should thy prowess want praise and esteem,
    But that 'tis shown ignobly and in treason.
YORK  So let it help me now against thy sword
    As I in justice and true right express it.        25
CLIFFORD  My soul and body on the action both!
YORK  A dreadful lay! Address thee instantly.
       [*They fight, and* CLIFFORD *falls*]
CLIFFORD  *La fin couronne les oeuvres.*       [*Dies*]
YORK  Thus war hath given thee peace, for thou art still;
    Peace with his soul, heaven, if it be thy will!    [*Exit*]  30

[*Alarums, then*] *enter* YOUNG CLIFFORD [*alone*]

Y. CLIFFORD  Shame and confusion! All is on the rout;

19] *Pope; What. . .Yorke? / Why. . .Pause* F    27 SD] *Capell subst.; not in* F    28 *oeuvres*] F2 *subst.; eumenes* F    28 SD]
F2; *not in* F    30 SD.1–2 *Exit. . .alone*] Q1; *Enter yong Clifford* F    31 SH] Q1 *subst.; Clif.* F    31 *confusion! All*] *Pope;*
*Confusion all* F

11 **carrion. . .crows** A species of crow larger
than the rook.
  11 **kites** See 3.2.191 n.
  13 Compare the proverb 'One dies when his
hour comes' (Dent H741.1).
  14 **chase** hunting ground (*OED* sv *sb* 3).
  19–30 For Q1's version of these lines see
Appendix 2, p. 233. Cairncross (p. xxviii) believes
that the F version represents a revision because of
the censorship: it makes the conflict between the
two men personal rather than political. However,
F's version may equally be an early draft – there is
no way of telling.
  21 **fast** fixedly.
  26 **action** fight (*OED* sv 11).

27 **lay** wager.
  27 **Address** Prepare (*OED* sv *sb* 3).
  *28 'The end crowns the works'; compare the
proverb 'The end crowns (tries) all' (Tilley E116),
and see 1.1.120 n. F's 'eumenes' was probably the
result of misreading MS 'euueres'.
  30 In performance York may kneel here as a
silent testimony to the nobility and 'brave bearing'
(20) of his adversary; see Lecercle, cited in 8n.
above.
  30 SD Directors might want to bring soldiers
on with Young Clifford to fly across the stage,
defying his command at 36.
  31 **confusion** destruction (*OED* sv 1).
  31 **on the rout** in disorderly flight (Wilson).

Fear frames disorder, and disorder wounds
Where it should guard. O war, thou son of hell,
Whom angry heavens do make their minister,
Throw in the frozen bosoms of our part                            35
Hot coals of vengeance! Let no soldier fly.
He that is truly dedicate to war
Hath no self-love: nor he that loves himself
Hath not essentially but by circumstance
The name of valour. [*Seeing his dead father*] O let the vile
　　world end,                                                     40
And the premised flames of the last day
Knit earth and heaven together!
Now let the general trumpet blow his blast,
Particularities and petty sounds
To cease! Wast thou ordained, dear father,                        45
To lose thy youth in peace, and to achieve
The silver livery of advisèd age
And, in thy reverence and thy chair-days, thus
To die in ruffian battle? Even at this sight
My heart is turned to stone: and while 'tis mine,                 50
It shall be stony. York not our old men spares;
No more will I their babes: tears virginal
Shall be to me even as the dew to fire,
And beauty, that the tyrant oft reclaims,
Shall to my flaming wrath be oil and flax.                        55

---

**40** SD] *Theobald; not in* F

**32 frames** fashions.

**34 minister** scourge. A scourge of God cleansed the world of evil but might be himself (as war is) evil; compare *Ham.* 3.4.177 and Calvin, *The Institution of Christian Religion*, trans. T. Norton, I, xviii, pp. 69–70; *1H6* 1.2.129 n.

**35 part** party.

**39 essentially** by nature *OED* sv 1b).

**41–2** Compare 2 Pet. 12, 'the coming of the day of God, by the which the heavens being on fire, shall be dissolved, and the elements shall melt with heat'.

**41 premised** literally 'sent before their time' (*OED* Premised 2), but here means, proleptically, 'preordained'. The scansion of the line may be improved if the word is pronounced with three syllables.

**43 general trumpet** the trumpet (of doomsday) that summons all men (1 Cor. 15.52).

**44 Particularities** Matters concerning individuals (*OED* Peculiarity 1b).

**46 lose** waste (Schmidt).

**47 advisèd** cautious (*OED* sv *ppl adj* 2).

**48 chair-days** old age.

**50–1 My…stony** Compare Ezek. 11.19, 'I will take the stony heart out of their bodies, and will give them an heart of flesh', and Dent H311, 'A heart as hard as stone'.

**51 stony** pitiless.

**53 dew to fire** Spraying a fire with water was supposed to make it hotter by reducing the flames to coals.

**54 reclaims** subdues (*OED* Reclaim 3) – with 'the tyrant' as object.

**55 oil and flax** Compare the proverbs 'Put not fire to flax' (Tilley F278) and 'To add oil to the fire' (Tilley O30).

Henceforth I will not have to do with pity:
Meet I an infant of the house of York,
Into as many gobbets will I cut it
As wild Medea young Absyrtis did;
In cruelty will I seek out my fame.                    60
        [*He takes his father's body up on his back*]
Come, thou new ruin of old Clifford's house:
As did Aeneas old Anchises bear,
So bear I thee upon my manly shoulders;
But then Aeneas bare a living load,
Nothing so heavy as these woes of mine.               65
                              [*Exit bearing off his father*]


*Enter* RICHARD *and* SOMERSET *to fight.* [*Somerset is killed under the inn-sign*]


RICHARD  So lie thou there:
        For underneath an alehouse' paltry sign,
        The Castle in Saint Albans, Somerset
        Hath made the wizard famous in his death.
        Sword, hold thy temper; heart, be wrathful still:   70
        Priests pray for enemies, but princes kill.    [*Exit*]

---

**60** SD] Q1 *subst.; not in* F    **65** SD.1 *Exit. . .father*] Pope (*following* Q1); *not in* F; *Exit. . .father.* / 5.4 *Oxford subst.*   **65**
SD.2–3 *Somerset. . .inn-sign*] *This edn* (*see* 0 SD); *not in* F    **67** For] F; Whats here, the signe of the Castle? / Then the
prophesie is come to passe, / For Somerset was forewarned of Castles, / The which he alwaies did obscrue. And Q1;
Fall'n *conj. Johnson*    **71** SD.1 *Exit*] *Theobald subst.; not in* F

**57–9** Prophetic, as Clifford will slay young
Rutland in 1.3 of *3H6*.
**59 wild** savage.
**59 Medea. . .Absyrtus** Absyrtus was Medea's
younger brother. When fleeing from Colchos
with her lover Jason she cut Absyrtus up and
strewed the pieces in the sea to delay her father
Aeëtes' pursuit of them. See Ovid, *Tristia* III,
9.25–8.
**61 thou. . .house** i.e. his father's body.
**62** Aeneas carried his father Anchises from
burning Troy (see *Aeneid* II, 720 ff.), an action
which provided an emblem of *pietas* or the proper
relationship with gods and family.

**65** Q1 has Richard enter here to fight and be
defeated by Young Clifford, who then resumes
the task of carrying his father's body to his tent
(see Appendix 2, p. 233). Again, this may represent a revision.

**65** SD.3 *inn-sign* See 0 SD.1 n.
**67–9** See 1.4.34–6 and 64–7.
**67 For** 'indicates an omission of which Q [see
collation] almost certainly gives the substance'
(Cairncross).
**69 wizard** Bolingbroke who appeared in 1.4.
**70 hold** maintain.
**71** SD.1 *Excursions.* Sorties, sallies.

*Fight. Excursions.* [*Alarums again, and then enter three or four bearing the*
DUKE OF BUCKINGHAM *wounded to his tent. Alarums still.*] *Enter*
KING, QUEEN, *and others*

MARGARET  Away, my lord! You are slow; for shame, away!
KING HENRY  Can we outrun the heavens? Good Margaret, stay.
MARGARET  What are you made of? You'll nor fight nor fly.
    Now is it manhood, wisdom, and defence                    75
    To give the enemy way, and to secure us
    By what we can, which can no more but fly.
            *Alarum afar off*
    If you be ta'en, we then should see the bottom
    Of all our fortunes: but if we haply scape,
    As well we may – if not, through your neglect –          80
    We shall to London get, where you are loved,
    And where this breach now in our fortunes made
    May readily be stopped.

*Enter* [YOUNG] CLIFFORD

Y. CLIFFORD  But that my heart's on future mischief set,
    I would speak blasphemy ere bid you fly:                   85
    But fly you must; uncurable discomfit
    Reigns in the hearts of all our present parts.
    Away for your relief! And we will live
    To see their day and them our fortune give:
    Away, my lord, away!                         *Exeunt*   90

---

71 SD.2–3 *Alarums again...still*] Q1 subst.; *not in* F    83 SD YOUNG] *Dyce; not in* F    84 SH] *Capell subst.;* Clif. F
86 discomfit] F; discomfort *conj. Capell in Cam.*    87 parts] F; part *Dyce;* party *Warburton*

71 SD.1–2 **three...tent** This detail, reported
in Q1, gives a final exit for Buckingham, who does
not appear in *3H6*. Holinshed (p. 241) and Hall
(p. 233) report his wounding at this first battle of
St Albans. The 'tent' may have been one of a
couple of tents erected on the stage (see Hattaway, p. 38) or, alternatively, the discovery space
could have been used.
73 **outrun the heavens** Compare Ps. 139.7–
12.
73 **outrun** escape by running.

76 **secure us** gain safety (*OED* Secure *v* 2b).
77 **what** whatever means.
86 **discomfit** defeat.
87 **present parts** remaining forces.
89 To win a victory like theirs and impose our
fortunes on them.

**[5.3]** *Alarum. Retreat. Enter* YORK, *[with his sons]* RICHARD *[and* EDWARD]*, WARWICK *[along with]* SOLDIERS, *with* DRUM *and colours*

YORK  Old Salisbury, who can report of him,
          That winter lion, who in rage forgets
          Agèd contusions and all brush of time,
          And, like a gallant in the brow of youth,
          Repairs him with occasion? This happy day          5
          Is not itself, nor have we won one foot
          If Salisbury be lost.
RICHARD                      My noble father,
          Three times today I holp him to his horse,
          Three times bestrid him; thrice I led him off,
          Persuaded him from any further act:          10
          But still, where danger was, still there I met him;
          And, like rich hangings in a homely house,
          So was his will in his old feeble body.
          But noble as he is, look where he comes.

*Enter* SALISBURY

          Now, by my sword, well hast thou fought today.          15
SALISBURY  By the mass, so did we all. I thank you, Richard:

Act 5, Scene 3     5.3] *Steevens; not in* F     0 SD.1–2 *with his...*EDWARD] Q3 *subst.; not in* F     1 Old] *Collier* (*following* Q1); Of F     3 brush] F; bruise *Warburton*     4 brow] F; blow *Johnson*     11 still there] F; there *conj. Vaughan*     14 SD] F; Enter *Salsbury and Warwick* Q1     15–16 *Wilson* (*conj. Pollard*); *Sal.* Now...day: / By...*Richard.* F

**Act 5, Scene 3**
**\*5.3** See 5.2 headnote. The chroniclers end their accounts of the battle with reports of a reconciliation between York and the king, the king forgiving the rebels and York on the grounds that Somerset had been removed, having forbidden his followers to harm the king (Holinshed, p. 241; Hall, p. 233).

**0 SD.1** *Alarum. Retreat* Sounded on drum or trumpet.

**0 SD.2 \*EDWARD** Edward's entrance is recorded only in Q3, but his presence is implicit in Q1's opening lines for this scene: 'How now boys, fortunate this fight hath been, / I hope, to us and ours for England's good, / And our great honour that so long we lost, / Whilst faint-heart Henry did usurp our rights' (TLN 2203–6). This may well have been a revision – see also 14 SD n.

**1 \*Old** F's 'Of' was presumably caught by the compositor from the 'of' later in the line.

**2 winter** aged (*OED* sv 3d).

**3 contusions** injuries, bruises.
**3 brush** attack (*OED* sv *sb*³ 1b).
**4 brow** countenance, aspect (*OED* sv 5c); compare *1H4* 4.3.83; Johnson's emendation 'blow' (blossom, spring) is, however, attractive.
**5 Repairs...occasion** Restores himself when he can fight.
**9 bestrid him** stood over in order to protect him (*OED* Bestride 2c).
**11 still** always.
**12 homely** humble.
**14 SD** Q1 delays Warwick's entrance until this point in the scene (see collation), bringing him on with his father. It also gives two lines to Edward (see 0 SD n.) to prepare for the entrance: 'See, noble father, where they both do come, / The only props unto the house of York' (TLN 2218–19). This may well represent a revision.
**\*15** I follow Wilson in continuing the line to Richard, whom Salisbury thanks in 16.

> God knows how long it is I have to live;
> And it hath pleased Him that three times today
> You have defended me from imminent death.
> Well, lords, we have not got that which we have:                    20
> 'Tis not enough our foes are this time fled,
> Being opposites of such repairing nature.

YORK  I know our safety is to follow them;
> For, as I hear, the king is fled to London
> To call a present court of parliament.                              25
> Let us pursue him ere the writs go forth.
> What says Lord Warwick? Shall we after them?

WARWICK  After them! Nay, before them if we can.
> Now, by my hand, lords, 'twas a glorious day:
> Saint Alban's battle won by famous York                            30
> Shall be eternised in all age to come. –
> Sound, drum and trumpets, and to London all:
> And more such days as these to us befall!            *Exeunt*

## FINIS

29 hand] F; faith *Malone (following* Q1)    32 drum] F; drums Q1 *subst.*

20 **we have...we have** our victory is not yet secure.

22 As they are enemies and so able to recover their fortunes.

23 **safety** safeguard (*OED* sv 3).

25 **present** immediate.

25 **court of parliament** an assembly, held by the monarch, of his councillors and great lords (see *OED* Court *sb*¹ 9, 10).

26 **writs** summonses (to attend the parliament).

29 **by my hand** a common asseveration (*OED* Hand 6), although Q's 'faith' may record an oath deleted after the Blasphemy Act (see 4.10.52n.).

# TEXTUAL ANALYSIS

The first edition of *2 Henry VI* appeared in 1594[1] as a quarto entitled *The First part of the Contention betwixt the two famous Houses of Yorke and Lancaster* (Q1).[2] It was printed by Thomas Creede for Thomas Millington.[3] This text was reprinted in 1600 by Valentine Simmes, again for Millington (Q2),[4] from a copy of Q1. In 1619, Thomas Pavier, to whom Millington had transferred his rights in the play in 1602, published the play for a third time in an undated quarto form (Q3)[5] as part of a set of ten plays printed by William Jaggard, who, four years later, was to print the First Folio of Shakespeare's works (F). This edition was the first to bear Shakespeare's name on its title-page, and its compiler seems to have had resort to a chronicle in order to attempt to make corrections to the corrupt version of York's pedigree found in 2.2, as well as, possibly, to a supplementary report of the play.[6]

F would seem to derive from Shakespeare's manuscript or 'foul papers', although it shares some readings with the quarto texts[7] (see below and Appendix 2). This gives rise to three conjectures: that F was set up basically from an authorial manuscript but with some reference to a quarto text, that certain quarto passages derive in part from a manuscript identical or related to that used for the preparation of F, or that copy for Q was annotated by someone (a player?) with memories of performance based on a version of the text recorded in the foul papers.[8] The first is the most likely.

These quarto texts are about a third shorter than the text which was printed in the Folio edition and which appeared some seven years after Shakespeare's death. There it is entitled *The second Part of Henry the Sixt, with the death of the Good Duke Humfrey*. The *Henry VI* plays are placed among the history plays after *Henry*

---

[1] It was entered on the Stationers' Register on 12 March.

[2] See William Montgomery, ed., '*The Contention of York and Lancaster*: a critical edition', unpublished DPhil thesis, University of Oxford, 1985.

[3] For an account of its setting by one compositor, see George Walton Williams, 'Setting by formes in quarto printing', *SB* 11 (1958), 39–53.

[4] W. Craig Ferguson, 'The compositors of *Henry VI Part 2* and *The First Part of the Contention*', *SB* 13 (1960), 19–29, demonstrated that Compositor A set most of Q2; see also Alan E. Craven, 'Simmes' Compositor A and five Shakespearean quartos', *SB* 36 (1973), 37–60.

[5] It was set up from a copy of Q1. See Peter W. Blayney, '"Compositor B" and the Pavier quartos: problems of identification and their implication', *The Library* 27 (1972), 179–206; Peter W. Blayney, 'The compositors of the Pavier quartos', *The Library* 31 (1976), 143–5; S. W. Reid, 'The compositors of the Pavier quartos', *The Library* 31 (1976), 392–4; Montgomery confirms this and notes that Q3 was corrected on perhaps six occasions by reference to some other authority, possibly a chronicle (Wells and Taylor, p. 176).

[6] See Appendix 2, pp. 235–6.

[7] For a general survey of Q > F transmission, see J. K. Walton, *The Quarto Copy for the First Folio of Shakespeare*, 1971.

[8] R. B. McKerrow, 'A note on *2 Henry VI* and *The Contention of York and Lancaster*', *RES* 9 (1933), 157–69 and 315–16.

*V*, in the order, that is, of monarchical reign and not the order of composition by Shakespeare. *2 Henry VI* occupies pp. 120–46 of the volume. The texts had been prepared by John Heminge and Henry Condell, Shakespeare's fellow players, and printed in the workshop of William Jaggard.

The texts in the subsequent seventeenth-century Folios (1632, 1664, 1685) are based ultimately on this first edition. Although F2 offers a number of metrical regularisations (see collation), these represent only conjectures emanating from the printing house responsible for that text.

The quarto texts bear all the signs of deriving from a playhouse (see Date and occasion, pp. 56–68). The stage directions are fuller (see, for example, 3.2.0 SD), and they contain short passages of dialogue or 'gag' that were probably improvised in rehearsal or performance (see, for example, 2.1.40, 2.3.85). They are now commonly agreed to be memorial reconstructions of London performances[1] – rather than, as scholars of earlier generations thought, sources or early drafts of the text found in the Folio. Peter Alexander demonstrated how Q's version of York's pedigree[2] could only have been written by a reporter who did not understand the facts of the case.[3] They also contain echoes of plays by Shakespeare and others,[4] which supports the case for memorial reconstruction and almost certainly destroys the case of those who would see the play as an early draft.[5] Besides being considerably shorter, the quarto texts show signs that the play was probably, as we would expect, subject to revision in performance, especially in the final act.[6] The omissions in Qq, in other words, are not to be accounted for simply by lapses in memory. For although these texts are commonly known as 'bad quartos', it may well be that behind them lie 'good acting versions', cut or adapted for a smaller playing company.[7] There is, however, no way of telling whether these revisions were made with or without Shakespeare's

---

[1] This was first demonstrated by Peter Alexander, *Shakespeare's 'Henry VI' and 'Richard III'*, 1929, and Madeleine Doran, *Henry VI, Parts II and III: Their Relation to the Contention and the True Tragedy*, 1928. Alexander conjectured that the text derived from the memories of two players, one who had played Warwick, another who had doubled Suffolk and Clifford, while Doran suggested that the text derived from a group effort. John E. Jordan, 'The reporter of *2 Henry VI*', *PMLA* 64 (1949), 1089–113, argues that the reporter was a bit player who took the parts of Horner, the Spirit, the Mayor, Vaux, and Scales. For the theoretical means of identifying reporters, see Wells and Taylor, *Modernizing Shakespeare's Spelling*, 1979, p. 129. Alexander's assumptions and conclusions are challenged but not convincingly overthrown by Steven Urkowitz, "If I mistake in those foundations which I build upon": Peter Alexander's textual analysis of *Henry VI Parts 2 and 3*', *ELR* 18 (1988), 230–56.
[2] 2.2.9ff.; see Appendix 2, pp. 234–5.
[3] Alexander, p. 62.
[4] See Appendix 2, pp. 236–41.
[5] See especially C. T. Prouty, *'The Contention' and Shakespeare's 2 Henry VI*, 1954, rebutted by James G. McManaway, '*The Contention* and *2 Henry VI*', in S. Korninger, ed., *Studies in English Language and Literature: Presented to Professor Doctor Karl Brunner*, 1957, pp. 143–54.
[6] This was suggested by A. Hart, *Stolne and Surreptitious Copies*, 1942, pp. 121ff.; see in particular the version of 5.2.31–65 in Appendix 2, p. 233.
[7] See Montgomery, and also Scott McMillin, 'Casting for Pembroke's Men: the *Henry 6* quartos and *The Taming of a Shrew*', *SQ* 23 (1972), 141–59.

authority,[1] and if they were, there is no compelling argument that allows a modern editor to decide whether the author's second thoughts are to be preferred over his first. I have therefore not included any passages that appear solely in the quarto texts in my own version of the play, but in the collation have alerted readers and directors to their presence in Appendix 2. It may well be decided that a quarto version of part of a sequence would suit a particular modern revival.

F therefore stands revealed as the only authoritative text for the play as a whole, although there is no doubt that Q records details of staging of performances with which Shakespeare was probably associated.[2]

The text of a Renaissance play was subject to alteration or corruption at up to seven stages: by the author (or authors) while still in preliminary drafts; by authors or scribes preparing a 'fair copy' for delivery to a company;[3] by an adapter connected with the company by whom it was performed; by the book-holder (who doubled as a prompter)[4] annotating the foul papers[5] or preparing a copy for performance; by an editor preparing copy for the printer;[6] by the compositors; and by the proof-reader. It is logical to look for evidence of changes of these kinds in reverse order and so produce a theory about the nature of the copy used by the compositors who turned the manuscript into the printed texts that survive. As a preliminary, we should note that proof-readers did not always check proofs against copy, that their aim was simply to correct typographical inaccuracies or irregularities, and that they might well thereby introduce corruption by correction.[7] In the case of *2 Henry VI*, however, the variants between copies of F are insignificant, involving only signatures or spaces that had risen high enough to be inked.[8]

It was established by Charlton Hinman that *2 Henry VI* was, like the remainder of the histories, set by two compositors, A and B, who in Jaggard's shop were responsible for setting most of the Folio.[9] Spelling tests (A preferred the forms 'doe', 'goe', 'here'; B the forms 'do', 'go', 'heere') and the tracing of individual pieces of type allowed Hinman to assign A, working from case x, and B, working from case y, the following stints:

| By set m2$^v$–m3$^v$ | pp. 120–2 | 1.1.1–1.2.79 |
| Ax set m4$^r$–n3$^r$ | pp. 123–33 | 1.2.80–3.2.61 |
| By set n3$^v$ | p. 134 | 3.2.62–3.2.187 |

[1] For an account of various kinds of textual 'piracy' see Stanley Wells and Gary Taylor, *Modernizing Shakespeare's Spelling*, p. 110 n.
[2] Hattaway, pp. 52–3.
[3] See Fredson Bowers, *On Editing Shakespeare*, 1966.
[4] W. W. Greg, *The Shakespeare First Folio*, 1955, p. 100.
[5] Greg, *First Folio*, p. 109.
[6] These have been studied by S. W. Reid, 'The editing of Folio *Romeo and Juliet*', SB 35 (1982), 43–66, and by Eleanor Prosser, *Shakespeare's Anonymous Editors*, 1981.
[7] Charlton Hinman, *The Printing and Proof-Reading of the First Folio of Shakespeare*, 2 vols., 1963, I, 274–5.
[8] Hinman, *Printing and Proof-Reading*, I, 274.
[9] Hinman, *Printing and Proof-Reading*, II, 53–69.

Ax set n4$^r$     p. 135     3.2.188–3.2.306
By set n4$^v$–o3$^v$     pp. 136–46     3.2.307–5.3.33

This analysis accounts for spelling inconsistencies that seemed to earlier scholars to point to manuscript copy, either produced by more than one hand or written by more than one author.

The next stage in our investigation must be to decide whether the copy used by the compositors derives from a manuscript used in the playhouse or not. Evidence of theatrical stage directions, added presumably by the book-holder, would suggest that the text passed through such a stage: we must decide whether the copy represented holographic or scribal copy marked up by the book-holder in preparation for the copying out of the promptbook, or a scribal copy of a fully annotated promptbook. As possible book-holder additions are few – there are, for example, no mentions of important properties like Margaret's hawk at 2.1.0 SD or the brigandine at 4.3.10 SD – it is reasonable to assume the former.[1]

We must now look to the text to see whether it presents positive signs of authorial copy[2] to support our hypothesis further. It does. First, we might note the confusion between Queen Margaret and the Duchess of Gloucester in 3.2 (see collation), which would almost certainly have been sorted out by a book-holder. It is much more likely to have been due to authorial carelessness than, as Wilson thought, revision by another hand.[3] Then we find descriptive, permissive, or vague stage directions: '*Fight at sea. Ordnance goes off*' (4.1.0 SD.1), '*Bolingbroke or Southwell reads*' (1.4.21 SD.1–2), '*Enter the King and State*' (2.3.0 SD.1), '*with infinite numbers*' (4.2.25 SD.2), '*Enter multitudes*' (4.9.9 SD). There is an example of extravagant casting in 1.3: the '*three or four petitioners*' (1.3.0 SD) are reduced to two in Q (TLN 291).[4] Necessary entrances and exits are missing,[5] speech prefixes designate both names and roles (Gloucester–Protector, Beaufort–Cardinal). We find examples of actors' names used as speech prefixes in 4.2 (Bevis and John Holland) and probably 4.7 (Michael and George), a sign of authorial copy.[6] It is also possible that lines in 1.1 (211–32) represent an undeleted early draft.[7]

Sir Walter Greg, however, argued that the copy for F of *2* and *3 Henry VI* was holographic with annotation: 'an author's fair copy which the book-keeper had annotated to serve as a prompt-book without troubling to make vague directions specific'.[8] Wilson disagreed on the grounds that the names of actors for

---

[1] The work of a book-holder may be discerned by comparing the stage directions of the quarto editions of *Richard II*, which derive ultimately from foul papers, with those in the Folio text, which derive from a promptbook. See A. Gurr, ed., *Richard II*, 1984, pp. 176–9.

[2] Greg, *First Folio*, pp. 124 ff.

[3] Wilson, p. xlv.

[4] The process is reversed at 4.5.0 SD, where F has '*Enters...two or three citizens*', and Q '*Enter three or four citizens*' (TLN, 1729). This may be due to high-handedness on the part of F's compositor; for a full discussion of these passages, see Wells and Taylor, *Textual Companion*, p. 177.

[5] See, for example, 1.3.95 SD, 2.3.16 SD, 2.4.16 SD.3, 5.1.116 SD, 5.1.122 SD.

[6] Greg, *The Editorial Problem in Shakespeare*, 1951 ed., p. 40.

[7] Compare Greg, *Editorial Problem*, pp. 61, 113, 127.

[8] Greg, *Editorial Problem*, p. 55. In *The Shakespeare First Folio*, 1955, p. 182, Greg lists all the stage directions and ascribes 'the very full provision of noises' to the book-holder. However the nature of the action surely demands them.

characters, etc., indicated that the manuscript would not have passed through the hands of a book-holder.[1] Cairncross followed Greg's basic suggestion but produced in addition a sophisticated argument that F was in part set from Q copy. He claimed that the compositors not only consulted a copy of Q3 and, on occasion, Q2, but copied lines from these into the margins of the original manuscript, enhancing the likelihood of metrical irregularities, or even cut up the quarto texts and pasted them onto the manuscript, having to use a copy of Q2 in order to recover portions of text on the side pasted down.[2] The last part of this argument is vitiated by the fact that the pagination of Q2 does not match that of Q3.

Cairncross's examples of mislineation common to all Q texts and F (2.1.137−8 and 4.6.1−5), his nine examples of non-substantive Q3/F agreement, his four examples of non-substantive Q2/F agreement, and his two examples of confused speech headings (at 4.6.10 and 5.2.8), however, do not seem to me to be numerous or conclusive enough to allow us to argue that the whole passages he designates were so constructed. There is no correlation with the stints of the two compositors, and his claim that the 'use of the Q copy seems to be determined by the Q page not by the F column'[3] is possible only if we accept the unlikely theory of the use of cut-up Q3 pages: the passages he cites are not coterminous with pages in Q3. On the other hand, 2.1.117−51 SD.2, most of 2.3.58 SD.1−2.4.0 SD, and 4.5.0 SD−4.6.5 are almost identical in Q and F, the most likely explanation for which is the hypothesis that Q was used for copy there. This confirms Greg's suggestion that portions of the copy of F had become illegible[4] – although the last may well be a passage restored after censorship (see below). Montgomery offers two other 'demonstrable instances of Q contamination': 1.1.55−9, and 2.1.66 SD.1−3.[5] All we can do is conclude that a copy of a quarto text, probably Q3,[6] may have been to hand in the printing house, but we cannot erect any theory for methodical consultation.

Cairncross thought that politically charged passages that occur only in Q[7] provided evidence that F was adapted after the book of the play had been relicensed by the censor, the original lines having been recalled by players in the first performances and included in Q. It is remarkable, however, that there seems to have been no detailed intervention by the censor in the Cade scenes – those that bear the closest resemblance to the Evil May Day riot sequences in *Sir Thomas More*, the manuscript of which survives bearing annotations by the Master of the Revels, Edmund Tilney.[8] He may, however, have excised 4.5.0 SD−4.6.5, a

[1] Wilson, 'The copy for *2* and *3 Henry VI* 1623', *3H6*, pp. 117−122.
[2] Cairncross, pp. xxxii−xxxix.
[3] Cairncross, p. xxxviii.
[4] Greg, *Editorial Problem*, p. 55.
[5] Wells and Taylor, p. 176; this is more plausible than Alexander's theory that the compilers of F had at their disposal fragments of the text used in original performances which they used to supplement their memories.
[6] See Montgomery; Wells and Taylor, p. 177; both F and Q3 were printed by Jaggard.
[7] See Appendix 2, pp. 230−5 and Cairncross, pp. xxv−xxix. These lines may, however, have been lost in the course of abridgement.
[8] See Janet Clare, '"Greater themes for insurrection's arguing": political censorship of the Elizabethan and Jacobean stage', *RES* 38 (1987), 169−83.

passage which dramatises the height of Cade's triumph. The two passages are almost identical in QI, 2 (but not Q3)[1] and F, which suggests that whoever was preparing the manuscript of F for the printer remembered that they had been recalled during the preparation of Q and included them to fill in a gap caused by censorship, possibly during a 'relicensing' in 1592.[2]

We may therefore conclude that the copy for *2 Henry VI* was a holographic one (or possibly a scribal copy of a holographic manuscript) which might have been lightly annotated by a book-holder and which was prepared with some reference to Q3 on occasion, either to make good illegible passages of the foul papers or, possibly, in one instance, to restore a sequence cut by the censor.

---

[1] The opening SD in QI, 2 for 4.5 substantively reads: '*Enter the* LORD SCALES *upon the Tower walls walking. Enter* THREE *or* FOUR CITIZENS *below*'; Q3 reads: '*Enter the* LORD SCALES *upon the Tower walls walking*'; F reads: '*Enter* LORD SCALES *upon the Tower walking. Then enters* TWO *or* THREE CITIZENS *below*'. This suggests that F depends upon Q3 here, with the second part of the SD being an addition derived from the following text, interpolated by whoever was preparing the text of F (see Wells and Taylor, p. 177).

[2] See Introduction, p. 60.

# APPENDIX 1: EXAMPLES FROM SHAKESPEARE'S SOURCES

Longer extracts from these texts are to be found in Bullough and Boswell-Stone.

## 1. The royal marriage (see 1.1)

[*In the margin*; An ominous marriage.] This marriage seemed to many both unfortunate and unprofitable to the realm of England, and that for many causes. First, the king had not one penny with her, and, for the fetching of her, the Marquess of Suffolk demanded a whole fifteenth in open parliament. And also there was delivered for her the Duchy of Anjou, the city of Mans, and the whole county of Maine, which countries were the very stays and backstands to the Duchy of Normandy. And furthermore, the Earl of Armagnac took such displeasure with the King of England for this marriage that he became utter enemy to the crown of England and was the chief cause that the Englishmen were expelled out of the whole Duchy of Aquitaine.

But most of all it should seem that God was displeased with this marriage: for after the confirmation thereof, the king's friends fell from him, both in England and in France, the lords of his realm fell at division, and the commons rebelled in such sort that finally, after many fields foughten and many thousands of men slain, the king at length was deposed and his son killed, and this queen sent home again with as much misery and sorrow as she was received with pomp and triumph. Such is the instability of worldly felicity, and so wavering is false flattering fortune. Which mutation and change of the better for the worse could not but nettle and sting her with with pensiveness, yea and any other person whatsoever that, having been in good estate, falleth into the contrary.

(Holinshed, p. 208; compare Hall, p. 205)

## 2. Eleanor, Duchess of Gloucester (see 1.2, 1.4, 2.3–4)

For, not content to be a duchess great,
I longèd sore to bear the name of queen,
Aspiring still unto an higher seat,
And with that hope myself did overween,
Since there was none, which that time was between
Henry the king and my good Duke his eme [uncle],
Heir to the crown and kingdom of this realm.

So near to be, was cause of my vain hope
And long await when this fair hap would fall.
My studies all were tending to that scope;

Alas, the while to counsel I did call
Such as would seem, by skill conjectural
Of art magic and wicked sorcery
To deem and divine the prince's destiny.

Among which sort of those that bare most fame
There was a beldam called the witch of Eye;
Old mother Madge her neighbours did her name,
Which wrought wonders in countries by hearsay.
Both fiends and fairies her charming would obey,
And dead corpses from grave she could uprear –
Such an enchantress as that time had no peer.

Two priests also, the one hight Bolingbroke,
The other Southwell, great clerks in conjuration,
These two chaplains, were they that undertook
To cast and calk [calculate] the king's constellation,
And then to judge by deep divination
Of things to come, and who should next succeed
To England's crown – all this was true indeed.

(*The Mirror for Magistrates*, pp. 434–5, 78–105)

## 3. Dissension breaks out in England and the conspiracy against Gloucester (see 1.3, 2.1, 2.3–3.2)

In the four and twentieth year of this king's reign [1446]...a certain armourer was appeached [accused] of treason by a servant of his own. For proof whereof, a day was given them to fight in Smithfield, insomuch that in conflict the said armourer was overcome and slain, but yet by misgoverning of himself. For on the morrow when he should come to the field fresh and fasting, his neighbours came to him and gave him wine and strong drink[1] in such excessive sort that he was therewith distempered and reeled as he went; and so was slain without guilt. As for the false servant, he lived not long unpunished, for, being convict of felony in court of assize, he was judged to be hanged, and so was, at Tyburn.

Whilst the wars between the two nations of England and France ceased (by occasion of the truce),[2] the minds of men were not so quiet, but that such as were bent to malicious revenge sought to compass their prepensed purpose, not against foreign foes and enemies of their country, but against their own countrymen and those that had deserved very well of the commonwealth; and this specially for overmuch mildness in the king, who by his authority might have ruled both parts and ordered all differences betwixt them, but that in deed he was thought too soft for governor of a kingdom. The queen, contrariwise, a lady of great wit and no less courage, desirous of honour and furnished with the gifts of reason, policy and wisdom, but yet sometime (according to her kind) when she had been fully bent on a matter, suddenly like a weathercock, mutable and turning.

[1] Shakespeare mentions 'charneco' and 'double beer' (2.3.61, 62), which suggests he used Holinshed here, since Hall mentions 'malmsey' and 'aqua vitae' (p. 207).
[2] Made at Tours: see *1H6* 5.5.

This lady, disdaining that her husband should be ruled rather than rule, could not abide that the Duke of Gloucester should do all things concerning the order of weighty affairs, lest it might be said that she had neither wit nor stomach which would permit and suffer her husband, being of most perfect age, like a young pupil to be governed by the direction of another man. Although this toy entered first into her brain through her own imagination, yet was she pricked forward to the matter both by such of her husband's council as of long time had borne malice to the duke for his plainness used in declaring their untruth...and also by counsel from King Reignier her father, advising that she and the king should take upon them the rule of the realm, and not to be kept under, as wards and mastered orphans.

What needeth many words? The queen, persuaded by these means, first of all excluded the Duke of Gloucester from all rule and governance, not prohibiting such as she knew to be his mortal foes to invent and imagine causes and griefs against him and his, insomuch that, by her procurement, diverse noblemen conspired against him. Of the which diverse writers affirm the Marquess of Suffolk and the Duke of Buckingham to be the chief, not unprocured by the Cardinal of Winchester and the Archbishop of York. Diverse articles were laid against him in open council and in especially one: that he had caused men adjudged to die to be put to other execution than the law of the land assigned. Surely the duke, very well learned in the law civil, detesting malefactors and punishing offences in severity of justice, got him hatred of such as feared condign reward for their wicked doings. And although the duke sufficiently answered to all things against him objected, yet because his death was determined, his wisdom and innocency nothing availed.

But to avoid danger of tumult that might be raised if a prince so well beloved of the people should be openly executed, his enemies determined to work their feats in his destruction ere he should have any warning. For effecting whereof, a parliament was summoned to be kept at Bury, whither resorted all the peers of the realm and amongst them the Duke of Gloucester, which, on the second day of the session, was by the Lord Beaumont, then High Constable of England, accompanied with the Duke of Buckingham and others, arrested, apprehended, and put in ward, and all his servants sequestered from him, and thirty-two of the chief of his retinue were sent to diverse prisons, to the great admiration of the people. The duke, the night after he was thus committed to prison, being the four and twentieth of February, was found dead in his bed, and his body showed to the lords and commons as though he had had died of a palsy or of an impostume.

But all indifferent persons (as saith Hall) might well understand that he died of some violent death. Some judged him to be strangled, some affirm that an hot spit was put in at his fundament, other write that he was smouldered [suffocated] between two feather-beds,[1] and some have affirmed that he died of very grief for that he might not come openly to his answer. His dead corpse was conveyed to St Albans and there buried. After his death none of his servants suffered, although

---

[1] These two latter barbarities were inflicted on Edward II and sketched in by Marlowe when he wrote the last act of his play about the monarch.

five of them...were arraigned, condemned, and drawn to Tyburn where they were hanged, let down quick, and stripped to have been bowelled and quartered; but the Marquess of Suffolk, coming at that instant, brought their pardons, showed the same openly, and so their lives were saved.

(Holinshed, pp. 210-1; compare Hall, pp. 207-9)

### 4. The miracle at St Albans (see 2.1)

Furthermore, as the learning of [Duke Humphrey of Gloucester] was rare and memorable, so was the discreet wisdom and singular prudence in him no less to be considered: as for the more manifest proof thereof, I thought here good, amongst many other his godly doings, to recite one example, reported as well by the pen of Sir Thomas More...to the intent to see and note not only the crafty working of false miracles in the clergy, but also that the prudent discretion of this high and mighty prince, the foresaid Duke Humphrey, may give us better to understand what man he was. The story lieth thus...

There came to St Albans a certain beggar with his wife, and there was walking about the town begging five or six days before the king's coming thither, saying he was born blind and never saw in his life, and was warned in his dream that he should come out of Berwick, where he said he had ever dwelled, to seek St Alban, and that he had been at his shrine and had not been holpen...When the king was comen and the town full, suddenly this blind man at St Alban's shrine had his sight again, and a miracle solemnly rung and *Te Deum* sung, so that nothing was talked of in all the town but this miracle. So it happened then that Duke Humphrey of Gloucester, a man no less wise than also well learned, having great joy to see such a miracle, called the poor man unto him, and first showing himself joyous of God's glory so showed in the getting of his sight, and exhorting him to meekness and to no ascribing of any part of the worship to himself, nor to be proud of the people's praise...at last he looked well upon his eyen and asked whether he could see nothing at all in all his life before. And when as well his wife as himself affirmed fastly no, then he looked advisedly upon his eyen again and said, 'I believe you very well, for me thinketh ye cannot see well yet'.

'Yes, sir', quoth he, 'I thank God and His holy martyr I can see now as well as any man.' 'Yea, can', quoth the duke, 'what colour is my gown?' Then anon the beggar told him. 'What colour', quoth he,' is this man's gown?' He told him also, and so forth without any sticking, he told him the names of all the colours that could be showed him. And when the duke saw that, he bade him walk traitor and made him to be set openly in the stocks. For though he could have seen suddenly by miracle the difference between diverse colours, yet could he not by the sight so suddenly tell the names of all these colours except he had known them before, no more than the names of all the men that he should suddenly see.

By this may it be seen how Duke Humphrey had not only an head to discern and dissever truth from forged and feigned hypocrisy, but study also and diligence likewise was in him, to reform that which was amiss.

(John Foxe, *Acts and Monuments*, 1583, 1, 704-5)

## 5. The Duke of York

When foreign war and outward battles were brought to an end and final conclusion, domestical discord and civil dissension began again to renew and arise within the realm of England; for when the care of outward hostility (which kept the minds of the princes in the realm occupied and in exercise) was taken away and vanished, desire of sovereignty and ambition of preeminence suddenly sprang out so far that the whole realm was divided into two several factions and private parts. For King Henry, descended of the House of Lancaster, claiming the crown from Henry IV his grandfather, first author of this division, and Richard, Duke of York, as heir to Lionel the third son to King Edward III, wrestled for the game and strove for the wager. By reason whereof, the nobles as well as the common people were into parts divided to the destruction of many a man and to the great ruin and decay of this region. For while the one part studied to vanquish and suppress the other, all commonwealth was set aside and justice and equity was clearly exiled. For the Duke of York, which sore gaped and more thirsted for the superiority and preeminence, studied, devised, and practised all ways and means by the which he might attain to his pretenced [intended] purpose and long-hoped desire. And amongst all imaginations, one seemed most necessary for his purpose, which yet again was to stir and provoke the malice of all the people against the Duke of Somerset, who only ruled the King...laying also great offences to King Henry, saying that he was a man neither of wit nor stomach, neither meet to be a king nor apt to govern a commonwealth, and therefore it was the duty of the noblemen and great princes not only to think on this weighty matter but speedily to provide a remedy and to set the realm in another stay. By which complaints and persuasions the Duke of York so altered the minds of many persons of high estate that they liked not the world as it then wavered nor approved th'acts of the king or his council. And because that ambition and avarice was newly entered into their hearts, they studied suddenly to change all things and to turn the world upsetdown. (Hall, p. 231; compare Holinshed, p. 237)

## 6. York's pedigree (see 2.2.10–52 and Appendix 2, pp. 234–5)

Edward the Third had issue, Edward, Prince of Wales; William of Hatfield, his second son; Lionel, the third, Duke of Clarence; John of Gaunt, fourth, Duke of Lancaster; Edmund of Langley, fifth, Duke of York; Thomas of Woodstock, sixth, Duke of Gloucester; and William of Windsor, seventh.

  The said Edward, Prince of Wales, which died in the lifetime of his father, had issue Richard, which succeeded Edward the Third his grandsire; Richard died without issue; William of Hatfield, the second son of Edward the Third, died without issue; Lionel, the third son of Edward the Third, Duke of Clarence, had issue Philippe his daughter and heir, which was coupled in matrimony unto Edmund Mortimer [third] Earl of March, and had issue Roger Mortimer [fourth] Earl of March, her son and heir; which Roger had issue Edmund[1] [fifth] Earl of

---

[1] The text reads 'of Edmund'.

March, Roger Mortimer, Anne, Eleanor; which Edmund, Roger, and Eleanor died without issue.

And the said Anne coupled in matrimony to Richard, Earl of Cambridge, the son of Edmund of Langley, the fifth son of Edward[1] the Third, and had issue Richard Plantagenet, commonly called Duke of York...To the which Richard, Duke of York, as son to Anne, daughter to Roger Mortimer, Earl of March, son and heir of the said Philippe, daughter and heir of the said Lionel, the third son of King Edward the Third, the right, title, dignity royal, and estate of the crowns of the realms of England and France, and the Lordship of Ireland, pertaineth and belongeth before any issue of the said John of Gaunt, the fourth son of the same King Edward.

(Holinshed, pp. 265–6)

## 7. The death of Winchester (see 3.3)

During these doings, Henry Beaufort, Bishop of Winchester and called the rich cardinal, departed out of this world and was buried at Winchester. This man was...more noble of blood than notable in learning, haught in stomach and high in countenance, rich above measure of all men and to few liberal, disdainful to his kin and dreadful to his lovers, preferring money before friendship, many things beginning and nothing performing. His covetise insatiable and hope of long life made him both to forget God, his prince, and himself in his latter days. For Dr John Baker, his privy councillor and his chaplain, wrote that he, lying on his death bed, said these words: 'Why should I die, having so much riches? If the whole realm would save my life, I am able either by policy to get it or by riches to buy it. Fie, will not death be hired, nor will money do nothing? When my nephew of Bedford died, I thought myself half up the wheel; but when I saw my other nephew of Gloucester deceased, then I thought myself to be equal with kings, and so thought to increase my treasure in hope to have worn a triple crown. But I see now the world faileth me, and so I am deceived, praying you all to pray for me.'

(Hall, pp. 210–11)

## 8. The causes of popular revolt (see 3.2, 4.2–9)

In [Normandy] were an hundred strong towns and fortresses, able to be kept and holden, beside them which were destroyed by the wars...Some say that the Englishmen were not of puissance either to man the towns as they should have been, or to inhabit the country, which was the cause they could not keep it. Other say that the Duke of Somerset, for his own peculiar lucre, kept not half the number of soldiers for which he was appointed and allowed, but put the wages in his purse. But the chief and only cause undoubtedly was the division within the realm, every great man desiring rather to be revenged on his foe at home than on the common enemy abroad, as by that which followeth you may plainly perceive.

---

[1] The text reads 'Henry'.

For whilst the French thus triumphed in Normandy, three cruel enemies among many (as by civil war and sedition ensuing appeared) sore urged the utter ruin of this realm at home. One was presumption in governance by some that were most unmeet to rule, as the queen and her privy councillors and minions; then the deadly malice and pride with insatiable covetise in the states both spiritual and temporal; and lastly the general grudge of the people for the universal smart that, through misgovernment, everywhere they suffered, who thus forwearied with the peise [weight] of burdens too heavy for them any longer to bear.

Herewith perceiving how (through want of provident wisdom in the governor) all things went to wrack as well within the realm as without, they began to make exclamation against the Duke of Suffolk, charging him to be the only cause of the delivery of Anjou and Maine, the chief procurer of the Duke of Gloucester's death, the very occasion of loss of Normandy, the swallower up of the king's treasure, the remover of good and virtuous counsellors from about the prince, and the advancer of vicious persons and of such as, by their doings, showed themselves apparent adversaries to the commonwealth.

(Holinshed p. 218)

## 9. Jack Cade (see 4.3–4)

Jack Cade, upon victory against the Staffords, apparelled himself in Sir Humphrey's brigandine set full of gilt nails, and so in some glory returned again toward London, diverse idle and vagrant persons out of Sussex, Surrey, and other places still increasing his number. Thus this glorious captain, guarded with a multitude of rustical people, came again to the plain of Blackheath and there strongly encamped himself: to whom were sent, from the king, the Archbishop of Canterbury and Humphrey, Duke of Buckingham, to common [confer] with him of his griefs and requests.

These lords found him sober in talk, wise in reasoning, arrogant in heart, and stiff in opinion; as who that by no means would grant to dissolve his army, except the king in person would come to him and assent to the things he would require. The king, upon the presumptuous answers and requests of this villainous rebel, beginning as much to doubt his own menial [household] servants as his unknown subjects (which spared not to speak that the captain's cause was profitable for the commonwealth), departed in all haste to the castle of Killingworth in Warwick-shire, leaving only behind him the Lord Scales to keep the Tower of London. The Kentish captain, being advertised of the king's absence, came first into Southwark and there lodged at the White Hart, prohibiting to all his retinue murder, rape, and robbery, by which colour of well meaning he the more allured to him the hearts of the common people.

After that, he entered into London, cut the ropes of the draw-bridge, and struck his sword on London Stone, saying, 'Now is Mortimer lord of this city'. And after a glozing [cajoling] declaration made to the mayor touching the cause of his thither coming, he departed again into Southwark; and upon the third day of July he caused Sir James Fiennes, Lord Say and Treasurer of England, to be brought to the Guildhall and there to be arraigned, who, being before the king's justices put to answer, desired to be tried by his peers for the longer delay of his life. The captain, perceiving his dilatory plea, by force took him from the officers and brought him to the standard in Cheap, and there (before his confession ended) caused his head to be stricken off, and pitched it upon an high pole which was openly borne before him through the streets.

And not content herewith, he went to Mile End and there apprehended Sir James Cromer, then Sheriff of Kent, and son-in-law to the said Lord Say, causing him likewise (without confession or excuse heard) to be beheaded, and his head to be fixed on a pole; and with these two heads this bloody wretch entered into the city again and, as it were in a spite, caused them in every street to kiss together, to the great detestation of the beholders. After this succeeded open rapine and manifest robbery in diverse houses within the city...He also put to execution in Southwark diverse persons, some for breaking his ordinance, and other, being of his old acquaintance, lest they should bewray his base lineage, disparaging him for his usurped surname of Mortimer.      (Holinshed, pp. 224–5; compare Hall, p. 221)

### 10. Wat Tyler's Rebellion

**10.1** [Tyler's rebels] began to show proof of those things which they had before conceived in their minds, beheading all such men of law, justices, and jurors as they might catch and lay hands upon, without respect of pity or remorse of conscience, alleging that the land could never enjoy her native and true liberty till all those sorts of people were dispatched out of the way. [*In the margin*: 'Lawyers, justices, and jurors brought to blockam feast by the rebels'.]

This talk liked well the ears of the common uplandish people, and by the less conveying the more, they purposed to burn and destroy all records, evidences, court-rolls, and other muniments, that the remembrance of ancient matters being removed out of mind, their landlords might not have whereby to challenge any right at their hands. [*In the margin*: 'The next way to extinguish right']

(Holinshed, II, 737)

**10.2** What wickedness was it to compel teachers of children in grammar schools to swear never to instruct any their art?...For it was dangerous among them to be known for one that was learned, and more dangerous if any man were found with a penner and inkhorn at his side; for such seldom or never escaped from them with life.                                                          (Holinshed, II, 737)

**10.3** [Ball] exhorted the people to consider that now the time was come appointed to them by God, in which they might (if they would) cast off the yoke of bondage and recover liberty. He counseled them therefore to remember themselves, and to take good hearts unto them that, after the manner of a good husband that tilleth his ground and riddeth out thereof such evil weeds as choke and destroy the good corn, they might destroy first the great lords of the realm, and after the judges and lawyers, questmongers [conductors of inquests], and all other whom they undertook to be against the commons; for so they might procure peace and surety to themselves in time to come, if, despatching out of the way the great men, there should be an equality in liberty, no difference in degrees of nobility, but a like dignity and equal authority in all things brought in among them.

(Holinshed, II, 739)

# APPENDIX 2: ASPECTS OF *THE FIRST PART OF THE CONTENTION* (Q1)

**1. Passages from Q1, the substance of which does not appear in F. Those passages marked with an asterisk (\*) may have been cut or altered by a censor:[1]**

1.1  The following takes the place of 1.1.24–31 in F. The hypothesis that the F version represents a first draft is unprovable:

> QUEENE  Th'excessiue loue I beare vnto your grace,
> Forbids me to be lauish of my tongue,
> Least I should speake more then beseemes a woman:
> Let this suffice, my blisse is your liking,
> And nothing can make poor Margaret miserable,
> Vnlesse the frowne of mightie Englands King.       (Q1, TLN 50–6)

1.2  The following may have been devised to give the Spirit a more prolonged and impressive exit, taking the place of 1.4.38–39 SD:

> He sinkes downe againe.
>
> BULLEN[BROOK]  Then downe I say, vnto the damned poule.
> Where Pluto in his firie Waggon sits.
> Ryding amidst the singde and parched smoakes,
> The Rode of *Dytas* by the Riuer Stykes,
> There howle and burne for euer in those flames,
> Rise *Iordaine* rise, and staie thy charming Spels.
> Sonnes, we are betraide.       (Q1, TLN 518–25)

1.3  The following takes the place of 2.1.38–43 – see note to 2.1.40:

CARDINALL  Euen when thou darest.
HUMPHREY  Dare. I tell [t]hee Priest, Plantagenets could neuer brooke the dare.
CARD.  I am Plantagenet as well as thou, and sonne to Iohn of Gaunt.
HUMPH.  In Bastardie.
CARDIN.  I scorne thy words. (Q1, TLN 585–91)

\*1.4  The following appears before 2.2.64 and stresses that York might easily win popular support for his uprising:

> WAR[WICK]  Then Yorke aduise thy selfe and take thy time,
> Claime thou the Crowne, and set thy standard vp,
> And in the same aduance the milk-white Rose,

---

[1]  In addition there is textual evidence that 4.5.0 SD–4.6.1, which are virtually identical in Q1, 2 and F, may have been censored (See Textual analysis, pp. 219–20).

> And then to gard it will I rouse the Beare,
> Inuiron'd with ten thousand Ragged-staues
> To aide and helpe thee for to win thy right,
> Maugre the proudest Lord of Henries blood,
> That dares deny the right and claime of Yorke.           (QI, TLN 788–795)

*1.5 *1 Contention* gives more specific details both of the insurrection in Ireland and of the means whereby it was to be quelled. In Q the queen sends York to Ireland, a cunning political act; in F it is suggested by Winchester. On the other hand, the reference to 'O'Neill' may have been suggested to the compilers of Q by the activities of Hugh O'Neill, Earl of Tyrone (1540?–1616), who, having been refused the regrant of Con Bacach O'Neill's lands in 1587, led a series of rebellions until his death. (It might equally derive from contamination by lines recollected from Marlowe's *Edward II* – see below, pp. 239–40.) Q also makes the queen much more overtly responsible for Humphrey's death (see Introduction, p. 35), as well as supplying Buckingham with lines for this part of sequence. Compare 3.1.282–330:

Enter a Messenger.

QUEENE How now sirrha, what newes?
MESSEN[GER]. Madame I bring you newes from Ireland,
    The wilde Onele my Lords, is vp in Armes,
    With troupes of Irish Kernes that vncontrold,
    Doth plant themselues within the English pale.
QUEENE What redresse shal we haue for this my Lords?
YORKE Twere very good that my Lord of Somerset
    That fortunate Champion were sent ouer,
    And burnes and spoiles the Country as they goe.
    To keepe in awe the stubborne Irishmen,
    He did so much good when he was in France.
SOMER[SET] Had Yorke bene there with all his far fetcht
    Pollices, he might haue lost as much as I.
YORKE I, for Yorke would haue lost his life before
    That France should haue reuolted from Englands rule.
SOMER[SET] I so thou might'st, and yet haue gouernd worse then I.
YORK What worse then nought, then a shame take all.
SOMER[SET] Shame on thy selfe, that wisheth shame.
QUEENE Somerset forbeare, good Yorke be patient,
    And do thou take in hand to crosse the seas,
    With troupes of Armed men to quell the pride
    Of those ambitious Irish that rebell.
YORKE Well Madame sith your grace is so content,
    Let me haue some bands of chosen soldiers,
    And Yorke shall trie his fortune against those kernes.
QUEENE Yorke thou shalt. My Lord of Buckingham,
    Let it be your charge to muster vp such souldiers
    As shall suffise him in these needfull warres.
BUCK[INGHAM] Madame I will, and leauie such a band

As soone shall ouercome those Irish Rebels,
But Yorke, where shall those soldiers staie for thee?
YORKE  At Bristow, I wil expect them ten daies hence.
BUC[KINGHAM]  Then thither shall they come, and so farewell.          *Exet Buckingham.*
YORKE  Adieu my Lord of Buckingham.
QUEENE  Suffolke remember what you haue to do.
And you Lord Cardinall concerning Duke Humphrey,
Twere good that you did see to it in time,
Come let vs go, that it may be performde.                          (Q1, TLN 1122–61)

*1.6  The following shows a Cade who boasts of his ability to dislodge the king, whereas F just shows him vaunting that he will become 'Protector'. Compare 4.2.151–4.3.16:

STAFFORD  Well sirrha, wilt thou yeeld thy selfe vnto the Kings mercy, and he will pardon thee and these, their outrages and rebellious deeds?
CADE  Nay, bid the King come to me and he will, and then ile pardon him, or otherwaies ile haue his Crowne tell him, ere it be long. [*There follows an abridged version of the fight with the Staffords*] [*To Dick*] Thou shalt haue licence to kil for foure score & one a week. Drumme strike vp, for now weele march to London, for to morrow I meane to sit in the Kings seate at Westminster.

(Q1, TLN 1674–94)

1.7  The following episode is added after 4.7.107. It indicates that Cade's order to set London Bridge on fire (4.6.11–12) has been executed, allows more time for the Says to be 'decapitated', and turns the rebels into rapists, which contracts an order which, according to Holinshed, Cade had promulgated (see Appendix 1, p. 227).

*Enter Robin.*

ROBIN  O Captaine, London bridge is a fire.
CADE  Runne to Billingsgate, and fetche pitch and flaxe and squench it.

Enter *Dicke* and a Sargiant.

SARGIANT  Iustice, iustice, I pray you sir, let me haue iustice of this fellow here.
CADE  Why what has he done?
SARG[EANT]  Alasse sir he has rauisht my wife.
DICKE  Why my Lord he would haue rested me,
And I went and entred my Action in his wiues paper house.
CADE  Dicke follow thy sute in her common place,
You horson villaine, you are a Sargiant youle,
Take any man by the throate for twelue pence,
And rest a man when hees at dinner,
And haue him to prison ere the meate be out of his mouth.
Go Dicke take him hence, cut out his toong for cogging,
Hough him for running, and to conclude,
Braue him with his owne mace.
                                        *Exet* with the Sargiant. (Q1, TLN 1834–53)

*1.8  The confrontation between York and Clifford lacks any magnanimity in the
Q version, and is both a demonstration of savage aristocratic factionalism and of
York's complete disdain for the monarch (compare 5.2.19–30):

> YORKE  Now Clifford, since we are singled here alone,
>        Be this the day of doome to one of vs,
>        For now my heart hath sworne immortall hate
>        To thee, and all the house of Lancaster.
> CLIFFORD  And here I stand, and pitch my foote to thine,
>        Vowing neuer to stir, till thou or I be slaine.
>        For neuer shall my heart be safe at rest,
>        Till I haue spoyld the hatefull house of Yorke.
>
>        *Alarmes, and they fight, and Yorke kils Clifford.*
>
> YORKE  Now Lancaster sit sure, thy sinowes shrinke,
>        Come fearefull Henry grouelling on thy face,
>        Yeeld vp thy Crowne vnto the Prince of Yorke.          (Q1, TLN 2153–2164).

1.9  Q offers a confrontation between Young Clifford and Richard of Gloucester
which is not in F but which may offer some evidence of authorial revision –
compare 5.2.31–65:

>                    *Alarmes, then enter yoong Clifford alone.*
>
> YOONG CLIFFORD  Father of Comberland,
>        Where may I seeke my aged father forth?
>        O! dismall sight, see where he breathlesse lies,
>        All smeard and weltred in his luke-warme blood,
>        Ah, aged pillar of all Comberlands true house,
>        Sweete father, to thy murthred ghoast I sweare,
>        Immortall hate vnto the house of Yorke,
>        Nor neuer shall I sleepe secure one night,
>        Till I haue furiously reuengde thy death,
>        And left not one of them to breath on earth.
>
>                    *He takes him vp on his backe.*
>
> And thus as old Ankyses sonne did beare
> His aged father on his manly backe,
> And fought with him against the bloodie Greeks,
> Euen so will I. But staie, heres one of them,
> To whom my soule hath sworne immortall hate.
>
> *Enter Richard, and then Clifford laies downe his father,*
> *fights with him, and Richard flies away againe.*
>
> Out crooktbacke villaine, get thee from my sight,
> But I will after thee, and once againe
> When I haue borne my father to his Tent,
> Ile trie my fortune better with thee yet.
>
>                    *Exet yoong Clifford with his father.* (Q1, TLN 2166–90)

## 2. Q's version of York's pedigree

(Compare 2.2.9 ff., and see Textual analysis, p. 216.) The compiler makes Edmund Langley, York's ancestor, not Edward III's fifth son but his second son, which makes nonsense of the attempt to argue that he was closer to the line of succession by virtue of his father's marriage to a descendant of the third son than the Lancastrians who derived from the fourth son, John of Gaunt.

> YORK My Lords our simple supper ended, thus,
>      Let me reueale vnto your honours here,
>      The right and title of the house of Yorke,
>      To Englands Crowne by liniall desent.
> WARWICK Then Yorke begin, and if thy claime be good,
>      The Neuils are thy subiects to command.
> YORK Then thus my Lords.
>      Edward the third had seuen sonnes,
>      The first was Edward the blacke Prince,
>      Prince of Wales.
>      The second was Edmund of Langly,
>      Duke of Yorke.
>      The third was Lyonell Duke of Clarence.
>      The fourth was Iohn of Gaunt,
>      The Duke of Lancaster.
>      The fifth was Roger Mortemor, Earle of March.
>      The sixt was sir Thomas of Woodstocke.
>      William of Winsore was the seuenth and last.
> Now, Edward the blacke Prince he died before his father, and left behinde him
>      Richard, that afterwards was King, Crownde by the name of Richard the second,
>      and he died without an heire. Edmund of Langly Duke of Yorke died, and left
>      behind him two daughters, Anne and Elinor.
>      Lyonell Duke of Clarence died, and left behinde Alice, Anne, and Elinor, that was
>      after married to my father, and by her I claime the Crowne, as the true heire to
>      Lyonell Duke of Clarence, the third sonne to Edward the third. Now sir. In the
>      time of Richards raigne, Henry of Bullingbrooke, sonne and heire to Iohn of
>      Gaunt, the Duke of Lancanster fourth sonne to Edward the third, he claimde the
>      Crowne, deposde the Merthfull King, and as both you know, in Pomphret Castle
>      harmelesse Richard was shamefully murthered, and so by Richards death came
>      the house of Lancaster vnto the Crowne.
> SALISBURY Sauing your tale my Lord, as I haue heard, in the raigne of Bullenbrooke,
>      the Duke of Yorke did claime the Crowne, and but for Owin Glendor, had bene
>      King.
> YORK True. But so it fortuned then, by meanes of that monstrous rebel Glendor, the
>      noble Duke of York was done to death, and so euer since the heires of Iohn of
>      Gaunt haue possessed the Crowne. But if the issue of the elder should sucseed
>      before the issue of the younger, then am I lawfull heire vnto the kingdome.
> WARWICK What plaine proceedings can be more plaine, hee claimes it from Lyonel
>      Duke of Clarence, the third sonne to Edward the third, and Henry from Iohn of
>      Gaunt the fourth sonne. So that till Lyonels issue failes, his should not raigne. It
>      failes not yet, but florisheth in thee & in thy sons, braue slips of such a stock.

> Then noble father, kneele we both togither, and in this priuate place, be we the
> first to honor him with birthright to the Crown.
> BOTH  Long liue Richard Englands royall King.                    (TLN 736–84)

## 3. Q3/Q1 variants

There are five significant variations between Q3 and Q1 which suggest, not as
Cairncross thought, that F shows some derivation here and elsewhere from Q3, but
that, as Montgomery concludes, 'Q3 somehow had access to a supplementary
report not available to those responsible for Q1'.[1]

### 3.1

QI:                        two, and on the ends were plac'd,
The heads of the Cardinall of *Winchester,*
And *William de la Poule* first Duke of Suffolke.

Q3:                        twaine, by whom I cannot gesse:
But as I thinke by the Cardinall. What it bodes
God knowes; and on the ends were plac'd
The heads o'th' Cardinall of Winchester,
And William de la Pole first Duke of Suffolke.

F:                        twaine: by whom, I haue forgot,
But as I thinke, it was by th'Cardinall,
And on the peeces of the broken Wand
Were plac'd the heads of *Edmond* Duke of Somerset,
And *William de la Pole* first Duke of Suffolk.          (1.2.26–30)

### 3.2

QI: But ere it be long, Ile go before them all.

Q3: As long as Gloster beares this base and humble mind:
Were I a man, and Protector as he is,
I'de reach to'the Crowne, or make some hop headlesse.
And being but a woman, ile not behinde
For playing of my part

F: Follow I must, I cannot go before,
While Gloster beares this base and humble minde.
Were I a Man, a Duke, and next of blood,
I would remoue these tedious stumbling blockes,
And smooth my way vpon their headlesse neckes.
And being a woman, I will not be slacke
To play my part in Fortunes Pageant.                   (1.2.61–7)

---

[1] Cairncross, pp. xxxii–xxxix; Wells and Taylor, *Textual Companion*, p. 180.

3.3

    QI: *Omits*

    Q3: She beares a whole reuennewes on her backe.

    F: She beares a Dukes Reuenewes on her backe.[1]           (1.3.75)

3.4

    QI: My Lord Protectors Hawke done towre so well,
            He knowes his maister loues to be aloft.
    HUMPHREY Faith my Lord, it is but a base minde
            That can sore no higher then a Falkons pitch.

    Q3: My Lord Protectors Hawkes doe towre so well,
            They know their maister sores a Faulcons pitch.
    HUMPHREY Faith my Lord, it is but a base minde
            That sores no higher then a bird can sore.

    F: My Lord Protectors Hawkes doe towre so well,
            They know their Master loues to be aloft,
            And beares his thoughts aboue his Faulcons Pitch.
    GLOUCESTER My Lord, 'tis but a base ignoble minde,
            That mounts no higher then a Bird can sore.     (2.1.10–14)

3.5

    QI: Vnder the title of Iohn Mortemer

    Q3: Vnder the title of Iohn Mortimer
          (For he is like him euery kinde of way)

    F: Vnder the title of Iohn Mortimer. . .
          For that Iohn Mortimer, which now is dead,
          In face, in gate, in speech he doth resemble.     (3.1.359, 372–3)

## 4. Recollections of lines from other plays which may have contaminated the memorial reconstruction from which QI derives.[2]

All of these plays could have belonged to Strange's or Pembroke's Men (see also 1.4.23 n.).

---

[1] Compare Marlowe, *Edward II* 706: 'He weares a lords revenewe on his back'. The phrase was, however, proverbial: see F. P. Wilson, *Oxford Dictionary of English Proverbs*, 1970 edn.
[2] Some of these were first listed by Alexander, *Shakespeare's Henry VI and Richard III*, 1929, pp. 91 ff. and by Hart, *Stolne and Surreptitious Copies*, 1942. Like Alexander, Cairncross (pp. 182–5) offers some further examples which I do not accept.

## 4.1  *1 Henry VI*

| | | |
|---|---|---|
| (a) | In crauing your opinion of my Title, | |
| | Which is infallible, to Englands Crowne | (*2H6* 2.2.4–5) |

| | | |
|---|---|---|
| Compare: | The right and title of the house of Yorke, | |
| | To Englands Crowne by liniall desent | (Q1, TLN 736–7) |

| | | |
|---|---|---|
| With: | But all the whole Inheritance I giue, | |
| | That doth belong vnto the House of Yorke, | |
| | From whence you spring, by Lineall Descent | (*1H6* 3.1.163–5) |

| | | |
|---|---|---|
| (b) | Heere shall they make their ransome on the sand. | (*2H6* 4.1.10) |

| | | |
|---|---|---|
| Compare: | And let them paie their ransomes ere they passe | (Q1, TLN 1473) |

| | | |
|---|---|---|
| With: | What ransome must I pay before I passe? | (*1H6* 5.3.73) |

## 4.2  *3 Henry VI*

| | | |
|---|---|---|
| (a) | ...he that breakes a sticke of Glosters groue, | |
| | Shall loose his head for his presumption. | (*2H6* 1.2.33–4) |

| | | |
|---|---|---|
| Compare: | ...he that breakes a sticke of Glosters groue, | |
| | Shall for th'offence, make forfeit of his head. | (Q1, TLN 226–7) |

| | | |
|---|---|---|
| With: | ...he that throwes not vp his cap for ioy, | |
| | Shall for the Fault make forfeit of his head. | (*3H6* 2.1.196–7) |

| | | |
|---|---|---|
| And: | And he that casts not up his cap for joie. | |
| | Shall for the offence make forfeit of his head. | (*True Tragedy* sig. B6ʳ) |

| | | |
|---|---|---|
| (b) | *Omitted in 2H6* | |

| | | |
|---|---|---|
| Compare: | And so thinke I Madame, for as you know, | |
| | If our King Henry had shooke hands with death, | (Q1, TLN 1107–8) |

| | | |
|---|---|---|
| With: | As I bethinke me, you should not be King, | |
| | Till our King Henry had shooke hands with Death. | (*3H6* 1.4.101–2) |

| | | |
|---|---|---|
| (c) | Away my Lord, you are slow, for shame away. | (*2H6* 5.2.72) |

| | | |
|---|---|---|
| Compare: | Away my Lord, and flie to London straight, | |
| | Make hast, for vengeance comes along with them, | |
| | Come stand not to expostulate, lets go. | (Q1, TLN 2194–6) |

| | | |
|---|---|---|
| With: | Away: for vengeance comes along with them. | |
| | Nay, stay not to expostulate, make speed | (*3H6* 2.5.134–5) |

## 4.3  *Titus Andronicus*

| | | |
|---|---|---|
| (a) | Lay hands upon these traitors | (*2H6* 1.4.40) |

Compare:    . . .laie hands on them, and bind them sure.            (Q1, TLN 528)

With:       . . .lay hands on them. . .
            And. . .binde them sure,                               (*Tit.* 5.2.159, 161)

(b)         For thousands more, that yet suspect no perill         (*2H6* 3.1.152)

Compare:    And thousands more must follow after me,
            That dreads not yet their liues destruction.           (Q1, TLN, 1064–5)

With:       Here comes a parcell of our hopefull Booty,
            Which dreads not yet their liues destruction.          (*Tit.* 2.3.49–50)

(c)         This Gloster should be quickly rid the world,
            To rid vs from the feare we haue of him.               (*2H6* 3.1.233–4)

Compare:    Then sit we downe againe my Lord Cardinall,
            Suffolke, Buckingham, Yorke, and Somerset.
            Let vs consult of proud Duke Humphries fall.
            In mine opinion it were good he dide,
            For safetie of our King and Common-wealth.             (Q1, TLN 1102–6)

With:       Then sit we downe and let vs all consult.
            My sonne and I will haue the wind of you:
            Keepe there, now talke at pleasure of your safety.
                                                                   (*Tit.* 4.2.132–4)

(d)         Oh Henry, let me pleade for gentle Suffolke.           (*2H6* 3.2.289)

Compare:    Oh Henry, reuerse the doome of gentle Suffolkes banishment.
                                                                   (Q1, TLN 1347)

With:       Oh reuerent Tribunes. . .

                              reuerse the doome of death. . .
            My euerlasting doome of banishment.                    (*Tit.* 3.1.23, 24, 51)


## 4.4 Shakespeare and others (?), *Edward III*[1]

(a)         Loe, I present your Grace a Traitors head,
            The head of Cade, whom I in combat slew. . .
            Iden, kneele down rise vp a Knight:
            We giue thee for reward a thousand Markes,
            And will, that thou henceforth attend on vs.
IDEN        May Iden liue to merit such a bountie. . .             (*2H6* 5.1.66–81)

Compare:    Lo here my Lord vpon my bended knees,
            I here present the traitorous head of Cade,

---

[1] Quotations from *Edward III* are taken from C. F. Tucker Brooke, ed., *The Shakespeare Apocryha*, 1908; for the analogous contexts see MacD. P. Jackson, '*Edward III*, Shakespeare, and Pembroke's Men', NQ 210 (1965), 329–31.

That hand to hand in single fight I slue...
Then rise vp sir Alexander Eyden knight,
And for thy maintenance, I freely giue
A thousand markes a yeare to maintaine thee...
I humbly thank your grace.                        (Q1, TLN 2015–2036)

With:        Lo, to repaire thy life, I guie to thee
             Three thousand Marks a yeere in English land...
             I took the king my selfe in single fight
                         ...I wil bend my knee...
             Kneele, therefore, downe: now rise, King Edwards knight;
             And, to maintayne thy state, I freely giue
             Fiue hundred marks a yeer to thee and thine...
             I humbly thank your grace.           (*E3* 4.9.48–9, 5.1.73, 4.3.52)

(b)          A world of earthly blessings to my soul          (*2H6* 1.1.22)

Compare:     A world of pleasures to my perplexed soule.      (Q1, TLN 50)

With:        From whom euen now my soule was much perplext     (*E3* 5.1.189)


## 4.5 Kyd, *The Spanish Tragedy*[1]

(a)          as free as heart can wish, or tongue can tell     (*2H6* 4.7.107)

Compare:     as free as hart can thinke, or toong can tell     (Q1, TLN 1833–4)

With:        I saw more sights than thousand tongues can tell,
             Or pens can write, or mortal hearts can think.    (*Sp. Trag.* 1.1.56–7)


## 4.6 Marlowe, *Edward II*[2]

(a)          Follow I must, I cannot go before.                (*2H6* 1.2.61)

Compare:     But ere it be long, Ile go before them all,
             Despight of all that seeke to crosse me thus,     (Q1, TLN 252–3)

With:        Nay all of them conspire to crosse me thus,
             But if I liue, ile tread vpon their heads.        (*E2* 897–8)

(b)          What, shall King Henry be a Pupill still,
             Vnder the surly Glosters Gouernance?              (*2H6*, 1.3.41–2)

Compare:     And nere regards the honor of his name,
             But still must be protected like a childe,
             And gouerned...                                    (Q1, TLN 347–9)

---

[1] Quotation taken from Philip Edwards, ed., *The Spanish Tragedy*, 1959.
[2] Quotations from Marlowe taken from C. F. Tucker Brooke, ed., *The Works of Christopher Marlowe*, 1910.

| With: | Did you regard the honor of your name...<br>As though your highnes were a schoole boy still,<br>And must be awde and gouerned like a child. | (*E2* 1323, 1335–6) |
|---|---|---|

| (c) | ...welcome were my Death | (*2H6* 2.3.14) |
|---|---|---|

| Compare: | Euen to my death, for I haue liued too long. | (Q1, TLN 815) |
|---|---|---|

| With: | ...euen to my death...<br>Nay, to my death, for too long haue I liued. | (*E2* 2331, 2651) |
|---|---|---|

| (d) | Rebels there are vp...<br>Th'vnciuill Kernes of Ireland are in Armes. | (*2H6* 3.1.283, 310) |
|---|---|---|

| Compare: | The wilde Onele my Lords, is vp in Armes,<br>With troupes of Irish Kernes that vncontrold,<br>Doth plant themselues within the English pale. | (Q1, TLN 1125–7) |
|---|---|---|

| With: | The wilde Oneyle, with swarmes of Irish Kernes,<br>Liues vncontroudle within the English pale. | (*E2* 966–7) |
|---|---|---|

| (e) | Then you belike suspect these Noblemen. | (*2H6* 3.2.186) |
|---|---|---|

| Compare: | But haue you no greater proofes then these? | (Q1, TLN 1268) |
|---|---|---|

| With: | But hath your grace no other proofe then this? | (*E2* 2611) |
|---|---|---|

| (f) | ...oppose himself against his King | (*2H6* 5.1.133) |
|---|---|---|

| Compare: | To leauy Armes against his lawfull King | (Q1, TLN 2073) |
|---|---|---|

| With: | And leuie armes against your lawfull king? | *E2* 1516) |
|---|---|---|

## 4.7 Marlowe, *Doctor Faustus* [1]

| (a) | *Omitted in 2H6* |
|---|---|

| Compare: | To pierce the bowels of this Centricke earth<br>And hither come in twinkling of an eye | (Q1, TLN 503–4) |
|---|---|---|

| With: | ...of this centricke earth<br>...in twinckling of an eie | (*Faustus* 648, 1327) |
|---|---|---|

| (b) | Aske what thou wilt; that I had sayd and, and, and done. | (*2H6* 1.4.27) |
|---|---|---|

| Compare: | Now Bullenbrooke what wouldst thou haue me do? | (Q1, TLN 508) |
|---|---|---|

| With: | Now Faustus, what wouldst thou haue me do? | (*Faustus* 270) |
|---|---|---|

---

[1] These were pointed out to me by Eric Rasmussen.

## 4.8 Anon, *Arden of Faversham*[1]

(a)          Some sodaine qualme hath strucke me at the heart.          (*2H6* 1.1.52)

Compare:   . . .a sodain qualme came ouer my hart          (Q1, TLN 79)

With:      . . .a sudden qualm come over my heart          (*Arden* 14.304)

(b)          Mischance and Sorrow goe along with you!. . .
             And three-fold Vegeance tend vpon your steps

                                                          (*2H6* 3.2.300, 304)

Compare:   Hell fire and vengeance go along with you.          (Q1, TLN 1356)

With:      Hell-fire and wrathful vengeance light on me.          (*Arden* 1.337)

[1] Quotations taken from T. W. Craik, ed., *Minor Elizabethan Tragedies*, 1974.

# APPENDIX 3: GENEALOGICAL TABLES

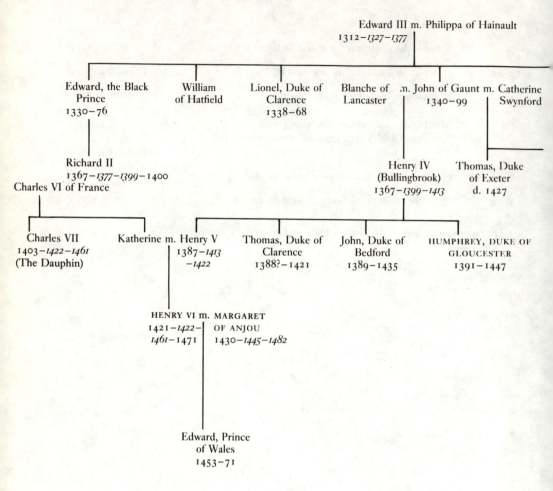

Edward III m. Philippa of Hainault
*1312–1327–1377*

Edward, the Black Prince *1330–76*

William of Hatfield

Lionel, Duke of Clarence *1338–68*

Blanche of Lancaster m. John of Gaunt *1340–99* m. Catherine Swynford

Richard II *1367–1377–1399–1400*

Henry IV (Bullingbrook) *1367–1399–1413*

Thomas, Duke of Exeter d. 1427

Charles VI of France

Charles VII *1403–1422–1461* (The Dauphin)

Katherine m. Henry V *1387–1413 –1422*

Thomas, Duke of Clarence *1388?–1421*

John, Duke of Bedford *1389–1435*

HUMPHREY, DUKE OF GLOUCESTER *1391–1447*

HENRY VI m. MARGARET *1421–1422– 1461–1471* OF ANJOU *1430–1445–1482*

Edward, Prince of Wales *1453–71*

Names of those in the play appear in capitals.
Italicised dates are those of reigns.
*See Notes to List of Characters, p. 76–7 above.

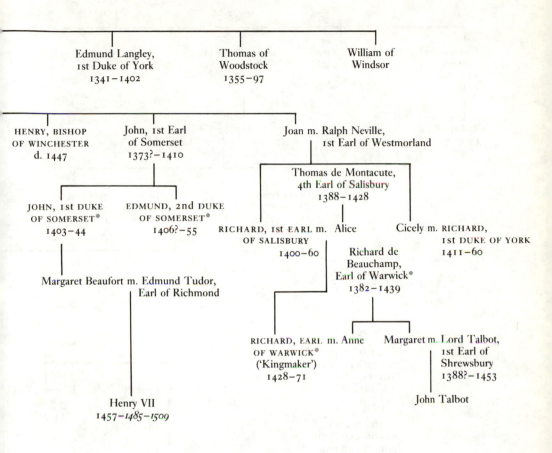

Table 1   THE HOUSE OF LANCASTER

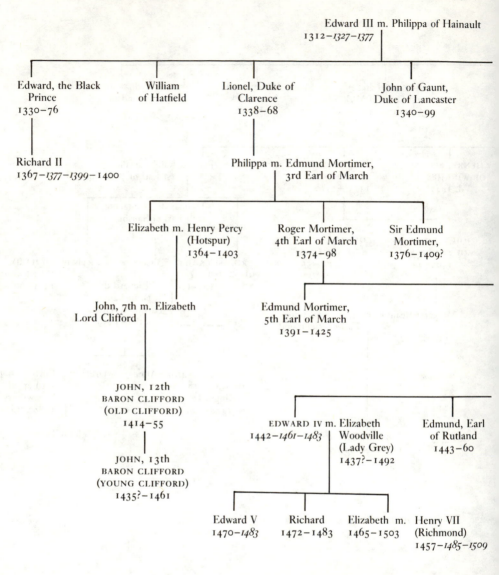

Names of those in the play appear in capitals.
Italicised dates are those of reigns.
*See Notes to List of Characters, p. 77 above.

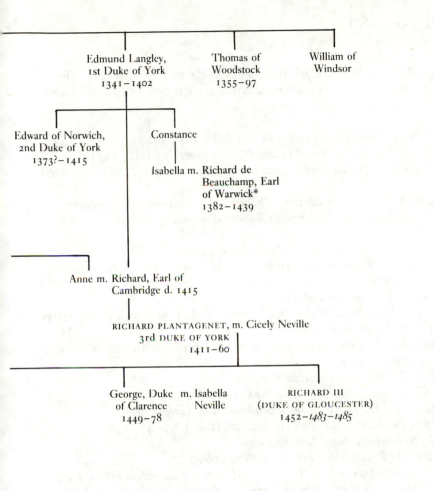

Edmund Langley,          Thomas of          William of
1st Duke of York          Woodstock          Windsor
1341–1402                1355–97

Edward of Norwich,        Constance
2nd Duke of York
1373?–1415

                          Isabella m. Richard de
                          Beauchamp, Earl
                          of Warwick*
                          1382–1439

Anne m. Richard, Earl of
Cambridge d. 1415

RICHARD PLANTAGENET, m. Cicely Neville
3rd DUKE OF YORK
1411–60

George, Duke   m. Isabella        RICHARD III
of Clarence       Neville       (DUKE OF GLOUCESTER)
1449–78                          1452–1483–1485

Table 2   THE HOUSES OF YORK AND MORTIMER

# READING LIST

A selection of critical texts central to the study of the play is listed here. The list also includes relevant works of reference, as well as some books and articles which might be found useful for further study.

Alexander, Peter. *Shakespeare's Henry VI and Richard III*, 1929
Baldwin, T. W. *Shakspere's 'Small Latine & Lesse Greeke'*, 2 vols., 1944
Berman, Ronald S. 'Fathers and sons in the *Henry VI* plays', *SQ* 13 (1962), 487–97
Berry, Edward. 'Twentieth-century Shakespeare criticism: the histories', in Stanley Wells, ed., *The Cambridge Companion to Shakespeare Studies*, 1986, pp. 249–56
　　*Patterns of Decay: Shakespeare's Early Histories*, 1975
Boswell-Stone, W. G. *Shakespeare's Holinshed, The Chronicle and the Historical Plays Compared*, 1896
Bristol, Michael D. *Carnival and Theater*, 1985
Brockbank, J. P. 'The frame of disorder – *Henry VI*', in J. R. Brown and B. Harris (eds.), *Early Shakespeare*, 1961
Brooke, Nicholas. 'Marlowe as provocative agent in Shakespeare's early plays', *S. Sur.* 14 (1961), 34–44
Brownlow, F. W. *Two Shakespearean Sequences*, 1977
Bullough, G. *Narrative and Dramatic Sources of Shakespeare*, III, 1960
Bulman, James C. *The Heroic Idiom of Shakespearean Tragedy*, 1985
　　'Shakespeare's Georgic histories', *S. Sur.* 38 (1985), 37–47
Burckhardt, S. *Shakespearean Meanings*, 1968
Burke, Peter. *The Renaissance Sense of the Past*, 1969
Campbell, Lily B. *Shakespeare's "Histories": Mirrors of Elizabethan Policy*, 1947
Carroll, D. Allen. 'Greene's "vpstart crow" passage: a survey of commentary', *RORD* 28 (1985), 111–27
Champion, L. *Perspective in Shakespeare's English Histories*, 1980
Clare, Janet. '"Greater themes for insurrection's arguing": political censorship of the Elizabethan and Jacobean stage', *RES* 38 (1987), 169–83
Clemen, Wolfgang. 'Some aspects of style in the *Henry VI* plays', in P. Edwards, I.-S. Ewbank, G. K. Hunter (eds.), *Shakespeare's Styles: Essays in Honour of Kenneth Muir*, 1980, pp. 9–24
Cohn, Norman. *The Pursuit of the Millennium*, 1970 edn
Colman, E. A. M. *The Dramatic Use of Bawdy in Shakespeare*, 1974
Cox, John D. *Shakespeare and the Dramaturgy of Power*, 1989
Dean, P. 'Shakespeare's Henry VI trilogy and Elizabethan "romance" histories: the origins of a genre', *SQ* 33 (1982), 34–48

Dessen, Alan C. *Elizabethan Stage Conventions and Modern Interpreters*, 1984

Eccleshall, Robert. *Order and Reason in Politics: Theories of Absolute and Limited Monarchy in Early Modern England*, 1978

Edmond, Mary. 'Pembroke's Men', *RES* 25 (1974), 129–36

Elton, G. R. *England Under the Tudors*, 1974

Fleischer, Martha Hester. *The Iconography of the English History Play*, 1974

George, D. 'Shakespeare and Pembroke's Men', *SQ* 32 (1981), 305–23

Goy-Blanquet, D. 'Images de la monarchie dans le théâtre historique de Shakespeare', in E. Konigson (ed.), *Les Voies de la création théâtrale, VIII: théâtre, histoire, modèles*, 1980

   *Le Roi mis à nu: l'histoire d'Henri VI de Hall à Shakespeare*, 1986

Griffiths, Ralph. *The Reign of King Henry VI*, 1981

Hammond, A. C. *The Early Shakespeare*, 1967

Hattaway, Michael. *Elizabethan Popular Theatre*, 1982

Hinchcliffe, Judith. *King Henry VI, Parts 1, 2, and 3*, Garland Shakespeare Bibliographies, 1986

Hinman, Charlton. *The Printing and Proof-Reading of the First Folio of Shakespeare*, 2 vols., 1963

Hobday, Charles. 'Clouted shoon and leather aprons: Shakespeare and the egalitarian tradition', *Renaissance and Modern Studies* 23 (1979), 63–78

Hodgdon, B. 'Shakespeare's directorial eye: a look at the early history plays', in S. Homan (ed.), *Shakespeare's 'More than Words can Witness'*, 1980, pp. 115–29

Honigmann, E. A. J. *Shakespeare: The 'Lost Years'*, 1985

   *Shakespeare's Impact on his Contemporaries*, 1982

Howard-Hill, T. H., ed., *2 Henry VI: A Concordance to the Text of the First Folio*, 1970

Hunter, G. K. 'Truth and art in history plays', *S. Sur. 42* (1990), 15–42

Jackson, Sir Barry. 'On producing *Henry VI*', *S. Sur. 6* (1953), 49–52

Jones, Emrys. *The Origins of Shakespeare*, 1977

   *Scenic Form in Shakespeare*, 1971

Kastan, David Scott. 'Proud majesty made a subject: Shakespeare and the spectacle of rule', *SQ* 37 (1986), 459–75

Kay, C. McG. 'Traps, slaughter, and chaos: a study of Shakespeare's *Henry VI* plays', *Studies in the Literary Imagination* 5 (1972), 1–26

Kelly, F. L. 'Oaths in Shakespeare's *Henry VI* Plays', *SQ* 24 (1973), 357–71

Kelly, H. A. *Divine Providence in the England of Shakespeare's Histories*, 1970

Leggatt, Alexander. *Shakespeare's Political Drama*, 1988

Long, J. H. *Shakespeare's Use of Music: The Histories and the Tragedies*, 1972

McCanles, Michael. *Dialectical Criticism and Renaissance Literature*, 1975

McFarlane, K. B. *England in the Fifteenth Century*, 1982

McMillin, Scott. 'Casting for Pembroke's Men: the *Henry VI* quartos and *The Taming of A Shrew*', *SQ* 23 (1972), 141–59

Manheim, M. *The Weak King Dilemma in the Shakespearean History Play*, 1973

Montgomery, William. 'The original staging of *The First Part of the Contention*

(1594)', *S. Sur.* 41 (1988), 13–22

Patrides, L. A. '"The beast with many heads": Renaissance views on the multitude', *SQ* 16 (1965), 241–6

Pettitt, Thomas, '"Here comes I, Jack Straw": English folk drama and social revolt', *Folklore* 95 (1984), 3–20

Rackin, Phyllis. 'Anti-historians: Women's roles in Shakespeare's histories', *Theatre Journal* 37 (1985), 329–44

Reese, M. M. *The Cease of Majesty*, 1961

Rhodes, E. L. *Henslowe's Rose: The Stage and Staging*, 1976

Ribner, Irving. *The English History Play in the Age of Shakespeare*, revised edn, 1965

Riggs, D. *Shakespeare's Heroical Histories: Henry VI and its Literary Tradition*, 1971

Robinson, Marilynne S. 'A new look at Shakespeare's *Henry VI, Part II*: sources, structure, and meaning', unpublished PhD dissertation, University of Washington, 1977

Saccio, Peter. *Shakespeare's English Kings: History, Chronicle, and Drama*, 1977

Shepherd, Simon. *Marlowe and the Politics of Elizabethan Theatre*, 1986

Siegel, Paul N. *Shakespeare's English and Roman History Plays: A Marxist Approach*, 1986

Slack Paul. *Rebellion, Popular Protest and the Social Order in Early Modern England*, 1984

Smidt, K. *Unconformities in Shakespeare's History Plays*, 1982

Sprague, A. C. *Shakespeare's Histories: Plays for the Stage*, 1964

Talbert, E. W. *Elizabethan Drama and Shakespeare's Early Plays: An Essay in Historical Criticism*, 1963

Tennenhouse, Leonard. *Power on Display: The Politics of Shakespeare's Genres*, 1986

Thomas, K. V. *Religion and the Decline of Magic*, 1971

Tillyard, E. M. W. *Shakespeare's History Plays*, 1944

Warren, Roger. '"Contrarieties agree": an aspect of dramatic technique in *Henry VI*', *S. Sur.* 37 (1984), 75–83

Watkins, Ronald. 'The only Shake-Scene', *PQ* 54 (1975), 47–67

Wells, Stanley, and Taylor, Gary. *William Shakespeare: A Textual Companion*, 1987

Wilders, John. *The Lost Garden: A View of Shakespeare's English and Roman History Plays*, 1978

Williams, Penry. *The Tudor Regime*, 1979

Williamson, Marilyn L. '"When men are rul'd by women": Shakespeare's first tetralogy', *Shakespeare Studies* 19 (1978), 41–60

Winny, J. *The Player King: A Theme of Shakespeare's Histories*, 1968

Yates, Frances. *Astraea: The Imperial Theme in the Sixteenth Century*, 1975